THE END OF THE MYTH

THE END OF
THE MYTH

. . . .

From the Frontier to the Border Wall
in the Mind of America

GREG GRANDIN

A Metropolitan Paperback

Metropolitan Books   Henry Holt and Company   New York

Metropolitan Books
Henry Holt and Company
Publishers since 1866
120 Broadway
New York, New York 10271
www.henryholt.com

Metropolitan Books® and m® are registered trademarks of
Macmillan Publishing Group, LLC.

The Library of Congress has cataloged the hardcover edition as follows:

Names: Grandin, Greg, 1962–, author.
Title: The end of the myth : from the frontier to the border wall in the mind of America /
    Greg Grandin.
Description: First edition. | New York : Metropolitan Books, Henry Holt and Company,
    2019. | Includes bibliographical references and index.
Identifiers: LCCN 2018027790 | ISBN 9781250179821 (hardcover)
Subjects: LCSH: Frontier thesis. | Borderlands—United States. | National characteristics,
    American. | Exceptionalism—United States. | Nationalism—United States—History—
    20th century. | Turner, Frederick Jackson, 1861–1932—Criticism and interpretation.
Classification: LCC E179.5 .G76 2019 | DDC 973—dc23
LC record available at https://lccn.loc.gov/2018027790

ISBN 978-1-250-21485-0 (trade paperback)

Our books may be purchased in bulk for promotional, educational, or business use. Please
contact your local bookseller or the Macmillan Corporate and Premium Sales Department at
(800) 221-7945, extension 5442, or by e-mail at MacmillanSpecialMarkets@macmillan.com.

Originally published in hardcover in 2019 by Metropolitan Books

First Paperback Edition 2020

Maps by Jeffrey L. Ward
Designed by Kelly S. Too

Printed in the United States of America

3 5 7 9 10 8 6 4

To the memories of Michael, Marilyn, Joel, Tani, Jean, Tom, and Emilia. And for Eleanor and her friends.

To live past the end of your myth is a perilous thing.

—Anne Carson

CONTENTS

THE END OF THE MYTH

Fleeing Forward

Poetry was the language of the frontier, and the historian Frederick Jackson Turner was among its greatest laureates. "The United States lies like a huge page in the history of society," he wrote in 1893. "Line by line as we read this continental page from West to East we find the record of social evolution."[1] Expansion across the continent, Turner said, made Europeans into something new, into a people both coarse and curious, self-disciplined and spontaneous, practical and inventive, filled with a "restless, nervous energy" and lifted by "that buoyancy and exuberance which comes with freedom." Turner's scholarly career spanned the late nineteenth and early twentieth centuries, during the height of Jim Crow and the consolidation of anti-miscegenation and nativist exclusion laws, with the KKK resurgent. Mexican workers were being lynched in Texas, and the U.S. military was engaged in deadly counterinsurgencies in the Caribbean and Pacific. But what became known as Turner's Frontier Thesis—which argued that the expansion of settlement across a frontier of "free land" created a uniquely American form of political equality, a vibrant, forward-looking individualism— placed a wager on the future.

The kind of Americanism Turner represented took all the unbounded optimism that went into the founding of the United States and bet that the country's progress, moving forward on the frontier and into the world, would reduce racism to a remnant and leave it behind as residue. It would dilute other social problems as well, including poverty, inequality, and extremism, teaching diverse people how to live together in peace. Frank Norris, in 1902, hoped that territorial expansion would lead to a new kind of universalism, to the "brotherhood of man" when Americans would realize that "the whole world is our nation and simple humanity our countrymen."[2]

Facing west meant facing the Promised Land, an Edenic utopia where the American as the new Adam could imagine himself free from nature's limits, society's burdens, and history's ambiguities. No myth in American history has been more powerful, more invoked by more presidents, than that of pioneers advancing across an endless meridian. Onward, and then onward again. There were lulls, doubts, dissents, and counter-movements, notably in the 1930s and 1970s. But the expansionist imperative has remained constant, in one version or another, for centuries. As Woodrow Wilson said in the 1890s, "a frontier people always in our van, is, so far, the central and determining fact of our national history." "There was no thought," Wilson said, "of drawing back."[3]

So far. The poetry stopped on June 16, 2015, when Donald J. Trump announced his presidential campaign by standing Frederick Jackson Turner on his head. "I will build a great wall," Trump said.

Trump most likely had never heard of Turner, or his outsized influence on American thought. But there, in the lobby of his tower on Fifth Avenue in Manhattan, he offered his own judgment on history. Referring specifically to the North American Free Trade Agreement and broadly to the country's commitment to free trade, he said, "We have to stop, and it has to stop now."

All nations have borders, and many today even have walls. But only the United States has had a frontier, or at least a frontier that has served as a proxy for liberation, synonymous with the possibilities and promises of modern life itself and held out as a model for the rest of the world to emulate.[4]

Decades before its founders won their independence, America was thought of as a process of endless becoming and ceaseless unfurling. In 1651, Thomas Hobbes described British colonialism in America as driven by an "insatiable appetite, or Bulimia, of enlarging dominion."[5] Thomas Jefferson, in a political manifesto he wrote two years before the Declaration of Independence, identified the right "of departing from the country in which chance, not choice" had placed settlers, "of going in quest of new habitations" as an element of universal law.[6]

True religion moved east to west with the sun, believed early American theologians, and if man could keep pace with its light, perhaps historical time itself could be overcome and decline avoided.[7] The West, said one frontier writer, was "the land of mankind's second chance."[8] It was, said Turner, a place of "perennial rebirth." Are there new frontiers? The historian Walter Prescott Webb, writing in the early 1950s, said that what that perennial question revealed was nothing less than a rejection of the death instinct. You might as well ask, Webb said, is there a human soul?[9] Faith in the regenerative power of the frontier resided in the fact that the West did offer, for many, a chance to shake off their circumstances. More than a few even got rich. The United States was great, in ambition as well as dimension.

The concept of the frontier served as both diagnosis (to explain the power and wealth of the United States) and prescription (to recommend what policy makers should do to maintain and extend that power and wealth). And when the physical frontier was closed, its imagery could easily be applied to other arenas of expansion, to markets, war, culture, technology, science, the psyche, and politics. In the years after World War II, the "frontier" became a central metaphor to capture a vision of a new kind of world order. Past empires established their dominance in an environment where resources were thought to be finite, extending their supremacy to capture as much of the world's wealth as possible, to the detriment of their rivals. Now, though, the United States made a credible claim to be a different sort of global power, presiding over a world economy premised on endless growth. Washington, its leaders said, didn't so much rule as help organize and stabilize an international community understood as liberal, universal, and multilateral. The promise of a limitless frontier meant that wealth wasn't a zero-sum proposition. It could be shared by all. Borrowing frontier language used by Andrew Jackson and his followers in the 1830s and 1840s, postwar planners said the United States would extend the world's "area of freedom" and enlarge its "circle of free institutions."[10]

The ideal of the frontier contained within itself the terms of its own criticism, which is another reason why it serves as so powerful a national metaphor. Martin Luther King, Jr., argued that the ideal fed into multiple reinforcing pathologies: into racism, a violent masculinity, and moralism that celebrates the rich and punishes the poor. For over a year, from early 1967 until his murder in April 1968—as the United States escalated its war in Vietnam—King put forth, in a series of sermons and press conferences, a damning analysis. Military expansion abroad, he argued, quickened domestic polarization. The "flame throwers in Vietnam fan the flames in our cities," he said; "the bombs in Vietnam explode at home." At the same time, constant war served to deflect the worst consequences of that polarization outward.[11]

King's point is as simple as it is profound: A constant fleeing forward allowed the United States to avoid a true reckoning with its social problems, such as economic inequality, racism, crime and punishment, and violence. Other critics at the time were coming to similar conclusions. Some scholars argued that imperial expansion let the United States "buy off" its domestic white skilled working class, either through social welfare or higher wages made possible by third world exploitation. Others stressed the political benefits of expansion, which allowed the reconciliation of competing interests.[12] Still others emphasized more Freudian, even Jungian, motives: deep-seated violent fantasies, formed in long-ago wars against people of color on the frontier, projected outward; soldiers sublimating their "own guilty desires," their own complicity in wartime atrocities, with ever more grotesque sadism.[13]

There is a lot to unpack in the argument that over the long course of U.S. history, endless expansion, either over land or through markets and militarism, deflects domestic extremism. How, for example, might historical traumas and resentments, myths and symbols, be passed down the centuries from one generation to another? Did the United States objectively need to expand in order to secure foreign resources and open markets for domestic production? Or did the country's leaders just believe they had to expand? Whatever the answers to those questions, the United States, since its founding, pushed outward and justified that push in moral terms, as beneficial equally for the people within and beyond the frontier. The idea of expansion, the historian William Appleman Williams wrote in 1966, was "exhilarating in a psychological and philosophical sense" since it could be "projected to infinity."[14]

Not, as it turns out, to infinity.

The United States is now into the eighteenth year of a war that it will never win. Soldiers who fought in Afghanistan and Iraq in the early 2000s are now seeing their children enlist. A retired Marine general recently said the United States will be in Afghanistan for yet another sixteen years, at least. By that point, the grandchildren of the first generation of veterans will be enlisting. Senator Lindsey Graham believes that the United States is fighting "an endless war without boundaries,' no limitation on time or geography."[15] Another former officer (referring to the expansion of military operations into African countries like Niger) said the war "will never end."[16] And grandchildren down the line will be paying its bill, now estimated to approach six trillion dollars.[17]

While the United States is mired in an endless war, it can no longer imagine endless growth. An entire generation's expectations have been radically foreshortened, as the 2007–2008 financial collapse has been followed by a perverse kind of recovery, marked by mediocre rates of investment, stockpiled wealth, soaring stocks, and stagnant wages.[18] The roots of the current crisis reach back decades, to the economic restructuring that began in the 1980s with farm failures and deindustrialization, and continued forward with financial deregulation, crippling tax cuts, and the entrenchment of low-paying service jobs and personal debt. The nation's political class, over the course of these decades, sold economic restructuring by ratcheting up the language of limitlessness. "Nothing is impossible," Ronald Reagan said. "There are no limits to growth."[19] The presidents who followed—George H. W. Bush, Bill Clinton, and George W. Bush—presided over an ideological bubble that proved as unrealistic as a prediction by one of Clinton's top economists, who in 1998 said that the soon-to-be-busted dot-com boom "will run forever."[20] All four presidents steadily upped the ante, pushing global "engagement" as a moral imperative, a mission that led the United States to the Persian Gulf and to its financially exhausting and morally discrediting global war.

Gaps exist in all nationalisms between ideal and experience. But in the years following defeat in Vietnam, the revival of the myth of rugged individualism and frontier limitlessness—at a moment when deindustrialization was making daily life precarious for an increasing number of people, when more and more people were reaching their limits—has created a punishing kind of dissonance. It was used to weaken the mechanisms of social solidarity, especially government-provided welfare and labor unions, just when they were most needed. In the mythology of the West, cowboys don't join unions.[21] The gap between myth and reality has now widened into a chasm.

The United States is a nation founded on the principle that government should leave individuals free to pursue their self-interest. Corruption and greed, even as the United States moved out in the world with a sense of moral mission, have not been foreign qualities. But it's hard to think of a period in the nation's history when venality and disillusionment have been so sovereign, when so many of the country's haves have nothing to offer but disdain for the have-nots.

The 2016 election of Donald Trump as president of the United States— and all the vitriol his campaign and presidency have unleashed—has been presented by commentators as one of two opposing possibilities. Trumpism either represents a rupture, a wholly un-American movement that has captured the institutions of government; or he is the realization of a deep-rooted American form of extremism. Does Trump's crass and cruel appeal to nativism represent a break from tradition, from a fitful but persistent commitment to tolerance and equality at home and defense of multilateralism, democracy, and open markets abroad? Or is it but the "dark side," to use Dick Cheney's resonant phrase, of U.S. history coming into the light? Breach or continuity?

What's missing from most commentary is an acknowledgment of the role that expansion, along with the promise of boundlessness, played in relegating racism and extremism to the fringe. To be sure, previous cycles of dislocation have given rise to demagogues similar to Trump, such as George Wallace and Pat Buchanan. But the movements those nativists led remained marginal and were contained—geographically, institutionally, and ideologically. And the United States has had other presidents who were open racists. Before Richard Nixon put his "southern strategy" into place to win the votes of southern neo-Confederates, Woodrow Wilson cultivated what was left of actual Confederates, and their sons and grandsons, into an electoral coalition, re-segregating the federal bureaucracy and legitimating the KKK. Before Wilson, there was Andrew Jackson, who personally drove a slave coffle between Natchez and Nashville and presided over a policy of ethnic cleansing that freed up vast amounts of land for white settlers, putting the full power of the federal government to creating a "Caucasian democracy."

What distinguishes earlier racist presidents like Jackson and Wilson from Trump, though, is that they were in office during the upswing of America's moving out in the world, when domestic political polarization could be stanched and the country held together—even after the Civil War nearly tore it apart—by the promise of endless growth. Trumpism is extremism turned inward, all-consuming and self-devouring. There is no "divine, messianic" crusade that can harness and redirect passions outward. Expansion, in any form, can no longer satisfy the interests, reconcile the contradictions, dilute the factions, or redirect the anger.

The "furies," as the writer Sam Tanenhaus described the conservative fringe that gained ground during Barack Obama's presidency, have nowhere left to go.[22] They whip around the homeland. Trump tapped into various forms of American racism: trading in birtherism, embracing law-and-order extremists, and refusing to distance himself from KKK and Nazi supporters, for instance. But it was the focus on the border and all that went with it—labeling Mexicans rapists, calling migrants snakes and animals, stirring up anger at undocumented residents, proposing to end birthright citizenship, and unleashing ICE agents to raid deep into the country, to stalk schools and hospitals, to split families and spread grief—that provided Trumpism its most compelling through-line message: The world's horizon is not limitless; not all can share in its wealth; and the nation's policies should reflect that reality. That argument isn't new. Over the years, there have been two versions of it. One is humane, a recognition that modern life imposes obligations, that nature's resources aren't infinite, and that society should be organized in a way that distributes fortune as fairly as possible. The other thinks that recognition of limits requires domination.

"To live past the end of your myth is a perilous thing," the Canadian poet Anne Carson once said. With Trump, America finds itself at the end of its myth.

To talk about the frontier is also to talk about capitalism, about its power and possibility and its promise of boundlessness. Donald Trump figured out that to talk about the border—and to promise a wall—was a way to acknowledge capitalism's limits, its pain, without having to challenge capitalism's terms. Trump ran promising to end the wars and to reverse the extreme anti-regulatory and free-market program of his party. Once in office, though, he accelerated deregulation, increased military spending, and expanded the wars.[23] But he kept talking about his wall.

That wall might or might not be built. But even if it remains only in its phantasmagorical, budgetary stage, a perpetual negotiating chip between Congress and the White House, the promise of a two-thousand-mile-long, thirty-foot-high ribbon of concrete and steel running along the United States' southern border serves its purpose. It's America's new myth, a monument to the final closing of the frontier. It is a symbol of a nation that used to believe that it had escaped history, or at least strode atop history, but now finds itself trapped by history, and of a people who used to think they were captains of the future, but now are prisoners of the past.

ONE

All That Space

"America was, if it was anything, geography, pure space."

1.

The British colonies in North America were conceived in expansion. America was an aspiration, an errand, and an obligation, born out of violent Christian schism and Europe's interminable religious and imperial conflicts. Depending on the intricacies of their particular interpretation of Revelation, the Protestants who settled New England might have understood flight across the Atlantic as a way of escaping European war. Or they might have seen migration as a chance to open a new front and win those wars on new soil. Here in the 1600s, in the eschatological nebula of the New World, was the first paradoxical image of America as simultaneously pristine *and* despoiled: empty and at the same time filled with primitives begging for deliverance, subordinated to Catholic Spain, which had conquered its part of the Americas a century earlier and stood as the great obstacle to Reformation England's rise as a world power. "All yell and crye with one voice *Liberta, liberta*," Richard Hakluyt, a clergyman and court minister, wrote in the late 1500s, hoping to convince investors and his queen to establish an American colony.[1]

As Puritan society frayed under the harsh conditions of settler life, the frontier threatened and beckoned. The dark woods were filled with witches. And they were witchy, inviting hither. The forest was the place where the community could be redeemed and given new purpose, a chance to once again start anew. Or it could be a place of more sorrows—"wilderness sorrows," as two early Puritan patriarchs described the hardships that awaited those who ventured into uncharted territory—where whatever solidarity existed would be smashed into atoms as settlers scattered to escape the rule of the clergy. "People are ready to run wild into the woods again and to be as heathenish as ever," warned Increase Mather. Expansion could be—often in the same sermon—held up as the cause of and solution to the difficulties of establishing Christian communities.

Either way, Native Americans had to get out of the way. They could die: "They waste, they moulder away, they disappear," said one Puritan chronicler of indigenous people who had succumbed to European pestilence years before the arrival of the *Mayflower* in 1620, thus clearing the earth for the establishment of the Massachusetts Bay Colony. "God made way for his people by removing the heathen and planting them in the ground," said another observer.[2] They could be murdered: the holy terror unleashed by the Puritans was, according to the historian Bernard Bailyn, driven by "fears of what could happen to civilized people in an unimaginable wilderness and fears of racial conflicts in which God's children were fated to struggle with pitiless agents of Satan, pagan Antichrists swarming in the world around them."[3] Survivors could be enslaved: the first patent granted in colonial America, in 1626, was to a Virginian merchant and planter, William Claiborne, for inventing a device that would not just restrain Indians but also make them work. Claiborne was given an Indian to experiment on, for the "tryall of his inventione."[4] Colonial records do not say what this innovation might have been, only noting that it wasn't successful.*

Or they could be pushed further and further west. The "prodigious

---

*Virginians turned decidedly to Africa for their labor needs, and Claiborne, a Puritan sympathizer, turned to Spanish America, launching, with backing from London merchant capital, a failed bid to establish a yet newer New England off the coast of Honduras.

and restless population," complained New Orleans's Spanish governor in 1794, "progressively drives the Indian nations before them and upon us, seeking to possess for itself this entire vast continent which the Indians occupy between the Ohio and the Mississippi Rivers, the Gulf of Mexico, and the Appalachian mountains."[5]

More than a century and a half later, writing in the early 1950s, the Mexican author and diplomat Octavio Paz made much the same point:

> America was, if it was anything, geography, pure space, open to human action. Since it lacked historical substance—ancient social classes, established institutions, religions, and hereditary laws—reality presented no obstacles other than natural ones. Men struggled not against history but against nature. And wherever there was an historical obstacle— indigenous societies, say—it was erased from history, reduced to a mere natural fact, and dispensed with accordingly. . . . Evil is outside, part of the natural world, like Indians, rivers, mountains, and other obstacles that must be domesticated or destroyed.[6]

The American Revolution is a permanent revolution, Paz went on, a nonstop expulsion of all "elements foreign to the American essence" and a "constant invention of itself." And anything that stands in the way of that invention, anything that is "in any way irreducible or inassimilable" to perpetual creation—be it Native Americans, Spanish America, or history itself—"is not American":

> In other places, the future is one of man's attributes: because we are men, we *have* a future. In Saxon America . . . the process is inverted, and the future determines the man: we are men because we *are* the future. And everything that has no future is not a man.

The United States, Paz said, "offers no room for contradiction, ambiguity, or conflict." The nation flies forward "swiftly, as if weightless," across the land. Trying to stop North Americans moving west, Stephen Austin, the founder of Texas, said over a century earlier, was like "trying to stop the Mississippi with a dam of straw."[7]

2.

The drive west waxed and waned and burst forth with great passion during key moments.

The first few decades of the 1700s were a period of relative theological calm. British colonists, still beset by wars, diseases, bad weather, and their own divisionism, recovered somewhat from the spiritual anguishes that had afflicted their Puritan settler forebears. Then came the Great Awakening in the 1730s, and hectoring jeremiads once again began to interpret global events—wars between European states—as the latest stage in the struggle between popery and true religion. Forest fever—the idea that migration was prophetic, that clearing the woods and filling the valleys with Christians was part of a messianic mission—returned. Settlers, who had begun to move over the Blue Ridge, into the Shenandoah and Ohio valleys, and through the Cumberland Gap, "were all great sticklers for religion and for Scripture quotations against the 'heathen.'"[8] They took it as a matter of faith—as was said of the Scotch-Irish who in the 1730s pushed the Conestoga people off nearly all of their land in western Pennsylvania—that it was "against the laws of God and nature, that so much land should be idle while so many Christians wanted it to labour on, and to raise their bread."[9]

Increasingly, in the decades before the American Revolution, western settlement was also understood in secular terms, as inducing not Christ's Coming but social progress. Benjamin Franklin previewed this way of thinking in 1751, in a short pamphlet titled "Observations Concerning the Increase in Mankind."[10] In Europe, Franklin wrote, an excess population pushed at the limits of subsistence, trying to coax food out of exhausted soil, filling cities, driving down wages. "When Labourers are plenty," he said, "their Wages Will be low." America, in contrast, escaped this demographic trap. Population growth, rather than working to subdivide finite resources into smaller and smaller shares, multiplied wealth. Abundant, cheap, and bountiful land meant laborers could give birth to as many children as they needed, since their children too could just clear a forest and plant their own crops. Markets would grow in tandem with supply, allowing America to avoid the distortions—too little food, too many workers, too cheap wages, too crowded cities, too much production of manufactured goods without enough demand—that afflicted Europe. "So vast is the Territory of North-America," Franklin wrote from his printing office in Philadelphia, "that it will require many Ages to settle fully; and till it is fully settled, Labour will never be cheap here."

Franklin was an optimistic Promethean. He imagined history as a propulsive movement across the sea and land, east to west. We are "scouring our planet," he wrote, "by clearing America of woods." There were, he estimated, a "million English souls" in America, a number that would double within a generation, until there would be more Englishmen on "this side of the water" than in Great Britain. Franklin here was putting forth a new way of thinking of racial differences, justifying his preference for people of his own "complexion" not by theological absolutes—of the kind that imagined Native Americans as agents of Satan and justified their removal from the land in the name of Providence—but by an assertion of a modern-sounding relativism. All people, he said, had a "partiality" for their own kind, as he did for white people: "I could wish their Numbers were increased." Africa was "black," Asia "tawny." Most of Europe, Franklin thought, was "swarthy," save for Great Britain and parts of Saxon Germany. In North America, white settlers were making "this side of our Globe reflect a brighter light to the eyes of inhabitants in Mars or Venus," Franklin wrote. It was a deist jab, substituting the judgment of other (extraterrestrial) sentient beings for that of an omnipotent god.

The Seven Years' War broadened horizons, spreading among an increasing number of people both Franklin's kind of optimism (which linked prosperity to expansion) and a darker impulse (by which settlers came to believe the land was their inheritance, bounty for blood shed). Between 1756 and 1763, Europe split into two great coalitions—one led by Catholic France, the other by Protestant Great Britain—and waged a war that spilled out over nearly all the earth, to India, Africa, Asia, the Caribbean, and South America. In northern America, Paris and London both deployed standing armies, settler militias, and indigenous allies, fighting for control of the continent.[11]

The war (which in America actually started in 1754, as British and French colonists skirmished for control of the Ohio valley) was bloody. It was a long low-intensity, high-mortality slog of exhausting treks through pathless woods, massacres, burned villages, frantic retreats, hunger, thirst, and cannibalism, which all sides practiced, either as retribution or for survival. British "rangers" copied the fighting style of Native Americans, learning how to move through the landscape stealthily, in small units, and conduct quick raids. Rogers' Rangers, for instance, dressed and lived "like the Indians," putting scalping knives to France's indigenous allies as they pacified the Connecticut valley. Upon approaching an Abenaki village near the Saint Lawrence River filled mostly with women and children, the rangers, according to one of its members, set about to "kill everyone without mercy." Within less than fifteen minutes, "the whole town was in a blaze, and carnage terrible." Hardly anyone escaped: "Those who the flames did not devour were either shot or tomohawk'ed." "Thus the inhumanity of these savages was rewarded with a calamity, dreadful indeed, but justly deserved," the ranger said.[12]

Such imitation served not only a tactical but a psychic function: by killing as pitilessly as they imagined their victims killed, they could justify killing their victims pitilessly. And by acting as if they themselves were as native to the land as Indians, they could claim the land once Indians were removed from the land. "Fraternal genocide" was how one writer described settler mimicry: slaughtered "Indian brothers" became the "unappeased ghosts in the unconscious of the white man."[13] This was, in a way, the beginning of the blood meridian that Cormac McCarthy writes about in his novel, the horizon where endless sky meets endless hate. Or at least it was the beginning of the continentalization of the "barbarous years," as Bernard Bailyn called the first decades of settler destruction of Native Americans.

Great Britain won that war, taking from France an enormous swath of forestland, north from the Great Lakes down through the Ohio valley and west to the Mississippi. But London soon lost the peace. With France defeated, Spain became Great Britain's last imperial competitor. The Spanish Crown, though, had by this time only a tenuous hold on its North American territories, leaving many British colonists, such as Franklin, anticipating one last battle, which would deliver all of North America and the Caribbean to Great Britain. In the coming "future war," Franklin wrote in 1767, English speakers would be "poured down the Mississippi upon the lower country and into the Bay of Mexico, to be used against Cuba, or Mexico itself."[14]

They already were pouring down, the "overflowing Scum of the Empire," as the British governor described the drifters and squatters who rushed over the mountains and into the Mississippi valley. Crown officials did what they could to stop them. But they were in a bind, since Great Britain's victory left it indebted to two opposing groups, whose interests couldn't be reconciled. On the one side were British colonists, from east of the Alleghenies and Appalachia, who had served as foot soldiers against the French. They had been promised plots of frontier land in exchange for their military service. On the other side were Britain's indigenous allies, who largely lived on the western side of the mountains in the trans-Appalachia valleys—Iroquois in the north, Cherokees, Choctaws, and Chickasaws in the south, and Seminoles in Florida, among others. Many of them too had fought for the Crown, and their contribution to London's victory was no less essential than that of the white colonists.

In October 1763, the Crown tried to clarify the situation. King George III issued a proclamation prohibiting European settlement west of a fixed partition line, which ran along the crest of the Alleghenies: "We do hereby strictly forbid, on Pain of our Displeasure, all our loving Subjects from making any Purchases or Settlements whatever, or taking Possession of any of the Lands above reserved." London even ordered settlers who had already crossed that line "forthwith to remove themselves" and return east. In issuing the decree, King George was

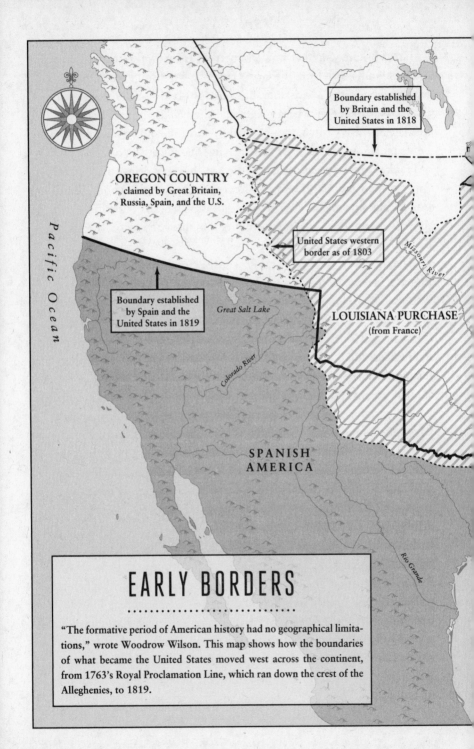

OREGON COUNTRY
claimed by Great Britain,
Russia, Spain, and the U.S.

Boundary established
by Britain and the
United States in 1818

United States western
border as of 1803

Boundary established
by Spain and the
United States in 1819

Great Salt Lake

Colorado River

LOUISIANA PURCHASE
(from France)

Missouri River

Pacific Ocean

SPANISH
AMERICA

Rio Grande

EARLY BORDERS

. . . .

"The formative period of American history had no geographical limitations," wrote Woodrow Wilson. This map shows how the boundaries
of what became the United States moved west across the continent,
from 1763's Royal Proclamation Line, which ran down the crest of the
Alleghenies, to 1819.

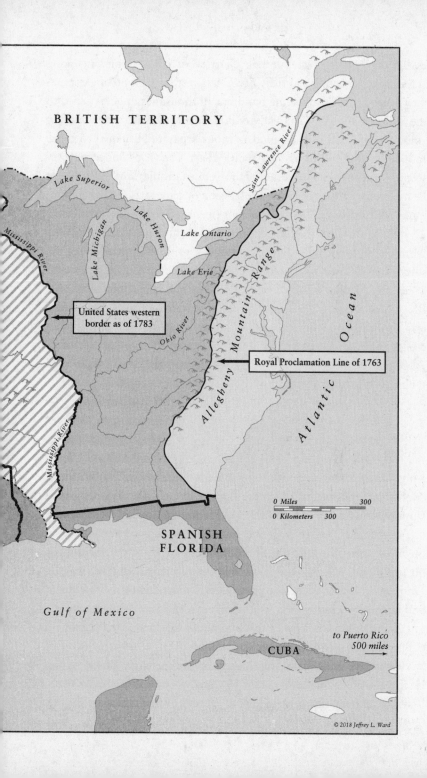

BRITISH TERRITORY

Lake Superior

Lake Michigan

Lake Huron

Lake Ontario

Saint Lawrence River

Lake Erie

Mississippi River

United States western
border as of 1783

Ohio River

Allegheny Mountain Range

Royal Proclamation Line of 1763

Atlantic Ocean

Mississippi River

0 Miles 300
0 Kilometers 300

SPANISH
FLORIDA

Gulf of Mexico

to Puerto Rico
500 miles

CUBA

© 2018 Jeffrey L. Ward

essentially voiding the founding charters of colonies and revoking standing concessions that the Crown had bestowed on private companies over the years, including hundreds of thousands of acres ceded to the Ohio Company.[15] In effect, London was recognizing a new kind of colony, comprised of indigenous nations separate but equal to those founded by Europeans on the Atlantic coast. They live "under our protection," the proclamation said of indigenous peoples, and "should not be molested or disturbed in the Possession of such parts of Our Dominions and Territories." The new arrangement wasn't disinterested. British merchants knew that continued access to fur depended on keeping white settlers out of indigenous hunting grounds. Still, to "let the savages enjoy their deserts in quiet," as the Lords Commissioners for Trade and Plantations said, was a powerful statement, as was George III's use of the word "nations" to describe native peoples. Indigenous leaders understood the proclamation to be an affirmation of their sovereignty.[16]

British colonists knew it to be a violation of theirs, since they defined their sovereignty as the right to move west.

3.

King George's partition was intolerable for squatter and squire alike, confirming to British colonists that their interests were now decoupled from the interests of the British Crown. Since God's law and nature's law were higher laws than George III's law, they claimed the right to set up a new society as they saw fit, where they saw fit, before, beyond, or on top of the Alleghenies. There was no reversing the flow, warned Franklin. "Neither royal nor provincial proclamations, nor the dread and horrors of a savage war, were sufficient," he wrote, "to prevent the settlement of the lands over the mountains." The facts were already on the ground, the settlers already on the land.

The partition of North America was unworkable. The proclamation itself was incoherent, offering land to white veterans of the Seven Years' War and protection of their land to Native Americans. The Crown stalled on the first and couldn't deliver on the second. Its representatives in America, loyal colonial governors, took desperate measures to stop the procession west and to remove squatters from Indian lands, even threatening the "felony of death without benefit of clergy." To no avail. Thousands of colonial volunteers in the war against France had received a firsthand view of the forbidden zone, the quality of its oaks and elms; its game and sources of water; the navigational potential of its rivers and tributaries; the nature of the soil; which crops would have to be planted, such as tobacco, flax, and cotton; and which ones grew unassisted. Native grapes and mulberries were just waiting to be plucked, hemp, said to spread spontaneously, to be cut. Witnesses to such bounty would not stay east of the Alleghenies.

As settlers moved forward, they terrorized Native Americans throughout the Ohio and Mississippi valleys. In 1763, the Scotch-Irish Paxton Boys rampaged through western Pennsylvania, murdering scores of Conestoga, scalping their victims and mutilating their corpses.[17] Another example of frontier barbarism is Frederick Stump, an American-born son of German immigrants, who in 1755 helped found Fredericksburg, Pennsylvania. Stump got caught up in the roil of war, which first enriched, then ruined, then enriched him again. He did well as a small-scale land speculator and store owner in eastern Pennsylvania. But without having obtained permission from Philadelphia, he moved his family somewhere "beyond the mountains." There, native people reportedly killed his wife and children, setting Stump, along with his bonded German servant, Hans Eisenhauer, on a course of retribution.* One sympathetic account describes Stump and Eisenhauer, who also went by the name John Ironcutter, hunting "savages through valley and mountain, and when their victims climbed trees to get away from the hounds, their pursuers shot them down like wildcats."[18] Stump became known as "Indian Killer": that is, he killed Indians and he killed like an Indian, fighting "the devil with fire" and using "methods practiced by his savage foes."[19]

The worst came in January 1768. In an eastern Allegheny hollow,

---

* Hans Eisenhauer was the great-great-great-grandfather of Dwight D. Eisenhower.

Stump and Eisenhauer murdered eleven "friend-Indians," as British officials called the victims: five men, three women, two children, and one infant. They scalped the dead and disposed of the bodies, throwing some in a hole hacked in a frozen river and burning the rest. News of the murders traveled through the region, especially throughout Indian lands. Quaker authorities in Philadelphia put a high bounty on Stump and Eisenhauer, and the two men were soon captured. A mob, though, made up of seventy to eighty white vigilantes and said to include members of the still-active Paxton Boys, came to their rescue. Armed with guns and tomahawks, the mob swarmed the old log jail where the two murderers were being held, in the town of Carlisle, and set them free.

Neither Stump nor Eisenhauer was ever brought to justice. Philadelphia issued another edict banning settlement on indigenous land. Again it was ignored. Stump fled to where no Quaker could touch him, down through Georgia and into Tennessee. There he became one of Nashville's wealthiest men, a plantation owner, profitable distiller of mash whiskey, and a slaver. He also earned the rank of captain in Tennessee's first militia expedition, clearing Creeks and Choctaws off the road from Nashville to Natchez.[20] Thus Stump was transformed from an outlaw into an agent of the law. He was part of a loose network of irregular rangers and formally organized militias that expanded the line of settlement outward, allowing whites to push north up to Maine and Canada, south into Spanish Florida, and west into the Mississippi valley.

Standing behind the squatters—behind men like Stump and Eisenhauer—were the squires who were also interested in western speculation, staking out enormous lots well west of the partition line, in what is now Kentucky, Tennessee, West Virginia, Ohio, west Florida, and western Pennsylvania. Many of these investors hailed from Virginia, including the men who would soon lead the revolt against royal authority: Thomas Jefferson, Patrick Henry, and George Washington. As did Stump, they assumed the 1763 proclamation didn't pertain to them. Unlike the plebeian Stump, however, they had ways to keep their hands hidden and unbloodied. Washington, a veteran of the

Seven Years' War, invested in frontier lands, instructing his "locator"—
as private surveyors were called—to venture west "under the guise of
hunting game" so as to avoid royal authorities. The future first president intended "to secure some of the most valuable lands in the King's
part"—that is, west of the partition line. Washington wrote that he
intended to do so "notwithstanding the proclamation that restrains
it at present, and prohibits the settling of them at all; for I can never
look upon that proclamation in any other light (but this I say between
ourselves) than as a temporary expedient to quiet the minds of the
Indians."

"It must fall," said Washington. It fell with the American Revolution.[21]

4.

The Declaration of Independence of 1776 was, among other things, the
colonists' counter to the Royal Proclamation of 1763. The document,
written by Thomas Jefferson, only referenced London's effort to partition North America obliquely, complaining that King George incited
"the inhabitants of our frontiers, the merciless Indian Savages" to wage
war on settlers. But two years earlier, Jefferson, in one of his first political tracts, had clearly condemned the Crown's effort to restrict migration. "America was conquered," Jefferson wrote in "A Summary View
of the Rights of British America," by its settlers, "at the expense of individuals, and not of the British public. Their own blood was spilt in
acquiring lands for the settlement, their own fortunes expended in making that settlement effectual; for themselves they fought, for themselves
they conquered, and for themselves alone they have right to hold."

"A Summary View" captures an argument, especially popular among
the Virginia rebels in the years leading up to the Revolution, that the
ideal of modern liberty, founded on property rights, can be traced back
hundreds of years to Saxon Germany. It was there, in the early centuries
of the millennium, where freemen first governed themselves as equals,
holding land "in absolute right," in Jefferson's words. When Old World

lords tried to encumber their rights, these Saxon heralds of American freedom fled, first to Britain and then to the New World.

Saxons to Britain, Brits to America, Americans westward. Where Benjamin Franklin, in the early 1750s, provided a compelling political economy to justify wilderness expansion, Thomas Jefferson now gave settlers a moral history along with a usable analogy to express their grievances. Just as Norman lords, after their 1066 invasion of the British Isles, trampled on the rights of Saxon freemen and placed the "yoke" of feudalism on their necks, so too was George III violating the rights of their Virginian descendants.

It was "universal law," Jefferson said, which "nature" had "given to all men," that allowed his "ancestors" the right to leave their country of birth and go "in quest of new habitations, and of there establishing new societies."

For Jefferson, the ability to migrate wasn't just an exercise of natural rights but the source of rights, or at least their historically necessary condition. Liberty was made possible by the right to colonize, letting freemen, when their freedom was threatened, move on to find free land and carry the torch from one place to another. Our "Saxon ancestors," Jefferson wrote, "left their native wilds and woods in the North of Europe" and "possessed themselves of the Island of Britain." As they did so, no German prince presumed to claim "superiority" over them. By what law, then, did the Crown presume to claim superiority over colonists to settle "the wilds of America"?

The American Revolution answered: none at all. Hostilities between Great Britain and its former colonial subjects formally ended in 1783, with the signing of the Treaty of Paris, which, in laying out the terms of London's defeat, set the new nation's western border at the Mississippi River. The republic came into the world doubling its size. King George III, in the treaty's first article, recognized the independence of the original thirteen colonies and, in the second article, ceded to them the territory between the Alleghenies and the Mississippi. The United States then proceeded to move swiftly—as if weightless, as Octavio Paz would say—across the west. The "numbers are increasing while we are writing," said Jefferson in 1786, of settlers moving into Kentucky.

The future president was here correcting a fashionable European opinion that the New World wasn't bountiful but degenerative. Its soil was said to be weak, its animals stunted, its people—both natives and transplanted Europeans—devoid of vitality, barely able to rouse themselves to reproduce. Jefferson and others countered by stressing American power, plenty, and fertility, reflected in high birth and low mortality rates. This optimism would later be reflected in the idea that nature was boundless and that the frontier would serve as a place of perennial rebirth.[22] When a European once insisted to Benjamin Franklin that Americans died young, Franklin answered that "the children of the first settlers are not yet dead!"*

That a line running down the middle of the Mississippi served for a short time as the western border of the United States is apt, for the river gives an illusion of fixity when in fact it is in constant flux, in a perpetual state of creation. It is "the crookedest river in the world," Mark Twain later wrote, making "prodigious jumps by cutting through narrow necks of land, and thus straightening and shortening itself."[23] U.S. diplomats used this mutability to press for a more liberal interpretation of the Treaty of Paris. The British still controlled Canada, but it was Spain (which in the 1780s and '90s controlled most of the land west of the Mississippi, as well as Florida) that stood in the path of the new nation.

Jefferson, now as secretary of state, and his diplomats began to demand from Madrid the right of U.S. ships to moor on the Mississippi's west bank (which according to the Treaty of Paris was Spanish territory), since in those pre-steam days tacking from bank to bank

---

* Happy insistence on longevity and large families can be thought of as a counterpoint to the sort of European gloom later associated with the English economist Robert Malthus, who soon would publish his famous essay on population growth, the foundational text still used by "race realists" (as today's white supremacists like to call themselves) to argue that the source of social conflict is that there are, or quickly will be, too many people in the world. Jefferson said there was plenty of room, fixing the upper limit at about ten people per square mile, after which inhabitants would run off "to search for vacant country," until "the whole of those two continents"—North and South America—"are filled up." "'Tis population, 'tis population alone, can save our bacon," the writer Parson Weems said a generation later, urging the country's unmarried men and childless women to live by the injunction from Genesis and multiply, so as to counter Europe's claims on the New World.

was the best way to ascend upriver. "It is," he said, "a principle that the right to a thing gives a right to the means without which it could not be used, that is to say, that the means follow the end." Such a principle, Jefferson told Spain, was but "natural reason," the "common sense of mankind." Spanish officials recognized this demand for easement as a stalking horse. The United States was then working to revise the terms of the Treaty of Paris, claiming the freedom to use and, implicitly, to settle and administer all the navigable rivers flowing into the Mississippi, along with all the portage roads connecting all the navigable tributaries. This was a formidable amount of land, since the Mississippi basin, the world's fourth-longest river system, sprawls across more than a million square miles. James Madison, as Jefferson's secretary of state, would also press for access to all of Florida's waterways. "Free communication with the sea," Madison insisted, "is so natural, so reasonable, and so essential that eventually it must take place."[24]

Where would such demands stop?, the Spanish governor of New Orleans, Baron de Carondelet, wanted to know. Soon, Carondelet warned, the United States would use the pretext of "free navigation" to dominate "the rich fur-trade of the Missouri, and in time the rich mines of the interior provinces of the very Kingdom of Mexico."[25] Spain, in response, tried to put into place a policy of "containment." "We have to figure out a way to contain them," one of its colonial governors said of Anglo settlers.[26] "We have to contain the Americans within their limits," wrote another.

But the United States was uncontainable. Nothing, Carondelet wrote, could check their "mode of growth." Settlers were "multiplying rapidly in the silence of the peace" that came after the American Revolution, the baron said, and, having pushed into the Ohio valley and Kentucky, resisted "all authority." When they "tire of one place, they move to another."

Well beyond any expansive definition of the Mississippi, a host of individuals and institutions—veterans granted bounty lands for fighting in the Seven Years' War, speculators, settlers who had purchased land from either Spain or France, real estate companies, and many of the original thirteen states—claimed western territory. Based on their old colonial charters, Georgia, South Carolina, North Carolina, and Virginia, for instance, said their territory ran all the way to the Pacific. "The land throughout from Sea to Sea" was how Virginia's charter, granted in the early 1600s, defined its territory. "All that Space," the charter said.[27]

The United States used these many claims, in different ways depending on the circumstance, to push forward. In other words, the United States won independence from Great Britain in a revolutionary war that was, among other reasons, fought to deny Great Britain the right to establish a western border; then, once independence was recognized by the Treaty of Paris establishing a western border, the United States cited earlier grants issued by Great Britain to hop-skip over that border.

What to do with all that space?

5.

Benjamin Franklin had one idea: in the 1750s, he had sketched out a rudimentary political economy, which posited the continent's abundant, affordable, and bountiful land as a safety valve, a way to ensure that families could grow and wages would stay high, demand would keep pace with supply, and agricultural production would harmonize with urban manufacturing. In the 1770s, Thomas Jefferson provided settlers a historical moral philosophy, telling them that their movement west wasn't just a fruit of freedom but the source of freedom. Now, in the 1780s, James Madison offered a political theory.

As the United States set about drafting a constitution in 1787, many delegates, despite Franklin's and Jefferson's odes to growth, fretted about size. They worried about the vices that come with vastness. The Spanish empire was vast; so was Spanish despotism and corruption. Received political philosophy at the time—handed down both by the ancients, Aristotle and Cicero, and the moderns, Machiavelli, Rousseau, and Montesquieu—held that republics were delicate flowers that could only be cultivated in small gardens. "It is in the nature of a republic to have only a small territory; otherwise, it can scarcely continue to exist,"

Montesquieu instructed in his 1748 *The Spirit of the Laws*. "In a large republic, the common good is sacrificed to a thousand considerations." What the "common good" was depended on perspective, but most republicans defined it as something greater than the sum total of individual interests. What republicans called virtue could be associated with culture, religion, blood, skin color, language, or martial courage, but in all cases it was a transcendent value that stood above personal pursuits and passions. Indeed, as Montesquieu writes, virtue was constantly threatened by those pursuits and passions, "sacrificed to a thousand considerations." This is why many philosophers, prior to Madison, thought that vastness and virtue contradicted each other. Republics couldn't be big and good, ambitious (in size) and virtuous. Too large a territory meant too many pursuits and passions, too many "considerations."

For Madison, Montesquieu's size limitations were unworkable. The United States was already large and getting larger. And there were too many seemingly irreconcilable ideas, held by merchants, farmers, and slavers, of how to define virtue. Madison figured out a way to harmonize these visions, offering a two-step revision of existing republican theory that was as simple as it was elegant. First, he said, Montesquieu's "thousand considerations" didn't threaten the common good. They *were* the common good. Madison's Federalist Paper No. 10, published in November 1787, offered a remarkably modern vision of society, rejecting a vision of republicanism that, in the name of virtue, sought to suppress what he called "diversity." Instead, Madison put forth an ideal that defined virtue *as* diversity, *as* society's plethora of uncountable impulses, opinions, desires, talents, thoughts, ambitions, and capabilities that create wealth, or "property." And it is government's "first object," its primary obligation, to protect such wealth-producing diversity.

At the same time, Madison knew that wealth could destroy virtue by dividing society into opposing factions: "those who hold and those who are without." Others who would participate in the drafting of the Constitution also recognized the problem that wealth posed to the general welfare. "The Rich will strive to establish their dominion and enslave the rest," thought Gouverneur Morris, who represented

Pennsylvania at the Constitutional Convention. "They always did," he said, and "they always will."[28] But they came up with cumbersome solutions: confiscate property every generation to prevent the formation of an aristocracy; establish a House of Commons and a House of Lords, each serving as a check on the other; or ensure an equal distribution of land among all households. Jefferson briefly had the idea of "subdividing" property, to avoid the growth of an impoverished wage "laboring poor."[29]

Madison had an easier solution, the second step in his revision of Montesquieu: "Extend the sphere."[30]

The word "sphere," at the time of the Constitution's drafting, was used to describe a number of issues related to politics, including the size of a nation's population, the number of people who enjoyed the right to vote, and the extent of its trading relations. But in Federalist 10, Madison used it to mean raw size, territory, and physical space. Not just a large republic but an ever-enlarging republic would dilute the threat of political conflict and factionalism. Citizens spread thin over a wide territory would be less likely to join "common interest or passion," to become "united and actuated" in their objectives, to "discover their own strength, and to act in unison with each other." Expansion would break up society "into a greater variety of interests and pursuits of passions, which check each other." The amalgamation of power would be prevented, making it unnecessary to take government action, either to regulate concentrated wealth or to repress movements organized in opposition to concentrated wealth. "Extend the sphere," Madison wrote, "and you take in a greater variety of parties and interests," and you make it difficult for either a mob majority or a tyrannical minority to unite "to invade the rights of other citizens."

Whatever one's take on any of the debates of the day (especially the debate over slavery), and whatever one's philosophical understanding of the relationship of republicanism to land, commerce, finance, and labor, most agreed on practicalities. All wanted to remove Spain from the Mississippi; all wanted the capacity to pacify hostile Native Americans and put down rebellions of poor people; and all wanted Great

Britain to get out of the way of their commerce. All wanted "room enough," as Thomas Jefferson would put it in his 1800 inaugural address, to be protected from Europe's "exterminating havoc."

Expansion became the answer to every question, the solution to all problems, especially those caused by expansion.

TWO

The Alpha and the Omega

*"It was the East when the sun set and
the West when the sun rose."*

1.

What kind of republic was the United States of America that its national border didn't just move occasionally, in response to episodic war or diplomacy, but constitutively as a quality of its being? What, exactly, lay on the other side of that moving border? And what happens to a nation when that line stops moving? These questions didn't haunt the United States. They animated it, giving life to its history as an exceptional nation.

The best way to identify the unique nature of something is to compare it to something else, so take a moment and consider Spanish America. By 1826—the year of Thomas Jefferson's and John Adams's deaths—all of Spain's former colonies in the Americas, with the exception of Cuba and Puerto Rico, had won their freedom. These new countries—among them Gran Colombia, the United Provinces, Bolivia, Peru, the Republic of Chile, and the United States of Mexico— immediately recognized the territorial integrity of the others, based on old colonial boundaries.

They had to, for each individual nation both legitimated and threatened the others in existential terms. "Legitimated" because the independence of one confirmed for the rest the right to rebel against colonial rule and establish self-governing republics. "Threatened" because all these new republics came into being at a time when reigning international law recognized war, conquest, and subjugation as valid means of obtaining territory and establishing sovereignty. In order to learn how to live with one another, Spanish American republicans, among the most famous being Simón Bolívar, rejected the legitimacy of the right of discovery, insisting that there was no "free land" left in Spanish America to be claimed. In its place, republicans dusted off an old Roman law, *uti possidetis*. In English, this phrase means "as you possess," and prior to Spanish American independence was mostly understood as an expression of power politics, justifying land grabs that came about as a result of wars of conquest: as you possess, so shall you possess. The strongest takes, and keeps. But this is not how the region's diplomats came to apply the doctrine.

American republicanism, both north and south, offered a theory of peace. Neither the founders of the United States nor those of Spanish America were pacifists. They all fought desperate wars to realize their goals, using violence to bring into existence the kind of New World they believed ought to exist, a more harmonious world, liberated from Europe's hatreds. To that end, Spanish American republicans argued that accepting fixed borders (as they existed in 1810, corresponding to colonial administrative divisions) would prevent conflict and help to establish a moral community of bounded nations. Gran Colombia's founders, for instance, agreed in 1823 that to "consolidate the liberty and independence" of any one republic, the territorial "integrity" of all republics had to be guaranteed.[1] As you possess, so shall you possess—not as a fruit of war but as a condition for peace.

This and similar statements denying the legitimacy of military aggression entailed a bold revision of existing international law. Spanish American republicans offered this revision both to limit conflict among the new republics and also to ward off monarchical Europe from trying to reconquer the New World. There was no undiscovered country, they said, no territory that lacked sovereignty, no *terra nul-*

lius, no space that wasn't already socialized. Old Europe marauded, plundered, expanded, conquered, and subjected. The New World's republics would contain themselves.

This principle of nonaggression was more ideal than reality. Clashes and wars broke out. Borders shifted. Many died. Gran Colombia splintered into Venezuela, Ecuador, and Colombia. What is now Uruguay went back and forth between Argentina and Brazil. The new Spanish American republics were subject to all the same pressures that, at that moment in the 1820s, were driving the United States like a whirligig across the northern continent. Seemingly infinite stretches of southern Argentina and Chile and northern Mexico were outside of the effective control of the national government, filled with unvanquished Native Americans, beckoning settlers to settle and central authorities to establish centralized authority. Hundreds of contested islands ringed the continent. And two million square miles of dense, deadly Amazon forest sat right in its middle, like a black hole, serving as the shared frontier of nine nations. Brazil coveted Peru's rubber trees, and took them. Chile wanted Bolivia's nitrate fields, and took them.

Still, over the course of the next century, efforts to resolve these transgressions by appealing to the doctrine of *uti possidetis* institutionalized the doctrine. We might, for the purposes of our comparison with the United States, rename the principle and call it the doctrine of "self-containment," the idea that a nation would stand pat with the territory it has. "I am going to insist one more time," an Ecuadoran diplomat told his Peruvian counterpart, as they negotiated a border dispute, "that the only line that can possibly serve as a basis for agreement is that of *uti possidetis* of 1810."[2]

South America's last major interstate war was in the 1930s, when landlocked and impoverished Bolivia and Paraguay, the two poorest in the region, clashed over hellish scrubland thought to contain oil. Standard Oil bankrolled Bolivia. Royal Dutch Shell financed Paraguay. And the two countries, whose armies were overwhelmingly made up of destitute indigenous conscripts, fell further into penury by running the third world's first arms race, buying up used World War I weapons and matériel from European dealers.[3] There was no oil, as the two nations soon realized. But the war and the arms race continued. Eventually, Argentina helped negotiate a cease-fire on the basis of *uti possidetis*, for which its foreign minister won a Nobel Peace Prize. From that point forward, the region's doctrine of self-containment worked its way out of the New World to become universal, serving as the legal and moral foundation of the United Nations and the guiding principle of twentieth-century decolonizing nations. The founding meeting of the Organization of African Unity, for example, held in Addis Ababa in 1963, tacitly affirmed the Latin American version of *uti possidetis*. "We must take Africa as it is," said Mali's president, Modibo Keita, by which he meant recognizing the borders imposed by European colonists as the fixed boundaries of independent nations.[4]

So Spanish America, starting in the 1820s, formed in effect the world's prototype league of nations, the first cooperative confederacy of republics: a community of sovereign, bounded, non-imperial, anti-colonial, formally equal and independent countries that rejected the legitimacy of aggression and vowed to resolve conflicts through multinational diplomacy.[5] Having been born into a large litter and raised, as one republican put it, in a shared New World household, Spanish American nations were socialized at an early age.

The United States, in contrast, was created lonely and raised thinking it was one of a kind.[6] It was, Thomas Jefferson said in 1809, the "solitary republic of the world, the only monument of human rights, and the sole depository of the sacred fire of freedom." *

2.

In 1787, four years after the Treaty of Paris fixed the United States' western line in the middle of the Mississippi, state delegates convened in Philadelphia to begin to debate a new constitution. As Alexander Hamilton, James Madison, and others began to publish their Federal-

---

* The United States wasn't the world's only republic: Haiti had declared itself a republic in 1804.

THE ALPHA AND THE OMEGA

ist series, staking out their positions, they, like their Spanish-speaking counterparts a bit later, were concerned with borders. Hamilton, for example, identified "territorial disputes" as the "most fertile sources of hostility among nations," from which "perhaps the greatest proportion of wars that have desolated the earth have sprung."[7] Similar to border disputes between, say, Chile and Bolivia, "discordant and undecided claims" between states such as Connecticut and Pennsylvania, or Maryland and Virginia, threatened the peace. There was, however, a key difference between the two regions. In Central and South America, territorial conflicts took place between sovereign nations over shared borders on what all agreed was (in principle) a fully occupied continent. That is, there was no free land left to claim. In the United States, in contrast, border conflicts more resembled competing empires fighting over newly discovered territory. As James Monroe wrote in a letter to Jefferson, the relationship of eastern states to western lands was much like "a colonial government, similar to that which prevailed in these states previous to the revolution."[8] What made the situation in the United States even more potentially combustible was that, to extend Monroe's analogy, there wasn't one colonial power but many—the thirteen original states—each jockeying for supremacy over their "western wastes," with, for example, New York and Virginia claiming the same patch of Appalachia. Hamilton worried that without a strong controlling authority, an "umpire or common judge," these conflicts could spiral out of control. States might turn to the "sword" as the final "arbiter."

The founders' solution to this threat was to create, with their Constitution, a central authority that could guide what Hamilton called America's "growing greatness." States agreed to cede their western-land claims to the national government to be administered as "territories." In turn, the Constitution's property clause empowered federal authorities to regulate the transformation of these territories, when they were ready, into states, equal in standing to the original thirteen. At first, around the time of the ratification of the Constitution, the discussion centered on the region west of the Alleghenies and east of the Mississippi (all that land that the British Crown had earlier, with its 1763 proclamation, tried to declare off-limits). But there was no outer parameter to the procedure incorporated into the Constitution for expansion. "It is impossible not to look forward to distant times," Jefferson wrote in 1803, "when our rapid multiplication will expand itself beyond those limits"—"limits" here referring to indigenous and British claims on western and Canadian lands—"and cover the whole northern, if not the southern continent, with a people speaking the same language, governed in similar forms, and by similar laws."[9]

Distant times came fast. Just two years later, Jefferson couldn't think of any limit to U.S. expansion. A few decades later in 1824, James Monroe, exactly at the moment Spanish Americans were winning independence, wouldn't even pause his multi-clausal exposition of limitlessness to insert a comma: "There is no object which as a people we can desire which we do not possess or which is not within our reach."[10]

The possibilities impressed James Wilson, an influential Pennsylvania judge who also saw the new federal structure as a machine for expansion. Wilson had signed the Declaration of Independence, helped draft the Constitution, and then served on the new nation's first Supreme Court. The Constitution, he said in a speech supporting ratification, "opens up immense vistas in space and time." Wilson let his thoughts drift to the future, imagining a time when the country would be comprised of "numerous states yet unformed, myriads of the human race, who will inhabit regions hitherto uncultivated."[11] Wilson turned rhapsodic at the very thought of the Constitution's power: "Calculations on a scale commensurate to a large portion of the globe" would be needed, Wilson said, to fully grasp its potential. "I have been often lost in astonishment at the vastness of the prospect before us . . . lost in the contemplation of its magnitude." *

---

* Wilson's political base was Carlisle, the town where Stump and Eisenhauer were first jailed and then liberated by a white-settler mob. Lettered and urbane, he was a station above those frontline killers. But the Revolution in Pennsylvania was powered exactly by an alliance of "staid gentlemen" like Wilson, who did the legal work, and "backcountry settlers," who did the dirty work. Wilson went bankrupt from his own speculation in western lands and fled to escape his creditors. He died on the run in Carolina, still a sitting Supreme Court justice.

Simón Bolívar too could get lost in the magnitude. He took off on flights of fancy as stratospheric as Jefferson's and did calculations commensurate with the size of the planet and beyond. Like Jefferson, who looked ahead to distant times and saw the United States spanning the continent, Bolívar "flew," in his mind, "across the years" and "fixed his imagination on future centuries, amazed by the region's prosperity, splendor, and vitality." There he saw the Absolute, calling the Americas the "heart of the universe" and the New World the "emporium of the human family":

> Radiating its riches, from its mountains of gold and silver, outward to all the precincts of the earth . . . distributing health and life through its divine [medicinal] plants to the sick men of the old world; I imagine [the Americas] sharing its precious wisdom with sages, who can't see that the sum of human enlightenment produced by nature is far greater than the sum of material wealth produced by nature. I see America sitting on the throne of freedom, holding the scepter of justice, crowned with glory, revealing to the ancient world the majesty of the modern world.[12]

Bolívar was an expansionist, at least in the realm of ideas. He hoped that one day not just Spanish America but the entire world would come together "to form a single nation spanning the universe—a federation."[13] He even predicted that Panama would someday be the center of this world government. Asia was on one side, Africa and Europe on the other, and when posterity searches for "origins of our public law," he wrote, it will find them in Panama. "What, then, shall be the Isthmus of Corinth compared to that of Panama?"

One doesn't read Bolívar's reveries and think of the words "restraint," "limit," or "containment." There was no boundary, no border, to Bolívar's republicanism, which he imagined someday unifying the world. But unlike that of Jefferson or Wilson, Bolívar's rhetorical inflation wasn't coupled to actual territorial expansion. Quite the opposite. Even as he floated to fabulous new heights, Bolívar was insisting that the best way to protect republican virtue and ensure its spread was for individual republics to submit to limits, to fix boundaries, to stop at the frontier.*

The United States, in contrast, kept going.

3.

In the middle of Thomas Jefferson's first administration as president, in 1803, the United States bought Louisiana from France (which had recently obtained the territory from Spain). The acquired territory was a rough and wide rhombus of over eight hundred thousand square miles of land west of the Mississippi, running from New Orleans to the northern Rockies. National security initially motivated the Louisiana Purchase. The threats to the young nation were many: Napoleon, Jacobins, slaves, freed slaves, Native Americans, Canada, Spain, and Great Britain. "Conspiracy, insurgency, treason, rebellion," Jefferson wrote to James Monroe, then governor of Virginia, referring specifically to a put-down slave uprising but also to a more general sense of siege, of claustrophobia, of feeling hemmed in by enemies at home and abroad.[14] With Louisiana, the United States broke out.

The purchase formally moved the U.S. border well beyond the Mississippi, roughly to the Continental Divide. But that boundary was so far away it was meaningless, for the enormous purchase of sprawling territory, yet to be fully charted, conveyed a sense of immeasurability. "Who can limit," Jefferson said, answering critics of the purchase, "the extent to which the federative principle may operate effectively?"[15]

Opponents said that the deal was illegal, since the Constitution did not include the ability to purchase territory as one of the powers assigned to the federal government. But neither, pointed out the pur-

---

*To the extent that Bolívar imagined republicanism expanding into a world government, it would be through the convergence of common ideals—not, as it occurred in the United States, by conquest. As to the specific doctrine of *uti possidetis*, the United States either refused to accept its legitimacy as Spanish America understood it or insisted on its *machtpolitik* interpretation, as it did in the 1840s when, during its invasion of Mexico, George Bancroft, secretary of the Navy, urged the United States to take California on "the basis of *uti possidetis*."

chase's supporters, did that document expressly prohibit such acquisi-
tions. The Constitution, said Virginia's representative John Randolph,
set no "particular boundary, beyond which the United States could not
extend." It was, Randolph said, "altogether uncomprehensible and inad-
missible" to argue that the founders of the republic meant to "tie us
down to particular limits, without expressing those limits."[16] "No such
bounds existed, or do now exist," Randolph argued; the United States
was "without limits." "The formative period of American history had
no geographical limitations," Woodrow Wilson would write ninety
years later, looking back.[17]

The most common justification for the purchase was that the "wilderness itself," as Maryland's representative Joseph Nicholson said,
would create "an almost insurmountable barrier to any nation that
inclined to disturb us."[18] Jefferson likened Louisiana's great wooded
expanse to the protection provided by an ocean, writing to his secretary of war that "the establishment of a strong front on our Western
boundary, the Mississippi" secures "us on that side, as our front on the
Atlantic does towards the East." Such arguments, based on defense and
national security, flung open the gate to other, more idealist visions.
"What is to hinder our extension on the same liberal principles of equal
rights," asked David Ramsay, a republican ally of Jefferson, in a speech
delivered at Charleston's St. Michael's Church in early 1804, "till we
have increased to twenty-seven, thirty-seven, or any other number of
states that will conveniently embrace in one happy union, the whole
country from the Atlantic to the Pacific ocean, and from the lakes of
Canada to the Gulf of Mexico?"[19]

"Great God!" Ramsay, like Wilson before him, could barely contain himself. Louisiana promised all: protection and liberty, which he
understood to be about "as much political happiness as ever yet has
fallen to the lot of man."

St. George Tucker, a Revolutionary War veteran and William and
Mary law professor, also supported the purchase. An energetic young
jurist in favor of the gradual emancipation of enslaved people, Tucker
shared the opinion, expressed later by Spanish Americans, that nearly
all of history's "bloody wars" were border wars. But Tucker came to a

position opposite that of his Spanish American counterparts, arguing that the best way to avoid conflict was not to fix borders but to do away with borders altogether, at least as they were understood as defining international boundaries. The Louisiana Purchase, he said, would allow the United States to replace its western border with a thousand-mile-wide buffer, an "impassable barrier against invasion." Like Ramsay's, Tucker's argument started out based on the dull terms of national defense. Yet it too, like Ramsay's, quickly turned rapturous. Jefferson's purchase was "utopian," Tucker said, equating security and liberty with bliss; never "was there a people who had their happiness so much in their own power."[20]

The Louisiana Purchase created something quite different from perpetual peace. Freed from the restraint of any "particular boundary, beyond which the United States could not extend," the United States moved forward over the land as surely as the sun across the sky. War followed like a shadow: the War of 1812, against the British and the Creek; the Texas secession from Mexico; the Mexican–American War; the long pacification campaign against Native Americans; along with a host of other, smaller conflicts, incursions, and slaughters.[21] Still, those wars were years off. Louisiana in the first decade of the 1800s was applied like a salve to all the sores that afflicted the new republic, an answer to every doubt, the allayer of every threat. Opposition existed, especially among New England Federalists who feared a dilution of their sectional power to the advantage of slave states, led by "imperial Virginia." But a majority of politicians, with starkly different visions of America's future and representing different interests and different parties—slavers, free traders, merchants, and agrarians—joined together in support. Even Alexander Hamilton, hostile to the thought of the United States becoming a sprawling rural republic of farmers, said the acquisition would "open a free and valuable market to our commercial states."[22] John Quincy Adams helped overcome opposition by defining the deal with the French not as a purchase but as a treaty and thus constitutional. The justification to expand into Louisiana contained every justification for expansion. Security was commerce, commerce was prosperity, prosperity was power, power nurtured virtue, virtue was freedom, and freedom had to be extended to be secured and secured to be extended.

So narrow was the gap separating interest from ideal that it made people giddy: St. George Tucker, when thinking of Louisiana, wanted to "break out in strains of rapture and enthusiasm."

4.

For its first generation of leaders, like Jefferson, the American Revolution was an enormous act of will. They defeated one of the most powerful empires on earth and then enshrined natural law in a political constitution, sending their diplomats east, across the Atlantic, to defend the legitimacy of their republic in Europe's royal courts. But they also moved west to erect a "government in the woods." The founders cited natural law—the "Laws of Nature and of Nature's God"—to justify American sovereignty. Yet the exercise of that sovereignty entailed the domination of nature. Settlers "pursued nature to her hiding places," and as they did, they created a new set of commandments: Establish "power over this world, everywhere naturally a wilderness." "Subdue nature." "Go forth." "Conquer a wilderness." "Take possession of the continent." "Overspread." "Increase." "Multiply." "Scour." "Clear."

Peter Onuf, a historian who has written widely on Thomas Jefferson, argues that westward expansion allowed the first generation of revolutionaries, including Jefferson, to project their original "glorious struggle into the future and across the continent," reenacting "the nation's beginnings in the multiplication of new, self-governing republican states." "It was," Onuf said, "a kind of permanent revolution."[23]

The implication of Onuf's point is profound. A key strut of the United States' exceptional sense of its history is that alone among the many Atlantic revolutions of its time—the French, Haitian, and Spanish American—the United States knew where, in the insurrection process, to stop. Republicans in the United States didn't, like the French and Haitians, push the premise of equality into the social arena and undermine the right of private property. They didn't think the state should try to conjure collective virtue out of individual interests (unlike, say, Simón Bolívar, who once wrote that the point of republican government was to produce "the greatest possible sum of happiness"). Indeed, they often argued that efforts to do so led to the vortex of terror and despotism that befell other revolutions, in France, Haiti, and Spanish America. The American Revolution understood, ideally, politics and economics to be two separate realms, going far enough to bring equality into the first but not too far to intervene in the second. Far, but not too far. Just so. Restraint when it comes to property rights, lack of restraint when it comes to territory. It's the heart of the Madisonian ideal: extend the sphere and you will protect individual liberty.

The American Revolution had no Jacobin terror, no guillotines lopping off the heads of aristocrats, no slave vengeance. The insurgency didn't devolve into tyranny-justifying anarchy. Republicans rose up, created order out of chaos, and then proceeded to extract wealth out of nature. And they kept doing so. Launching themselves into the frontier, they staged, over and over again, Onuf's permanent revolution. Expansion was "*the* principle of our institutions," Edward Everett, the influential editor of the *North American Review*, told a group of Ohioans in 1829. "It is civilization personified and embodied, going forth to take possession of the land . . . like the grand operations of sovereign Providence."[24]

But endless revolution requires power and force, of the kind that makes—in practice, and despite whatever ideal imagining otherwise—little distinction between politics and economics, between the state and the economy. An activist federal government had to deploy its full array of political, military, and financial power: to pacify, remove, transfer, settle, protect, punish, irrigate, drain, build, and finance. Jefferson himself was quite clear that the power of the state was needed to assimilate Native Americans into a settled way of life, compelling them to give up free-range hunting and fishing and to instead grow crops, spin, and weave, thus opening up their hunting forests to white settlers. He offered detailed instruction on how to use government-subsidized predatory debt to induce assimilation. "We shall push our trading houses," Jefferson wrote to Indiana's territorial governor in

1803, the year he acquired Louisiana, and "be glad" when Native Americans fell into debt and had to sell their land.[25] The trading houses needed to be government run, Jefferson said, since they could do "what private traders cannot do." That is, they could sell goods at prices low enough to begin the cycle of debt: when "debts get beyond what the individuals can pay, they become willing to lop them off by a cession of lands." And if state-orchestrated debt wasn't sufficient to the task, more direct force could be used to compel Native Americans into economic life. It would be preferable "to cultivate their love," Jefferson said, but "fear" would also work. "We presume that our strength & their weakness" is obvious to them; they "must see we have only to shut our hand to crush them." Jefferson was a man of the Enlightenment, who respected Native Americans as rational beings capable of choosing between assimilation and extermination. "All our liberalities to them proceed from motives of pure humanity," he said. Yet "should any tribe be foolhardy enough to take up the hatchet at any time, the seizing of the whole country of that tribe, and driving them across the Mississippi, as the only condition of peace, would be an example to others, and a furtherance of our final consolidation."

Most native peoples didn't give up their way of life willingly. But Jefferson had someone to blame: Great Britain. After recognizing the independence of the United States, London continued to cultivate indigenous associates in the Mississippi valley, both as part of the fur trade and as allies during the War of 1812. Great Britain's ongoing presence in the New World allowed Jefferson to hold it responsible when some Native Americans refused to assimilate or when others had a "relapse into barbarism." "The interested and unprincipled policy of England has defeated all our labors for the salvation of these unfortunate people," Jefferson wrote in 1813, and "they have seduced the greater part of the tribes, within our neighborhood, to take up the hatchet against us."[26]

Jefferson's generation broke through history, carrying forward a revolution that began the world anew. The event was a remarkable act of political resolve, and the acquisition of Louisiana allowed it to be restaged down the generations. Yet when he discussed the effects of his policy toward Native Americans, about the violence heaped on them when various legal and market mechanisms failed to convince them to part with their land, he lapsed into passive voices and hapless tenses. Even after he gave precise instructions for how to lock Native Americans into predatory debt, followed by a threat of destruction, Jefferson, upon contemplating the consequences, acted as if he stood impotent before history, as if he and the government he brought into the world were not the means of the destruction. Britain's actions, Jefferson said, "will oblige us now to pursue them to extermination, or drive them to new seats beyond our reach."[27] The United States "shall be obliged to drive them, with the beasts of the forest into the Stony mountains." *Will oblige us. Shall be obliged.* Gone are the unqualified action verbs—to conquer, to establish, to possess, to go, to act—as Jefferson here talked of the United States almost as if it were being carried away by forces beyond its control.

In South America too, Simón Bolívar, like Thomas Jefferson, believed that New World republicanism inherited its "Indian Problem" from Old World colonialism. But it is one thing to advocate, as Bolívar advocated, for a strong, virtuous state that would turn Indians into citizens. It is quite another to say, as Jefferson did, that mass murder might be the only solution, for which only the British would be culpable, and that Europe would be liable for the failure of New World republicans to deliver on their promise of perpetual peace: "the extermination of this race in our America is therefore to form an additional chapter in the English history of the same colored man in Asia, and of the brethren of their own color in Ireland and wherever else Anglo-mercantile cupidity can find a two-penny interest in deluging the earth with human blood."

The passive phrasing continued down the line. The United States would soon deploy an extraordinary amount of federal force to uproot and drive Native Americans west, many to their deaths. And yet its leaders described their fate as the result of an "unavoidable operation of natural causes." "Their misfortunes," said Lewis Cass, who as Andrew Jackson's secretary of war executed Indian removal, "have been the consequence of a state of things which could not be controlled by them or us."[28]

Thus the United States was hurled forward, an act of will against its will.

5.

In James Madison's formulation, freedom depended on expansion, needed to dilute and fragment factions. As the settlement line moved west, however, expansion came to be identified not just as a condition of freedom but as freedom itself. The identification took place in a disorienting manner. "Effects would be confused with causes," Peter Onuf writes, and the "irresistible westward tide of settlement appears to be its own cause, the manifest destiny of nature's nation" rather than the orchestrated outcome of federal policy.[29] This confusion of cause and effect—which mystified the way public force makes private power possible—multiplied outward, resulting in other confusions: of means and ends, of idealism and realism, of isolation and internationalism, even of time and space.

Others have noted the phenomenon by which the immensity of the new United States, both of the territory and the psychic task of filling it, created a new relationship, as Judge James Wilson put it, of time to space. "Pure space," Octavio Paz wrote in the 1950s, describing the United States. It sounds like a description of the Absolute, except that the political scientist Louis Hartz, also writing in the 1950s, said that Americans didn't so much confront the Absolute as believe themselves to be the Absolute. "The American absolute," Hartz said, manifested itself in a compulsive, obsessive individualism and timeless "innocence of mind."[30] "Time was abolished for God's country," the historian Loren Baritz wrote a bit later, of American mythology. "Lifted out of history, free from a limiting past, Americans were presumably more self-determining than any other national people had ever been." Having defeated the Old World, Baritz said, they resisted the very idea of "old," the thought that limits, decline, and death might pertain to them. The vast, open West, Baritz wrote, "contributed its share to the notion that Americans swung free in seemingly limitless space unhampered by the dead and deadening hand of the past."[31]

Madison's equation of the republic with an ever-inflating sphere is a good symbol of the American Absolute (whether understood as something Americans confronted or something they were). The argument that republicanism depended on expansion, when considered fully and extended logically, allowed no distinction between what was inside and what was outside. The welfare of those inside required the gradual incorporation of what was outside. "The greater the expansion," as President James Monroe would say in 1822, "the greater the advantage."[32] There might be some "practical limits," Monroe admitted, to the inflation. But he couldn't think of any.

We had to take all so we could be all, so the republic could, in Jefferson's words, realize its "final consolidation."[33] The beginning became the end of things, the Alpha and the Omega, as Columbus, sailing west to get east, first wanted to call America.*

---

* On his first journey across the Atlantic, Columbus, according to the sixteenth-century Milanese historian Peter Martyr, wanted to name the extreme western point of Cuba "Alpha and Omega," because he thought that "it was the east when the sun set and the west when the sun rose." Later, in 1697, the Puritan Samuel Sewall, in his *Phaenomena quaedam Apocalyptica*, wrote: "America's being the Beginning of the East, and the End of the West; was that which moved Columbus to call some part of it by the Name of Alpha and Omega."

THREE
....

A Caucasian Democracy

"All beyond was wilderness."

"Frontier," "border," "boundary." These words were essentially inter-changeable at the beginning of the 1800s, at the time of the Louisiana Purchase. They were used to indicate the limits and confines of a country, "the *marches*, the utmost verge of any territory." "Frontier" held no special civilizational or emotional meaning, as it would come to later, as a liminal zone associated with a distinct culture. Essentially, "frontier" was either synonymous with boundary, the juridical outer limit of a nation, or, more commonly, it was used to mark a line of national defense.[1] If anything, of these three words, "border" was more often used to convey the vexed experience of living on the edge. A "borderer," rather than a frontiersman, identified "he that dwells on the borders," and "bordrage," now obsolete, meant "to plunder the borders."[2] Neither the first English dictionary published in the United States, in 1788, nor the first dictionary written by someone born in America, in 1798, even included the word "frontier." But throughout the 1800s, as the United States executed one "removal" operation after another, driving Native Americans west and freeing up their land for settlers and speculators, "frontier" came more frequently to mean the line separating Indian

Country from white settlement. By the end of the 1800s, though, there was no more Indian Country, at least apart from fragmented reservations, and the word "frontier" had come to mean not a line but a way of life, synonymous with freedom.

1.

The first run of United States presidents—who comprised what might be called the founders' coalition—was dominated by Tidewater and Piedmont slavers from Virginia. Washington, Jefferson, Madison, and Monroe all speculated in land west of the Alleghenies. And they all fully expected that the indigenous peoples who lived on this land would vanish, either as a culture, through assimilation, or as individuals through death, as the United States moved toward the Pacific.

Yet these early presidents were constrained. Jefferson had promised to "bend" his entire administration to acquiring indigenous land and transforming their hunting grounds into private property, and he lived long enough to witness the breakup of entire communities. But, really, the federal government lacked the resources, military and financial, to expedite his western vision as quickly as many would have hoped. Having read the full ancient and modern library on moral government, the men who ruled the United States for its first half century of existence did imagine themselves responsible administrators. They weren't Pennsylvania Quakers, the authorities who drove an Indian Killer like Frederick Stump to Tennessee and who came close to imagining Native Americans as full equals. But neither were they Stumps. In representing their new republic to the international community, some of the nation's leaders felt compelled to prove themselves good stewards of its land and people, contrary to European opinion, and that meant respecting what George Washington called the "interior frontiers" of indigenous sovereignty.

With independence from Great Britain, the United States had inherited a tome of treaty obligations London had made to indigenous communities. Then it signed a volume more, promising protection and recognizing their borders and boundaries. Washington, for example, negotiated a treaty with the Creek nation that granted it the authority to punish trespassers "as they please."[3] "Foreign nations" was the way Washington's secretary of war, Henry Knox, understood indigenous tribes.[4] The federal government required Anglo travelers to carry passports as they entered these nations south of the Ohio River, the borders of which were marked by a line of cleared forest twenty feet wide.[5] The new republic, in other words, was a jigsaw of indigenous nations within a nation, some holding extensive forested hunting grounds. In the Old Northwest Territory, these nations included the Iroquois, Ojibwa, Ottawa, Potawatomi, and Winnebago; in southern Appalachia were the Cherokees, the Creeks in western Georgia and Tennessee, the Choctaws and Chickasaws in the eastern Mississippi valley, and the Seminoles in Florida, along with many other groups. All told, nominal indigenous sovereignty stretched west of the Alleghenies from a large region around the Great Lakes down to northwestern Ohio, most of Georgia, Alabama, and Mississippi, the western third of Tennessee, and western Kentucky.

The new United States also inherited settler lust for the land.[6] It was a nation founded on the right of freedom, a right not just exercised *by* but originating *in* movement. And so ever more vicious variations on a theme extended the blood meridian: the hostility British settlers felt toward the British Crown was now, after independence, transferred to the federal government brought into being by that hostility, especially as that government began to promise to protect indigenous sovereignty, as London had earlier.

The clash was fundamental to the United States' foundation. In 1783, for instance, the same year the Treaty of Paris recognized the existence of the United States and fixed its western boundary at the Mississippi, the Continental Congress did what George III had done two decades earlier: ban settlement in land inhabited or claimed by Indians. And so some states did what the American revolutionaries did: they ignored the ban. For instance, North Carolina, also in 1783, passed what became known as its "Land Grab Act," declaring that all the territory west of the Alleghenies (which included the soon-to-be-incorporated state of

Tennessee) was open to surveys and claims. Within seven months, upward of four million acres, mostly of Cherokee and Chickasaw land, was taken by settlers and investors.

Earlier, in the years prior to the American Revolution, George Washington himself pushed against British efforts to limit his Ohio valley land ventures, saying that the Royal Proclamation of 1763 line had to "fall." But decades later, as he shepherded the United States into existence, he complained of the "land jobbers, speculators, and monopolizers" who were streaming into that same valley, acting like a law unto themselves, contributing nothing to the support of the government.[7] Their insistence, Washington wrote, of living in what they considered absolute liberty would cause a "great deal of bloodshed." In the conflict between settlers and Indians, Washington's secretary of war, Henry Knox, was sympathetic to the Indians. Indigenous people, he said, "possess the right of the soil of all lands within their limits." But he was pessimistic that the federal government could protect such a right: "The angry passions of the frontier Indians and whites are too easily inflamed by reciprocal injuries, and are too violent to be controlled by the feeble authority of the civil power."[8] In 1807, the federal government passed an "Intrusion Act," which made the unsanctioned settlement of western public land a crime and empowered the executive branch to use military force to remove squatters. It was hard to enforce, however. "The disposition of the people of the States to emigrate into the Indian country," Knox said, "cannot be effectually prevented." Though he did hope it could be "restrained and regulated."

There's an 1811 story about Andrew Jackson that captures this irony, of a government that came into being as the agent of settler spirit only to become the target of settler animus, of a refusal to be "restrained and regulated." Jackson, an advocate of vigilantes like Stump (who, after settling in Tennessee, served as a captain under Jackson's military command), was still seventeen years away from winning the presidency and ending the rule of the founders' coalition. But he was well established in Nashville. As a regional public figure, he had been elected Tennessee's first representative to Congress and to the state's Supreme

Court and also headed the Tennessee militia. As a private businessman, General Jackson had grown wealthy as a lawyer, merchant, horse breeder, and planter, profiting greatly from the nexus of slavery, slave trading, and Indian dispossession that continued to pull settlers through the Cumberland Gap into Tennessee and Kentucky.[9] As a lawyer, Jackson earned significant fees processing the claims of land taken from Native Americans. And he's the only president, as far as we know, to have personally driven slave coffles—a "coffle" being a procession of enslaved people, often roped by the neck, marched from one place to another.[10]

In the winter of 1811, Jackson was moving a coffle along the Natchez Trace—an ancient Indian road that ran alongside the Mississippi, connecting Nashville to Natchez—when he was stopped by Silas Dinsmore, a federal agent. The Trace passed through Chickasaw and Choctaw lands, nominally protected by federal treaty, and government Indian agents like Dinsmore were charged with checking the passports of travelers. They did so for a number of reasons: to monitor white settlers and traders entering indigenous lands; to keep a lookout for escaping slaves, who hoped to slip into Indian country; and to enforce the growing number of federal laws attempting to regulate slavery. Three years earlier, Congress had banned the trans-Atlantic slave trade, so the checkpoint was intended to ensure that the only chattel being moved along the road were bona fide slaves, either imported prior to 1808 or American-born.

"Yes, sir," Jackson answered Dinsmore when the agent asked for his papers, "I always carry mine with me." He meant the U.S. Constitution—which was "sufficient passport to take me where ever my business leads me," including on a road that "was by law free for every American citizen." Another version of the story has the general showing his pistols and saying, "These are General Jackson's passports!"[11] Whatever exactly transpired, Jackson made it clear that he was "unwilling . . . to submit the American name to such an insult as to request permission to travel on the public highway." Jackson was waved through, but he launched a campaign to remove Dinsmore from office. In a series of letters to government officials, the future president warned that the

agent, who faced similar complaints from other slavers that he had
hindered their free movement, would face vigilante justice. Jackson
threatened to burn "Silas Dinsmore in the flames of his agency house"
and to "cut" the agent off at his "roots."[12] "The citizens say," Jackson
warned, "they will remove the nuisance, if Government does not"; the
people were "ready to burst forth in Vengeance."

"*My God*, is it come to this?" Jackson asked (the emphasis in the
original transcription). "Are we *freemen or are we slaves? Is this real
or is it a dream?*"

Dinsmore was hardly a radical. Appointed to his position by Washington and reappointed by Jefferson, he served as one of those predatory debt agents Jefferson described, working to convince the Choctaw
and other indigenous groups to cede land to the federal government.
But as Dinsmore wrote in his defense, "gentlemen in the Western Country" such as Jackson believed that no laws pertained to them. They
practically hallucinated freedom. "*Is it a dream?*" They also took the
mere request for documents proving their ownership of slaves to be a
form of slavery, to be (as Jackson wrote in one of his letters) an "evil"
and affront to the "bravery and blood of our forefathers." At Jackson's
urging, the state legislature condemned Dinsmore and directed Tennessee's representatives in the Senate and House to press, successfully,
for his removal.[13]

Here on a frontier back road more than half a century before the
Civil War, two different, racialized definitions of sovereign liberty faced
off against each other. The first, represented by Jackson, imagined "free
born" to mean white born and "liberty" to mean the ability to do whatever they wanted, including to buy and sell humans and move them,
unrestrained by interior frontiers, across a road that by treaty belonged
to an indigenous nation. To be asked for a passport was akin to slavery itself, and to be so asked in front of actual enslaved people signaled
"that their owners were not the sovereigns after all."[14] The second,
embodied by Agent Dinsmore, authorized federal authorities to take
action to provide minimal protection to the subjugated and vanquished
victims of the "free born."

With men like Jackson loose upon the land, the fragile authority of an overstretched state, which had enough capacity to roll the frontier west but not enough to moderate the treatment of those ground down under the roll, was easily routed.

2.

In October 1812, a year after Jackson's dustup on the Natchez Trace, Tennessee's state legislature ordered the creation of a "sufficient force to exterminate the Creek Nation."[15] Jackson, in charge of the west Tennessee militia, complied. The white settlers around Nashville had been in a low-intensity war with the Creeks for years. Leaders like Jackson had complained continually of federal inaction, of temporizing when it came to punishing the Creeks for raids on white communities. Jackson instructed his men—including Stump and his sons—to "pant with vengeance" and turn themselves into "engines of destruction." Jackson laid waste to Creek villages and declared himself "Justifiable." He threatened to continue burning houses, killing warriors, mutilating their bodies (he ordered his men to cut the noses off the Indian corpses, so as to more easily tally the dead), and enslaving their wives and children "until I do obtain a surrender."

Jackson had long criticized federal treaties for dealing with Native Americans too deferentially. Now Jackson imposed a new kind of treaty on the defeated Creeks, previewing the misery he would later, as president, nationalize. Dispossessed of over twenty million acres, the Creeks were, according to the treaty's text, "reduced to extreme want" and denied "the means of subsistence." A once self-sufficient people were made dependent on government corn—which, according to Jackson's treaty, the United States would provide free of charge out of "motives of humanity"—and forced to accept the establishment of trading houses in their territory. As Jefferson had earlier suggested, these were meant to increase debt bondage and compel the Creeks to give up even more of their hunting grounds. (Later, Henry Clay, one of the last great pre-Jacksonian statesmen, said that all of the history of human diplomacy, including that of "all-conquering and desolating Rome," would not yield a more hateful document than Jackson's Creek treaty, filled as it was with humiliating demands imposed on a "wretched people reduced to the last extremity of distress, whose miserable existence we have to preserve by a voluntary stipulation to furnish them with bread!" Taking special exception to the treaty's demand for the Creeks to turn over their religious leaders, whom Jackson blamed for leading opposition to white settlers, Clay begged, "Sir, spare them their prophets!")[16]

Victory over the Creeks cleared the road for Jackson to make a national name for himself. He'd go on to defeat the British in the War of 1812's Battle of New Orleans, the Seminoles in Florida, then the Chickasaw in Tennessee and Alabama. Scholars sometimes describe the "madman" theory as a modern kind of diplomacy, the tactical use of the threat of irrational violence to leverage negotiations. But Jackson in the 1810s warned one indigenous group after another that they would be hunted to extinction if they didn't agree to terms. "Fire shall consume their towns and villages," he told Native Americans considering supporting the Creeks, and "their lands shall be divided among the whites." Jackson kept the skulls of Indians he killed as trophies, and his soldiers cut long strips of skin from their victims to use as bridle reins. Terrorize, bribe, legalize. Jackson used that sequence—threaten death, pay off those tribal leaders who could be paid off to break unified resistance, and then formalize the arrangement with a treaty—to propel himself to the presidency. "We have seen the ravens and the vultures preying upon the carcasses of the unburied slain," Jackson told his troops, following an especially gruesome 1814 massacre. "Our vengeance has been glutted."[17]

Jackson was more brutal in dealing with Native Americans than his predecessors had been. Madison and Monroe distrusted Jackson. Jefferson disliked him intensely, saying he was "much alarmed" at the idea of Jackson becoming president: "He is one of the most unfit men I know of for such a place. He has had very little respect for laws and constitutions. . . . His passions are terrible . . . he is a dangerous man." Yet all three of them came to depend on Jackson. Madison wanted the British out of the Mississippi valley, for which he started the War of

1812. General Jackson won it. James Monroe wanted Spanish Florida. Jackson gave it to him; his murderous 1818 raid into Pensacola convinced Spain to cede the territory to Washington. As to Jefferson, he believed that the "final consolidation" of American liberty wouldn't be achieved until the surface of the continent was occupied by white, English-speaking people, with neither "blot" nor "mixture on that surface." But three obstacles stood in the way to this vision of a continent scoured white: Native Americans; Africans and African Americans (both enslaved and free); and the multihued citizens of Mexico, which, after winning its independence from Spain in 1821, claimed territory as far north as modern-day Utah, blocking access to the Pacific.

Jackson sensed the tension in the founders, of wanting it all but not wanting to do all it took to have it all. Thomas Jefferson, in particular, came to embody for Jackson a failure of will. Jefferson swung widely, for instance, between issuing instructions for how to use predatory loans to break up indigenous culture, fantasizing genocide ("to pursue them to extermination"), and dreaming that sex would solve the problem of difference (he once told a delegation of Delaware and Mohegan that "we shall all be Americans, you will mix with us by marriage, your blood will run in our veins"). Jefferson knew that if the federal government wanted to establish new states, it would have to extinguish indigenous title in western Georgia "at some point in the future."[18]

Jackson was the future.[19]

By the mid-1820s, with Jacksonians on the march, the founders' coalition fell apart. The last president to represent that coalition, even though he was a few years too young to be a founder himself, was John Quincy Adams (in office for one term, from 1825 to 1829). Adams opposed slavery. He opposed the dispossession of Native Americans. And he resisted pressure, placed on him by members of the nascent Jacksonian coalition, to escalate tensions with Mexico. Adams did, though, favor expansion. The United States, he said, was "destined by God and nature to be coextensive with the North American continent." But he couldn't square the circle. He couldn't come up with a way to make the country and continent coterminous and at the same time extirpate slavery, avoid war with Mexico, and protect Native Americans.

Adams couldn't even use his executive authority to stop southern states, especially Georgia, from driving what was left of their subdued indigenous populations west.[20]

The Jacksonians had a simpler solution, which aligned theory, or desire, with action: remove Indians, wage war on Mexico, and defend and extend slavery.

3.

Andrew Jackson defeated John Quincy Adams in 1828 to become the seventh president of the United States. Many historians still consider Jackson's two terms (1829–1837) the fulfillment of the promise of the American Revolution's anti-aristocratic aspirations, a moment of boisterous egalitarianism in which restless white workers armed with the vote became a political force.[21] "A proletarian orgy" was how one writer later recalled the scene at Jackson's inauguration, as the president's crude supporters "descended upon the city like a great swarm of locusts, by stagecoach, cart, and wagon, on horseback and on foot."[22] Wearing homespun dresses and rough canvas jackets, they made the White House their own for a day, leaving the rugs muddied and porcelain shattered when the festivities were over. This was a time of vast and fast-paced change, marked by the growth of cities, the arrival of increasing numbers of European immigrants, and the rise of manufacturing and finance capital. More families than ever before depended on wages to survive. Paper currency flooded local markets, as banks spread across the nation. Personal debt grew and rent increased. The Atlantic market for cotton boomed, with southern slave plantations growing to keep pace with demand.

The nation was gripped by a sense of upheaval, an expectation that the republic stood on the brink of a fundamental rupture with its past. Many worried that rapid extension of electoral democracy might result in some kind of social tyranny, that the Jacksonians, in response to popular demands—especially those voiced by the country's growing number of urban wage workers—might turn out to be coonskin Jacobins. "The hobgoblin of Caesarism haunted universal imagination," one writer described the "terror" that pervaded Whig circles, as the well-heeled opponents of Jackson were called.[23]

Jackson, though, took the country in a different direction. He responded to the growing complexity of daily life by promising to bring back "primitive simplicity and purity," to "restore" government institutions to what he said was their original minimal design.[24] The federal government, Jackson said, should be "limited to a general superintending power," prohibited from restricting "human liberty" and used only to "enforce human rights," chief among them "free enterprise" and property rights, including the right to own human beings as property. Washington's duties should be "plain." Its "machinery" should be "so simple and economical as scarcely to be felt."[25] Jackson often used the image of a stripped-down machine, reduced to minimum operations, to describe what should be the proper, limited relationship of the federal government—"that simple machine which the Constitution created"— to the individual states. The specter of a "machine" could be monstrous in the 1830s, on the eve of the industrial revolution. But the Jacksonian machine hummed like a waterwheel.

Some social demands were met, either at the federal or state level, leading to an extension of the vote and public education and an end to debtors' prison. But the cult of primitive simplicity was designed to forestall one particular demand, then being made with increasing insistence, especially by northerners: emancipation and the destruction of chattel slavery. A minimalist vision of federal power—supported by new legal doctrines offered by slavers and their defenders, among them nullification, "state sovereignty," and states' rights—was meant to legally arm the South against an increasingly hostile and abolitionist North.[26]

Mobilized to defend a system of racial domination, the ideal of a limited federal government is itself inescapably racialized. It's an extension of that resentment unique to white American supremacy carried forward since at least the Paxton Boys: the idea that the central government wasn't doing enough to protect settlers, that indeed it was hostile to settlers, and that settlers had to take matters into their own hands. Jacksonians understood freedom as freedom from restraint, including, as Andrew Jackson himself insisted on the Natchez Trace, from authorities telling them they couldn't slave or settle.

The Age of Jackson, or what some scholars have called the Jacksonian consensus, entailed a radical empowerment of white men. At the same time, though, it witnessed an equally radical subjugation of African Americans. "The adoption of universal white male suffrage," wrote the historian Lerone Bennett, Jr., in 1970, "led directly to the disenfranchisement of black males who had voted since the colonial period." As chattel cotton slavery spread into the Deep South, into Alabama, Arkansas, Louisiana, and Texas, free people of color (that is, former slaves or descendants of slaves who had gained their emancipation through manumission, escape, or, in northern states, abolition) saw their rights greatly curtailed, with new second-class-citizenship laws passed in many states. "As Jacksonian democracy reached new heights," Bennett continued, "racism in America reached levels never before known to man."

"Poor whites rose" and "poor blacks were pushed down." But poor whites could only rise so far in cramped cities and squalid quarters, earning low wages and paying high rent. Many, looking around at their miserable conditions, began to organize workingmen's and mechanics' associations and to ask the same question Jackson asked of his encounter on the Trace: "Are we freemen or are we slaves?"

The Indian Removal Act let Jackson answer: freemen. The act, which Jackson signed into law in early 1830, about a year into his first term, mandated federal troops to push Native Americans beyond the Mississippi and extinguish their titles to their land. On the southern frontier, Florida Seminoles fought back. They were slaughtered, and survivors fled into the Everglades. Within just a few years, about fifty thousand people had been driven from their homes east of the Mississippi and marched west, herded across the river into territory that today comprises Oklahoma and parts of Kansas. It was a "wise

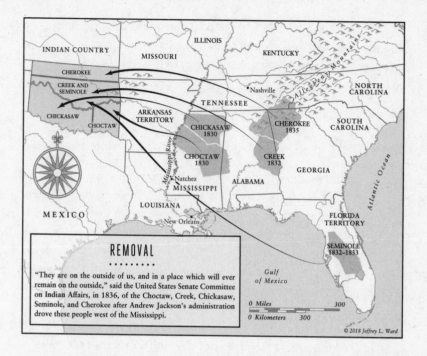

REMOVAL

"They are on the outside of us, and in a place which will ever remain on the outside," said the United States Senate Committee on Indian Affairs, in 1836, of the Choctaw, Creek, Chickasaw, Seminole, and Cherokee after Andrew Jackson's administration drove these people west of the Mississippi.

and humane policy," Jackson told Congress in 1832, to transfer our "remnants" to the western side of the Mississippi, and the work was fast approaching "its consummation."[27] Thousands had died in the transfer. Many more thousands fell ill.

This first removal resulted in about twenty-five million acres of formerly Indian land, including large tracts of Georgia and Alabama, freed up for the market and slave economy. Jackson's predecessor, John Quincy Adams, had tried to use the proceeds generated by the sale of western public land to fund what he called a "national program," to build roads and canals but also hospitals, schools, and other social institutions. Jackson, though, pledged to "put an end forever" to this "subversive" use of public land for government revenue. He instead started to distribute, or let states distribute, land at low cost to his slaver and frontier constituents, to those Jackson called the "adventurous and hardy," the "true friends of liberty."[28] Settlers and planters poured into the suddenly "free land," extending cotton planting up and down the Mississippi and into the lands of the Cherokee, Creeks, Choctaws, and Chickasaws. And they didn't have to carry a passport to do so.

4.

In 1837, on the cusp of a fearsome seven-year recession, the United States prepared for war on its many frontiers. "There is not," the *New York Journal of Commerce* wrote, "at this moment, a single portion of our vast frontier, whether inland or maritime, that does not require attention. On the south, we have the Seminoles to contend with; on the S.W. is Mexico, with which we have unsettled relations."[29] Enemies were everywhere, harrowing the geopolitical imagination of second- and third-generation republicans. The Canadian "frontiers" are "overhanging us from sea to sea like a lowering storm-cloud," warned Caleb Cushing, a Massachusetts member of the House of Representatives.

The threat gathering on the west—a "long inland frontier, of river, and plain, and lake," as Cushing described it, "utterly incapable of being guarded by fortifications or armies"—dominated public debate.[30] With Indian removal well under way, some feared retribution. An anonymous artillery officer, writing from east Florida to the *Charleston Courier* in 1838, described the horrors he had helped inflict on the recalcitrant Seminoles. He and his fellow soldiers had driven them "into the swamps and unwholesome places of their country," where they clung "with the last efforts of despair to their beloved homes." He reminded readers that "equilibrium" is a moral as well as physical concept and that "retribution will inevitably follow dereliction." The penitent soldier continued: "Like the Southern winds of a summer's day, congesting thunderous clouds in the north, we have been crowding and condensing disaffected Indian tribes between the Mississippi and the Rocky Mountains, and as by an electric spark, these clouds turn and rush forth, lavishing their fury upon the earth, so may a foreign enemy, or one among themselves, arouse these tribes to come down upon us in such numbers as shall desolate a large portion of our new happy country."[31]

Others were less soul-searching yet still understood that a policy of biblical-level dispossession would most likely provoke some kind of reaction. In France, when republicans executed the king, deposed the aristocracy, and launched a reign of terror, they incited all the various branches of Europe's *ancien régime* to mobilize against them and lay siege to their revolution. In North America, republicans presided over a different sort of terror, not class terror but race terror. Decades of horrific violence against Native Americans didn't so much provoke as produce enemies. "We must bear in mind," said the *Journal of Commerce* essay cited above, "that the many thousand Creek, Chickasaw, Cherokee, Seminoles, and other Indians, who have been, or will be, removed to the far west, will cherish there a lurking spirit of hostility against the people who have injured them, which ever and anon may break out into open war. A general war waged by the Indians, who will soon be concentrated on our western frontier." *Or will be* is a powerful tense shift, moving swiftly from the past—discussing the possible effects of something the United States did do—to the expectant future, the predicted consequences of something it would do. In 1837, the Bureau of Indian Affairs estimated that there existed 66,499 potential "warriors" among the remaining Indian population in North America and that if they "ever combined" they would make a "formidable" force capable of sweeping "away the whole white population west of the Mississippi."[32]

The Indian Removal Act, in addition to removing Native Americans, mandated the federal government to protect Native Americans once they were removed. The United States was to assure removed nations that it would "forever secure and guaranty" their new lands and protect them from "all interruption or disturbance" from "any other person or persons whatever." "We are as a nation," Jackson's successor, Martin Van Buren, wrote, "responsible in *foro conscientiae* to the opinions of the great family of nations" regarding the post-removal treatment of Native Americans, "a people comparatively weak, upon whom we were perhaps in the beginning unjustifiable aggressors, but of whom in the progress of time and events, we have become the guardians, and, as we hope, the benefactors."[33] It wouldn't be too contrived a point to make that the United States was charging itself with the duty of protecting its victims from itself.

The act blurred the line between foreign and domestic policy. Was Indian Country a different country, outside the authority of the United States? A series of Supreme Court rulings in the early 1830s answered the question by splitting the difference, saying that the Cherokee nation was and wasn't sovereign, was and wasn't part of the United States. "Perhaps," said one decision, indigenous polities could be called "domestic dependent nations." "Indian Country" was foreign, in the sense that removal treaties—the agreements Washington signed with specific indigenous peoples that formalized their expulsion—acknowledged the sovereignty of individual nations. But to hold to the letter of those documents and to treat Indian Country as a foreign sovereign power would give an opening to European rivals, especially the British, who were still being regularly accused of using indigenous grievances to destabilize frontier society. "They were neither foreign nations, nor states of the union, but something different from either," said one newspaper of Native American communities, following a particularly confusing Supreme Court ruling on the Cherokees.[34] "Baffling," wrote one historian of the situation.[35]

The location of Indian Country, in relation to what was considered the United States proper, added to the bafflement. At this point, in the 1830s, the United States' outer reaches were laid out thusly, east to west: First there was the Mississippi River. Not too far beyond that was the line of Anglo settlement, from Lake Superior down to Natchez. Next was the Army's military defense perimeter, plotted along a series of forts running from the Great Lakes to Louisiana. Then came Indian Country, generally used to describe Oklahoma and a portion of Kansas but sometimes also referring to land running up to the Dakotas. Past Indian Country was the nation's internationally recognized legal limit, north out of the Gulf of Mexico, first along the Sabine River (which today separates Louisiana from Texas), then the Red and Arkansas Rivers.

Beyond that border was Mexico, which reached north to Utah and Montana and west to California.

By 1836, the Senate Committee on Indian Affairs considered these lines more or less fixed. But fixed didn't mean clear-cut. Indian Country was *east* of—that is, *within*—the international boundary of the United States, but it was *west* of the settler line. The committee unintentionally conveyed the muddiness of it all when, referring to expelled Indians, it pronounced: "They are on the outside of us, and in a place which will ever remain on the outside."[36] The committee here is obviously referring to the settlement line. Whatever the case, they wouldn't be outside for long.

The lines were in constant movement, driven west by settlers over Indian Country. As they moved, more removals followed, in Ohio, Michigan, Indiana, Illinois, Wisconsin, Iowa, Minnesota, up and down and across the west, a repeating cycle that advanced with a propulsive force. John Quincy Adams knew that this rotation—with Indians finding themselves inside, outside, then inside the boundary once more—couldn't go on forever. The continent was vast but not infinite. "In the instances of the New-York Indians removed to Green Bay, and of the Cherokees removed to the Territory of Arkansas," he wrote in his private diary in 1828, the last full year of his presidency, "we have scarcely given them time to build their wigwams before we are called upon by our own people to drive them out again." The best policy, he confided to himself, would be assimilation, to make Native Americans equal citizens. But this, he knew, "the People of the States within which they are situated will not permit."

Throughout the nineteenth century, some indigenous peoples did make a move to sedentary agriculture. But they still had their lands taken and they still were removed. Georgia's Cherokees, for instance, had even adopted a written constitution, using the constitutional relationship established between states and the federal government to justify their existence. Adams, the president most sympathetic to the plight of Native Americans in U.S. history, thought the constitution "impracticable," as he noted in his diary. Some communities, including

Native Americans in the Old Northwest Territory, around the Great Lakes, successfully participated in the commercial fur trade while maintaining a distinct sense of cultural identity. Lewis Cass, who served as Michigan's territorial governor before he became Jackson's secretary of war, took this hard-won achievement—maintaining cultural and political autonomy while mastering the commercial market—as proof of backwardness. They had "successfully" resisted, he wrote in 1830, "every effort to meliorate their situation."[37]

5.

The decades following Jackson's Removal Act witnessed an evolution in the meaning of the word "frontier." It went from identifying a military front or a national border to indicating a way of life: the "outer edge of the wave," as Frederick Jackson Turner would later describe the concept, separating civilization from savagery. The metaphor "edge of the wave" would seem to work against itself, since it combines an image that suggests definitional sharpness—an "edge"—with one that conveys constant flux and decomposition—a "wave." But it perfectly describes its object.

The frontier, especially after removal, had to be precise, like an edge, because it was the measure of civilization. "Well-defined lines marked the onset of civilization at the far West, and all beyond was wilderness," wrote an early observer of the frontier. The American Revolution advanced a theory of political self-governance based on an individual's ability to self-govern, to use capabilities, virtues, strength, and reason to contain passions and control vices. People of color—enslaved peoples within the United States or dispossessed peoples on its border—helped define the line between proper liberty, which justified self-governance, and ungovernable licentiousness, which justified domination. Native Americans especially, in their "wild freedom"—a refusal to cultivate the earth and a desire instead to roam, hunt, and gather—created what many identified as an almost childlike relationship to nature, held up as the opposite of the self-cultivation and self-possession of white people worthy of political self-rule. "The Indians are children," Horace Greeley, editor of the *New-York Tribune*, wrote, and "any band of schoolboys from ten to fifteen years of age, are quite as capable of ruling their appetites, devising and upholding a public policy, constituting and conducting a state or community as an average Indian tribe." The Indian "is a slave of appetite and sloth, never emancipated from the tyranny of one passion save by the ravenous demands of another . . . These people must die out," Greeley said. "God has given the earth to those who will subdue and cultivate it."[38]

But like a wave, the frontier was also blurry, indistinct, a place where white settlers fled to escape routinization, even as they defined their self-command against the wildlings on the other side. In the east, it was becoming increasingly difficult for families to reproduce themselves, as the spread of capitalism—with its low wages, high prices of basic goods, and even higher rents—placed increasing pressure on the family structure. In order to survive, many households moved west. As they did, not only was the ideal of the family, including domestic order and fatherly authority, redeemed, it was sharpened in contrast to the wildness of the frontier. A little house on a big prairie, sheltered from "unrestrained" and "lawless iniquity," as one observer described life on the frontier. There existed in the pages of western romances, poems, and newspaper reports an intense, simultaneously rageful and rueful, menacing and maudlin identification with Native Americans. "A life in the open air," went another early description of the frontier, "freedom from restraint, and a vigorous appetite, generally finding a hearty meal to satisfy it, make difficult a return to the humdrum of steady work and comparative respectability."[39] Settlers might imagine Native Americans as their "brothers" who had a primogeniture right to the land, even as they donned hide skins and took up tomahawks to slaughter them and claim that right as their own. "Voluptuary and stoic; swept by gusts of fury too terrible to be witnessed, yet imperturbable beyond all men, under the ordinary excitements and accidents of life; garrulous, yet impenetrable," as one Bureau of Indian Affairs agent wrote, in describing the "curious compound and strange self-contradiction" of "the red man" in his "wild life."[40]

Also like a wave, the frontier had to move, it had to be "fleeting," as the western traveler George Catlin described the line in the late 1830s, "a moving barrier" advancing over the continent as civilization progressed. The western frontier was "a zigzag, ever-varying line," a government official in charge of Indian affairs once said, "more or less definitely marked" yet "always slowly moving west," a threshold of constant, endless war: "an almost incessant struggle, the Indians to retain and the Whites to get possession."[41]

For tactical reasons, though, the U.S. military had to continue to think of the frontier as fixed, and their mission clear-cut: "to protect . . . border settlements, extending along a line of one thousand miles, against the incursions of numerous savage tribes."[42] Yet however much the military imagined the frontier as stable and well defined, the boundary separating Native Americans from white settlers was constantly changing. As the United States moved west, any given major river—the Mississippi, the Missouri, the Arkansas, or the Red River—along with the tributaries that ran perpendicular into that river would become part of the defensive frontier. In this vision, the frontier looked more like a comb, or half a fishbone.

Military strategists wanted to defend a firm line, and they produced one survey after another trying to plot the frontier's exact coordinates. Tactical requirements, however, imagined not one but three separate lines dividing the United States from "Indian Country." The first, according to an Army report, was the line of white settlement, of traders, farmers, ranchers, hunters, and trappers. The second was a militarized "interior line," required for "the special protection of the settlements," and entailed a series of outposts and forts that "must necessarily be *within* our boundary." The third was an "exterior line," west of the settlement line, identified as advancing "into Indian country far *beyond* our boundary."[43] *Within* or *beyond* (the emphasis is in the original report) the boundary, the geography was baffling indeed.

However they were defined, and wherever they ran, none of these lines were steady. Each interacted with the other to move the whole operation forward. Two years before Jackson's Removal Act, the office of the secretary of war complained to Congress about the policy of "pushing our military posts"—including Fort Snelling on the Mississippi and Fort Leavenworth on the Missouri—"so far within the Indian country, and so far ahead of the regular advances of our population," that the advance kicked off a violent cycle: the outposts "only serve to invite wild and profitless adventures into the Indian country," leading to "personal collisions with the natives"; the government then had to mount "a military expedition, to vindicate the rights of these straggling traders." This dynamic, in which danger caused by the United States going over the line pulled the U.S. over the land, was repeated over and over again.

Indian removal opened the floodgates, allowing, as one legal theorist would describe the Age of Jackson, "an irresistible tide of Caucasian democracy" to wash over the land.[44] King Cotton extended its dominion through the South, creating unparalleled wealth, along with unparalleled forms of racial domination over both enslaved and free blacks. At the same time, Native Americans were driven west, and the white settlers and planters who got their land experienced something equally unprecedented: an extraordinary degree of power and popular sovereignty. Never before in history could so many white men consider themselves so free. Jacksonian settlers moved across the frontier, continuing to win a greater liberty by putting down people of color, and then continuing to define their liberty in opposition to the people of color they put down.

FOUR

The Safety Valve

"There is no longer any controlling of the mania."

1.

Consider the safety valve. Invented, apparently, in its basic form in the late 1600s, in France, after a pressure cooker used to break down horse hooves and mutton bones into jelly exploded, the device had within a century been forge-welded onto steam engines, boilers, locomotives, and furnaces—a necessary, though too often unreliable, last line of defense against accumulating gases and unsustainable pressures. Thomas Jefferson had urged Spain to let U.S. barges and keelboats moor on the west side of the Mississippi, which they needed to do to be able to tack upstream against the current. Soon, though, U.S. boats would have their own means to ply the river's main trunk and many tributaries, moving upriver with ease and racing down with speed: steam revolutionized the pan-Mississippi world.

Steamboats carried more and more passengers and freight, including slavers and slaves, west along the Ohio and Arkansas, and south down the Mississippi, into newly incorporated U.S. territory. It was easier, though, to build steam than to release steam, and boilers began to blow ships to tinder with a startling frequency. Steam, the *North Amer-*

ican Review wrote in 1840, in a long essay on riverboat disasters, remained "an enigma even to the learned."[1]

The first engineers on these boats came from the east, from New York, Philadelphia, and England, and their experience was purely practical. They had little understanding of what one contemporary report called the "theoretical idea of steam."[2] They knew how much water, more or less, they should maintain in a heated boiler. And they knew that as their boat picked up speed, they could build pressure by closing the safety valve. But their understanding of the "expansive power" of steam was intuitive and inexact. A popular idea among engineers held that only dry boilers exploded, and that as long as water remained in the tank all was well. That was not true. "Theoreticians of steam" had already worked out that the expansion created in a closed boiler filled with water increases as heat increases but at a higher rate, with expansion doubling with every fifty additional degrees. This made on-the-spot guesswork volatile. "Why not call it witchcraft?" wrote one doctor, referring to the idea that water-filled boilers can't explode.

Worse, the rapidly advancing technology of boilers, which made it possible to generate more steam with less water, fast outstripped the technology of safety valves and outpaced the intuition of engineers. Well into the 1830s, what was called a "safety valve" was little more than a few weights levered over a three-inch hole in the boiler, controlled by a rope and pulley or a rod. It could be, and often was, easily circumvented to build more steam. River travel became considerably safer later in the decade, with the adoption of Philadelphia inventor Cadwallader Evans's "Patent Safety Guard against explosion of Steam Engine Boilers," which used a fusible alloy that melted when exposed to excessive heat, triggering a release of built-up steam.[3] Still, riverboat crews and travelers were "launched into eternity" with some regularity.

The problem with steam wasn't just magical thinking and too-quickly-developing technology. The "expansive power" of expansion—the ability to move swiftly through the landscape of the American West, to embark in the morning after daybreak and get to where one was going before the sun set—fired recklessness, as engineers drove faster, notwithstanding whatever steam theory they might possess. "Among the many singular phases in which the human character presents itself, few have appeared to us more unaccountable than this frantic desire to get ahead, no matter at what risk, or for what object, or haply for no object at all," said the *North American Review* on the continuing dangers of the steamboat.

According to the opinions of well-heeled Boston or London passengers, the engine-room workers—the firemen, oilers, and engineers, made up of either poor whites or enslaved African Americans—were the problem. They were as volatile and ill-regulated as an overheated boiler. Explosions were often blamed on drunk braggarts, incapable of distinguishing between power and recklessness. They, as one Scottish traveler described an African American crew, lacked "thought" and "moral dignity." "What a horrid accident was that on the Ohio, where my good friend and thirty other good fellows were sloped into eternity at the bidding of a thick-headed engineer, who knew not a valve from a flue," wrote Herman Melville in "Cock-A-Doodle-Doo!" Unable to govern themselves responsibly, members of the working class were, some complained, easily misgoverned by others, unable to resist the demands of pilots and passengers to go faster, and faster still. During Mississippi boat races, slaves were made to sit on the safety valve to build steam. Travelers excited by speed and boat owners wanting to shave off a few minutes from a trip's duration urged the stokers to throw more combustibles into the fire, to jam the valve down, with only the "quivering throes of the over-worked boat" gauging the danger.

"There is no longer any controlling of the mania," wrote the *North American Review*.

2.

Potent imagery, the workings of a safety valve: expanding gases seeking release. It's a wonder it took until the 1820s for the device to be invoked on a regular basis as a metaphor. By that time, a kind of madness had overcome young America, according to the historian Gordon

Wood. "Everything seemed to be coming apart," Wood writes in his *The Radicalism of the American Revolution*, "as if all restraints were falling away." Many worried that the public was increasingly confusing freedom with debauched egoism. "A new competitiveness was abroad in the land," Wood says, "and people seemed to be almost at war with one another."[4] It was a season of "inward and outward revolution, when new depths seem to be broken up in the soul, when new wants are unfolded in multitudes, and a new and undefined good is thirsted for," as the theologian William Ellery Channing described his times.[5]

Dueling and brawling increased, as did alcoholism and murder. Doctors saw a spike in cases of *mania a potu*, or delirium tremens. The *American Journal of Insanity* didn't start publishing till mid-century, but the number of public and private asylums multiplied. The tally of citizens confined to such institutions nearly doubled between 1808 and 1812, though an exact count is hard. Many people suffering from physical diseases like consumption and epilepsy were put in asylums, and others, suffering from mental illness, were locked up in prisons and poorhouses. The list of causes of "mental illness" captures the competitive stresses of the era. Along with traditional explanations such as "intemperance" and family "inheritance," doctors now added "disappointment in business," "loss of property," or "disappointment in ambition" to account for emotional breakdowns. "Mania" was, by far, the leading cause of asylum deaths. Other fatalities were described as "fatuous," "melancholic," and "furious and melancholic."[6]

Americans, thought William Gilmore Simms, a southern author writing a bit later, had an "imagination continually on the stretch," their ambitions "always ready to overboil and overflow." There existed, he said, a "rage" for "strange doctrines," including Mormonism and Millerism (according to one of the directors of the New York State Lunatic Asylum, "religious excitement or despondency" was the third-leading cause of "insanity" in 1824). Youth in particular often fell "victim to wild and exaggerated sentiments—startling delusions—gloomy desolating terrors—the chimeras of a deeply roused imagination." Perhaps, Simms hoped, such "phrenzies" might serve "the purposes of moral safety-valves, and carry off," on their flight beyond settled society to create new religious communities, "the blood and bile" that otherwise might destroy the commonwealth.[7]

The fires of republicanism, which had burned just right a generation earlier, flared dangerously during the Age of Jackson. America needed a safety valve, something that could release the unsustainable pressure placed on the machinery of democracy, now that an increasing number of unlettered and unpropertied white men had the vote. During these years, the phrase mostly referred to procedural brakes on public passions. Newspaper correspondents, preachers, and politicians identified any given institutional check and balance—rotation of office-holders, access to a legal system, power-sharing between state and federal authorities, and so on—as the "safety valve in the political engine." The value of a free press, said one Fourth of July orator in Norwich, Connecticut, in 1822, derived not from any moral principle but from the fact that it worked as a "safety-valve for the vapor of popular ebullition." Giving people the right to speak out against politicians allowed "the bad passions of society [to] find an easy vent," a "safety valve" to release "boiling indignation."[8]

Jackson's Whig opponents imagined the newly enfranchised masses to be a "congregation of vapors" requiring spewing. Jacksonians, in turn, reminded their would-be betters that they weren't promised "life offices." The right to elect representatives was the "safety valve of the Constitution," checking "the frailty of the most ambitious."[9] Reformers called their whole agenda—including abolition of debtors' prison, an end to chartered monopolies, a more equitable law system, free and universal education, and an extension of the vote—the "principal safety-valve to our system," which, no matter how much the rich might complain, worked to save their privileges and status by defusing demands for more-radical change. Plain old "grumbling," one writer noted in 1833, protected the social hierarchy by reminding elites to act with a bit more social conscience: grousing served as a "safety valve that lets off what is within." Its "hissing and its noise" warned those in power "not to apply too much fuel."[10] On the slave plantation, Frederick Douglass wrote, the music- and drink-filled days between Christmas and New Year's served as "safety-valves to carry off the explosive elements inseparable from the human mind when reduced to the condition of slavery." Enslaved for two decades, between his birth in 1818 and his escape in 1838, Douglass wrote that such yearly rituals damped "down the spirit of insurrection."[11]

The psychic workings of democracy, no less than constitutional mechanisms and guarantees (such as the ability to vote out leaders, to take grievances to court, to speak and assemble in public), were discussed in the language of vapor release. Philosophers and theologians easily bolted the "safety valve" onto their moral premises, to the idea that vices and weaknesses had to be controlled or balanced by virtues and strengths. "Reason or mind," wrote "Rusticus" in 1831 for the *National Gazette*, "is supposed to have control over the animal instinct, and to repress effects which might occasion general confusion and violence—like the safety valve to a steam engine, to correct the natural instigations of sense and physical impulse." Christian theologians worried that America's "unprecedented" wealth was increasing worldliness, dissipation, and vice. "How important is it that some safety valve," recommended one preacher, "should be provided for this excess of prosperity!"[12]

Just under the surface of these discussions of animal instincts, passions, and "phrenzies" lurked sexual violence. All women, of every class, status, and skin color, were subject to the threat, enslaved women especially so. Increasingly through the decades leading to the Civil War, abolitionists began to identify slavery as a moral evil, corrosive of republican principles, and slavers responded by defending the institution as a "positive good," helping to elevate republican virtue. Slaves were commodities, bought and sold in the market. But owning a large number of slaves, southern cavaliers said, allowed slavers to rise above the grub of the market and cultivate more refined, chivalric qualities. Rape was an instrument of this refinement. Enslaved women were, as defenders of slavery put it, "safety valves," helping to redirect the lust of white men away from white women and allowing southerners to distinguish their section of the country as genteel and mannerly. Samuel Rutherford, a Knoxville, Georgia, slaver, wrote New York's

Jamestown Journal to complain about its anti-slavery editorial, which described the regime of sexual terror enslaved women lived under in the South. Rutherford admitted the truth of the editorial but said that sexual access to enslaved women worked as a "safety valve to the virtues of our white females, who are far superior in virtue to your northern females."[13]

3.

People write and think with all kinds of metaphors. But the utility of the idea of the safety valve, coming into rhetorical service just as the actual industrial device was helping multiply humanity's capacity for power and speed, was particularly meaningful. The phrase worked, especially when used to refer to western expansion, to reconcile the dissonance, the crying contradiction, of Jacksonian America, a nation founded on unparalleled freedom and unmatched unfreedom.

The Reverend Elizur Wright was among the first to apply the image to slavery. A New England abolitionist and founder of the American Anti-Slavery Society, Wright was a fierce critic of colonization: the idea that the problem of slavery could be solved by removing emancipated slaves to Africa. Such a scheme, he said in 1833, served as "the safety valve to an engine otherwise tremendously oppressive."[14] Abolitionists like Wright didn't want to vent the machine. They wanted to break the machine.[15] And they accused northern proponents of colonization of working to ensure slavery's survival. Colonization was a "safety valve," another critic later said, a way of saving slavery "by getting rid of its encumbrances."[16] "Encumbrances" here referred to the growing numbers of free people of color. This free population—numbering about four hundred thousand in the early 1840s—presented a singular problem. For defenders of slavery, they were a threat, both to their ideology (which held that people of color couldn't live free) and to their institutions (which imagined them as criminals, subversives, unproductive dependents, or competitors for jobs). For slavery's opponents, the implacable hatred large segments of white people directed at freed people—manifest in new laws disenfranchising African American men, in the segregation of housing, education, and public services, and in a panic concerning "amalgamation," or intermarriage—suggested that the evil created by slavery would outlive the institution of slavery, that abolition wouldn't abolish the problem racial inequality posed to the promise of republican equality.

Aside from dissident voices such as Wright, advocates and adversaries of slavery joined together to push for colonization, which the Pennsylvania affiliate of the American Colonization Society said was "the only safety valve to our domestic slave question." That "only" bears weight, carrying both an appreciation of the forces aligned against equality and an accommodation to their power. Thousands of emancipated African Americans did migrate to Africa, to Liberia, Sierra Leone, and other state-sponsored colonies (Maryland, Georgia, and Pennsylvania had all set up colonies in West Africa), but not in enough numbers to make a noticeable difference in public life. So abolisher, reformer, and defender turned their attentions west.

Those committed to saving the institution pointed their vent at Arkansas, Alabama, the lower Mississippi valley, and beyond, at Texas. If freedmen and freedwomen could be shipped out, it would remove a source of social conflict from the coastal South. If white settlers could be sent, it might eventually lead to the addition of slave states to the Union, thus giving southerners more political leverage in dealing with the North.[17] Timothy Flint, the editor of the *Western Monthly Review* and a vocal advocate of pushing on to the Pacific, proposed in 1830 the acquisition of Mexican territory, which would serve as "the proper escape valve from the danger of too great an accumulation of blacks in the slave states . . . thinning the population by diffusing it over great surfaces."[18] Flint was opposed to slavery in the abstract, but he said he "could see both sides of the question." The promise of expansion gave men like Flint the liberty of never having to stand firmly on one or the other of those sides. Texas, though then still part of Mexico, could "operate as a safety valve to let off the superabundant slave population from among us," thought South Carolina senator George McDuffie, a Jacksonian defender of states' rights and slavery.[19] It wasn't just new land and new markets that would provide relief. The extremity of life and work on the frontier lands of the Deep South was itself a valve. When a Virginia planter was asked, in 1840, if he feared for his life at the hands of his slaves, he said he had no such worries. The hardness of the frontier offered him protection. "God, in his Providence, had opened for them a safety valve in the extreme southern states, which purchased their slaves and worked them to death in seven years."[20]

4.

At the same time, the metaphor of the "safety valve" was deployed in proposals to solve the class problem. That problem was two problems, actually. The first, economic: How to ensure that wages would remain high enough to support the rapidly growing number of urban laborers? The second, political: How to protect against the threat of increasing numbers of illiterate, unpropertied male voters (Andrew Jackson's key constituency)? How to stop them from coalescing into a faction—a "Labor Party"—and casting their ballots for a program trespassing on property rights? The answer, for many, was simple: have them go west, and give them land.

The call to distribute public lands could be a radical one.[21] Self-identified socialists—such as the brothers George Henry Evans and Frederick Evans, who arrived in the United States from Great Britain in the 1820s—helped organize what became known as the "Free Soil" movement. In its early years, the movement imagined western lands fulfilling the egalitarian promise not just of the American and French Revolutions but also the Protestant Reformation: many Free Soilers were radical Christians, including Frederick, who helped found a number of Shaker communes.[22] An early list of the demands of Free Soilers reveals as militant a program as ever advanced in U.S. politics:

> *Vote yourself a farm;*
> *Down with monopolists;*

Freedom of public lands;
Homesteads made inalienable;
Abolition of all laws for the collection of debt;
Equal rights for women with men in all respects;
Abolition of chattel slavery and wage slavery.

Here were white men calling themselves slaves—wage slaves—not to distance themselves from Africans and African Americans but to establish solidarity, including with women. What became known as "Evans's safety valve" was almost as simple as the mechanical one: making western public land available to immigrant workers at affordable prices, said the New York Industrial Congress, a confederation of the city's most radical unions, would ease competition not just for wages but for housing. Wages would rise, rents lower, and the "mechanic and laborer" would have a "better footing for the maintenance of his rights and interests."

In practice, "free land" didn't serve this function, for the most part. Speculators, railroads, ranchers, and corporations were claiming the best of it. And it wasn't that easy for most poor working families to move west. In the late 1830s, spikes in inflation made the cost of moving prohibitive (though the later spread of railroads lessened the burden of migration). At the same time, the fast introduction of labor-saving technology in eastern factories counterbalanced whatever wage-raising pressure western land might have exerted. Still, if the frontier wasn't a "standing retreat" for the country's surplus labor, it could be effective as a "standing threat."[23] It wasn't necessary that workers should actually leave their mills, workshops, and factories during labor troubles and go west. Owners only had to know that they might do so, moving, just a bit, the "balance wheel" of power between labor and capital.[24]

Others, however, proposed the distribution of "free land" to solve social contradictions in a different manner, along the lines of what Andrew Jackson imagined when he pledged to return the federal government to its "primitive simplicity." For instance, the Massachusetts congressman Caleb Cushing, the son of a wealthy shipbuilder with sympathies for southern slavery, spoke of the frontier in a holistic fashion, as a solution to *all* the major problems inherent to Jacksonianism: the problem slavery posed to republican virtue; the problem of freed slaves demanding equal rights in a society that was overwhelmingly white; and the growing problem of white, enfranchised workers whose wages were depressed in a larger labor system dominated by chattel slavery and European migration. But he did so in a way designed not to advance socialism, much less Shaker communism, but rather to elevate the ideal of a minimal government committed to the protection of property rights.[25]

In a Fourth of July oration given in Springfield in 1839, Cushing identified the West as "the great safety-valve of our population," a protection from the kind of dangers caused by "poverty, and discontent, and consequent disorders" that occur when an overpopulated society has "outrun its capacity to afford due recompense to honest industry and ambition." The danger here, for Cushing, wasn't poverty, disorder, or unfair recompense in itself. Rather, the danger resided in the possibility that the federal government, in order to address those problems, would increase its powers and, in so doing, curtail the liberty of both individuals and states. Westward movement provided a way out, allowing the federal government to focus its force on extending the frontier. In turn, an extended frontier would leave individuals free to develop their capacities, pursue their interests, and satisfy their passions, Cushing said, with neither an overly repressive nor overly redistributive state stifling civil society. By directing its operations west, the government could remain simple, he suggested, maintaining the "guardianship of the great constitutional principle" of states' rights and ensuring the proper balance between "public and private virtue." By "private virtue," Cushing meant the protection of private property.

In the South, the Mississippian Robert Walker, an influential senator and planter, also thought the West might serve as a "safety-valve," allowing the problem slavery posed to the republic to be solved without resort to either a slave revolution or a civil war between states. Walker was writing in the depressed early 1840s on behalf of fellow southerners who felt hemmed in, under siege by northern abolitionists and cramped by a contracting economy, when the fear of violence was a growing concern. Expansion would lessen the pressure.[26] "Free blacks" who could never be "tolerated" to "roam at large in the limits of the South" might "find a home" beyond the line of white settlement. Like many defenders of slavery, Walker conceded that the institution would eventually have to come to an end. Expansion west would allow it to do so quietly: "Slavery will slowly recede and finally disappear into the boundless regions." And the slaves themselves too might "disappear" into the horizon, "beyond the limits of the Union."

The Mississippi senator pitched his proposal as much to readers in the North as to those in the South, looking to deflect abolitionist criticism. Previewing the kind of racialization of public policy that would come to infect U.S. political culture—which holds African Americans responsible for a range of social ills and for the expansion of government bureaucracy needed to respond to those ills—Walker predicted that emancipation would drive an "immense free black population" into northern cities. Crime would rise, and the wages of the "white laborer" would fall. The "poor-house and the jail, the asylums of the deaf and dumb, the blind, the idiot and insane, would be filled to overflowing."[27] Government would have to grow to tend to such misery. Taxes would increase, "depressing the value of all property." "Universal bankruptcy," Walker warned, would follow.

For both Cushing and Walker, the North's "class problem" and the South's "race problem" were intertwined and unsolvable within existing U.S. borders. There was only one acceptable solution: go west. Expansion, Walker insisted, was "the only practicable outlet for the African population," the "only safety-valve for the whole Union." The West, Cushing said, was America's "asylum."

5.

Cushing and Walker, along with many others, advanced an ideal of republican freedom as freedom from a too-intrusive federal government and posited expansion as both an expression and guardian of this ideal. Subsidized by an enormous amount of public land acquired through

Indian dispossession (and, later, by the annexation of Texas and the conquest of Mexico), such a vision was hard to resist, and it led to the capture of other, more egalitarian ideals by the Jacksonian cult of Caucasian democracy.

The line between being anti-slavery and anti-black blurred. "The poor white" laborer, as W. E. B. Du Bois later put it, transferred "all the dislike and hatred which he had for the whole slave system"—blamed for keeping wages low—to the victims of the system.[28] The promise of free land facilitated this transference. George Henry Evans, for instance, moved away from his radical abolitionism, which had called for the end of both chattel and wage slavery. He went from saying that the existence of chattel slavery kept down wages to worrying that the abolition of chattel slavery would keep down wages by glutting the labor market. He too proposed removing freedmen and freedwomen to someplace west of the Mississippi—not as part of the great universal stream of young America realizing its fullest possible expression of equality, but as two separate, segregated currents, with African Americans confined to their own homeland. "You of the North find land for the slaves," Evans reported being told by a southern slaveholder, "and we will emancipate them." "We have got rid of the Indians, who were more numerous, by removing them to the west," his journal *Young America* pointed out in 1845, and asked: "Why not the negro?" Emancipation was inevitable, the anonymous author said, but he feared the harm that might be done by the sudden release of three million wage workers into the labor market "at one fell stroke." Freed slaves would fill the nation's "jails, penitentiaries, and poorhouses" and reduce the wages of "white laborers." Instead, the author suggested removal: "The United States possess an ample domain on west side of the Mississippi, in a climate suited to the negro constitution and habits, which is unoccupied. Let Congress lay out a State there for the negroes, giving every family a freehold of forty acres forever, with one year's provision, and implements of husbandry, tools, &c., to make a beginning for themselves."[29]

There were counter-visions to expansion.[30] "What more than this has earth to offer to social man?" wondered George Perkins Marsh,

Vermont's House representative, in 1848. Marsh thought the United States had become big enough and opposed it all, all the mulled-over dreams of Texas, Mexico, and California. Stop, he said, in his book *Man and Nature*, published in 1864, making an ecological argument that the philosophy of natural rights gave man not a warrant to conquer nature but an obligation to tend to it, to protect it. Marsh's critique of expansion sounds farsighted today, especially his warning that constant war would turn republicanism into Caesarism. "The soldiery raised to protect the frontier may supersede your electoral colleges," he said in a House speech, "and impose upon you a dictator." But Marsh's small-state republicanism proved, in a way, James Madison's expansionist premise. Madison said an enlarging sphere was necessary to protect a vision of a modern citizenry bound by its diversity of interests, not by blood, race, culture, religion, or martial virtue. Marsh, in contrast, "lauded racial, linguistic, and cultural homogeneity," according to his biographer.[31] The Vermonter was partial to the Prussian philosopher Johann Gottfried von Herder's 1794 insistence that "the most natural state is *one* people with *one* national character."

There was only one way forward: forward.

Theoreticians of social steam—ministers, politicians, reformers, abolitionists, slavers, states' righters, and Free Soilers—deployed their metaphor in wildly differing ways, with opposing hoped-for effects: the dissipation of class tensions; the weakening of slavery; the extinction of slavery; the salvation of slavery. Yet when it comes to understanding the metaphor's power, these differences matter little. What matters is that invocation of a "safety valve" allowed individuals to simultaneously answer and evade a question. Inherent in the metaphor is the *recognition* of the profundity of the problem that Jacksonian democracy represented and *resignation* that the problem wouldn't be solved within the existing terms of social relations and political power. The point of the image was to take social conflicts that seemed irresolvable in the here and now (between the interests of enslaved people and wage workers; abolitionists and slavers; states' righters and federal consolidators; agrarians and industrialists; free traders and tariff makers) and imagine their resolution in the there and then: there beyond the line of settlement, and then when the federal government annexes Texas, or takes California from Mexico, or distributes public land, or opens the China market.

In antebellum America, the star of empire guided all. Just a few generations earlier, during the drafting of the Constitution, anti-federalist advocates for states' rights feared that the administration of an expanding empire would necessitate a too-powerful central government, which in turn would run roughshod over states' rights. Now, though, by the 1840s, expansion was understood as key to checking the power of the federal government (if not when it came to removing Indians, then at least when it came to responding to demands for social reform, including demands for the abolition of slavery). The great defender of slavery and theorist of state sovereignty, the South Carolinian John Calhoun, Andrew Jackson's vice president, defined expansion as a function of government, necessary to "preserve domestic institutions."

"Empire," said Cushing in 1850, was a "safety valve for all the pent up passions and explosive or subversive tendencies of an advanced society." The nation had to keep moving. Cushing even coined a new word to describe American ceaselessness: "expansibility." Citizens of the United States, he said, needed a "scope for the free action of our characteristic national qualities of activity, expansibility, individualism, love of land."

Deny them that range of free action by sitting on the safety valve— "check it, stop it, shut it up, force it back on itself," Cushing said—and you'll have hell to pay.

FIVE

Are You Ready for All These Wars?

"The cause of the cause."

1.

Late in his life, after he had left the White House at the end of his one-term presidency, John Quincy Adams came to grasp the viciousness of the cycle, the way expansion west simultaneously hastened and stemmed crisis, the way the effects of one war became the cause of the next, and he oscillated between two fears. The first was that a perpetual war for the frontier, which Adams believed U.S. settlers had started with Andrew Jackson's destruction of the Creeks in 1814 and had expanded with Indian Removal in 1830, would rend the nation "asunder," like the "kingdoms of Ephraim and Judah." The "violent and heartless" war-driven enlargement of Washington's jurisdiction was polarizing the republic, the former president said. The country was dividing into two hardened camps—free and slave—that would eventually turn on each other. Adams's second fear was that perpetual war on the frontier wouldn't break the nation but rather bind it together in iniquity, with racist terror against Native Americans and Mexicans working like glue, uniting the country's diverse population in shared hatred.

After having lost the presidency to Andrew Jackson, Adams won, in 1830, a seat in the House of Representatives. There, he cultivated his growing skepticism as he watched his Jacksonian opponents dismantle his political legacy and, he felt, set the country on the road to ruination. As it became increasingly clear that Indian removal was but a prelude to a full-scale assault on Mexico, Adams, on May 25, 1836, rose to give one of the most powerful anti-war speeches in this country's history. The topic was Texas, which had just won its independence from Mexico. All the same arguments made earlier for the Louisiana Purchase were now marshaled to justify the new republic's annexation. As a "barrier," President Andrew Jackson said, Texas would make the United States "invincible," at the same time expanding its "area of freedom" and extending its "circle of free institutions."

The territory was anything but free, however. "Texas must be a slave country," said Stephen Austin, who led the rebellion against Mexico, in 1835.[1] It was in fact a slaver's utopia, founded earlier in the 1800s on Spain's mistaken idea that it could win the loyalty of Anglo settlers, who in turn might serve as a bulwark against the encroaching United States. In the hope of keeping the settlers loyal, Spanish officials promised them land (the more slaves they had, the more land they were granted) and freedom (that is, a hands-off policy when it came to trading and slaving). The colony, though, had barely been established when Mexico won its independence in 1821 and, shortly thereafter, abolished slavery. After Mexico City began intercepting their slave ships, Anglo Tejanos revolted. During its time as a short-lived stand-alone republic, Texas tried to enshrine slavery in perpetuity, passing laws that prohibited masters from freeing slaves and black people from being considered anything other than slaves. (Later, in the run-up to the U.S. Civil War, Texas became the last stop on an underground railroad running in reverse: slavers kidnapped freedmen and women from other places and re-enslaved them in Texas. Mexico tried to shut it down, but Texas effectively reestablished an international slave trade; Galveston, in the late 1830s, became the largest slave market west of New Orleans.)[2]

Adams, representing Massachusetts, didn't oppose the annexation of Texas just because it would tilt federal power even further to the slave states, though that was a concern. Adams also opposed annexation because he'd come to despise Jacksonianism. And Texas represented Jacksonianism in extreme form. Most of the Texas republic's Anglo settlers were from the Deep South, including Tennessee, and many shared Andrew Jackson's profile: they were land speculators, slavers, militia leaders, and Indian killers. Taking Texas, Adams feared, would lock in the worldview that Jackson represented. The country was already fighting what Adams considered a perpetual war on Native Americans, a crusade that Jacksonians used to create a racist solidarity among whites and to beat back demands for a more robust state capable of addressing social problems. Violent dispossession of indigenous peoples also made possible the alliance between the worst, most retrograde elements of the country: "The slave-holders of the South," Adams wrote in his diary, "have bought the cooperation of the Western country by the bribe of the Western Lands."[3] Now, he warned, a fight with Mexico over Texas would deepen the nation's habituation to racist wars, leading to the point where racism and war would be the only thing that gave the republic meaning.

2.

Adams's speech in the House is a stunningly prophetic exposition of what today is called "blowback." He used the word "recoil" to argue that the kind of settler violence Jackson had made national policy created an addictive cycle of expulsion, expansion, and repression that led to lust for Texas but wouldn't end with Texas. Removal, Adams said, was "the cause of the cause," the "cause of this state of things."[4]

"By force or by compact," the federal government had expelled:

all the Indian tribes from their own territories and dwellings, to a region beyond the Mississippi, beyond the Missouri, beyond the Arkansas, bordering upon Mexico; and *there* you have deluded them with the hope that they will find a permanent abode—a final resting place from your never ending rapacity and persecution. *There* you have undertaken to lead the willing, and to drive the reluctant, by fraud or by force; by treaty, or by the sword and the rifle; all the remnants of the Seminoles, of the Creeks, of the Cherokees, of the Choctaws, and of how many other tribes I cannot now stop to enumerate. In the process of this violent and heartless operation, you have met with all the resistance which men in so helpless a condition as that of the Indian tribes, could make.

Such violence, Adams said, would meet natural resistance. Scalping, he said, was but "retributive justice from heaven" and the scalping knife God's instrument. Indigenous retaliation represented the "last agonies of a people." Their raids on settlers were the "last convulsive struggles of their despair." Mexico too would resist. Adams predicted that any attempt by the United States to annex Texas would lead to war. Eventually, he added, the United States would have to fight Spain, which still ruled Cuba and Puerto Rico.

Adams continued his dissent as a series of questions, whose answers he left implicit. Was hatred of the "Indian savage"—whom the United States had already driven "back to the foot of the Rocky Mountains"— the glue that bound together the nation's diverse white population in "harmony, concord, and patriotism"? Directing his anger at the speaker of the House, James Knox Polk, whom Adams addressed as "the slaveholder sitting in the chair," he asked:

Do not you, an Anglo-Saxon, slave-holding exterminator of Indians, from the bottom of your soul, hate the Mexican-Spaniard-Indian, emancipator of slaves, and abolisher of slavery?

Is your southern and southwestern frontier not sufficiently extensive? . . . Are you not large and unwieldy enough already?

Have you not Indians enough to expel from the land of their fathers' sepulchres, and to exterminate?

War would lead to more war, Adams warned, including with Mexico. In that war, he said, "the banners of freedom will be the banners of

Mexico; and your banners, I blush to speak the word, will be the banners of slavery."

The United States was supposed to be something new, rushing into the future, which for many meant rushing into the West. But, Adams said, constant war had trapped Jacksonians in a state of constant historical grievance, transposing ancient enemies faced by their imagined forebears—including the Normans, who in 1066 invaded Great Britain to conquer Saxon freemen—onto their current opponents. "Is there not yet hatred enough between the races which compose your southern population and the population of Mexico," Adams asked Polk, that "you must go back eight hundred or a thousand years, and to another hemisphere, for the fountains of bitterness between you and them?"

Adams eventually came to his main point: that the promotion of what he described as one endless frontier war would soon boomerang home, leading to war against slavery in the heartland. The territorial expansion that resulted from war had split the United States into two irreconcilable sections, as free and slave state alternated entering the Union. (Free: Ohio, Indiana, Illinois, Maine, and Michigan. Slave: Louisiana, Mississippi, Alabama, Missouri, and Arkansas.) The addition of Texas would, by tipping the balance of power to the South, make conflict certain.

"Are you ready for all these wars?" Adams asked.

Polk became president in March 1845, promising that the pending annexation of Texas would secure the "frontier" and make possible "perpetual peace." Three months later, he presided over the incorporation of Texas into the union. "They have sown the wind," Adams wrote in his diary, and would reap the "whirlwind."* In early 1846, Polk declared war on Mexico.[5]

---

* It's important to point out that Adams wasn't opposed to expansion. Earlier, as secretary of state, he had even been one of the few members of James Monroe's administration who supported Jackson's violent raid into Spanish Florida (which allowed Adams to negotiate Spain's transfer of the territory to the United States). Even much later, in the 1840s, he supported the incorporation of Oregon into the union (to offset the influence of Texas). His opposition to the Jacksonians, whom he described as a party of "slave breeders," radicalized him. "The Constitution," he wrote in 1845, on the eve of Texas's annexation, "is a menstruous rag, and the Union is sinking into a military monarchy."

3.

Until recently, most historians in the United States described the war on Mexico as small, inevitable, or largely inconsequential, save for helping the United States fill itself in across the continent, below Oregon and Canada to the Pacific. Scholars, though, have now come around to confirm most of Adams's fears. The conflict was one of the "most costly" and "most politically vexing episodes in American history," writes the historian Steven Hahn, requiring "a major mobilization of military manpower and financial resources" and inflicting "depredations and atrocities on the Mexican people, motivated in large measure by bitter racism and anti-Catholicism among American troops."[6] Casualties were high on both sides, and the fighting "emboldened some of the most aggressive political and cultural tendencies in American life," Hahn notes, united (as Adams said they would be) under "the banners of slavery." It was, General Ulysses S. Grant said, reflecting back at the end of his life on a war he helped win, "one of the most unjust ever waged by a stronger against a weaker nation."

The military conflict began in April 1846, when a detachment of U.S. soldiers crossed the Nueces River and occupied territory claimed by Mexico. Mexican troops responded, attacking the detachment and giving Polk the pretext he needed to ask Congress for a declaration of war. Within weeks, the Senate voted 40 to 2 for war, and the House 174 to 14. Adams led the opposition, but the former president's influence was reduced to a little more than a dozen votes.

Most accounts say Polk sent troops over the Nueces either to intimidate Mexico into negotiating away territory or to provoke a short war that would quickly lead Mexico to such negotiations. But once war was declared, the fighting lasted much longer than anyone in Washington thought it would. Mexicans put up strong resistance, setting off within the United States simultaneously centrifugal and centripetal energies. Expansion through war drove forward the conflict over slavery that would soon result in the Civil War. At the same time, though, it stemmed that polarization, at least momentarily, as the "motley compound" of white ethnics Adams described came together in a racial victory.

There was some opposition to the war, especially among Whigs. But once it was under way, the country fell in line. The cause was popular in New York: only one New York House member (New York City's Erastus Culver) voted against funding the invasion, while both of the state's senators voted in favor. It was popular in Vicksburg and Illinois (Abraham Lincoln, running for a House seat, largely avoided the issue, only speaking out forcefully against the war once elected). And it was popular in the West.

Like Adams, Herman Melville had in his youth been an enthusiastic supporter of continental expansion. But his views changed as he too came to worry that the war needed to bring about such expansion had created an emotional attachment to bloodshed, an addiction to the type of sensation that only war can provide. In a letter to his Jacksonian brother, Melville said that Polk's declaration of war had created a cross-class "delirium": gentry colonels joined with "'prenticeboys" to run off "to the wars by scores," dreaming about spending a night in the Halls of Moctezuma.[7] "Lord, the day is at hand," he wrote, when the Revolutionary War's "Battle of Monmouth will be thought child's play." War, Melville predicted, would beget more war. "A little spark kindleth a great fire," the future author of *Moby-Dick* quoted Proverbs, before asking: "And who knows what all this may lead to?"*

Congress appropriated money to pay volunteers, so the war created jobs for the masses. It also made careers for the classes. Jefferson Davis, after losing his first race for a seat in the House, joined the war effort, thinking—correctly—that it would help him win a future bid. The next two elected presidents after Polk, Zachary Taylor and Franklin Pierce, were veterans of the war, and a third, James Buchanan, served as Polk's secretary of state. Like Jackson before him, Taylor, a Mississippi cotton

---

* Like Adams, Melville would use the word "recoil" to refer to the blowback he expected from westward expansion: the "wild western waste" did help the United States "overflow" its "redundancies"—that is, avoid social problems. But soon the West would be full. "And then, the recoil must come."

planter who owned dozens of slaves, found Indian killing to be a good path to the White House, working up to the rank of general by fighting Shawnee and Black Hawks and hunting Florida Seminoles with bloodhounds imported from Cuba's slave plantations. There's no better example of how the war simultaneously stayed and worsened the country's disaggregation than that it functioned as a "training ground" for cadets and officers who would later serve on opposing sides during the Civil War. Grant, Davis, Robert E. Lee, and William Sherman, along with thousands of enlisted men, worked together, gaining experience in a way that would expand the country territorially even as it began to break it apart geographically, over slavery.[8]

The nation's elites "placed their most restless and desperate citizens upon the throat of Mexico," as the historian Paul Foos described the looting, civilian murder, and terror that U.S. troops—comprised of state militia volunteers and Army regulars—inflicted on Mexicans.[9] On February 9, 1847, for one example, a member of an Arkansas volunteer regiment raped a Mexican woman near the regiment's camp at Agua Nueva, in the state of Coahuila, and Mexicans retaliated by killing a U.S. soldier. Afterward, over one hundred Arkansans cornered a group of war refugees in a cave. According to one eyewitness, the volunteers screamed "like fiends" as they raped and slaughtered their victims, with women and children "shrieking for mercy." By the time the killing had ended, scores of Mexicans lay dead or dying on the cave floor, which was covered with clotted blood. Many of the dead had been scalped (more than a few of the volunteers in the U.S. Army had, before the war, made their living on the borderlands scalping Apaches for bounty money, or "barbering," as one infamous Texan scalp hunter called his trade).* Even before this massacre, General Winfield Scott, commander of U.S. forces, wrote Washington to complain of other atrocities committed by volunteers, who'd been organized under the command of future president Zachary Taylor. The crimes of Taylor's men, Scott said, were so heinous they would "make Heaven weep, & every American, of Christian

---

* Cormac McCarthy's novel *Blood Meridian*, which follows a band of Anglo scalp hunters around the time of the Mexican–American War, is largely based on *My Confession*, the memoir of Samuel Chamberlain, who rode with an infamous borderland scalping gang.

morals blush for his country. Murder, robbery, & rape on mothers & daughters, in the presence of the tied up males of the families, have been common all along the Rio Grande."[10]

"The smiling villages which welcomed our troops on their upward march are now black and smoldering ruins, the gardens and oranges groves destroyed, and the inhabitants . . . have sought refuge in the mountains," was how one regular officer described the atrocities committed by U.S. forces on Mexicans. "The march of Attila was not more withering and destructive."[11] The rampage led Scott to declare martial law over U.S.-occupied Mexican territory and to establish military tribunals to try war criminals. Technically, Scott's declaration, issued shortly after the massacre committed by the Arkansas regiment, applied to both citizens of Mexico and the United States. But the list of crimes it covered—including rape, the desecration of churches and cemeteries, and the interruption of religious ceremonies—makes it clear that Scott intended to discipline U.S. soldiers, especially state volunteer militias, who terrorized Mexican women and despoiled Catholic churches.*

In the eastern United States, the press stirred up war fervor by depicting Mexicans as a degenerate and servile people. The "imbecility and degradation of the Mexican people" caused by the "amalgamation of races"—Spanish, African, and Native American—meant a quick victory, assured the *New York Herald*.[12] Some argued against the war, opposed to the possibility of incorporating millions of dark-skinned people into the United States. But James Gordon Bennett, editor of the *Herald*, wasn't concerned. "Amalgamation has been always abhorrent to the Anglo-Saxon race on this continent," he wrote; but just as indigenous "barbarism" had "receded before the face of civilization," the "imbecile" Mexicans were "sure to melt away at the approach of Anglo-Saxon energy and enterprise as snow before a southern sun."[13]

---

* Scott's order was the first time the United States put into place a formal mechanism to administer justice outside its borders. Though Scott was primarily trying to prevent atrocities committed by the United States against citizens of another country, his precedent would be cited by the administration of George W. Bush after 9/11 to work out how to try foreigners in the "Global War on Terror" (see the Congressional Research Report, "Terrorism and the Law of War: Trying Terrorists as War Criminals," December 11, 2001, p. 18).

Native Americans and African Americans had long been used to mark the line between freedom and abandon. Now Mexicans helped secure that psychic border. "Mexico and the United States are peopled by two distinct and utterly unhomogeneous races," said Indiana senator Edward Hannegan, and "in no reasonable period could we amalgamate."[14] "Mexicans," said Hannegan (who was an "all-Mexico" Jacksonian, meaning that he wanted to annex the entire country), are utterly unfit for the blessings and the restraints of rational liberty, because they cannot comprehend the distinction between regulated freedom, and that unbridled licentiousness which consults only the evil passions of the human heart."[15] Charles Bent, the provisional governor of New Mexico Territory during the war, proclaimed that "the Mexican character is made up of stupidity, obstinacy, ignorance, duplicity, and vanity."[16] And while their resistance might have been unexpectedly energetic, Mexicans remained nonetheless torpid in their essence. "The majority of the Mexicans seem rather to vegetate than otherwise," wrote one infantry officer to his wife.[17]

The war dragged on, and President Polk took Mexico's tenacity as confirmation of its barbarism. Polk complained to Congress that Mexicans avail "themselves of every opportunity to commit the most savage excesses upon our troops."[18]

But the U.S. Army finally took Mexico City in September 1847, planting "the banner of burning stars, and ever-multiplying stripes on the towers of the city of the Aztecs," as future secretary of state William Seward described the unfurling. On February 2, 1848, Mexican officials signed the Treaty of Guadalupe Hidalgo, which (along with the subsequent Gadsden Purchase) transferred all of northern Mexico— Arizona, New Mexico, California, Nevada, western Colorado, Utah, and southwestern Wyoming—to the United States: a total of about five hundred thousand square miles, home to an estimated eighty to one hundred thousand people. Three weeks later, John Quincy Adams, at the age of eighty, died, having collapsed at his desk in the House of Representatives just after voting "no" on a resolution giving commendations to the military generals for their service in the war on Mexico.

When the war was done, the United States finally had a permanent

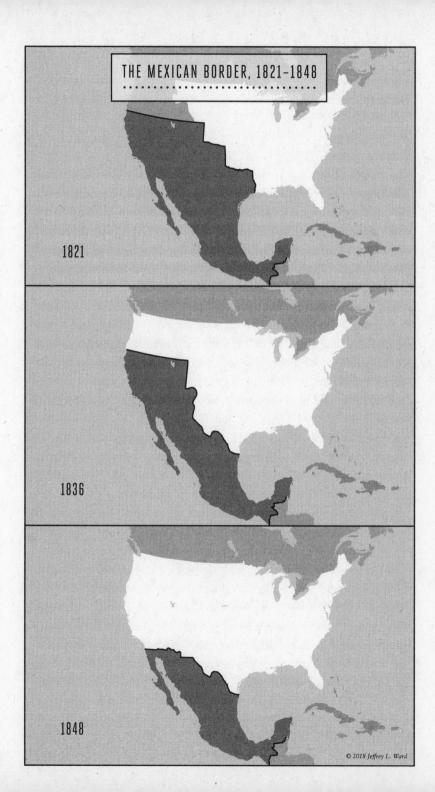

THE MEXICAN BORDER, 1821–1848

1821

1836

1848

© 2018 Jeffrey L. Ward

southern border, running about two thousand miles from Brownsville, Texas, to San Diego, California.

4.

The Mexican citizens who suddenly found themselves inside what was now, as a result of the Treaty of Guadalupe Hidalgo, United States territory were a diverse population. They included old-line Spanish families, who could trace their land claims back generations, centuries even; their mestizo and mulatto servants and ranch hands, along with other laborers; thousands of migrants in California, prospecting for gold; and scores of indigenous peoples, including Apache, Navajo, Pueblo, Ute, Yaqui, and Tohono O'odham. Under the terms of Mexico's constitution, most, regardless of color, were considered Mexican citizens. Now, though, they had become foreigners in their own land. They had the option of moving to a truncated Mexico. But it wasn't clear what their status would be if they opted, as the majority did, to stay in their homes. The Supreme Court still hadn't worked out the legal status of Native Americans within the United States' prior boundaries, or indeed whether they could even be considered "persons within the meaning of the law."[19] And most of the protections and rights associated with citizenship, including the right to vote, were at that time left to the discretion of individual states, which resisted granting U.S. citizenship to many of the former Mexicans, especially if they were people of color.

They found themselves in a nation that was becoming inured to its brutality and accustomed to a unique prerogative: its ability to organize politics around the promise of constant, endless expansion. A comparison with Europe is instructive. In 1848, on the day of John Quincy Adams's death, European workers revolted, with uprisings starting in Paris and then spreading to Vienna, Prague, Hamburg, Lyon, Milan, Palermo, Amsterdam, Budapest, Munich, Berlin, Naples, and elsewhere. Insurgents built barricades out of cobbles and waved the red flag, cutting society in two, as Alexis de Tocqueville later put it: uniting those who possessed nothing against those who possessed everything. The insurgents were defeated, but their revolt began the social-democratization of European politics, which eventually came to entail the growth of unions, the establishment of labor parties, and the extension of what came to be called social, or economic, rights, including the rights to welfare, education, health care, and pensions.

The United States too had crowded cities and hungry workers, fighting efforts to subordinate their lives to mechanical routine. But instead of waging class war upward—on aristocrats and owners—they waged race war outward, on the frontier. 'Prenticeboys didn't head to the barricades to fight the gentry but rather joined with the gentry to go west and fight Indians and Mexicans. After which, in 1848's November presidential election, they divided their votes between a Democratic Party Indian killer and a Whig Party Indian and Mexican killer.* The choice was between Lewis Cass, who as governor of Michigan Territory and then Jackson's secretary of war eliminated Native Americans from the Mississippi valley, and Zachary Taylor, that Mississippi slaver whose troops in Mexico committed atrocities "sufficient to make Heaven weep," and who earlier had hunted Seminoles with Cuban bloodhounds.[20] During the campaign, a political cartoon circulated of Taylor in full military uniform, holding a bloody sword and sitting on a pyramid of skulls. Taylor won the election, and his "war-clan," as one observer noted, "grew as big as the nation" itself.[21]

In the years that followed, Jacksonian domination of the executive branch seemed near absolute. Slavery's statesmen especially exercised monopoly control over the country's foreign policy and war-making apparatus. The Cotton Kingdom wasn't, in these years, moving to split from the republic but to command it, going on the offensive, committed to defend slavery in those countries where it still existed (Brazil and

---

* By this point, most national elections, either for the presidency or Congress, had become a contest between Whigs and Jacksonians over the "question of who could kill Indians with more fanfare," as the historian Daniel Scallet writes in his study on the second Seminole War.

Cuba), protect it where it was under siege (in the southern states), and extend it where they could, as far west as possible.[22]

5.

The Jacksonian consensus was powerful. It unleashed market capitalism by stealing Indian property and celebrated a minimal state, even as it increased the capacity of that state to push the frontier forward. During the first half of the nineteenth century, until Abraham Lincoln's election in 1860, a series of Jackson's successors continued to unite slavers and settlers under a banner of freedom defined as freedom from restraint—freedom from restraints on slaving, freedom from restraints on dispossessing, freedom from restraints on moving west. As they did, the nation's sense of morality became dependent on outward movement: the virtuous commonweal was defined as expansion and the common woe as anything that stood in the way of expansion (like that federal agent who stood in the way of Andrew Jackson on the Natchez Trace). This is what Octavio Paz meant when he said that for the United States "evil is outside, part of the natural world, like Indians, rivers, mountains, and other obstacles that must be domesticated or destroyed."

Expansion, though, had a corrosive effect, habituating, as Adams feared, the nation to war. The Mexican–American War helped overcome what could be called Seminole Syndrome. Just a few years prior to invading Mexico, the United States had fought its exhausting "second war" against holdout Seminoles in Florida. The war dragged on for years, with troops, including those led by Zachary Taylor, literally bogged down in an everglade quagmire. As the fighting continued, disillusionment set in among the officer class, a sense that politicians were using the fight for domestic politics but not giving them the resources needed to win. The public even began to show some sympathy toward the enemy, turning against the brutality of U.S. soldiers. The army eventually removed most Seminoles from Florida, though a small band remained undefeated.[23] The U.S. claimed victory in 1842, but it was, as many said, an "inglorious" victory that cost thousands of lives and millions of dollars. In contrast, triumph over Mexico wasn't easy, but when it came it was total, helping to restore, especially among upper-class officers, a romantic vision of war.[24] Martial style became associated with republican virtue, with a praetorian class increasingly involving itself in democratic governance, best symbolized by Taylor and his "war clan."

Common soldiers developed a personal investment in military nationalism, as war became an even more effective venue of social mobility. Not only were veterans of the Mexican campaign promised "bounty land" for their service, but the sudden annexation of new territory led veterans of past wars—many of whom had been promised, but had never received, similar bounties—to demand compensation. Republican civic life took on a militaristic cast, as old soldiers, including veterans of the War of 1812, began organizing pressure groups and marching on Washington. Few questioned this new militarization of public sentiment, or the increasingly commonsense notion that soldiers deserved exceptional deference. Between 1850 and 1855, Congress, suddenly the executor of a near-entire continent to dispense, overwhelmingly passed a series of laws that granted land to *all* veterans of *any* past war, going back to 1790. Hundreds of thousands of veterans, or their widows and heirs, received warrants for over thirty-four million acres (if they didn't want the land, they could redeem the warrants for cash).[25]

At the same time, serial wars greatly buttressed the power of the federal government. "There is no king, prince, or sultan more thoroughly above and beyond all legal restraint," a Whig journal complained of President Polk in 1847, "than the President of the United States."[26] As war expanded the power of the presidency—to mobilize men, spend money, tax, extend contracts, make appointments, and distribute land—so it expanded corruption. Yet rather than criticizing the way war enabled profiteering, graft, and patronage, many started holding up more war as an antidote to corruption: war, especially war to spread liberty across the continent, would provide the transcendent purpose needed to curb avarice. Walt Whitman strongly supported Polk and the taking of much of Mexico for such a reason. "Less liberal" governments were motivated by "greediness," Whitman wrote in 1846. But the United States made war to "reach the truer good, the good of the whole body of the people." In the years ahead, the expected virtues that would come from the next war were regularly prescribed as the solutions for the vices generated by the previous one.

Constant expansion continued to blur the line between foreign and domestic politics, bringing a battle-hardened brutalism back to an ever-growing homeland. When the war was over, some soldiers went back east, to New England's manufacturing towns or to New York's Bowery, their war-sharpened racism working its way into local politics, labor associations, and the Free Soil movement.[27] Others spread out into the newly conquered western land, into California and up into Oregon. They were armed with federally supplied rifles and an ample stock of bullets, ready to deal with Native Americans the way they had with Mexicans. "A war of extermination," the first U.S. Anglo governor of California predicted in 1851, "will continue to be waged between the races, until the Indian race becomes extinguished." The Mexican–American War had been fought in an extremely decentralized manner, with officers barely exercising control over their troops. In other words, soldiers experienced the violence they committed—"the repetition of the most heinous offenses, murder, rapine, robbery, and rape," as one newspaper wrote of U.S. atrocities committed on Mexicans— as a form of liberty. As they gave up soldiering for settling, they carried this blood-soaked entitlement forward. "Popular sovereignty"—a rallying cry for settlers who wanted to be free of federal control—had become a "synonym for racist brutality and wanton usurpation," advancing the sectional crisis that would soon lead to the Civil War.[28] In this sense, then, war came to be both valve and throttle, with each conflict simultaneously venting the hatreds produced by the last while creating the conditions for the next.

Some reformists, including Christians, labor radicals, and writers, reached for a definition of the general welfare as more than an increasingly strident defense of minimal government and property rights. They wanted a national identity based on something other than the letting loose of "twenty millions of monarchs" to do as they pleased. A "monster of a million minds" was how Melville described a society founded on radical individualism. Writing from intellectual exile in Europe, Margaret Fuller criticized what she called a "boundless lust of gain," which she held responsible for the "wicked war" the United States waged on Mexico. A "new, undefined good is thirsted for," as Reverend William Ellery Channing wrote a bit earlier. But what would that good be, other than martial nationalism?

For many, abolition was a primary, nonnegotiable demand. Beyond that, though, there weren't many practical options upon which to organize a national identity that were not inherently exclusionist or supremacist. Radicals continued to hope for a society in which both chattel and wage slavery would be abolished, and a few founded more utopian communities, but they were a minority.[29] Others who supported emancipation still imagined putting into place some kind of removal scheme, where freedmen and freedwomen could be relocated to Africa or somewhere in the west. Jefferson once talked about stocking the continent with people who spoke and looked like him, "descendants to the thousandth and thousandth generation." Settlers in Oregon, which officially joined the United States as a territory in 1848, didn't want slavery. But they didn't want black people either, passing a number of expulsion laws calling for the deportation of all people of color and prohibiting them from owning property or entering into legal contracts.[30] They wanted their arcadia white.

The reality of the country, however—its sudden gaining of tens of thousands of former citizens of Mexico, its soon-to-be emancipated four million African Americans, its growing population of already free people of color, its rising numbers of migrants, including many Irish-Catholic workers, and its multiplicity of faiths—meant that the United States would be populated by something other than Saxons to the thousandth generation.

SIX

The True Relief

"A kind of life not incompatible with health."

1.

Earlier, in 1748, Montesquieu gave a sense of what a republic organized around something other than same-stock racism and property
rights might look like. The French political theorist, who influenced
Madison and other founders, provided a list of what good government
"owed" its citizens: "a certain subsistence, a proper nourishment, convenient clothing, and a kind of life not incompatible with health."[1] It
was a list that would later reflect the demands of some radical labor
organizations in the United States. But to refound the country as a social
republic would have required breaking the Jacksonian coalition and
refuting its justifying premises.

Such a break finally came with the Civil War. In other places, the
kind of carnage the United States inflicted on itself in that war forced
governments to attend. In 1848, for instance, a Prussian doctor who
treated Berlin's revolutionary victims of counterrevolutionary violence
would go on to transform the first premise of liberalism—that people
have a "right to life"—into a new socialized "right to health and health
care."[2] In subsequent upheavals, in wars, epidemics, and famines that
took place in Crimea, France, and the Rhine, among other places, phy-

sicians and nurses continued to develop the principles of social medicine and public health. In nineteenth-century South America, a war fought between Brazil, Paraguay, Argentina, and Uruguay that brought an unimaginably high death toll laid the foundation of more socially active states. And in the early twentieth century, Mexico's prolonged, violent revolution—millions dead, millions displaced—culminated in the world's first social-democratic constitution.

War itself rapidly spurred improvements in trauma treatment, in fixing gunshot wounds, stemming bleeding, amputating limbs, setting bones, and figuring out how to improve collective hygiene to contain infectious diseases. In the early 1880s, when Peruvian soldiers returned to Lima from the battlefield carrying smallpox, government intervention in the economy to prevent an epidemic—forcing the cleanup of market stalls, for example, or regulating the sale of meat—was cast as patriotic.[3] Throughout human existence, as the sociologist Karl Polanyi wrote, death and decay had been the most elemental part of daily life. But starting in the late 1700s, and increasingly through the 1800s, the rapid expansion of capitalism gave ever-greater numbers of people a sense that maybe it didn't need to be that way, that escape from worldly misery might be possible. The same capitalist technology, though, also greatly increased the capacity of states to kill and maim. Battlefields grew in size. Death tolls rose to new heights. So did the numbers of soldiers coming home wounded, since advances in medicine meant more men were surviving amputations, infectious diseases, and bullet wounds. Writing at the end of World War II, Polanyi said that this clash brought about by industrial capitalism—between an expanding sense of possibility and an equally expanding experience of destruction—led to "knowledge of society," a realization that the freedom created by industrial growth did have limits, and that laissez-faire, if left unchecked, could destroy on the same scale that it created.[4]

A direct confrontation with the physicality of death and dismemberment—with having to dispose of severed limbs and rotting corpses, settle and feed uprooted refugees, tend to dysenteric fevers, and calm shell-shocked veterans—expanded social consciousness. In continental Europe, Prussia created the first fully developed welfare state after a deadly war with France. In the United Kingdom, the National Health Service was established after World War II. In the United States, the unprecedented bloodshed of the Civil War—in the heartland, not on the borderlands where it could be more easily ignored—forced questions about "union, citizenship, freedom, and human dignity," as Drew Gilpin Faust writes in *This Republic of Suffering*, and pushed the state to address "the needs of those who had died in its service." "From the stump of the arm, the amputated hand," Walt Whitman wrote in a poem capturing his experience as a volunteer nurse in camp hospitals, "I undo the clotted lint, remove the slough, wash off the matter and blood."[5]

The fulfillment of such duties, Faust writes, provided an "important vehicle for the expansion of federal power that characterized the transformed postwar nation. The establishment of national cemeteries and the emergence of the Civil War pension system to care for both the dead and their survivors yielded programs of a scale and reach unimaginable before the war. Death created the modern American union—not just by ensuring national survival, but by shaping enduring national structures and commitments."[6] Such battle-forged commitments laid the foundation of the country's modern welfare system. In addition to the provision of pensions and burial plots, they included bounty land; hospital care; support for widows, mothers, and the elderly; disability insurance; and an increasing concern for the mental health of veterans.[7]

2.

The Bureau of Refugees, Freedmen, and Abandoned Lands, which Faust doesn't discuss, is an especially powerful example of how war led the state to attend to needs. The Freedmen's Bureau, signed into law by Abraham Lincoln just before his assassination in 1865, functioned as a branch of the Department of War. Sending out thousands of agents across the South and setting up hundreds of offices, the bureau distributed basic necessities, including food, medicine, and clothing. It also founded thousands of schools, colleges, and hospitals, resettled refugees (white and black), administered confiscated properties, made and executed ad hoc laws, regulated labor relations and minimum wages, and levied taxes. W. E. B. Du Bois, writing in the early twentieth century, called the Freedmen's Bureau the "most extraordinary and far-reaching institution of social uplift that America has ever attempted."[8]

The bureau was, in potential and practice, the antithesis to Jacksonianism, an instrument of extraordinary power. "The federal government's assumption of responsibility for the welfare of a large body of its citizens," one historian describing the agency's mandate put it mildly, was "a concept of national authority alien to the constitutional thought of the day." Gone were the pastoral images of government as a "simple machine," like a lazily turning millwheel on a stream. The state was now hissing and screeching, a hurtling locomotive, its Freedmen's Bureau the "symbol and substance of military occupation." The bureau helped poor people of all colors, both "low down whites" and "venerable negroes," as one of its agents put it. As the historian Nancy Isenberg writes, it treated them not "as cutthroat adversaries but as the worthy poor." In the Deep South, in Alabama, Arkansas, Missouri, and Tennessee, "the bureau extended twice—and in some cases four times—as much relief to whites as to blacks."

The bureau promised universal equality and provided substantial assistance. Its actual operations were somewhat different from what a socialist like Du Bois wanted them to be. Underfunded and understaffed, the bureau made enormous concessions to the old planter class, especially when it came to getting the cotton economy started again. And it didn't have anywhere near the personnel to protect freed people from violence. Yet to appreciate the force of the backlash against the agency, it's useful to consider not just what it did but what it represented, its potential, as Du Bois imagined it, as an organic form of American socialism-in-embryo, a model for a "vast and single-eyed" instrument of centralized government needed to "guide us up from murder in the South and robbery and cheating in the North into a nation whose infinite resources would be developed in the interest of the mass of the nation—that is, of the laboring poor."

If ever there was a time for the birth of a social republic—for an end to expansionist morality, where the solution to all problems was to flee forward—this was it. The South was under military occupation, its plantations seized and planter class surviving at the sufferance of its vanquishers. But that social republic was not to be.

3.

Chattel slavery was a three-hundred-year-old institution, "congealed," Du Bois writes, "in law." Slave traders "took millions upon millions of men, human men and lovable, light, and liberty-loving children of the sun, and threw them with no sparing of brutality into one rigid mold." Slavery, he continued, was a "school of brutality and human suffering" whose pedagogy was the "darkening of reason," serial rape, and "spiritual death."[9] Destroyed by the Union Army, slavery left millions of survivors, stretching out from the Potomac to the Rio Grande, from Florida to Missouri.

Andrew Johnson, who became president upon Abraham Lincoln's assassination in April 1865, thought these survivors should help themselves.

"Slaves were assisted to freedom," said Johnson, with the expectation that "on becoming free they would be a self-sustaining population." Johnson here was explaining why he had vetoed a bill extending the Freedmen's Bureau. He did so, he said, because any legislative action based on the idea that freedmen and freedwomen wouldn't quickly "attain a self-sustaining condition" would be "injurious" to "their character and their prospects."[10] Congress overrode Johnson's veto, and the bureau went on for seven more years.

Johnson did all he could to stymie the empowerment of former slaves, including pardoning their former masters-turned-rebels and returning much of their property. His attacks on the bureau were heartfelt.[11] He hated the idea of the institution. But his campaign was also strategic. Upon taking office, Johnson, a member of the Democratic Party, quickly fell out with congressional Republicans who wanted to extend Reconstruction. The demonization of the bureau, then, allowed Johnson a way to use racism to build up his own political base among

poor whites, even as he signaled to southern planters, known as Bour-
bon Democrats or Redeemers, that he would do what he could to preserve their power and privileges. Just as today, when simply mentioning
a topic ("Obamacare," say) can call forth a whole racialized worldview
whose details needn't be filled in, the phrase "Freedmen's Bureau" alone
whistled its meaning. Here's the transcript from one of Johnson's
speeches: "Now, my countrymen, let me call your attention to a single
fact, the Freedmen's Bureau. [Laughter and hisses.]"[12]

Most of Johnson's northern and southern audiences had been raised
in the church of Andrew Jackson's "primitive simplicity and purity,"
with its already racialized understanding of the federal government,
when any publicly administered social program would be seen as but
an opening for "extraneous corrupting influences." So their shared,
already-understood animosity to the Freedmen's Bureau, which needed
nothing but laughter and hisses to convey, made it easy for the president to shift all the many problems of post–Civil War America—its
corruption, concentration of power, low wages, and inadequate
housing—onto African Americans and their "blood-sucker" advocates
in Congress, radical Republicans such as Thaddeus Stevens and Wendell Phillips, who were trying to fund the bureau.

"You, the people," Johnson told an audience in Indianapolis in 1866,
"must pay the expense of running the machine out of your own pocket."
Johnson presided over a period of unmitigated venality, with land
speculators and railroad magnates supping at the public trough. Yet
he decried the bureau's modest efforts as the essence of corruption and
patronage. He portrayed its "draw day" distribution of corn as creating a new class of dependents attached to the government—a class composed of both the bureaucrats who administered the provision and
the recipients of the largesse. Then, just in case anyone in the audience missed the point, Johnson asked what his veto of the bureau
meant. An answer came back from the crowd: "It is keeping the nigger
down."[13]

As portrayed by Johnson and others, the bureau, along with other
civil legislation, was unnatural in its interventionism, in its effort to use
political power to impinge on economic activity, to extend political

equality into the social realm—or, in the words of Missouri Republican House member James Blair, "to force the negroes into social equality." Blair stood with the Union during the war, opposed formal slavery, and said he supported "equality before the law." But he was opposed to legislation that tried to use the ideal of political equality to force tavern and hotel owners to serve freedmen and women, or ministers and doctors to care for them. "Ethiopia," Blair said, referring to efforts to desegregate churches, "is now stretching forth her hand and demanding rights that white men never dared demand," the right "to regulate the worship of the white people."[14] Emancipation, for Blair, blurred the line between foreign and domestic spheres, introducing an alien threat into the heartland of liberty: "Ethiopia, with her million of voters at her back, is demanding that one of the most sacred principles"—the right to free worship—"of American freemen be trampled under foot."[15]

The Civil War destroyed the Jacksonian political coalition but not its myths. The backlash to the Freedmen's Bureau retooled all of its old ideas—concerning the virtues of a minimal state, the racialization of any welfare-providing bureaucracies, the sanctity of property rights, individualism, and a definition of freedom as freedom from restraint—and cast them forward. President Johnson described the bureau as a giveaway to blacks. At a moment when freedmen and freedwomen were being murdered in staggeringly high numbers, the president of the United States said he favored "the emancipation of the white man as well as the colored ones," complaining that the bureau was both trapping African Americans in a new form of slavery and giving African Americans preferential jobs. Resurrecting the Jacksonian opposition of "free" men fighting federal "enslavement," Johnson described the agency as an effort "to transfer 4,000,000 of slaves in the United States from their original owners to a new set of task masters" (to this, the crowd cheered and yelled back, "Never"). The bureau was an "agency to keep the negro in idleness" and create a culture of dependency through the "lavish issuance of rations."

Johnson's racist gambit didn't help his political fortunes. He did not get his party's nomination for reelection in 1868. General Ulysses

S. Grant won the presidency, allowing the radical phase of Reconstruction, already launched by congressional Republicans, to carry on. The military continued to occupy the South, and national laws and constitutional amendments were passed that allowed black men to vote and run for office, in principle and in fact. In 1867, no African Americans held any office. Within three years, they held fifteen percent of all elected positions, at the local, state, and national level.[16] The bureau's work went on, though still underfunded. Many of its functions passed to other agencies of the Army.[17]

4.

Then, in 1872, the bureau's chief commissioner, General Oliver Otis Howard, was reassigned by the Department of War to Arizona. The politics behind this new commission was complicated, yet the symbolism of the reassignment itself was stark. It captured the priorities of a nation now unified, industrializing, and ascendant in the world turning away from the past—from the bloody obligations of Reconstruction—toward the future, to the frontier, a place not of obligation but opportunity.[18]

Howard was a Christian opponent of slavery, a believer in the true religion, who called the bureau he ran the "true relief." He deployed that bureau's power with a single-mindedness of purpose that realized Andrew Jackson's nightmare, the apotheosis of that federal agent on the Natchez Trace, now in the form of the federal government itself. When Johnson had earlier vetoed the bureau's renewal, he described Howard as an "absolute monarch" with the power to "determine the rights of persons and property." Howard himself described his work as advancing a different, more social understanding of "freedom" than those individualistic ones used as a cudgel by Jackson, Johnson, and others to keep people of color down. The bureau, Howard said, "was bound to put its foot firmly upon *every* form of slavery" in an effort to help freedmen achieve true emancipation—from unregulated labor markets and from "old masters" who, if left unchecked, would use any ploy to create new forms of bondage, including vagrancy laws, debt peonage, and collective contracts. Howard deeply believed in the virtues of "individuality," of initiative and self-control. But he knew concerted government force—to protect emancipated people from night-rider terror, to guarantee them their right to vote, and to provide food and education—was needed to make "individual independence" a reality for the victims of slavery.[19]

Howard, in other words, was no Jacksonian, to say the least. But Howard's management of the bureau had been controversial. The bureau, naturally, remained a target of unrelenting criticism by southern planters and politicians, who leveled charges of corruption, incompetence, and despotism at Howard. Understaffed and greatly underfunded, especially considering the geographic range the agency was meant to administer, Howard couldn't offset these criticisms by pointing to efficient, clear accomplishments. The sprawling and often contradictory nature of the bureau's mandate—to contain planter power, administer basic welfare, establish schools and hospitals, and revive the cotton economy—sparked conflict. The bureau tried to create a wage economy, but pay on cotton plantations remained unsustainably low, leading to what some have called "slavery by another name" and to the spread of debt peonage and sharecropping.

In any case, rather than leaving him to finish his work with the bureau, Howard's superiors sent him west, where he was put to blazing his own trail of tears.

First he was sent to Arizona Territory to negotiate a peace with the Apaches. Then he was assigned to the Pacific Northwest to deal with Chief Joseph, who was resisting federal efforts to force the Nez Perce to vacate the Wallowa valley to make room for white settlers. Howard was still facing criticism over his zealous administration of the Freedmen's Bureau, not just by southern planters but in the national press and in the ranks of the military, where his enemies were investigating his management of the bureau for abuse. The Wallowa white settlers had followed the Civil War and Reconstruction closely, and they knew of Howard's reputation. Though far removed from the South, they nonetheless had carried forth a Jacksonian hostility to federal power and were ready to treat Howard the way the general was treated by southern whites. For his part, Howard, as his biographer notes, felt that if he "took it upon himself to champion and then enforce a policy that favored Joseph," that if he did in Wallowa what he tried to do with the Freedmen's Bureau—"testing the law to its limits in order to achieve something unpopular but just"—he'd continue to be pilloried and would perhaps even put his military career at risk.[20]

So Howard took a hard line against Chief Joseph. He gave the Nez Perce an ultimatum to surrender their homeland, which they rejected. Joseph fought back, then retreated, setting out on a brutal fifteen-hundred-mile trek. Howard pursued the Nez Perce for nearly four months, over the Rockies and across Montana's plains. His troops killed scores, and only about half of the eight hundred who had started out on the march survived. They were packed into boxcars and taken to Oklahoma.

Meanwhile, with Howard in the West, opponents of the Freedmen's Bureau in the War Department managed to shut the agency down. By this point, in the middle of the 1870s, white vigilantism against African Americans had grown so intense that President Ulysses S. Grant considered trying to acquire the Dominican Republic as a homeland for freedmen and women. Grant had initiated his annexation effort prior to a massacre that took place on Easter Sunday 1873, in Colfax, Louisiana, which left between sixty-two and a hundred and fifty African Americans dead at the hands of a white mob. But that atrocity must have been on his mind when in his last address to Congress in 1876 he explained his reasons for wanting the Dominican Republic: "Thus in cases of great oppression and cruelty, such as has been practiced upon them in many places within the last eleven years, whole communities would have sought refuge in Santo Domingo. I do not suppose the whole race would have gone, nor is it desirable that they should go. Their labor is desirable—indispensable almost—where they now are. But the possession of this territory would have left the negro 'master of the situation,' by enabling him to demand his rights at home on pain of finding them elsewhere."[21]

Grant, in other words, imagined the Dominican Republic as a

substitute for the Freedmen's Bureau, achieving all the things that government agency was meant to accomplish—specifically, protecting African Americans and making sure that their labor was adequately compensated. The proposal didn't go forward. But Grant, in proposing a place where emancipated slaves might be masters of their situation, both acknowledged the depth of the problem—in this case, the deadly post–Civil War combination of racial terror and the southern plantation economy's starvation wages—and admitted that the problem wouldn't be solved under existing political and economic arrangements.

5.

The bureaucratic machinery for western expansion—including the Department of Agriculture, the Morrill Land-Grant Act, the Pacific Railroad Act, and the Homestead Act—was put in place even before the Civil War had ended. In fact, the ability of the Union to win the war, historians Boyd Cothran and Ari Kelman write, was based on a trade-off. Men could "enlist to fight for Lincoln and liberty, and receive, as fair recompense for their patriotic sacrifices, higher education and Western land connected by rail to markets. It seemed possible that liberty and empire might advance in lock step."[22]

The Homestead Act embodied that imperial liberty, the fruit of the Free Soil movement. Promising large lots to any settler who would work them, the federal government distributed a bit under three hundred million acres of public land to about four hundred thousand families. But this was less than half of the acreage private interests acquired through purchase. Within a decade of the act's passage, large capitalists and speculators had laid claim to the most fertile, best irrigated, and, via railroad lines, best connected portion of public "free land." The corruption and fraud that marked the Johnson administration continued through the 1870s and 1880s, at an even greater scale; the federal government had land to distribute, patronage to dispense, contracts to award, and other favors, including tariffs and subsidies, to shower on its allies.[23] It was a "great barbecue," was how the historian Vernon

Parrington in 1927 described the post–Civil War seizure of the West, with the largest portions going to the most powerful corporations and conglomerates. "It was a splendid feast." Everybody was invited. Democracy promised to feed all: "The eating and drinking went on till only the great carcasses were left. Then at last came the reckoning. When the bill was sent in to the American people [they] discovered they had been put off with giblets while the capitalists were consuming the turkey."[24]

By this point, energy to fuel all this activity was becoming its own economic sector, and the increasing demand for power was leaving marks on the land. Coal capitalists, followed by the pioneers of petroleum, swarmed into the the valleys of Appalachia, dispossessing smallholders and stripping the hills and hollows. "Denuded of their forests," was how one turn-of-the-century witness imagined the near future, "the valleys lighted by the flames of coke-ovens and smelting furnaces; their vegetation seared and blackened with soot and gasses; derricks rising like skeletons along the streams . . . yawning mines and piles of slack disfiguring the once pleasing landscape—and one could wish that such an Arcadia might have been spared such ravishment. But the needs of the race are insatiable and unceasing. They must be supplied; and one after another the reserves stored by nature in the hidden places of the earth must be brought out to feed the perpetual hunger of the world's commerce."[25]

In the 1870s, a severe economic downturn accompanied by a wave of militant strikes led some to worry that a "second civil war seemed imminent," this time a class war, along with intensified terror directed at freedmen and women now that the federal government had withdrawn its protection to focus on the final campaign to pacify the West. Later in the decade, after years of contraction, the economy revived, rapidly. Such cycles of extended busts followed by dizzying booms only served to deepen commitment to the idea of expansion. During the busts, expansion was the proposed solution, the validity of which was confirmed when the eventual boom finally came: onward.

And as foreign markets opened, large-scale export-oriented agriculture reinvested its soaring profits in technology and mechanization, making it even more competitive, allowing those who stood at the summit of this sector of the economy to consolidate even more political power. The same dynamic held for manufacturing. "How much longer are we to continue blind to the demands for new markets for our already excessive and rapidly increasing production?" asked Iowa representative John Kasson in 1881. Kasson's question captures the post–Civil War extension of the expansionist premise to overseas markets. Extend the sphere to create new outlets for the country's growing agricultural and manufacturing exports and you will avoid cyclical business crises, as well as the popular unrest that comes with such crises. You will have domestic peace. "We are rapidly utilizing the whole of our continental territory," Kasson said. "We must turn our eyes abroad, or they will soon look inward upon discontent."[26]

War produced death and revealed decay, and death and decay demanded public policy. But public policy threatened to lead to socialism, or at least to a more interventionist government empowered to stir up, as General Howard described the work of the Freedmen's Bureau, "all social life." There was an alternative, a chance to turn away from the Civil War's bloody battlefields and hence away from reminders of the death and decay that forged the modern American union.

"Read but your history aright, and you shall not find the task too hard," Woodrow Wilson wrote in 1895. Recommit to the "heroic work" of moving outward in the world, Wilson said, and we "shall renew our youth and secure our age against decay."[27]

The frontier, said Frederick Jackson Turner at around the same time, "was a magic fountain of youth in which America continually bathed and was rejuvenated."[28]

SEVEN

The Outer Edge

"This great continent, then wild and silent."

1.

In the last decade of the 1800s, the historian Frederick Jackson Turner emancipated the concept "frontier," unhitching it from its more mundane, earthbound meanings—used to indicate a national border or a military front—and letting it float free as an abstraction. One sentence alone, which subsequent historians cite the way monks chant a creed, captures Turner's revolution: "The existence of an area of free land, its continuous recession, and the advance of American settlement westward, explain American development."

Turner was an unnoticed assistant professor at the University of Wisconsin in 1893 when he first presented his "Frontier Thesis," at the World's Congress of Historians and Historical Students, held in Chicago during its World's Fair—the one stalked by a serial killer made famous in Erik Larson's *The Devil in the White City*. Thirty-two professional historical writers and credentialed university scholars had gathered at Chicago's Art Institute, located some distance from the loud fairground, with its Buffalo Bill's Wild West Show and mock-ups of Native American villages. Last on a late-in-the-day panel, Turner read his paper, titled "The Significance of the Frontier in American History."

His sparse audience might have been tired, for no one asked a question. Turner returned to his boardinghouse, his biographer writes, "burdened with a heavy sense of failure."[1] But his argument grew quickly in reputation.

Many of the scholars at the Chicago conference thought of history writing as mostly a compendium of facts, dates, and names. Turner, in contrast, was part of a new generation that was beginning to make and revise arguments about the past—trying to "explain," as Turner wrote, the relationship between economics, migration, ideas, science, culture, and politics. There was, though, one influential historical argument prior to the Turner thesis, popular among New England Protestant historians: the "germ theory," which had nothing to do with literal bacteria or infections.

The germ theory held that what was good and strong about American institutions germinated in Europe, in ancient Saxon and Teutonic villages filled with "freemen" not yet subordinated to feudal lords. Applied to Germany and England, this theory was one of romantic decline, of a once-free people weighted down by the sediments of history, bureaucracy, ecclesiastical strictures, and aristocratic caste. "Untrammeled in the liberty which he enjoyed," the "primitive Aryan" came to represent "what the world had once possessed, but which it possessed no longer."[2] In North America, it was a theory of ascent, of Saxon freedom spreading first to medieval England, then to New England. The "old Anglo-Saxon race" is "destined to plant amid the wilds of the New World the germs of free institutions . . . extending over a vast continent," read one succinct statement of the theory.[3]

The germ principle was straightforwardly racist, a celebration of the "blood gene," or the "great Teutonic race," as one of its most prominent practitioners, Herbert Baxter Adams, put it, and a confirmation of the continuity and superiority of Britain and North America's Saxon lineages (such as the Adamses, including John, Samuel, and John Quincy, down to Herbert himself). If the study of history is the study of change, these early historians of the United States were decidedly ahistorical. Their germs were something like physicists' Big Bang, sudden and pristine. When the Puritans landed, "their institutions were already perfected," George Bancroft, among the country's most influential historians prior to Turner, wrote.[4] Woodrow Wilson, who studied with Turner under Adams at Johns Hopkins, argued in 1899 that early Christian settlers "were inventing nothing"; ideas that would later result in the Declaration of Independence and the Constitution were already fully formed upon their arrival in the New World. Americans, Wilson said, were "simply letting their race habits and instincts"—as developed in Europe—"have natural play."[5] Another historian wrote that the origins of the independent spirit of the American West was "found to be in the forests of Germany," and that American frontiersmen were but replicas of Saxon, Teutonic, and Aryan "independent freemen."[6]

Turner, in contrast, flipped the focus. He said that what was good in America was made in America, by settlers transforming frontier wilderness: "Free land," he wrote, and "an abundance of natural resources open to a fit people, made the democratic type of society in America." America's unique democratic individualism, Turner held, was a "new product that is American." American democracy "came out of the American forest and it gained strength each time it touched a new frontier."[7]

The use of the word "frontier" had evolved as the United States grew. Whereas in the late 1700s the term, as discussed earlier, nearly exclusively referred to a boundary, border, or military front, by the time of Turner's Chicago presentation it had come to mean much more. What exactly it meant was subject to debate. Over the course of its existence, the United States' political boundary moved forward rather steadily, from the crest of the Alleghenies to the Mississippi River to the Sabine and Red Rivers to, finally, its current limit at Mexico and the Pacific Ocean. But its line of white settlers, along with the line of military force used to protect those settlers, moved forward in fits and starts, zigs and zags, sometimes east of the political boundary, sometimes west of it. Anglo society moved forward not as a uniform front against Native Americans but more fluidly, as if it were poured into the interstices separating Indian nations and communities. As it did, the meaning of the word "frontier" diverged from that of "border," which continued, more or less, to indicate a fixed line. "Frontier" became fuzzier. It came to suggest a cultural zone or a civilizational struggle, a way of life: a semantic change electrified by the terror and bloodshed that went along with settler expansion.

Turner's genius was to embrace the unsettledness of the concept, to not try to fix the "frontier" as any one thing. "The term is an elastic one," he wrote, and "for our purposes does not need sharp definition." He then went on, in his 1893 thesis, to define "frontier" in at least thirteen different ways, to indicate, among other things, "a form of society rather than an area"; "a return to primitive conditions"; a "field of opportunity"; "the outer edge of the wave—the meeting point between savagery and civilization"; something that lies "at the hither edge of free land"; the "line of most rapid and effective Americanization" for European migrants (especially those who started arriving in the 1880s in increasing numbers from central and southern Europe); a harsh "environment" that is almost "too strong for the man"; and "a gate of escape from the bondage of the past." There was a "trader's frontier," a "rancher's frontier," a "miner's frontier," and a "farmer's frontier."

These many different frontiers had many different functions. In this sense, the power of Turner's thesis, or theory, was not that it was refutable or provable, from a scientific or logical standard, but that it wasn't. The frontier could be posited as numerous things and speculated as the cause of multiple effects. It cultivated a "love of wilderness freedom"; nurtured "the formation of a composite nationality for the American people," which in turn led to the "evolution of American political institutions"; "promoted democracy"; combined "coarseness and strength" with "acuteness and inquisitiveness" to create an archetype personality uniquely American, at once "practical" and "inventive," fast "to find expedients," displaying a "masterful grasp of material things, lacking in the artistic but powerful to effect great ends."

Such multifunctional complexity! The frontier, here and henceforth, was a state of mind, a cultural zone, a sociological term of comparison, a type of society, an adjective, a noun, a national myth, a disciplining mechanism, an abstraction, and an aspiration. At the same time, though, such explanatory simplicity: "The existence of an area of free land, its

continuous recession, and the advance of American settlement westward, *explain* American development."

Within a decade of the 1893 paper, it became difficult to grapple
with any of the main themes of American history without passing
through Turner. By 1922, Arthur Schlesinger, Sr., in his popular survey
of U.S. history, said that so many books applied Turner's arguments
that it would be impossible to list them all, and, anyway, there was
no point to summing up the Frontier Thesis, since it was "too well
known."[8] Not just historians, but economists, sociologists, philosophers, literature professors, psychoanalysts, politicians, and novelists,
both dime-store and highbrow, adopted Turnerian ideas. Two of Turner's fellow historians of the West, Theodore Roosevelt and Woodrow
Wilson, became president. Having moved from the department of history at the University of Wisconsin to Harvard, Turner tutored the
country's ruling class, its intellectuals, policy makers, businessmen, and
career foreign-service officers. Franklin Delano Roosevelt was one of
his students.

2.

The midwesterner Turner had seized the discipline of history from its
Brahmin ministers, from the Adamses and Bancrofts, disenchanting the
Saxon fairy tale that located the origins of Madison's Constitution
in primeval German mists, to be carried forth by Saxon germs. Turner,
instead, emphasized what he called the "germs of processes," the material
and ideological forces—trade, legislation, technology and science, law
and the rise of new ideas concerning the relationship of the individual
to the state—churning below the froth of great events and great men.

Turner's main argument, which he advanced in his 1893 essay as
well as in subsequent writings, is straightforward: America's vast, open
West created the conditions for an unprecedented expansion of the ideal
of political equality, an ideal based on a sense that the frontier would
go on forever: "The wilderness seemed so unending."[9] Left alone with
their visions of unlimited resources, pioneers would transform nature

and deepen democratic values: independence, personal initiative, and, above all, individualism. But also fairness, honesty, and trust, a kind of frontier mutualism. In a harsh land, prior to the arrival of the state, pioneers had to find a balance between self-reliance and cooperation, extending relations of commerce and rules of law. When the government did show up, and as local markets evolved into a national economy, these frontier values spread throughout the country, shaping its institutions. Frontier individualism, Turner said, didn't just exist on the frontier. It was found everywhere in the country, in its cities, villages, and ports, "*because* of the existence of the frontier"—that is, because individualism was generated on the frontier and because the frontier kept a check on other, less wholesome tendencies, including demands for wealth redistribution. That, more or less, is what Turner's argument is. But to understand Turner's revolution, one has to know what Turner's argument isn't.

It isn't elitist. Other historians of the time might have credited Virginia's Tidewater "gentlemen" for developing the West, saying that it wasn't backwoods grit but copious amounts of capital that cleared the land (the "meaner sort of people," wrote one British report of western settlement, "seat themselves" under "the shade and protection of the greater"). Turner, anticipating by many decades the modern impulse to document "history from below," instead celebrated the hunters, traders, dirt-farming families, as the executors of progress. In this sense, he was building on the Jacksonian impulse to exalt and empower the common man, not the man of substance but of the soil.

Jacksonian exaltation and empowerment, though, was racist. And Turner isn't, at least not overtly. He wasn't concerned with identifying racial purity as history's kick-starter, the way that others searched for the originating Saxon "germ" of American greatness. For instance, one of Turner's mentors, Hubert Howe Bancroft, hailed the "great Aryan march of centuries," the "mother race," and "Anglo-Saxon blood," as carrying forward everything good about America.[10] The power driving the United States out in the world, said Senator Albert J. Beveridge, not long after Turner presented his Chicago paper, was "racial." And it was divine: God had been "preparing the English-speaking and Teutonic peoples for a thousand years," the senator continued. "He has made us the master organizers of the world to establish system where chaos reigns." "This," said Beveridge, "is the divine mission of America."[11] Turner, in contrast, didn't have much to say about religion, positing neither the dynamism of Protestantism nor the decadence of Catholicism as the cause of civilizational success or failure.

Also muted in Turner's writing are the celebrations of the conquering passions that accompanied the removal of Native Americans or the U.S. invasion of Mexico, which imagined the Mexicans disappearing from the earth. Turner wrote no sentence anywhere near as callous as this one composed by Theodore Roosevelt in 1889, which cited the march of civilization to condone the elimination of Native Americans: "The settler and pioneer have at bottom had justice on their side: this great continent could not have been kept as nothing but a game preserve for squalid savages."[12] Turner deemphasized genocidal hatred as a justification of U.S. expansion, unlike, say, the historian Bernard Bailyn, who has recently identified a "deep, pervasive racism" as motivating settler terror. There's no rape as a shock strategy in Turner's account of the frontier, though that strategy was used by settlers and soldiers. There's no burning indigenous peoples out of their villages, no slaughtering their children as they fled the flames, no retaliatory killings, no Andrew Jackson rousing his men to "pant with vengeance" and turn themselves into "engines of destruction" to slaughter Creeks and mutilate their bodies. "When American history comes to be rightly viewed," Turner wrote, dismissing the importance of forced labor to the creation of U.S. wealth, "it will be seen that the slavery question is an incident."

Just three years before Turner's Chicago panel, the 7th Cavalry murdered upward of 250 Sioux men, women, and children at Wounded Knee, South Dakota. Yet of all the many things the frontier is in Turner's 1893 paper, one thing the frontier is noticeably not much of is a military front. Turner does note in passing that each successful frontier—the fall line of the Alleghenies; the Mississippi; the Missouri; and the

99th meridian (the longitude where the moist prairie gives way to the arid plains)—was "won by a series of Indian wars." But he then proceeds to muffle the violence of these wars. Theodore Roosevelt, again, is illustrative. His many-volume *The Winning of the West*, published in the 1880s, begins with a classic statement of the germ principle, identifying Andrew Jackson's victory over the Creeks as one battle in a war that started with the Saxon "conquest of Britain" and continued forward in a larger crusade to conquer the "world's waste spaces."[13] Roosevelt's history reads like an epic poem to the doctrine of discovery, a brutalist's answer to those who were beginning to show concern about the extermination of Native Americans: "Let the sentimentalists say what they will, the man who puts the soil to use must of right dispossess the man who does not, or the world will come to a standstill."[14] Like Turner, Roosevelt believed that the frontier created a particular kind of political culture. Unlike Turner, however, Roosevelt identified the first step in this creation as wild terror and rough justice.

At least since the late eighteenth century and continuing well past the publication of *The Winning of the West*, frontier vigilantism was used to suppress people of color. Roosevelt celebrated such vigilantism. When threatened, "good men" would band "themselves together as regulators and put down the wicked with ruthless severity, by the exercise of lynch law, shooting and hanging the worst off-hand." He admitted that torture was often used but argued that, in general, such rough justice was "healthy for the community" and would eventually evolve into more rational forms of state-administered jurisprudence.* On the frontier, each man—even when he wasn't banding with others in a

---

*Later, as president, Theodore Roosevelt, in signing some of the world's first multinational legal treaties, attempted to subordinate the United States to international jurisprudence. But at home, he couldn't even subordinate the frontier justice he had earlier celebrated. In *The Winning of the West*, Roosevelt said vigilantism would transform into law. It didn't. Faced with what he called an "epidemic" of lynching, President Roosevelt blamed the victims: "The greatest existing cause of lynching," he said in 1906, "is the perpetration, especially by black men, of the hideous crime of rape." Worse still, having been forced to lynch, white men debased themselves, falling to "a level with the criminal," spreading chaos. "Lawlessness," Roosevelt said, "grows by what it feeds upon; and when mobs begin to lynch for rape they speedily extend the sphere of their operations and lynch for many other kinds of crimes."

posse—was a law unto himself, each living in the "perfect freedom" to work out his own morality. Pioneers were "men of lawless, brutal spirit" who, by subduing nature and natives, also eventually subdued their own violence, calling forth civilization; "thus the backwoodsmen lived on the clearings they had hewed out of the everlasting forest; a grim, stern people, strong and simple, powerful for good and evil, swayed by gusts of stormy passion, the love of freedom rooted in their very hearts' core."[15]

There's none of this drama in Turner. None of this "wild half-savage romance," as Roosevelt described U.S. history, which posited civilization as emerging out of cruel, relentless war, not just against nature and Native Americans but against one's own base instincts. If the advance of Turner's civilization was inevitable, it was a gentle inevitability. And if his writing presented an ode to individualism, it was a restrained individualism, more James Stewart than John Wayne. There was struggle, but it wasn't racial or class struggle. What moved the frontier forward, according to Turner, were laws, courts, and commerce.[16] Not for him Roosevelt's wolfish frontier. The Wisconsin historian wrote in a soothing prose, at its most tumultuous when it was describing the frontier as a "wave." But his analysis is more like the calm lapping of water onshore. Turner sings softly of American vitality, yet denies heroism. He celebrates nameless "types," like the "hunter" or the "farmer." It's the frontier, not men, that "leaped over the Alleghenies" and "skipped the Great Plains and the Rocky Mountains."

There's an interesting backstory to Turner's calming of American passion. As a child growing up in Portage, Wisconsin, he had gone canoeing and hiking among the Winnebago and Menominee, a memory that he later described to a colleague as bucolic. "I remember a voyage down the Wisconsin, poled by Indians in a dugout from near Wausau, and hearing a duet-like conversation between the boatmen and the squaws as we passed their Indian village—the guttural of the buck and the sweet, clear laughing treble of the squaw. I remember the antlered deer who stood at the bend among the balsam firs, drinking at the river's edge, and how close we got to him in our silent canoe."[17] The Indians, though, would soon be gone, removed by federal troops and boarded on federal trains and disappeared—troops that were invited to do the work by Portage leaders, including Turner's father, a namesake of Andrew Jackson.

Andrew Jackson Turner was, according to his contemporaries, a good man and an upstanding and responsible leader in his town. He was also a man who wanted the Winnebago and Menominee villages destroyed. They were "worthless savages," as he described them in the paper he edited and published, the *Wisconsin State Register*, and he demanded that the army drive them from the community, since they were "utterly despised, disgusting everyone with their filthiness and alarming timid women by their frightful appearance." The military did so. According to Turner's biographer, "a detachment of troops arrived early in 1873 to drive the red men to their Nebraska reservation."[18] They resisted, but soldiers pushed them "westward all that summer, some almost at bayonet point." Some escaped into the Wisconsin woods, to be rounded up by federal troops, marched through Portage, and "herded on railroad cars that would carry them westward." Frederick was thirteen years old, and none of the events he witnessed— not the actions of his father, not the "disgust" that must have been as much a part of family conversation as it was the *Register*'s editorial— made it into his scholarship.[19]

3.

Turner depicted the borderlands as a place where individualism sprouted from the land like prairie weeds, and only later did government and big business arrive. "Complex society," he wrote, "is precipitated by the wilderness." "Steadily, almost calmly, they extended," Woodrow Wilson similarly wrote of frontier settlers, across "this great continent, then wild and silent."[20] But what we think of the West, since its inception, has been the domain of large-scale power, of highly capitalized speculators, businesses, railroads, agriculture, and mining. "Settlement tended to follow, rather than precede, connections to national and international markets," Richard White, a historian of the West, argues. These markets were created through federal action, by, among other things, federal gunboats.[21] Western movement required a strong state. The U.S. Army removed Native Americans and Mexicans. Government-backed bonds financed the purchase of Louisiana. Federal surveyors plotted out their baselines and principal meridians well in advance of the settled frontier, and federal engineers laid out roads. Public-works projects, many of them carried out by the Corps of Engineers, irrigated arid lands in the West and drained swampy lands in Florida. And the secretary of war distributed rifles and ammunition to settlers.

Turner, raised in the maelstrom of Indian removal, knew full well the power of the state, based on his experience of watching government soldiers round up Native Americans around his Wisconsin hometown and remove them west. He also knew that the state *preceded* the frontier. In notes he took on an 1887 essay that detailed the various ways frontier society generated an "exaggerated" sense of liberty and an "abnormal" anti-government ideology, Turner included a telling comment: "The West of our day relies on national gov[ernment] because gov[ernment] *came before the settler*, and gave him land, arranged his transportation, gov[ernment], etc. etc."[22]

Yet in Turner's case studies, as well as in his more sweeping generalizations, he advances a different sequence, one that goes more or less like this: First there's nature, either in its raw, untouched state or cut through by Indian trails. Then come settler families, who apply their labor to wrest a clearing in the woods and create fields and pastures. As they do this work, individual families begin to aggregate, forming communities and voluntary associations, including law-and-order vigilante groups (which Turner, like Roosevelt, celebrates, but in toned-down, sanitized form). Dispersed communities start to "touch hands with each other," along old indigenous roads or along river valleys, creating what political scientists call civil society. They develop commercial relations and nurture frontier values, including initiative, optimism, trust, cooperation, individualism, along with a refusal to tolerate despots. Trade deepens, local and national markets extend, mining and manufacturing spring up, "as by magic." And then the state arrives.[23]

Turner's sequence—nature, settlement, labor, society, security, trade, trust, more trade, which leads to more security and trust, and then government—is important in that it crystallizes a number of uniquely American ideals about the relationship between the economy, rights, and sovereignty: Labor mixed with nature creates property. Property creates virtue. Private property–based virtue exists prior to the state. And the state's only legitimate function is to protect virtue, not create virtue. It's a sleight of hand, this sequence, for, as Turner wrote in his notes, "government came before." But it was, and remains, a powerful move, one that premises the virtue of freedom as existing independently of the state and restricts the role of the state to only guarding virtue. That premise makes possible the ongoing refusal of the United States to accept the legitimacy of social or economic rights. Individual, inherent rights, found in nature—*to have, to bear, to move, to assemble, to believe, to possess*—were legitimate, as was a state that protected them. Social rights—*to receive health care, education, and welfare*—made possible by state intervention were perverse.[24]

4.

Turner didn't publish much after his frontier essay, but he lectured often. Mostly optimistic, these public presentations did contain dark notes. In 1890, the U.S. Census Office had declared that it would no longer use the word "frontier" as a descriptive category. There were so many people in the West, the office said, that "there can hardly be said to be a frontier line." Even more important than population density, Turner knew, was the fact that the power of capital—or, borrowing from Andrew Jackson, what he called "money power"—was outrunning what was left of the frontier. The West's effectiveness as a safety valve was, he believed, diminishing.[25]

   "The age of cheap land, cheap corn and wheat, and cheap cattle has gone forever," Turner wrote in 1914; "the free lands are gone, the continent is crossed, and all this push and energy is turning into channels of agitation."[26] Increasingly, now in the early twentieth century, "masters of industry"—the "coal baron, the steel king, the oil king, the cattle king, the railroad magnate, the master of high finance, the monarch of trusts"—claimed to be the true heirs to the western ideal, fashioning themselves as "pioneers" as they seized "new avenues of action and of power . . . to expand the horizon of the nation's activity, and to extend the scope of their dominion."[27] Turner, though, rejected efforts by capitalists to apply the frontier metaphor to capital itself as a way to mollify social protest with the promise of endless economic growth. Instead, he repeatedly used the metaphor to describe government action. "In place of old frontiers of wilderness," he wrote, there are "new frontiers" in public policy, and "better social domains yet unexplored."[28]

But the scale of the problem seemed to dwarf any political solution on offer. Monopolies, Turner said, had come to exercise a "unified control over the nation's industrial life." "Colossal private fortune" was corrosive.[29] Turner could sound as damning as Karl Marx: "Capital began to consolidate in ever greater masses," subordinating the self-driven and sovereign individual—who emerged during the earlier, open-range stage of frontier capitalism—to "system and control." In the factories: to repetitive motion and the assembly line. In the fields: to mechanized farming and industrial mining. In daily life: to debt. "Political democracy," Turner said, was now "an appearance rather than a reality."[30]

Other social ills included: "congested tenements" filled with growing numbers of not-yet-assimilated immigrants; "long hours of work, the death rate"; slum diseases, like typhoid. All these evils threatened to turn America's "industrial energy and vast capital" into a "social tragedy."[31] Tenancy increased, ownership declined. Wages fell. "It's all gone, all done, all over," was how another frontier writer, the novelist Owen Wister, registered a similar pessimism. Earlier, in 1902, Wister's *The Virginian* had described the West as a "world of crystal light, a land without end, a space across which Noah and Adam might come straight from Genesis." But just a few years later, Wister published another novel that imagined the frontier not so much closed as commandeered, seized by the barons and bankers. "There's nothing united about these States any more, except Standard Oil and discontent. We're no longer a small people living and dying for a great idea; we're a big people living and dying for money." "The world," Turner said in 1925, "has never before seen such huge fortunes exercising complete control over the economic life of a people . . . has never seen such a consolidation of capital and so complete a systematization of economic processes."[32]

Turner didn't pine for smallness as a solution to the problem created by "huge aggregations of capital."[33] He knew that society in the twentieth century would be mass, industrial, and large. But he hoped somehow that the experiences gathered in the nineteenth century's wide and vast West would teach "the United States how to deal with the problem of magnitude."[34] Turner was having a hard time finding a middle ground, something between corporate plutocracy and socialism, that could manage the transition from the frontiers of the West to the frontiers of public policy, taking America to what he said would be the next stage of its development: "to the realm of the spirit, to the domain of ideals and legislation."[35]

There was another option: to define the frontier not as a line to stop at but one to cross over. To link—as two other frontier theorists, Theodore Roosevelt and Woodrow Wilson, often did—progressive reform at home to war abroad.

In 1898, the United States launched itself overseas. Washington annexed Hawaii and declared war on Spain, after which it took Puerto Rico, Guam, and Manila and established a protectorate over Cuba. The United States built an interoceanic canal across Panama, which it had separated from Colombia, and invaded, occupied, and fought counterinsurgencies in Nicaragua, Haiti, and the Dominican Republic. Meanwhile, in the Philippines, troops engaged in a lengthy pacification campaign.* Theodore Roosevelt described the 1898 deployment overseas of occupying troops as a "righteous war," necessary to prevent the country, now that its frontier was closed, from getting too comfortable with itself, to avoid falling into a languor he associated

---

* The war in the Philippines gave English a successor word to "frontier," used to refer to remoteness: "boondocks," from the Tagalog, "a distant, unpopulated place," adopted by U.S. soldiers fighting a shadowy war against hit-and-run enemies. Its usage was expanded in World War II and then shortened in Vietnam to "boonies."

with Asia: "We cannot, if we would, play the part of China, and be content to rot by inches in ignoble ease within our borders." Fighting "medieval tyranny," as Roosevelt described Spain, would steel political leaders to confront modern tyranny in the form of corporate corruption and monopolies at home. For his part, Woodrow Wilson—who, like Roosevelt, would become a president noted for progressive reforms—identified America's post-1898 wars in the Pacific and the Caribbean as part of its permanent revolution on the frontier. A "great revolution in our lives," he said, a "new revolution. . . . No war ever transformed us quite as the war with Spain transformed us."[36] The military campaign that brought Puerto Rico, the Philippines, and Guam under U.S. occupation and made Cuba an informal colony wasn't *just* transformative. It "completed" the "transformation" (transformed into what, Wilson didn't say, but Turner once used the phrase "imperial republic" to describe the post-1898 United States). "We made new frontiers for ourselves beyond the seas," Wilson said.[37] As president, he dispatched troops to Mexico, twice, and in 1915 ordered a Marine occupation that over the course of two decades left fifteen thousand Haitians dead, many more tortured, and extended Jim Crow–like rule, including the establishment of a form of public-works forced labor, over the black republic.

These were tumultuous, consequential wars that extended the United States' military and legal frontier seven thousand miles into the Pacific and at least as far south as Panama. They brought tens of millions of people, most of them of color and speaking Spanish and Tagalog, under U.S. authority, raising vexed constitutional questions.[38] And yet Turner describes the period with aloof phrasing, especially when compared to his contemporaries Roosevelt and Wilson. "Having colonized the Far West, having mastered its internal resources," he wrote in 1910, "the nation turned at the conclusion of the nineteenth and the beginning of the twentieth century to deal with the Far East, to engage in the world-politics of the Pacific Ocean. Having brought to its logical conclusion its long continued expansion into the lands of the old Spanish empire by the successful outcome of the recent war, the United States became the mistress of the Philippines at the same time that it came into possession of the Hawaiian Islands, and the controlling influence in the Gulf of Mexico."[39]

Became the mistress. Came into possession. It all floats by like a dream, as if the United States had empire thrust upon it.[40]

Turner was reluctant to extend his arguments concerning the rejuvenating power of the frontier to the realm of imperial expansion. Yet he went with the flow. He first supported Wilson's initial policy of staying out of World War I. But when Wilson reversed himself, Turner reversed himself.[41] The Germans, the original repository of the mother seed, became the evil seed. If social conditions couldn't be reformed at home to protect actual individuals, then at least the ideal of individualism could be sharpened in the fight against its opposite: Germanic militarism. Turner's defense of Wilson's war, presented in a series of lectures in 1918, rehearsed all his old arguments but in exaggerated form. Turner went so far in casting Germany's militarism as the absolute antithesis to American individualism that he slipped into a rare, explicit race consciousness: "The Prussian discipline is the discipline of Thor, the War God, against the discipline of the White Christ," he wrote.[42]

5.

Turner's cooling of the racist heat that powered Jacksonian settler colonialism was indispensable. By 1898, the United States stood at the threshold of global power. And there were just too many different kinds of people abroad for the United States to treat the world as Louisiana or the Mexican Cession writ large. It would take some time for the legal and political system to catch up and shed its explicit Saxonism: "We are mainly Anglo-Saxon," said Texas representative James Slayden in 1909, while Puerto Ricans "are a composite structure . . . largely mongrels."[43] But in the first years of the twentieth century, expansion, be it commercial, political, or military, couldn't be justified as but a new edition of Teutonic conquest and the latest victory of the "blood gene." They found themselves by losing themselves, Turner once said of Europeans who had been transformed on the frontier into Americans. And that's what happened, in a way, to America's "manifest destiny" (a phrase coined in 1845 to describe the belief that Providence was guiding Anglo-Saxons across the continent, to take Texas and California and establish dominion from the Atlantic to the Pacific). It found its universalism by losing its racial and religious particularism.

White supremacy continued, keeping the beat moving forward, in Jim Crow, in lynchings, in anti-miscegenation, exclusion, and "second-class citizen" laws, and in the racism of the ruling class, including in President Woodrow Wilson's ongoing arias to "wholesome blood."[44] But Turner's soothing processional became the official public anthem of a nation moving out in the world, not as a conquering race, much less a woodland Germanic tribe, but in the name of humanity.

Turner also put forward his version of American universalism at a moment when class conflict was on the rise. Demands for a redistribution of wealth were growing increasingly militant, as industrial capitalism swung between ever more dramatic booms and busts and the number of strikes, fueled by immigrant workers from countries with strong socialist traditions, increased. In fact, the 1893 World's Fair, where Turner first presented his Frontier Thesis, was something like one large labor action: plasterer, gas fitter, carpenter, bricklayer, and mechanic unions took advantage of the concentration of work to press for higher wages and shorter hours.[45] That year, a financial crash led to a wave of factory closings and rising labor conflict. Organized by the socialist Eugene Debs and the American Railway Union, striking Pullman Company railroad workers effectively closed access to the frontier, making sure no freight or passenger trains rolled farther west than Detroit. President Grover Cleveland sent tens of thousands of troops, redeployed from western territories, to break the strike and get the trains running again. Debs's union was dissolved and scores of workers lost their lives.

A few years later, the progressive Woodrow Wilson used the considerable resources of the federal government to execute one of the most violent crackdowns on radical labor unions and left-wing political parties in the country's history, a repression that increased after the country entered World War I. The war and its aftermath, as Adam Hochschild has written, was a "period of unparalleled censorship, mass imprisonment, and anti-immigrant terror."[46] The Industrial Workers of the World and the Socialist Party were destroyed. Wilson's 1917 Espionage Act (which Turner endorsed as a "temporary sacrifice of individual freedom" necessary to counter German efforts to destroy "freedom everywhere") targeted thousands of activists.[47] A. Philip Randolph and Eugene Debs were thrown in jail for opposing the war. Patriotic fever empowered vigilantes to go on the hunt for any perceived subversion of Americanism. A pro-Wilson crowd assaulted Alice Paul and other members of her anti-war National Woman's Party as they protested in front of the White House. In Elaine, Arkansas, white vigilantes, with help from the U.S. Army, slaughtered 237 sharecroppers for trying to organize a union, just one episode in the relentless race terror African Americans faced since the end of Reconstruction, which included over four thousand lynchings.[48]

The IWW had plenty of cowboy radicals among its ranks, drawing much support in western and border states, from mine workers, lumberjacks, and ranch hands. Debs himself often tried to offer an alternative, socialist version of the Frontier Thesis.* But the myth of rugged individualism was applied more effectively *against* socialists and anti-war activists, used to draw a bright line between Americanism and anti-Americanism.[49] Theodore Roosevelt matched up the hands on his Dakota ranch against Chicago's Haymarket labor anarchists: "My men here in Dakota are hardworking, laboring men, who work longer hours for no greater wages than the strikers; but they are Americans through and through." "Nothing," he said, "would give them greater pleasure than a chance with their rifles at one of the mobs."[50] The western nov-

---

*Debs in 1902: "The rise of class-conscious trades-unionism in the West was not the result of mere chance or personal design, but obedient to the rising tide of the revolutionary spirit of the proletariat of the rugged and sparsely settled mountain States, a composite population composed of pioneers, the most adventurous, brave and freedom-loving men from all States of the American continent." In 1924: "The bold, assertive spirit of the pioneer—the one-time 'free' American could not survive in this generation of concentrated wealth and power and intensified wage-slavery. The spy system and the black-list are especially effective in these one-company towns—be they lumber, coal, copper, oil, or money—to destroy the free spirit that once was the glory of America."

elist Owen Wister agreed, celebrating the dispatch of "United States troops, just come from fighting Indians," to disperse Chicago strikers. For Wister, the use of troops against radicals—"rats" who "swarm over our body social"—served a double purpose. It put down the radicals, but it also focused the energies of the soldiery, now that there were no more Indians left to fight, preventing them from becoming attracted to the radical doctrines offered by the "Debses" of the country. Wister was particularly enraged at Debs's ability to shut down train service west, since he considered the continental railroad one of civilization's greatest achievements. "Vigilance," wrote Wister, "is the price of liberty not only from foreign but domestic foes."[51]

The power of frontier Americanism is found in its ability to marginalize Rooseveltian-style racism (with deep roots in America's settler reality) and Debsian-style social democracy (also with deep roots, in America's promise of equality) and to reconcile them into a vibrant, progressive ideal that presented itself as the highest expression of liberal universalism. Turner imagined the experience of westward expansion overcoming sectional loyalties and racial animosities, leading to a true humanism, nurturing open-minded citizens capable of addressing the problems of mass industrial society with applied, progressive, and responsible policies. Turner also thought that the experience of the West, of different states coming together to cooperate over resources and trade, would serve as a model for Woodrow Wilson's League of Nations. His centrist pioneer progressivism even found expression in popular culture, in the "Cowboy Code" of the beloved western entertainer Gene Autry, star of rodeo, radio, and screen. On one hand, the cowboy, according to Autry's commandments, must not "advocate or possess racially or religiously intolerant ideas."[52] On the other, the cowboy must also "be a good worker" and be "a patriot."

Born out of ceaseless expansion, Turner's frontier universalism, along with its imagined suppression of extremes, could only be maintained through ceaseless expansion.

EIGHT

The Pact of 1898

"Peace among the whites."

In the fight that broke out during the presidency of Barack Obama over whether Confederate flags and Confederate statues should be taken down as racist symbols or kept in place as heritage mementos, nearly all the public discussion focused on domestic history. Most of the country's Lost Cause monuments were put up in the decades after the Freedmen's Bureau was shut down and Reconstruction troops were withdrawn from the South, when the Klan was on the ride and lynching trees scarred the land. As to the flags, most commentary traced them back to the post–World War II backlash to the Civil Rights Movement. Columnist Eugene Robinson, for instance, on *Meet the Press*, said that South Carolina raised the Confederate battle flag over its statehouse in 1961 as part of its "massive resistance to racial desegregation."

All true. Yet like many discussions of the history of America's white-supremacist right, this account misses the role foreign expansion, especially the country's many overseas wars, has played in keeping the symbols of the Confederacy alive. Starting around 1898, well before it became an icon of redneck reaction, the Confederate flag served for half a century as a symbol not of polarization but of national unification, a prideful pennant in an extending American empire. It was a reconciled army that moved out into the world after the Civil War, as new wars allowed those who fought for the Confederate Army, and the children of those who fought, to be readmitted into the nation. But reconciliation took place not just between soldiers who wore the blue and those who wore the gray. Also reunited was an unstoppable combination of northern law—bureaucratic codes, hierarchies of command and control, industrial might, and technology—and southern spirit, an "exaltation of military ideals and virtues," including valor, duty, and honor.[1]

1.

In the years after the Civil War, northerners and southerners found "rare common ground," write historians Boyd Cothran and Ari Kelman, on the need to acquire more ground. They agreed on nearly nothing, only that the "Army should pacify Western tribes." White southerners bitterly opposed Reconstruction, a military occupation imposed on the entire defeated Confederacy, but they came together with northerners "on the subject of Manifest Destiny."[2]

Demilitarization from the Civil War freed up resources for the militarization of the frontier, as the end of Reconstruction in 1877 allowed the U.S. Army to focus its attention on the final pacification of Native Americans. Thousands of northern and southern soldiers were sent west to fight the end stage in the long war for the continent, which, between 1865 and 1891, included thirteen different campaigns and over one thousand separate battles against the Cheyenne, Lakota, Navajo, Arapaho, Sioux, Ute, Bannock, Modoc, and other peoples.

It was too soon for Confederate generals, colonels, and captains to be admitted into the Union Army. So distinguished northern officers—men like George Armstrong Custer and Philip Sheridan—commanded the troops who committed most of the atrocities against indigenous peoples. Even before the Civil War was over, Lincoln had sent General John Pope to put down the Dakota Sioux. Pope, who had lost to Robert E. Lee at the Second Battle of Bull Run, presided over the "largest mass execution in the nation's history: 38 Dakotas were hanged the day after Christmas 1862."[3] Another Union hero who also had fought in the Mexican–American War, pioneer legend Kit Carson, drove eight thousand Navajo men, women, and children on a three-hundred-mile "Long Walk" from Arizona to New Mexico, where they endured years of "humiliation, suffering, death, and near starvation"—one of many "trails of tears" that took place during and after the Civil War, as removal never really ended.[4]

But southern veterans and their sons used the pacification of the West, and beyond, as their rehabilitation program. The military career of Luther Hare, the son of a Confederate captain and among the first class of southerners readmitted into West Point, is illustrative. After Hare graduated from the academy in 1874, his detachment was assigned to the western frontier, where he took part in Custer's campaign against the Sioux. It was still too early to fly the Confederate battle flag, which was treated like contraband during Reconstruction. Not, though, to let out a Texas-style battle cry. Cornered in a skirmish that preceded Little Big Horn, Hare "opened fire and let out a rebel yell. 'If we've got to die, let's die like men! I'm a fightin' son of a bitch from Texas!'" he reportedly said. Hare survived and then went on to fight Native Americans in Montana, Texas, the Pacific Northwest, and Arizona. He joined with Oliver Otis Howard to help pacify the Nez Perce, fought the Sioux, and, as he put it, pacified the "last of the renegade Apaches," before being sent to the Philippines as a colonel.[5] There, he led the Texas Volunteer Cavalry against the Spanish.

With Reconstruction over and Jim Crow segregation installed in every southern state, Washington sent tens of thousands of troops to take the Philippines, Cuba, Puerto Rico, and Guam from Spain in the War of 1898, a turning point in Confederate reintegration. Earlier, when slavery was a going concern, southerners had yearned to separate Cuba from Spain and turn it into a slave state (Cuba and Puerto Rico had remained under Spanish rule after the rest of Spanish America won its independence in the 1820s). Now, conquering the island served a different purpose: a chance to prove their patriotism and reconcile with the North.

War with Spain over Cuba had been predicted for decades. An insurgency led mostly by former slaves and free people of color against Spanish rule had raged, off and on, since 1868, creating the kind of chaos on the island that easily justified intervention. The rebels had already won the abolition of slavery and now were demanding independence. In response, Spain had sent its military to put down the insurrection. President Grover Cleveland almost went in in 1896, on the justification that the fighting was threatening U.S. trade; the United States, he said, needed to "protect its own interests and those of its citizens, which are coincident with those of humanity and civilization generally."[6] Then, on February 15, 1898, the USS *Maine* exploded in the port of Havana, killing hundreds of sailors. When William McKinley, who succeeded Cleveland as president, blamed Spain for the explosion and used it as a pretext to go to war, North and South came together.

What's done is done, and the Civil War won't be forgotten, said the *News* of Lynchburg, Virginia, two days after the explosion. But "thousands of persons in the South are now ready to admit that secession," the South's attempt to break from the Union over slavery, "was a mistake."[7]

2.

The nation called. All sections responded. "Yes, sir, I fought with Stonewall and faced the fight with Lee," ran a poem in the *Atlanta Constitution*, "but if this Union goes to war, make one more gun for me." To which the *Minneapolis Journal* responded: "Make it two, old fellow, I want to stand once more beneath the old flag with you as in the days of yore. Our fathers stood together and fought on land and sea the battles fierce that made us a nation of the free."[8] Georgia's governor said he would personally lead his state's militia into war. In New York, at the Knickerbocker Theatre, John Philip Sousa introduced a new march, "Unchain the Dogs of War," into his comic operetta *The Bride-Elect*, and "audiences went wild with patriotism." The play toured the country, with that song, a newspaper noted, "encored again and again."

Southern ports like New Orleans, Charleston, and Tampa were used as staging areas for the invasions of Cuba and Puerto Rico. Northern soldiers passing through New Orleans were glad to see "grizzled old Confederates" cheering them on and saluting the Union flag. Newspapers throughout the South, along with Dixie's largest veterans association, the United Confederate Veterans, reveled in the exploits of former Confederate generals, including Robert E. Lee's nephew, Fitzhugh Lee, and Alabama's Joseph Wheeler, who had been appointed to the military by President McKinley as "a token that henceforth we were one country with one flag over all."[9]

Wheeler had served as cavalry general in the Civil War and then, after the end of Reconstruction in 1877, he was elected to the House of Representatives. "This and this alone," he said, referring to the invasion of Cuba, "will cause the flag of our country to continue to soar higher and higher and the prestige of this Great Republic to extend its power for good in the farthest corners of the earth."[10] The conversion to Unionism wasn't seamless. Showing southern grit at the command of a cavalry division, Wheeler, at age sixty-one, disobeyed the orders of his northern superior officer and led a charge against a Spanish fortification. Upon dispersing enemy troops he, according to legend, shouted, "Let's go, boys! We've got the damn Yankees on the run again!"[11]

Representatives from all sections of the country voted in favor of funding the war, but southerners—and their cotton-growing constituents, looking for tariff-free overseas markets—were especially enthusiastic. As President Cleveland had put it, U.S. interests were coincident with those of humanity. "The boys who wore the blue and the boys who wore the gray," Texas representative Reese De Graffenreid said, "reconciled and reunited in the great and grand bonds of true brotherhood and love, side by side, heart in heart, hand in hand, will go marching on with the one purpose, the one intention, and one exclamation, that is, woe, irretrievable woe, shall betide that country, that nation, and that people against whom a brother American's blood shall cry to us from the ground." The senator from Mississippi, a Confederate veteran with the improbable name of Hernando De Soto Money, thought the war an opportunity to teach traits associated with southern valor and strengthen a bourgeois culture that had grown overripe. Any war was better than a "rotting peace that eats out the core and heart of the manhood of this country," he said. All wars, the senator continued, taught devotion, abnegation, courage, and forced nations to "rise above the petty, the unworthy, the selfish." But a war for "human liberty and human life" would have an especially "wholesome," even "purgatorial effect upon this nation." The United States "will come out of it," he predicted, "like the Phoenix from its ashes, renewed and with glory."[12]

In June 1898, just weeks after U.S. troops landed in Cuba, two train-car loads of Confederate flags arrived in Atlanta for a coming reunion of southern veterans of the war. The southern battle flag would soon festoon the city that Union general William T. Sherman had burned to the ground. At the very center of the celebration's main venue stood a thirty-foot Confederate flag, flanked by a Cuban and a U.S. flag.

Speech after speech extolled "sublime" war, not just the Civil War but all the wars that made up the nineteenth century—with Mexico, on Native Americans, and now against Spain. One southern veteran spoke of "the gallantry and heroism of your sons as they teach the haughty Spaniard amid the carnage of Santiago to honor and respect the flag of our country, which shall float forever over an 'indissoluble union of indestructible states.'" War with Spain allowed "our boys" to once more be "wrapped in the folds of the American flag," said General John Gordon, commander of the United Confederate Veterans, in remarks opening the proceedings.[13] Their heroism had led "to the complete and permanent obliteration of all sectional distrusts, and to the establishment of the too long delayed brotherhood and unity of the American people."[14] A year later, in Nashville, a regiment arrived home from Manila just as the local Daughters of the Confederacy had raised a Confederate reunion, with soldiers marching "under old battle torn rebel flags intertwined with the stars and stripes."[15]

The War of 1898 was alchemic. It transformed the "Lost Cause" of the Confederacy—the preservation of slavery—into humanity's cause for world freedom. "The Spanish yoke was about to be lifted," as Evelyn Scott remembers the excitement of her Tennessee childhood, "and by southerners!"[16] The South, General Gordon said, was helping to bring "the light of American civilization and the boon of Republican liberty to the oppressed islands of both oceans."[17] General Wheeler, before he shipped out to Cuba, gave a speech on the House floor in which he folded the South's seditious war for slavery into the country's long war for freedom.

"Cast a glance backward," he said, and "reflect." American history was one long war: first for the frontier against the "wild beasts and savage Indians"; then the American Revolution, followed by the War of 1812 and the War on Mexico. Into this stream of progress Wheeler slipped the Civil War, when "a million brave men" flew "to arms," not so much to fight each other but to fight for their understanding of freedom.[18] The liberation of Cuba would be the next chapter in the procession.

At subsequent meetings of United Spanish War Veterans, the theme that 1898 united a fractured country was repeated over and over again. "I know of no incident that so well indicates the reunion of the North and South," said Chaplain Arthur Sykes, than the fact that the first two U.S. fatalities in the war were a son of a Union soldier and a son of a Confederate major. "The blood of the North and the blood of the South mingled," Sykes said, and "forevermore the North and South of the United States were to be united."[19]

With Spain defeated, McKinley took a victory tour of the South, pinning a Confederate badge to his lapel and hailing "the valor and the heroism [that] the men from the south and the men of the north have within the past three years . . . shown in Cuba, in Puerto Rico [and] in the Philippines." "When we are all on one side," the president said, with northern industrial power and southern spirit conjoined once again, "we are unconquerable." Around this time, Congress, after much delay, authorized the return of Confederate flags captured by Union forces during the Civil War to the United Confederate Veterans.

3.

Nothing was truly reconciled, nothing transcended, at least when it came to the country's founding paradox: the promise of political freedom and the reality of racial subjugation. The alchemy of war didn't transform chivalric dross into universal humanism. On the contrary, as southerners gradually took the lead in the United States' military campaign outward, all the dread, resentment, and hate generated by that campaign "poured back within the frame of the South itself," as the southern writer W. J. Cash wrote in his 1941 classic, *The Mind of the South*.

The overseas frontier—wars in Cuba, the Dominican Republic, the Philippines, Nicaragua, and Haiti—acted as a prism, refracting the color line abroad back home. In each military occupation and prolonged counterinsurgency they fought, southerners could replay the dissonance of the Confederacy again and again. They could fight in the name of the loftiest ideals—liberty, valor, self-sacrifice, camaraderie—while putting down people of color. The body count in the Caribbean and Pacific was high. U.S. troops killed about fifteen thousand Haitians in battle between 1915 and 1935; tens of thousands of Dominicans between 1916 and 1924; fifty thousand Nicaraguans between 1912 and 1933; and thousands upon thousands of Filipinos between 1898 and 1946. Many more hundreds of thousands from these countries died from disease, famine, and exposure.

In the first rushes of the campaign against Spain, in the spring of 1898, the skin color of the people who lived in Cuba, Puerto Rico, and the Philippines wasn't commented on much in the press. It was enough to report that the United States was freeing a trampled-down people. But then Spain was defeated and began to clear the field. And all of a sudden, without an enemy on which to focus attention, newspapers and soldiers started to note the color of the people they were sent to liberate. Letters from soldiers, first in the 1898 campaign and then later in Nicaragua, Haiti, and the Dominican Republic, are notably similar, lightheartedly narrating to family and friends how they would shoot "niggers," lynch "niggers," release "niggers" into the swamp to die, water-torture "niggers," and use "niggers for target practice."[20]

It was all poured back in and blended together, as W. J. Cash said. Over there, foreign enemies could be called nigger, and over here, domestic enemies—labor, farmer, and civil rights organizers, both people of color and their white allies—could be called subversives and anti-American. The Ku Klux Klan was organized in 1865 by Confederate veterans but had lain dormant for decades. Now what historians call the "second Ku Klux Klan" emerged, in 1915, led by veterans of 1898. One of the new Klan's founders, William Joseph Simmons, repeatedly highlighted his military service in testimony he gave to Congress: "I am a veteran of the Spanish–American War. I am a past commander of my Spanish–American war veterans' post. I am a past national aide-de-camp of the Spanish–American War Veterans' Association and also a past provisional division commander. I was at one time the senior colonel in command of five regiments."[21] A "heroic veteran of the Spanish–American War" was how one Congressional ally described Simmons (though the historian Linda Gordon writes that Simmons arrived in Cuba after the fighting had ended). Simmons even took the opportunity of his testimony to paraphrase Abraham Lincoln: "I have fought a good fight," Simmons said, "with love toward all, with malice toward none. I shall pursue the right as God shall give me a vision of the right."

Such Lincolnesque borrowings nicely capture how the War of 1898 both re-legitimated the Confederacy and allowed resurgent racists to drape themselves in the high ideals of a now-reconciled national history. It was all patriotic. Simmons imagined the new Klan as transcendent, a fraternal organization meant to "memorialize" the nation's great war heroes, including Confederate heroes, a tribute that would "destroy from the hearts of men the Mason and Dixon line" and establish instead "a great American solidarity and a distinctive national consciousness."[22] "Look away, look away, look away, freedom calls," wrote the *Florida Times-Union* in 1898, providing new words to an old song, "Dixie." "We are all Yankees now, Yankee Lee and Yankee Grant." Eventually, the United Confederate Veterans and the United Spanish War Veterans all but fused into one organization. Brothers!

Not so for the thousands of African Americans who signed up for the U.S. Army in early 1898. African Americans, in general, viewed the war with the same ambivalence they viewed the United States. Many identified with the Cuban rebels, overwhelmingly made up of dark-skinned field hands, many of them former slaves. Others saw the war

as their ticket to admission into the U.S. nation, a chance to win a war
of liberation for their brothers and sisters overseas and fight at home
for full "title to all the privileges of citizenship."* McKinley, even as he
courted the South, made it easier for African Americans to join the military. And many volunteered, joining African American regulars in
Florida (many of whom had arrived from the West, buffalo soldiers
who were used to fight the Apache, Comanche, Sioux, and Ute). There
they waited, mostly in Tampa and Key West, for orders to invade Cuba
and Puerto Rico. Throughout the South, with the hardening of Jim
Crow rule, African Americans had suffered decades of lynchings, confiscation of property, disenfranchisement, "rifle clubs," as some white
terrorist organizations dubbed themselves, arbitrary prosecution, and
chain gangs. The dismantling of Reconstruction in 1877 transformed
public spaces into venues of racial domination.

It was not, in other words, an auspicious moment to mix thousands
of gun-carrying white men with thousands of gun-carrying black men
in Tampa.

A backlash followed. White soldiers and residents rioted and rebelled
against the public presence of African American soldiers. In one incident, drunken white soldiers grabbed a two-year-old African American
baby from his mother's arms and used him for target practice (white
soldiers would later repeat similar "games" in Haiti). Newspapers
throughout the old Confederacy were initially color-blind when it came
to celebrating the courage of white soldiers, largely overlooking the fact
that their cavaliers were fighting on the side of people of color against
Europeans. As the war progressed, however, they gradually woke to
the fact that the people the United States was fighting *against* were white
Europeans and that the rebels they were fighting *for* were black. As captured Spanish prisoners were transported to Florida, the *Savannah Tribune* expressed "outrage" that "white men" should be "subjected to the

---

* Some civil and religious leaders urged African Americans not to take the bet—that is,
the bet that if they proved their loyalty and demonstrated their bravery they would be
admitted as full citizens into the nation. Henry M. Turner, a bishop in Atlanta's African
Methodist Episcopal Church who had earlier worked with the Freedmen's Bureau, advised
staying out of a "death struggle for a country that cares nothing for their rights and manhood." Turner said, "Negroes who are not disloyal to the United States deserve to be lynched."

humiliation of having negro guards over them."[23] The *Atlanta Constitution* urged the government not to send African American troops to Cuba to "assault white Cubans."[24] Let them go back west, the paper said, where they could fight Indians and be less noticeable.

African Americans were denied a chance to share in the glory, even as they watched the war reconcile North and South and mingle the confederate battle flag with the U.S. flag. White soldiers, like Theodore Roosevelt's Rough Riders, had their valor praised; the boldness of black soldiers was proof that they didn't "know their place." African Americans continued to represent both a foreign and domestic threat. After the Civil War, opponents of civil rights worried that Ethiopia was "stretching forth" her black hand to destroy American freedom. Now, in the early twentieth century, blacks were seen as stalking horses for a different kind of subversion, the kind of cross-class and cross-race anti-imperialism that powered opposition to U.S. occupation in Cuba, the Philippines, Nicaragua, Haiti, and the Dominican Republic ("The American Negro returning from abroad," the southerner Woodrow Wilson would soon confide to his doctor, about African Americans fighting in World War I, "would be our greatest medium in conveying Bolshevism to America").[25]

"If war among the Whites brought peace and liberty to the Blacks," Frederick Douglass had asked years earlier, "what will peace among the Whites bring?"[26] In 1898, the black editor of the Norfolk *Recorder* had an answer: "The closer the North and South get together by this war the harder [the African American] will have to fight to maintain a footing."* Also answering the question were the thousands of white

---

*The Yale sociologist William Graham Sumner was a racist anti-imperialist, with little regard for African Americans, but in an 1899 lecture he precisely captured the way the seizure of Puerto Rico and the Philippines bought national reconciliation on the backs of African Americans. "For thirty years the negro has been in fashion, he has had political value and he has been petted," Sumner said. But now, with the war against Spain, northerners and southerners "are all united. The Negro's day is over. He is out of fashion." Freedmen and freedwomen were anything but "in fashion" in the decades prior to the war, but Sumner's point is important: that victory in the War of 1898 affirmed the racial logic of Jim Crow. The conquest of racially distinct peoples, and the categorization of them as subjects, not citizens, reinforced the arguments of white supremacists, who wanted to do the same thing to African Americans. Northern expansionists were "enunciating doctrines which proved that, for the last thirty years, the Southerners have been

men in Wilmington, North Carolina, who in November 1898, shortly after Spain surrendered to the United States, staged a coup against the elected, multiracial coalition governing the city. The white mob, many of them veterans of the Cuban campaign just returned from the war, killed between sixty and three hundred African Americans, ransacked African American businesses, and set fire to African American homes.

The war was won, the North and South reconciled, and the white people of Wilmington liberated themselves from one of the South's last vestiges of Reconstruction rule.

4.

More war brought more goodwill, at least to white southerners, and more proud displays of the Confederate flag. In June 1916, Woodrow Wilson began to push through Congress a set of laws and actions militarizing the country, expanding the Army and National Guard, constructing nitrate plants for munitions production, funding military research and development, and enforcing the Espionage Act. Also that month, Confederate veterans descended on Washington, D.C., to show their support for the coming war in Europe.

The *Brooklyn Eagle* reported, wrongly, that it was the first time an encampment of former Confederates was allowed in the nation's capital. In fact, Grover Cleveland earlier had allowed Fitzhugh Lee and his men to serve as the honor guard at his two inaugurations. But it was the first time Confederates arrived in large numbers, tens of thousands according to reports, "wearing the gray." They were joined by "several thousand who wore the blue," marching down Pennsylvania Avenue to be reviewed by Wilson. *The Eagle* described the scene: "In the line were many young soldiers now serving in the regular army, grandsons of those who fought for the Confederacy and of those who fought for the Union. The Stars and Bars of the Confederacy were proudly borne

---

right all the time": that if it was correct to deny Puerto Ricans and Filipinos the vote on the grounds that they weren't ready for citizenship, then it was correct to do the same thing to African Americans.

at the head of the procession. . . . As the long line passed the reviewing stand the old men in gray offered their services in the present war."[27] "We will go to France or anywhere you want to send us!" the elderly veterans shouted to Wilson. "Call on us if the boys can't do it!"

Wilson won reelection later that year running on the slogan "He kept us out of war." He could, however, then betray his anti-war supporters, knowing that a rising political coalition (made up, in part, of men looking to redeem a lost war by finding new wars to fight) had his back. Decades before President Richard Nixon bet his reelection on winning the Dixiecrat vote, Wilson worked his own southern strategy. Even as he moved the nation to war, Wilson re-segregated Washington, purged African Americans from federal jobs, and legitimated the Ku Klux Klan (earlier having described its members as "frolicking comrades," veterans bored by civilian life).

It was Wilson who dedicated Arlington Cemetery's Confederate War Memorial. In 1916, having just dispatched thousands of troops (including many southerners) to Haiti, Wilson turned that memorial ritual into a war rally. "America is roused," Wilson said to a large gathering of Confederate veterans, conscripting their "Lost Cause" into a new brand of universalism, "roused to a self-consciousness she has not had in a generation." "It is this spirit," he said, that "is going out conquering and to conquer until, it may be, in the Providence of God, a new light is lifted up in America which shall throw the rays of liberty and justice far abroad upon every sea, and even upon the lands which now wallow in darkness and refuse to see the light."[28] The next year, at the same ceremony, Wilson said that war (which Wilson had entered two months earlier) offered a chance "to vindicate the things which we have professed" and "show the world" that America "was born to serve mankind."[29]

The frontier wars to come—occupations and counterinsurgencies in Haiti, the Dominican Republic, and Nicaragua, along with the ongoing pacification of the Philippines—allowed the South's gentry-officer class to continue the pact of 1898. They could prove their worth to the reconciled nation, even as they saw these campaigns as a chance to avenge their ancestors. Virginians, including the sons of old-line Tidewater slavers, played a large role leading the Caribbean counterinsurgencies. Colonel Littleton W. T. Waller, for instance, led troops in Cuba, the Dominican Republic, and the Philippines, where he developed a "ruthless" reputation. Waller was the son of Piedmont slavers whose ancestors were killed in Virginia's 1831 Nat Turner slave rebellion (which was inspired by the Haitian Revolution). "I know the nigger and how to handle him," said Waller. "The same quality is going to be needed in San Domingo as well as here."[30] Troops under Waller's command, the majority southerners, committed widespread torture and cruelty. They could kill "niggers" abroad—and instead of being punished by the federal government and the Union Army, they were celebrated and welcomed home with pomp and parades.

Not just a war-hardened racism but also undiagnosed trauma and unprocessed guilt returned home from these campaigns. Private First Class Emil Thomas shipped out of Quantico, Virginia, for Nicaragua in the late 1920s, writing to his fiancée that he looked forward to killing "a few niggers" and bringing back some "nigger toes" and "scalps" as trophies.[31] Thomas's letters home reveal an unalloyed hatred: "I'd like to break spick noses, necks, heads, legs, and all," as revenge for "causing me to come down here." Over the course of a year, Thomas guessed he had killed a dozen people, and he hinted in letters home that he participated in war-crime atrocities. He mostly recounted his experiences in a jaunty tone, but his letters often turned dark. "I wonder if I'll ever learn to forget some of the things I saw and done down in Nicaragua. Do you think I will? Some days I can lay here all day and never give it a thought and other days I just can't drive it out of my mind and it makes me so damn mad and bitter that I can't even bear being in the same bed with myself."

As soldiers like Thomas had their private nightmares, American history was fast turning into an endless public parade of war and more war. The sectional reconciliation that went with it meant that the "conquered banner" could fly pretty much anywhere, with little other than positive comment.[32] It flew in every war after 1898, with "entire divisions" sewing "Confederate patches instead of Federal ones" on their uniforms. In World War II, after more than eighty days of fighting to take Okinawa, it was the first flag raised over the captured head-quarters of the Japanese Imperial Army, carried into battle by a Marine captain from South Carolina.*

With the Korean War, the NAACP's journal, *The Crisis*, would report a staggering jump in sales of Confederate flags, from forty thousand in 1949 to sixteen million in 1950. Much of the demand was coming from soldiers overseas in Germany and Korea. *The Crisis* wished for the best, writing that the banner's growing popularity had nothing to do with rising "reactionary Dixiecratism.[33]

"A fad," the magazine hoped, "like carrying foxtails on cars."[34]

5.

The War of 1898 was—as one orator after another said, one editorial after another insisted, and one poet after another declaimed—a pact. The deal allowed southerners to atone for their sedition against the nation, even as they carried the banner of that sedition to the "farthest corners of the earth."

This war, and all the many wars that followed, updated the Jacksonian consensus for the twentieth-century world, a world in which African Americans were nominally free citizens and there was no more land to take from Native Americans and give to the white working class. Overseas war had the effect of unifying the country, this time not some sections against others but the whole nation.

The military, as an instrument of war, expanded the overseas frontier. But as a rationalized bureaucracy, the military also served as its own

---

* Leading the United States' invasion of Okinawa was the Kentuckian Lieutenant General Simon Bolivar Buckner, Jr., whose father, General Simon Bolivar Buckner, fought in the Mexican–American War and the Civil War. Before Okinawa, Buckner, Jr., was in charge of the military defense of Alaska, where he objected to the deployment of African American troops, writing his superiors that he worried they would stay on after the war: "with the natural result that they would interbreed with the Indians and Eskimos and produce an astonishingly objectionable race of mongrels which would be a problem." As to the Confederate flag over Okinawa, most of the Marines present cheered when its hoister gave out a rebel yell: "Yip-tjip-yeee!" The flag reportedly flew for days with Buckner's support: "My father fought under that flag," he said.

kind of frontier. As the promise of "free land" receded, the various branches of the armed forces became the primary means of social mobility, allowing both whites and, increasingly after 1898, blacks shelter from the capitalist market, along with access to education, health care, and decent pay. Even W. E. B. Du Bois, who had previously resisted all efforts to deflect race and class conflicts outward, felt he had to give the promise of integration through militarization a chance and tentatively support Wilson's war. "Let us, while this war lasts," Du Bois wrote, "forget our special grievances and close our ranks shoulder to shoulder with our own white fellow citizens and the allied nations that are fighting for democracy."[35]

The Pact of 1898 included two elements. First, southerners could fuse their Lost Cause into humanity's cause, even as they kept their emblems and practices of supremacy. Second, African Americans could claim a seat at the nation's table by being willing to fight for the nation. But the pact could only remain in place so long as people of color didn't publicly question their subordinated role. Because once they did—as previewed by those African American soldiers in Tampa in 1898—southerners would be reminded that their "cause" was no longer the nation's cause, that it was in fact a lost cause. Korea would be the end of the line, the last place the Confederate battle flag could be unfurled as a pennant of reconciliation. For as the Civil Rights Movement evolved and the Black Power Movement emerged, as Korea gave way to Vietnam, the Confederate flag returned to its original meaning: the bunting of resentful white supremacy. Later, Dixie would find itself in Da Nang.

NINE

A Fortress on the Frontier

"It all started with the border.
And that's still where it is today."

People like to study borders, to do research, take pictures, sing songs, write poems and stories, and even tell jokes about them because they represent the absurdity of human efforts to force the concrete to conform to the abstract, to take the world as it is and try to make it be as it ought. "A line, half water, half metal," writes the Chicano poet Alfred Arteaga. Borders, not to mention walls, represent domination and exploitation. But they also announce the panic of power, something that overcomes a political state similar to the way dread comes over an individual with the realization that their psyche isn't theirs to control alone, that it's formed in reaction to others. "The phobia is thrown before the anxiety like a fortress on the frontier," Sigmund Freud wrote, around the same time that Frederick Jackson Turner was advancing his Frontier Thesis. Freud's controlling image here—a fortress on the frontier—implies that the society being defended by the fortress is as unstable as an individual's ego, that it's constantly in danger of being undone, and that its border defenses are a sideshow to the main issue. It would be inadequate, Freud writes, to treat the outward phobia without also addressing its underlying causes.

The same is true on the United States' border with Mexico, where an obsession with fortification against what's outside is symptomatic of trouble that exists inside.

"Something there is that doesn't love a wall," Robert Frost wrote. But people do take enjoyment in efforts to subvert walls, especially when they are used to mark international boundaries. Even if the subversion only lasts a moment, such as when citizens of Naco, Sonora, and Naco, Arizona, today play an annual volleyball game over the border fence, or when people come together to gossip, or when couples get married through the spaces separating the slats. If people didn't keep coming up with new ways to beat the border—tunnels, ramps, catapults and homemade cannons (to launch bales of marijuana to the other side), Radio Shack drones—then the United States wouldn't have to keep trying to find new ways to fortify the border. When Janet Napolitano, former governor of Arizona and Barack Obama's director of Homeland Security, said, "Show me a fifty-foot wall, and I'll show you a fifty-one-foot ladder," she was advancing a theory of history, positing a dependent relationship between technology and resistance.

Borders can't stop historical change, as Napolitano's comment suggests, but they do highlight moments when history goes one way instead of another. As when the settlement of the United States–Mexico War brought the United States' march to an abrupt halt, at least in the direction south. Or when what was thought of as one thing split into two. In the twentieth century, the idea of the frontier continued to advance, even as the border stayed put.

1.

The line was first established by the Treaty of Guadalupe Hidalgo at the end of the war between the United States and Mexico. On its run out of the gulf, the border moves west along rivers that curlicue back and forth, their banks shifting and water rerouting to serve towns, ranches, mines, and (starting in the 1960s) increasing numbers of factories, passing over arid sands, mesquite and creosote scrub, before

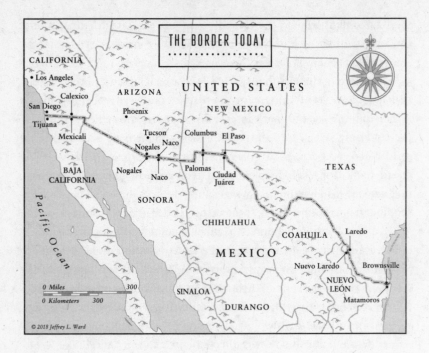

THE BORDER TODAY

© 2018 Jeffrey L. Ward

finally hitting coastal brush and the Pacific beach. As it goes forward, the border divides dozens of indigenous communities, among them the Tohono O'odham, Yaqui, and Apache; small farms and large ranches; herds of cows and desert deer and packs of gray wolves; archaeological sites, bird and butterfly reserves, towns, streams, canals, canyons, roads, paths, cemeteries, and city streets. The Mexican town of Nogales became Nogales, Arizona, and Nogales, Mexico; Laredo split into Laredo and Nuevo Laredo.

The border is long, and the specifics of its fortification vary across the whole of its span, from Brownsville in the east to Tijuana in the west. But a general pattern is clear. There was no fence at first, just some stone markers when a joint United States–Mexico boundary commission finished its work in the 1850s. Humans and animals and water and goods passed back and forth, as they had for centuries, creating an integrated ecology. Most of it was hard and unromantic, but people—Mexicans, Mexican Americans, and Native Americans—

survived with fortitude worthy of the awe that Roosevelt, Turner, Wilson, and other frontier lyricists reserved for Anglo settlers. The commissioners who drew the line generally ignored the region's people, focusing only on its geography. "Much of this country," wrote a U.S. surveyor, "is a sterile waste, utterly worthless for any purpose than to constitute a barrier or natural line of demarcation between two neighboring nations."[1] The commissioners might have gone on not noticing the people who lived in the borderlands were it not for the fact that those people, including the Pima, gave them shelter when they were threatened by hostile Apaches.

The United States was still rolling west when this boundary with Mexico was created, and there'd be new frontiers in wars throughout the Caribbean, Central America, the Pacific, and Southeast Asia. But for some, it was hard to accept that this one line in the country's south was permanent. During the Mexican–American War, Sam Houston, the former president of the Republic of Texas, rallied in New York City in February 1848 on behalf of the All-Mexico Movement. Mexico, all of it, was the Anglo-Saxon "birthright," he said. "Take it," wrote the *New York Herald*. As did the "Sabine virgins," Mexicans would "learn to love her ravishers."[2] Trying to stop the "American people" from annexing all of Mexico, wrote Lewis Cass, who as Jackson's secretary of war presided over removal and was now a Michigan senator, was like trying "to stop the rushing of the cataract of Niagara."[3] The founder of the Anglo colony in Texas, Stephen Austin, had earlier used the same imagery to describe efforts to slow western migration, which would be like "trying to stop the Mississippi with a dam of straw."

Ultimately, though, the All-Mexico Movement couldn't carry the argument. The expected burden of taking Mexico in its entirety, and of having to rule over millions of Spanish-speaking people, cut into the movement's ability to gain sufficient support in Congress. Some continued to push the point. Settlers, having crossed into Mexico to set up farms and mines in Sonora, kept calling on Washington to annex their land. They argued that the border was artificial and arbitrary, cutting in half a shared export-oriented economy that should enjoy common access to roads and ports, uniform property rights, and reliable military protection.[4] Mercenaries like William Walker, who in 1854 landed on Mexico's Pacific coast and declared Ensenada the capital of a very short-lived Republic of Lower California, also kept trying to extend the frontier forward. But the boundary stayed where it was. The line, said one of its first surveyors in 1857, was "a good one," halting, finally, what earlier had seemed to be "the inevitable expansive force" of Anglo "institutions and peoples" from sweeping all the way down to Panama.[5]

Anglo capital faced no such limits.

2.

It's a wonder Mexico survived the nineteenth century at all. Some in the United States had their sights on the territory even before Anglo settlers started arriving in its Tejano northern reaches, when it was still a colony of Spain. Aaron Burr, just after his successful duel with Alexander Hamilton, was accused in 1806 of trying to "establish an empire west of the Allegheny Mountains, of which he, Burr, was to be the Sovereign, and New Orleans the emporium, and to invade and revolutionize Mexico."[6] Burr was acting on behalf of planters, who in those early years of the republic—before Andrew Jackson's presidency—felt the federal government wasn't supportive enough of their slaving and real estate ventures (Jackson too was suspected of being involved in the scheme). Burr's conspiracy collapsed, but Mexico, after breaking from Spain in the early 1820s, suffered one calamity after another, including a series of palace coups and civil wars. It lost Central America, which briefly after independence had been part of Mexico. It lost Texas in 1836. It almost, in 1847, lost the Yucatan, to a significant revolt of Mayan peasants. A year later, the United States took its northern territory, and then, soon after, in 1862, France's Napoleon III used Mexico's inability to pay its foreign debt as pretext to invade the country. After occupying Mexico City, Napoleon installed an Austrian archduke, Ferdinand Maximilian, and his wife, Carlota, as emperor and empress, with support from Mexican conservative Catholic elites. Mexicans fought back. This time, unlike their earlier failure to withstand the United

States, liberal rebels waged a five-year-long guerrilla war that drove out the French, after which they executed Maximilian.

Maximilian's short reign in Mexico crisscrossed in strange, opposing ways with the politics of slavery and empire in the United States. On the one hand, the war against French occupation was a southern front in the broader battle against New World servitude. The liberal forces who arrayed against Maximilian saw themselves as allies of Lincoln's Union, fighting a shared campaign against the forces of reaction; Maximilian's government, for his part, purchased southern cotton, sent supplies to southern troops, and even enlisted Confederate refugees into its military.* And if it weren't for the liberal insurgents' ability to keep the pressure on Maximilian's government, the Catholic emperor might have provided even more active help to the Confederacy.

On the other hand, though, late in the U.S. Civil War, when it was clear the North was going to win, both Confederate and Union officials separately proposed a temporary armistice so the armies of the North and South could join together to invade Mexico. In February 1865, the Confederacy's vice president, Alexander Stephens, made the proposal directly to Abraham Lincoln himself, saying that with the issue of slavery out of the way (the South had by then accepted its impending defeat), both sides might come together in defense of "the Right of Self-Government of all Peoples" on "this Continent." Lincoln demurred. The idea that foreign war might provide, as Stephens suggested, a "peaceful and harmonious" solution to domestic conflict was premature (it wouldn't be until 1898 that North and South came together in a high-minded crusade to drive a monarchy out of the New World).[7]

---

* In 1865, during the last months of the Civil War, Confederate soldiers and southern slavers fled into Mexico, ahead of advancing Union troops. So many of them had landed in Mexico City that the ornate Hotel Iturbide was turned into a kind of Confederate capital-in-exile. A few had been in Mexico before, as conquering troops during the U.S. occupation in 1847. Now they came escaping Reconstruction and the rule of the Freedmen's Bureau. Maximilian was sympathetic, granting Confederates five hundred thousand acres near Veracruz to establish a colony. Though slavery remained abolished in Mexico, some southerners had taken their slaves with them into Mexico, as Tejano settlers did years earlier. But one Confederate complained, "All our Negroes decided to leave us upon our arrival here." The colony collapsed in 1867 after Maximilian's execution.

The North did, on its own, supply aid to the Mexican liberals. New York, Boston, and Philadelphia banks extended loans to buy muskets, cannons, and other needed equipment, while New England weapons manufacturers advanced guns to anti-French forces on credit. Then, after the French were defeated, U.S. creditors began demanding payment. Mexico, bankrupted from its many wars, couldn't pay. Over the next few years, businesses from nearly every sector of the United States' fast-growing, post–Civil War economy made demands on Mexico City. Among them were financial houses recalling loans; arms dealers wanting payment; border ranchers complaining that Mexico City wasn't doing enough to protect them from rustlers; merchants claiming to have lost goods in transit; shipping interests reporting damages during the war; real estate and mining companies insisting that Mexico recognize land grants issued by Emperor Maximilian.[8] Caleb Cushing, himself a real estate speculator in Baja California, represented many of these plaintiffs before a special United States–Mexico General Claims Commission.[9]

The liberals in Mexico—in command of the government after having beaten the French—rejected most of these cases and refused to recognize debt incurred and concessions granted by Maximilian. But Ulysses S. Grant's secretary of state, Hamilton Fish, pressed Mexico. Powerful voices demanded payment, calling on Washington to take Mexico "in hand" and establish a "protectorate" over the country, or seize the country entirely and lead it "to a higher plane of civilization."[10]

In the end, though, it wasn't annexation or war but the leverage provided by debt, along with the promise of more loans and investments to build railroads, that brought Mexico to heel. With no other options, Mexico's leaders practically handed over the national economy to foreign investors. Led by some of the most storied names in U.S. corporate history—including J. P. Morgan, John Rockefeller and Standard Oil, Edward Harriman, the Astors, the Guggenheims, Joseph Headley Dulles (John Foster Dulles's great-grandfather), William Randolph Hearst, Phelps Dodge, Union Pacific, and Cargill—U.S. capital radically transformed Mexico. "To revolutionize" became a popular phrase during this period in the U.S. press (much like the verb "to disrupt" today signals the creation of new markets by breaking up old production practices). U.S. agricultural firms were, as one report noted in 1899, moving "across the border into Mexico" and were "revolutionizing and will continue to revolutionize the farming methods of the country."[11] Within half a century, the United States' interests would come to control, nearly absolutely, oil production, railroads, utilities, livestock, agriculture, and ports. Almost all of Mexico's exports—wheat, beef, henequen, minerals, and petroleum—went to the United States, and a good percentage of U.S. manufactured goods went to Mexico. Everything from artificial limbs to surgical supplies, from paints, pianos, and preserves to safes, stoves, and sewer pipes, from heavy machinery to acids and oils, and every finished product in between, was exported south.[12]

Investment led to a dramatic transformation of the border region, where, starting in about 1870, corporations and individuals dispossessed long-term inhabitants of a massive amount of property. North of the border, in California, Arizona, New Mexico, and Texas, miners, ranchers, and railroad companies used "litigation, chicanery, robbery, fraud, and threat" to take millions of acres from indigenous communities and former Mexican citizens (*former* in the sense that, prior to the 1848 Treaty of Guadalupe Hidalgo, they or their families lived within the border of Mexico).[13] With Washington hosting its "great barbecue"— Vernon Parrington's term for the post–Civil War giveaway of public resources—Congress passed a number of new "homestead" acts (such as 1873's Timber Culture Act and 1877's Desert Land Act), facilitating the transfer of property from Mexicans and Native Americans who didn't have title to land or who held land collectively. The dispossessed appealed to U.S. courts. But in nearly all cases judges ruled against them. In upholding the takings, courts cited as precedent decades-old rulings issued in support of Jackson's removal policy, including judgments that upheld the doctrine of discovery: "Conquest gives a title which the courts of the conqueror cannot deny."[14]

Below the border, the rapid expansion of export agriculture took millions more acres. In an expulsion that rivaled the brutality of Jackson's removal policy, tens of thousands of Yaqui were driven from their homes in Sonora and deported south, to the Yucatan and Oaxaca. There, they were put to work on sugar, tobacco, and henequen plantations (though Mexico had long abolished chattel slavery, the post–Civil War spread of export-led capitalism intensified various mechanisms of forced labor, including those based on peonage and vagrancy laws). Tens of thousands more died in the assault. Women and children were forced into servitude. Confiscated Yaqui property in Sonora went to large firms, including Hearst, Phelps Dodge, and Cargill, who transformed the stolen land into export plantations, turning Sonora into the second most profitable Mexican state for U.S. investment (after Veracruz, which had oil).[15]

Decades earlier, Jacksonians justified removal in the name of settler sovereignty.[16] Now, though, it was mostly capital, and only a few settlers, advancing forward.

3.

In 1910, the model of economic development the United States had been promoting in Mexico for over half a century gave way. The country was thoroughly "revolutionized," though not in the way U.S. financial and business interests had been using that word, as peasants, students, the middle class, and national capitalists launched what turned out to be a violent, wild, multi-fronted insurgency. Campesinos arrayed against planters, secularists against Catholics, and workers against the owners. Fields were burned, factories sacked, mines flooded, and railroads requisitioned. Oil rigs and plantations were nationalized. Running through many different phases as it raged for many years, the Mexican Revolution was, as the historian John Mason Hart describes, the "first great third world uprising against American economic, cultural, and political expansion."

Anglo vigilantes had already, over the half century that preceded the revolution, lynched an unknown number of Mexicans and Mexican Americans in the Southwest. Conservative estimates put the number in the thousands.[17] The court system in the United States supplemented mob violence, with southwestern judges ordering, and marshals and sheriffs carrying out, the execution of more than two hundred Mexicans and Mexican Americans during this period. Borderland repression was conducted equally by law officers and night-riding groups such as the Mounted Rifles, the White Owls, and the Wolf Hunters. They enforced the subordinated position of Mexican Americans, disenfranchising them at the ballot box, terrorizing them in their homes, breaking strikes, and helping to reinforce a segregated labor market with at least three pay grades: white, Mexican, and migrant.[18]

But violence increased even more as a result of the revolution. As refugees from the fighting came north—into, for instance, the border city of Juárez, and then over the border into El Paso, with as many as forty thousand arriving there, nearly twice the city's Anglo population— so too came rumors that subversives were organizing a "Liberating Army of Races and Peoples" to reconquer the Southwest and establish a "social republic."[19] In response, the Texas Rangers, which had been turned into an official branch of state law enforcement in 1902, and their sheriff adjuncts carried out "mass executions." They lynched scores of Mexicans and Mexican Americans and drove many more from their homes. A stunning counter-memory project, "Refusing to Forget," put together recently by the scholars Trinidad O. Gonzales, John Morán González, Sonia Hernández, Benjamin Johnson, and Monica Muñoz Martinez, documents the reign of terror Mexican Americans lived under during this period:

> The dead included women and men, the aged and the young, long-time residents and recent arrivals. They were killed by strangers, by neighbors, by vigilantes and at the hands of local law enforcement officers or Texas Rangers. Some were summarily executed after being taken captive, or shot under the flimsy pretext of trying to escape. Some were left in the open to rot, others desecrated by being burnt, decapitated, or tortured by means such as having beer bottles rammed into their mouths.[20]

Bodies of Mexicans and Mexican Americans piled up, victims of a killing spree that "was welcomed," as the project notes, "and even insti-
gated at the highest levels of society and government." Similar to earlier
calls in support of Indian removal, one Texas paper described "a serious surplus population that needs eliminating." The authors of "Refusing to Forget" write that high-level politicians "proposed putting all
those of Mexican descent into 'concentration camps'—and killing any
who refused. For a decade, people would come across skeletons in the
south Texas brush, marked with execution-style bullet holes in the backs
of their skulls."

The mobilization that preceded entrance into World War I worsened
matters. On the border itself, Woodrow Wilson encouraged a crackdown
in the name of national security, dispatching the cavalry to cities like
El Paso. The fight against the Germans created in the minds of many U.S.
politicians and intellectuals the idea that their country faced a single
enemy, over there in the Rhineland and over here at the border (Frederick Jackson Turner felt that Wilson, despite his dispatch of troops, wasn't
taking the threat of German influence in Mexico seriously enough). New
Mexico's senator warned that the United States might lose access to stra-
tegically vital coal and copper and worried about an overreliance on
migrants to run southern rail lines: "For 800 miles from the border back
into the States the railroads are entirely in the hands of Mexicans of old
Mexico," a "majority of such Mexicans were ex-bandits."[21]

The Texas Rangers—now led by an elite wartime core of "Loyalty
Rangers"—policed anti-war activity, as did private citizen vigilante
groups, such as El Paso's County Council of Defense and Home Defense
League. Rangers defined their mandate liberally, identifying "anti-war
activity" as anything from trying to organize a union to trying to vote.
In 1918, according to "Refusing to Forget," the Rangers radically
reduced the number of Mexican American voters across south Texas,
humiliating and disarming Mexican American politicians and terrorizing their families: "A new, more brutal white supremacy had come to
the border." Radicals associated with the Industrial Workers of the
World, who proposed an alternative to this supremacy, were targeted.
Labor conflicts were common on the border, but miners and ranchers

could count on their vigilante and law enforcement allies to intervene. Strikers were rounded up by the thousands and deported, as law officials, including the sheriff's office in Maricopa County (later famous as the headquarters of Joe Arpaio), ransacked IWW offices across the border states.

4.

Border policing, distinct from the vigilantism described above, evolved gradually over time but also in bursts, usually related to war and economic crises. The United States had started to regulate border migration in the late nineteenth century, expanding customs houses and setting up checkpoints, mostly aimed at preventing Chinese workers— targeted by a number of exclusion laws since 1882—from entering from Mexico. But it wasn't until 1907 that the border line was even cleared of brush, after President Theodore Roosevelt ordered that a sixty-foot strip running its length be kept open to prevent smuggling.

Prior to World War I, the border was relatively free. As the historian Mae Ngai points out, before the war the United States "had virtually open borders," with the exception of laws explicitly excluding Chinese migrants. "You didn't need a passport," says Ngai. "You didn't need a visa. There was no such thing as a green card. If you showed up at Ellis Island, walked without a limp, had money in your pocket, and passed a very simple [IQ] test in your own language, you were admitted."

The same was true in much of the world. Then, suddenly, "the frontiers seem to close in" until there was "scarcely room to breathe," as a character in a Charles Isherwood novel describes the restrictions on mobility brought about in Europe by world war. In April 1917, the month the United States entered the war, Wilson signed into law a set of sweeping constraints on immigration, which included literacy tests, entrance taxes, and quota restrictions.

The legislation mostly applied to Europeans and Asians. Mexican migrant workers, who were needed to labor in the fields and mines of the Southwest and the West, were exempt from the quotas ("Western farmers were completely dependent on Mexican workers," as the historian Kelly Lytle Hernández writes). They were, however, supposed to go through established checkpoints, where they were subjected to health inspections and delousing.* It was an odd system, half enforced, half not—half water, half metal. Border towns turned into waiting rooms, as thousands of Mexicans every day submitted to the new rituals.[22] Nearly half a million Mexicans entered the country legally between 1920 and 1928, according to immigration records.[23] But probably at least that many just quietly walked over Tijuana's unguarded chaparral or ferried across the Rio Grande, going back and forth every day to jobs in smelters, mines, fields, and households. Others stayed longer, catching the Rock Island Line at El Paso north to Chicago.

The years after World War I witnessed booms and busts and, in the United States, labor shortages and gluts. Two distinct but interdependent opinions took shape during the 1920s within white society regarding Mexican migration. Political and economic elites, including the business community of border towns like El Paso and Laredo and southwestern and California farmers and northeastern industrialists, wanted Mexicans to remain exempt from entrance restrictions. At the same time, though, the deadly racism documented by the authors of "Refusing to Forget" increased. Hatred focused on Mexicans for depressing Anglo wages, even as that hatred ensured that wages remained depressed, shattering the solidarity that had allowed a common fight for better terms.

Anti-Mexican terror spiked in the early 1920s, as a revived Ku Klux Klan began to influence the national debate on immigration. With more than a million members by the early 1920s—including two hundred thousand in Texas—the Klan helped elect state officials from Arkansas

---

* On January 28, 1917, a group of migrant day laborers, led by a domestic worker, Carmelita Torres, refused to strip naked and submit to a delousing cryolite bath at the El Paso crossing, leading to three days of protests. A year earlier, a similar "bath" at the El Paso jail had ignited a fire, killing scores of Mexicans. In the 1920s, writes the historian David Dorado Romo, "U.S. officials at the Santa Fe Bridge deloused and sprayed the clothes of Mexicans crossing into the U.S. with Zyklon B"—subsequently used in Nazi death camps—in a room that U.S. officials called "the gas chambers." Romo also cites an article in a German science journal published in 1938 that "praised the El Paso method of fumigating Mexican immigrants with Zyklon B."

to California; so influential was the Klan on the Democratic Party that one newspaper sardonically called its 1924 national convention a "Klanbake."[24] The "invisible empire," as the Klan leaders referred to their organization, paralleled the rise of post–World War I European fascism, but with a particularly American sensibility.[25]

The Klan was frontier fascism, the return of the racism at the heart of settler colonialism that Frederick Jackson Turner three decades earlier had tried to suppress. El Paso's chapter, established in 1921, called itself Frontier Klan Number 100. "Our pioneers were all Protestant" and "Nordic," said the Klan's Imperial Wizard, Hiram Wesley Evans, in the 1920s.[26] "My people," a Georgia Klan leader said, "are all plowmen." Turner idealized the West. So did the Klan. Be they from Georgia's upcountry, the Midwest, upstate New York, the Southwest, or the West, Ku Kluxers also tended to be members of fraternal societies, including faux frontier associations such as the Woodmen of the World, Foresters of America, and the Eleven Tribes of the Improved Order of Red Men. The new Klan, said one Oklahoma supporter, was born of the same compulsion that "made necessary on the western frontier the 'vigilance committee' that put a stop to crime by using a rope." The Oklahoman expressed a kind of opposition to taxes that is common today among law-and-order racists, saying that the Klan provided a means for "taxed to the limit" citizens to protect themselves without adding to public expenditure.[27]

The Klan focused on many of the Roaring Twenties' threats: jazz, immorality, Jews, high taxes, and African Americans. But it also increasingly fixated on the border, harassing migrants as far away as Oregon.[28] "Thousands of Mexicans," Evans said, "many of them communist, are waiting a chance to cross the Rio Grande and glut the labor marts of the Southwest." Prohibition had turned many border towns honky-tonk, with liquor, marijuana, and narcotics run in from Mexico. The "cesspools of El Paso" was how one Baptist minister described the city's dance halls, speakeasies, and brothels, which many Protestants blamed on Catholic Mexicans and Mexican Americans.[29] El Paso's Frontier Klan Number 100 vowed to "strive for the eternal maintenance of white supremacy." The border Klan infiltrated fraternal organizations and

Protestant churches, took over school boards, and quickly established a presence in local police and state national guards, where they
helped reinforce minority white rule by suppressing the Mexican
American vote.[30]

By 1922, violence on the border had grown so acute that the Department of State—an office that usually attends to foreign policy—felt
compelled to intervene. Secretary of State Charles Evans Hughes wrote
to the governor of Texas, pleading with the governor as if he were a
sovereign foreign leader presiding over a rogue government carrying
out an illegal occupation. "I beg urgently," Hughes said, "to request that
adequate measures be immediately taken to afford complete protection
for Mexican citizens." Hughes was concerned about an incident in the
oil boomtown of Breckenridge. In November, a mob organized under
the name White Owls had lynched a Mexican migrant and then marched
through town threatening all people of color. This show of white power
provoked a "sudden exodus" of Mexicans, Mexican Americans, and
African Americans. It wasn't "too extravagant to say," wrote the *New
York Times* of the incident, "that there is an open season for shooting
Mexicans in unpoliced districts along the Rio Grande" (though it was
often police doing the shooting). Mexico's envoy to Washington started
compiling a list of victims of vigilantism, counting "between fifty and
sixty Mexicans" who had been violently murdered in 1922 alone.

"The killing of Mexicans without provocation," the *Times* wrote,
"is so common as to pass almost unnoticed."[31]

5.

The United States Border Patrol was officially established two years
later, as part of the comprehensive 1924 Immigration Act, and immediately became arguably the most politicized branch of law enforcement, even more so than J. Edgar Hoover's Federal Bureau of
Investigation. The debate leading up to the passage of the act was
intense; nativists warned that with its open-border policy, the country
was committing "race suicide" and was in danger of "mongrelization."

Forty thousand Klansmen marched on Washington demanding entrance restrictions. The 1924 law codified into immigration policy a xenophobia that had deep roots in the nation's history. Immigration from Asia fell to practically zero, while arrivals from central and southern Europe were sharply reduced. Most countries were now subject to a set quota system, with western European countries assigned the highest numbers.

Mexico, though, was exempt, as those in favor of restriction lost out to business interests. "Texas needs these Mexican immigrants," said the state's Chamber of Commerce.[32] There were also other indications that, despite having passed the 1924 law, Anglo-Saxonists were losing their grip on the country's political and legal institutions. Puerto Ricans had been declared citizens by the Supreme Court, while Congress, in June 1924, voted to grant citizenship status to Native Americans born in the country. Wilson, despite his racism, had opposed immigration restrictions. And though his successors, Warren Harding and Calvin Coolidge, were strong for limits, Harding (rumored to be both part African American and a member of the KKK) was the first twentieth-century president to give a speech specifically addressing civil rights. Speaking in 1921 in Birmingham, Alabama, he called for the granting of "full citizenship" to African Americans. Harding's call was explosive: "untimely and ill-considered," the Birmingham police rebuked the twentieth-century president, while a Mississippi senator said that if the "president's theory is carried to its ultimate conclusion, then that means that the black man can strive to become President of the United States."[33] The Caucasian democracy was starting to come undone.

Having lost the national debate when it came to restricting Mexicans, and fearing they were losing the larger struggle in defense of Anglo-Saxonism, white supremacists took control of the newly established U.S. Border Patrol and turned it into a vanguard of race vigilantism. The patrol's first recruits were white men one or two generations removed from farm life, often with military experience or with a police or ranger background. Their politics stood in opposition to the big borderland farmers and ranchers who wanted cheap labor.[34] Unlike the Chamber of Commerce, they didn't think that Texas—or Arizona, New Mexico, and California—needed Mexican immigrants. Earlier, in the mid-1800s, the Mexican–American War had unleashed a broad, generalized racism against Mexicans throughout the nation. That racism, in the years after 1924, distilled and concentrated along an increasingly focused line. Whatever the specific provisions of national immigration law, it was the agents who worked for the border patrol, along with customs inspectors, who decided who could legally enter the country from Mexico. They had the power to turn what had been a routine daily or seasonal event—crossing the border—into a ritual of abuse. Hygienic inspections became more widespread and even more degrading. Migrants had their heads shaved, and they were subjected to an ever-more-arbitrary set of requirements and to the discretion of patrollers, including literacy tests and entrance fees.

The Juárez–El Paso bridge became something like a stage, or a gauntlet; as Mexicans crossed, they were showered with spit and racial epithets by federal employees of the U.S. government. Border patrol agents beat, shot, and hung migrants with regularity. The patrol wasn't a large agency at first, and its reach along a two-thousand-mile line was limited. But its reported brutality would grow as the number of its agents, over the years, increased. Migrants had no rights, which gave the patrol absolute impunity. Two patrollers, former Texas Rangers, were accused of tying the feet of migrants together and dragging them in and out of a river until they confessed to having entered the country illegally. Other patrollers were members of the resurgent Ku Klux Klan, active in border towns from Texas to California. "Practically every other member" of El Paso's National Guard "was in the Klan," one military officer recalls, and many had joined the border patrol upon its establishment.[35]

In 1929, before the stock market crash and onset of the Great Depression, President Herbert Hoover signed a law that, as the historian Kelly Lytle Hernández puts it, advanced the "criminalization of informal border crossings." The law had been introduced into Congress by Coleman Blease, South Carolina's white supremacist senator, who as governor of his home state had publicly encouraged the lynching of African American men as "necessary and good." Blease was brokering

what Hernández calls a compromise between employers and restrictionists. Accepting the fact that Mexican migrants would be exempt
from national quotas, the new law made it a crime to enter the country outside official ports of entry.[36]

Then, after Wall Street collapsed and unemployment spread, Hoover
tried unsuccessfully to politicize anti-Mexican nativism to win reelection in 1932, hiring more agents and activating previously lax provisions
of immigration law to place pressure on Mexican communities. At the
same time, states like California and Texas took severe action against
migrants and Mexican Americans, with some of the country's leading
intellectuals associating Mexicans with peril, disease, and menace
(including one prominent professor of zoology who in the pages of the
mainline *North American Review* worried about "racial replace-
ment").[37] The federal government encouraged agencies set up to deal
with unemployment to cull the labor force. Charles Visel, head of the
Los Angeles chapter of Hoover's unemployment relief agency, sent a
telegram to the administration counting "four hundred thousand
deportable aliens" in the United States. "We need their jobs," he said.
Visel suggested that police and sheriff's offices stage high-profile raids
"with all publicity possible and pictures," a "psychological gesture" that
would "scare many thousand alien deportables" into leaving the country. The White House gave the go-ahead.[38] As employment rolls, and
farm prices, collapsed, many migrants and Mexican Americans did
leave, either because they were deported or in response to such threats.
Estimates of how many vary, ranging from three hundred thousand to
two million.[39]

"The present administration," the *New Republic* observed in 1931,
"is pursuing a general policy toward aliens which would delight the
most fanatical member of the Ku Klux Klan."

The 1924 Immigration Act, then, had an explosive effect. On the one
hand, the limits it placed on the numbers of European and Asian
migrants who could enter the United States reinforced Mexico's

importance as a source of cheap labor for the United States' expanding economy. On the other hand, it created an agency—the U.S. Border Patrol—that institutionalized a virulent form of nativism and concentrated its animus on Mexican migrants.

To understand the nation's current crisis—especially the way anti-migrant nativism has become the binding agent for what is now called Trumpism—one has to understand that the border, over the long course of its history, has effectively become the negation of the frontier. The long boundary separating Mexico from the United States served as the repository of the racism and the brutality that the frontier was said, by its theorists, to leave behind through forward motion into the future. To say that the frontier "marginalized" extremism isn't just a metaphor or a turn of phrase. Anglo-Saxonism was literally pushed to the margins, to the two-thousand-mile border line running from Texas to southern California. Other kinds of racist extremism certainly found expression throughout the whole of the country, from lynching and Jim Crow to northern segregation.[40] Supremacism was also kept sharp in the country's serial wars. But an important current that has fed into today's resurgence of nativism flows from the border.

One example in particular captures what could be called the nationalization of border brutalism, or the border-fication of national politics. In 1931, Harlon Carter, the Laredo son of a border patrol agent, shot and killed a Mexican American teenager, the fifteen-year-old Ramón Casiano, for talking back to him. Carter then followed his father into the patrol, becoming one of its most cruel directors. Presiding over Operation Wetback in the 1950s, Carter transformed the patrol into, as the *Los Angeles Times* wrote, an "army" committed to an "all-out war to hurl tens of thousands of Mexican wetbacks back into Mexico."[41] Carter was already a member of the National Rifle Association when he murdered Casiano, and he remained a high-ranking officer with the organization through his years with the border patrol. Then, in 1977, after his retirement from the patrol, he led what observers called an extremist coup against the (relatively) more moderate NRA leadership, transforming that organization into a key institution of the New Right, a bastion of individual-rights absolutism—in this case, for the right to bear arms. Likewise, it was a border patrol agent who in 2015 invited Donald Trump to tour Laredo's port of entry, just a few days after Trump announced his presidential candidacy.

"It all started with the border. And that's still where it is today," run the first two lines of the Drive-By Truckers' 2016 song "Ramón Casiano." The song ends: "And Ramón still ain't dead enough."

TEN

A Psychological Twist

"To subdue the social wilderness."

1.

Frederick Jackson Turner had originally conceived his Frontier Thesis as a sociology of vastness, using it to explain how seemingly infinite free land created a unique, vibrant political equality. It was then amended, by politicians, into an ideology of limitlessness, used to justify wars as far away as the Philippines. But starting around the second decade of the twentieth century, critics began to turn the thesis against itself. Turner and his followers had posited "the frontier" to account for all the bad things that the United States had managed to avoid: despotism, militarism, collectivism, class conflict, servility. Now, others started to give the same answer—"the frontier"—whenever they asked why the United States couldn't have good things, like social rights, or a government with the capacity to respond to social problems, or a culture that wasn't mawkish.

Turner especially valued individualism as a national virtue. But those who inverted Turner now regarded individualism, at least in its extreme form, as a vice, responsible for many of America's ills. Walter Weyl, an editor of the *New Republic*, where much of this criticism took place, wrote in 1912:

The westward march of the pioneer gave to Americans a psychological twist which was to hinder the development of a socialized democracy. The open continent intoxicated the American. It gave him an enlarged view of self. It dwarfed the common spirit. It made the American mind a little sovereignty of its own, acknowledging no allegiances and but few obligations. It created an individualism, self-confident, short-sighted, lawless, doomed in the end to defeat itself, as the boundless opportunism which gave it birth became at last circumscribed.[1]

Weyl accepted Turner's premise. Frontier democracy, "raw, crude," was powerful, creating the nation's wealth. But its "evil" lingered, in a reflexive anti-government sentiment that prevented adequate solutions to the country's many problems: plutocracy, racism ("Our ten million Negroes, considered as a whole, are the most exploited section of the community"), class domination, and corruption. Where romanticists of the frontier said that its resources were unlimited, its vistas infinite, Weyl warned of the "new preëmptor," a phrase he used to describe the economic monopolies that were exhausting the country's raw material. "Like the pioneer, though on a much greater scale," the preemptor "wasted, ravaged, and laid fire." "Vast forests were destroyed by machinery with the rapidity of fire," he wrote. Capitalism, Weyl said, had created a "social surplus" of wealth that the state should seize and distribute, in the form of education, health care, and other forms of economic security. Weyl argued for new forms of rational conservation in rural areas to save the natural world. For the urban "slum"—a phrase Weyl used with almost the same frequency that Turner did "frontier"— he urged applied policy to lift its residents out of poverty and illness.

Writing prior to World War I, Weyl was an optimist, believing that with the landed frontier closed, the "wild excesses" of "ultra-individualism" had come to an end. Citizens now had to develop the tools to address the crises of modern life. He called himself a socialist. But socialism for Weyl was as much a psychological as an economic state, an emotional recognition of limits, a check on a boundless id, which often expressed itself as a nostalgic yearning for a limitless frontier. Turner said that the American found himself by losing himself in the woods. Weyl said that, upon having hit the end of the road at the Pacific, the American found himself by "falling back upon" himself— and falling back on others, to realize that he is, indeed, a social being. The "soul of our new democracy is not the unalienable rights, negatively and individualistically interpreted, but those same rights, 'life, liberty, and the pursuit of happiness,' extended and given a social interpretation."

Another critic who inverted Turner was Lewis Mumford. Nothing good took place in the woods, Mumford said, and nothing virtuous came out of them either. "The life of the pioneer was bare and insufficient," he wrote in 1926, in a long essay called *The Golden Day*; "he did not really face Nature, he merely avoided society." Human beings were social animals, and no individual, culture, or nation could withstand, in any healthy way, the "raw savagery" of frontier life, its wars, massacres, its "barbarities in dealing with the original inhabitants." The "crudities of the pioneer's sexual life," which sublimated eros into violent trauma, were made manifest in an unrelenting "warfare against Nature, cutting down the forest and slaughtering its living creatures," a "blind fury" that was then remembered with syrupy melancholy. The pioneer scalps an Indian, and a well-thumbed copy of Longfellow's "Song of Hiawatha" slips from his pocket. "Woman," insomuch as she interrupted this romance, "was the chief enemy of the pioneer," Mumford wrote. She reminded men that the world was made up of more than just them, nature, and Indians, and that there was such a thing as society and responsibility.[2]

Weyl hoped that Americans were on the cusp of developing a rational, social-democratic political culture, rooted in a clear-eyed understanding of class relations. Mumford didn't think so. "When, after the long journey was over" and the pioneer came out of the woods, all he could do was respond to social problems in "covert pathological ways," with spastic, hysterical panic prohibitions, against cigarettes, for example, alcohol, or even "the length of sheets for hotel beds."

Weyl and Mumford provide a sense of the modernist backlash against the Frontier Thesis but also of the degree to which that thesis set the terms of the debate: expansion west through a wilderness cre-

ated a unique form of individualism and gave shape to America's exceptional democracy. Most agreed that the frontier had served as some
kind of safety valve, defusing passions and dissolving class conflict, and
that it had closed sometime in the late nineteenth century, when population density reached a critical mass and there was no more "free
land" to divvy out. What it all meant, though, depended on one's
politics. Turner and his followers thought frontier individualism was
something to be celebrated. Socialists like Weyl, not so much.

"Utopia shut up shop forty years ago," wrote Stuart Chase, an economist who was part of Franklin Delano Roosevelt's "brain trust."
Chase was writing in the wake of the 1929 stock market collapse, at
the beginning of the Great Depression; his book, titled *A New Deal*,
gave FDR, as a presidential candidate in 1932, the term he would use
to describe his reform agenda. "The realization that our future is not
boundless is only now thrusting home," Chase said. "There is no escape;
we have to fight our economic battles at home." He continued: "Laissez-
faire rides well on covered wagons; not so well on conveyor belts and
cement roads. The great reaches of the continent of North America
stamped into our fathers the idea that our future was boundless." But
"the frontier has collapsed" and the country's "perpetual motion
machine"—its constant flight forward that allowed it to psychologi-
cally avoid dealing with its contradictions—has "stripped its gears."[3]

2.

Franklin Delano Roosevelt had taken a class with Frederick Jackson
Turner at Harvard in 1904, though it seems that he skipped out about
halfway through the semester to go sailing in the Caribbean. But Roosevelt did read Turner's essay collections, which he found in "Uncle
Ted's" library.[4] FDR was influenced by other important syntheses
explaining the meaning of American expansion (including *The Law of
Civilization and Decay* and *The New Empire* by John Quincy Adams's
grandson Brooks Adams). But it was from the Frontier Thesis that Roosevelt, and many other reformers, most often drew to make sense of

the crisis, to translate more-abstract scholarly analyses of its causes into an accessible language.

FDR announced Turner's influence on him during his campaign for the presidency, in a September 1932 speech given at San Francisco's Commonwealth Club.[5] Turner had died a few months earlier, and Roosevelt's opening remarks—which recited the whole frontier liturgy, free land, individualism, opportunity, all of it—channeled his spirit. Back then, Roosevelt said, depressions came and went. But since men worked only part of their time for salary, if wages ever fell, or dried up completely, they could always retreat to their farms. That period of the nation's history was "long and splendid." Starvation and dislocation were "practically impossible."

> At the very worst there was always the possibility of climbing into a covered wagon and moving west where the untilled prairies afforded a haven for men to whom the East did not provide a place. . . . Traditionally, when a depression came a new section of land was opened in the West; and even our temporary misfortune served our manifest destiny.

But then came industrialization and rapid advances in communication, transportation, and farm machinery. As a result, capitalism began to outrun the pioneer, and political and economic power conglomerated. For a while, Roosevelt said, the benefits derived from this mode of production were enormous. Unprecedented wealth was created. America rose in the world, and so did its people. "So manifest were the advantages of the machine age," he said, "that the United States fearlessly, cheerfully, and, I think, rightly, accepted the bitter with the sweet." But the tide turned when the century turned: the United States had reached its "last frontier." The end of free land tipped the balance of political power to "industrial combinations." "There is no safety valve in the form of a Western prairie to which those thrown out of work by the Eastern economic machines can go for a new start," Roosevelt said.

Roosevelt didn't use this argument (that the closing of the frontier safety valve made the United States' brand of laissez-faire more prone to crisis) to put forward a coherent alternative economic policy. He was too spontaneous a politician, as his biographers have noted, too extemporaneous a policy maker.

Instead, he used the argument to put forward a new way of conceiving of the relationship between the individual and government. As he did at the Commonwealth Club, FDR often provided a "thumbnail sketch," as one writer put it, of the Frontier Thesis "to explain why a democratic government that had historically done very little regulating had to give way to a government that regulated a good deal."[6] In Little Rock, Arkansas, in 1936, for instance, FDR offered one such sketch, taking time in particular to celebrate Andrew Jackson's opening of the Mississippi valley, before dismissing it all with two sentences: "Today that life is gone. Its simplicity has vanished and we are each and all of us, whether we like it or not, parts of a social civilization which ever tends to greater complexity."[7] "We must lay hold of the fact," Roosevelt said elsewhere, making the case for Social Security, "that the laws of economics are not made by nature. They are made by human beings."[8] "This man-made world of ours," Roosevelt called it, conveying a new ethics of social solidarity.[9]

The Great Depression was as much an ecological crisis as an economic one, and the Frontier Thesis helped New Dealers understand the link between the two.* In a striking 1935 essay titled "No More Frontiers," undersecretary of agriculture Rexford Tugwell said that centuries of easy U.S. expansion across the continent had resulted in "riotous farming."[10] "It was all very romantic," Tugwell said, this "national epic" of pulling up stakes and moving on. But it had habituated U.S. farmers to unsustainable techniques, which produced widespread soil erosion. In the nineteenth century, the Homestead Act distributed good land to the powerful, including lumber barons who stripped the trees off the land and assigned the rocky margins to the poor. The act was a "death warrant" for the soil, accelerating the practice by which farmers farmed

---

* "Twenty-five years ago, when we had all the land in the world," Roosevelt explained, in off-the-cuff remarks he made from the rear platform of a train as he inspected drought conditions in Colorado in 1936, there was no need for government intervention. "Today the unlimited land of the old days of the frontier is gone," he said, making a pitch for the rational use of land for flood control.

until depletion and then moved on to a new plot. The United States' entrance into World War I worsened the situation. Earlier, Theodore Roosevelt had managed to conserve some public land. But now, wrote Tugwell, farmers were told to "grow wheat to win the war," with stepped-up production fueled by wartime demand sweeping away many of Roosevelt's protections.

Tugwell blamed the crisis on a frontier tradition that bred ignorance of methods that would allow more sustainable "intensive farming." Assuming infinity, Americans didn't farm so much as strip-mine the soil, ignoring limits until they hit, in the Great Depression, the final limit. Technology that was introduced, such as the tractor and thresher, only served to spread wasteful practices across even larger areas—"to cut and burn away the vast screen of the dense and daunting forest," as Turner himself wrote, deforesting the southlands and destroying the Great Plains at ever greater rates while rendering the labor of tenant farmers unneeded.[11] By the 1920s, dust storms were blowing huge clouds of topsoil east, darkening cities and raining down "mud over the rest of the country. . . . Feed crops withered, the water courses dried up, starving cattle had to be salvaged," and "millions of economic refugees" marched desperate across the land, looking for food. The New Deal's response to this ecological crisis was spectacular and, in those years prior to World War II, offered the most far-reaching vision of the collective public good since the Freedmen's Bureau: the government resettled families, put people to work, planted trees, restored the loam, reseeded soil, expanded national parks, returned land to Native Americans for pasture, and tamped down the dust.

Other reformers too used the Frontier Thesis to make their case for a new social ethics.[12] Frances Perkins, FDR's secretary of labor, similarly argued that extensive frontier expansion led to a different kind of erosion, not of soil but of human worth: a "deflation" and "devaluation of human life." Surplus people worked the land until their early deaths, and their children continued the process. She agreed that the nation's prosperity was created on the frontier—not, however, because the distribution of "free land" created value. Rather, Perkins, in a 1934 book titled *People at Work*, drew out the gendered underpinnings of the Frontier Thesis. Wealth was created by the "free labor" provided by household production (free in the sense of not being paid for). The uncompensated toil of women and children resulted in a "pure gain in national wealth." The "freedom" of the frontiersman, in other words, depended less on having a gate of escape across an endless frontier than on being able to control the labor of his family.[13] Perkins argued for a new "awakened conscience," based, at the very least, on adequate compensation, dignified working conditions, and limitations placed on child labor, which were the goals of the Fair Labor Standards Act of 1938.

The "frontier" was good to think with, to help make sense of the crisis, a way to explain economic theory with commonsense terms, including the argument that the Depression was caused by industrial overproduction: the end of the landed frontier, it was believed, threw the economy out of sync, leading to supply greatly outstripping demand. Tugwell, Perkins, and others also thought that reference to the frontier might be a way to use the past to move beyond the past. "The future," Tugwell said, needed to "usurp the functions of the past." He hoped that critics and politicians would eventually give up using the word "frontier" to describe human aspirations.

Still, the frontier wasn't just a rhetorical device but, for many New Dealers, living memory. Nearly all of FDR's advisors and millions of his supporters were born before the frontier was proclaimed closed in the 1890s (some, like FDR's top economist, Alvin Hansen, were born on the frontier) and they'd witnessed firsthand the relationship between the frontier and crisis.[14] Some "frontier states" had only recently been admitted into the union, such as Oklahoma in 1907. Traveling to Tulsa in 1933, the head of FDR's National Recovery Administration, Hugh Johnson, said his bureaucracy was the successor to "the great American frontier," acting as "a safety valve against depressions." Johnson had been raised in Oklahoma Territory in the 1890s, so he knew of what he spoke when he identified the state as a long-standing haven for refugees fleeing economic crises. "There are no more Oklahomas," Johnson said, "there is no more frontier." (The exception being Alaska, which the FDR administration, in building up its roads and parks as part of the federal public works program, often referred to as the "last frontier.")[15]

Hoping to socialize the country, New Dealers attached the adjective "social," or "socialized," to old Turnerian categories. Progressive educators started a journal called *The Social Frontier*. "Non-social individualism," one sociologist wrote, is "detrimental to our further progress; non-social should therefore give place to social individualism." "New frontiers beckon with meaningful adventure," Henry Wallace, Roosevelt's secretary of agriculture, who would go on to serve as his vice president, said in 1934. "We must invent, build, and put to work new social machinery." And of course there was a "social surplus" to be distributed by the "social republic" as a "social wage," through programs including "social security."[16] We ourselves might attach the adjective to these critics, who weren't so much anti-Turnerians as "social Turnerians." "We are each and all of us, whether we like it or not, parts of a social civilization," FDR told his Little Rock audience.

"To subdue the social wilderness," Wallace said, one needs "not a new continent but a new state of heart."

3.

The New Deal's socialization of the Frontier Thesis allowed reformers to rebut racism and white supremacy. Leaders of nativist movements imagined Anglo, Saxon, and Nordic plowmen moving forward on the frontier toward greatness. New Dealers, though, read the frontier less as mythology and more as pathology, a social disorder manifested in an insistence on national uniqueness. Such a reading made space for a new kind of tolerance and openness. Roosevelt himself was Hudson Valley Dutch-descended gentry, as inside a member of the country's sacred Saxon lineage as one could be ("this is a Protestant country," he once said to an economic advisor who was the son of Irish immigrants, "and the Catholics and Jews are here on sufferance"). To FDR's everlasting discredit, he would order the internment of Japanese Americans during the war and, in order to keep southern Democrats happy, he cut African Americans out of many New Deal reforms.

But FDR's advisors were the first to signal something like cultural pluralism, that there was a place for all in the nation.[17] "Your generation," Rexford Tugwell told the 1935 graduating class of the University of New Mexico—which included students with last names such as Montoya, Sánchez, Chávez, Cobos, and Rainwater—will "assume the full stature of Americans," and the country will recognize not only your "rootedness but also the sun, the air, the water, and the soil of your environment as a definition of your sphere of interest." "You are part of this nation; and this nation is part of you," Tugwell said, promising that the federal government would "protect them from the destructive forces of reaction." Referring to a willingness of the federal government to let indigenous communities return to collective farming, Tugwell said that Native Americans might become "once more themselves in their own ways." "A fog of casuistry" was how Tugwell described laws meant to enforce Anglo-Saxonism. For her part, Frances Perkins, even before she became secretary of labor, had already criticized border patrol brutality. In office, she worked to limit the abuses of immigration officials as much as she could, curtailing warrantless arrests and allowing detained migrants a telephone call (the U.S. Border Patrol remained under the authority of the Department of Labor until 1940, when it passed to the jurisdiction of the Department of Justice). Perkins also tried to make abusive migrant labor contracts more equitable.[18]

To socialize the Frontier Thesis also meant to de-exceptionalize, or relativize, American history. Turner thought that the development of the United States was unique, based on a just-right amount of "free land" and a just-so balance between individuals, capital, and government. He was an internationalist, supporting Wilson's League of Nations. But a new world order would only become a reality, he thought, when other nations figured out how to emulate the United States' singular history. New Dealers, in contrast, emphasized commonalities, shared national histories of oppression and political struggle. A new rural sociology, represented by studies such as Rupert Vance's *How the Other Half Is Housed* and Arthur Raper's *Preface to Peasantry*, not only informed federal agricultural policy but suggested that the United States had something in common with one country in particular: Mexico, a nation whose experience of racial domination, peonage, squalid housing, and planter power mirrored the history of large parts of the United States, especially in the South and Southwest.

By the time of Roosevelt's election, the various factions that made up the Mexican Revolution—which was fought to overcome this history of oppression—had consolidated into a stable government that, in 1917, put into place the world's first social-democratic constitution, guaranteeing citizens the right to receive education, health care, and decent wages and to organize unions. Mexico's president Lázaro Cárdenas, upon his election in 1934, accelerated a program of economic reforms, including land reform. By the time he left office in 1940, Cárdenas had distributed close to forty-five million acres (many expropriated from U.S. companies) to 810,000 families. This redistribution included restoring a good part of the Yaqui homeland as a single indigenous *ejido*, a land grant to be held, worked, and governed collectively (Cárdenas's actions would have been the equivalent of FDR restoring to the Cherokees their original Georgia lands, or returning western Tennessee to the Creeks). Mexico also nationalized a significant amount of U.S.-held property, including that of Standard Oil.[19]

Earlier, starting with the Wilson administration, the Department of State and business interests had united to condemn the Mexican Constitution as a perversion of the ideal of individual rights, especially property rights.[20] Now, though, members of FDR's cabinet were making pilgrimages to Mexico, holding up its land reform as something that might be tried in the United States, and reading its constitution, wondering if they could get similar social rights inserted into the U.S. Constitution.[21] Tugwell and Wallace—along with others further to the left of the New Deal, such as the leaders of the socialist Southern Tenant Farmers Union—began to visit Mexico for lessons that might be applied at home. The United States, said the head of Roosevelt's Farm Security Administration, could "learn much" from Mexico's communal farm system.[22] The goals of Mexico's "social revolution," wrote one historian around this time who was trying to move beyond Turner's parochial vision, were "rights for the common man," a slogan that he hoped was starting to "sound familiar to Anglo-Americans."[23]

The admiration was mutual. Mexican revolutionaries pointed out the similarities between their agrarian policies and Roosevelt's effort to emancipate the "North American campesino" from the "social cancer" of "peonage." Reformers in both countries, a Cárdenas ally said, were working for "common social ideals for human betterment."[24]

4.

The New Deal's inversion of the Frontier Thesis allowed some of its most dynamic and committed officials to come up with a fairly comprehensive diagnostic of society's ills, a way to critique laissez-faire individualism. In doing so, they put forth a new, commonsense ethic that freedom in a complex industrial society required government intervention and that, in a phrase FDR would use over and over again, "necessitous men are not free."

The actual economic policies of the New Deal were nowhere near as coherent. Prior to the country's entrance into World War II, FDR presided over an eight-year trial-and-error experiment. His New Deal lurched forward, leaned left, leaned right, then left again, rehearsing one program (regulating the banks) then another (public works), being told by the Supreme Court that something wasn't constitutional (the National Recovery Act, for instance) before trying some other thing (Social Security and the Farm Security Administration). Much of this activity brought enormous relief to workers and farmers, helping to reconstitute a viable rural, family-farm economy. At the same time, though, such policies—whether the provision of immediate aid, the political empowerment of unions, or technical and financial assistance to small-scale farmers—took second place to supporting the creation of large, export-oriented industry and agriculture.

Pearl Harbor in 1941 focused the nation's collective energies, as the federal government raised taxes, rationed, conscripted, set price controls, and requisitioned nearly the entire industrial plant of Detroit and

Dearborn to produce needed matériel. In the run-up to the war, the word "frontier" increasingly reverted to one of its original meanings, referring to a defensive front or cordon. As the United States began to organize Latin American nations into a mutual defense treaty, analysts started to identify America's "frontiers" as the perimeter of the entire Western Hemisphere: "All of the hemisphere is thus incorporated in the theoretical defensive frontier of the United States," with the U.S military committed to protecting "the entire continent from the northern wastes of Canada to Tierra del Fuego."[25] Earlier, as Germany started to make moves against France, a Republican senator leaked to the press that Roosevelt, in a meeting with the Senate Committee on Military Affairs, said that "America's frontier is on the Rhine." Roosevelt denied the remark; public opinion was still not ready to support a war in Europe. But the country's defensive line was indeed pushing outward as never before (in response, Italy said it had moved its frontier to the Panama Canal).

Roosevelt might or might not have thought the Rhine America's frontier. But his success in creating a new and stable political coalition ultimately did depend on moving outward (economically, but that meant projecting diplomatic and military power into Asia, in competition with Japan's growing influence). The New Deal's endurance rested on two pillars. First, Roosevelt's government did everything it could to open foreign markets, which helped consolidate a powerhouse economic sector of highly capitalized industries. These industries—which included banking, along with chemical, petroleum, pharmaceutical, electronic, and Detroit's automobile companies—for the most part supported what would be over the next three decades the twin objectives of the New Deal coalition: expanding capitalism abroad and allowing a gradual extension of political liberalism, including civil rights, at home.[26]

The second pillar related to the nation's agricultural sector and entailed keeping its labor costs low while similarly opening foreign markets for its exports.[27] In general, this sector, comprised of southern cotton and sugar planters, midwestern farmers, southwestern ranchers, and California growers, was not, to put it mildly, an ally of New Deal reform. Southern planters, for instance, their power restored upon the withdrawal of Reconstruction troops in the 1870s, saw pretty much anything that people like Tugwell or Perkins did as, at best, a stalking horse for integration or, at worst, a step toward revolution. Amid news that the Mexican government was seizing vast amounts of private property and giving it to Native Americans, among other groups, and with memories of the Freedmen's Bureau still fresh, even the mildest of agrarian reform policies elicited condemnation. A "giant bureaucracy which can be used to prosecute a philosophy of state land socialism" was how Oscar Johnson, head of the National Cotton Council, described the Farm Security Administration, which, alongside other initiatives, helped tenant farmers buy land.[28]

As with the Freedmen's Bureau, opposition was driven more by what New Deal agencies represented than by what they actually did. The reach of federal agencies remained limited, particularly in the South, where planters controlled the Democratic Party.[29] The White House, to keep Dixiecrats happy, decentralized the administration of many of its programs, effectively allowing local white supremacists to run them. This meant that African Americans were shut out of many government benefits. One of the most important pieces of legislation passed by the New Deal—the National Labor Relations Act, which increased the power of workers to unionize and negotiate collectively—excluded rural workers, many of them African American, from its protections, again to appease southern planters.

"It really is too bad," Tugwell wrote FDR in 1937, complaining of what he thought was the timidity of federal assistance to farmers, "that the tenant bill as it passed allowed nothing for communal and cooperative activities." "I shall have to go to Mexico," he said, "if I am to see the aims" of the New Deal in practice. "Do you see what Cárdenas does to the big farmers [who] object to the confiscation of their estates?"[30]

FDR had no intention of doing what Cárdenas did to planters: breaking their political power by confiscating their property. In any case, soon the most dynamic, experimental phase of both countries' reform movements would start winding down. Cárdenas's successor was relatively conservative, and Roosevelt, focused by the early 1940s on fighting the war, took steps to ensure that agriculturalists would continue to have a reliable supply of low-wage farmworkers.

What became known as the Bracero Program started in the depths of world war, in late 1942, as the Wehrmacht laid siege to Stalingrad and the United States began pushing the Japanese back in the Pacific, still more than a year away from D-Day. Over the next two decades, nearly five million Mexican workers migrated legally, with travel permits, to the United States. The steady supply of low-wage labor was a dream for U.S. farmers, especially those based in California, Florida, the Southwest, and the Pacific Northwest, providing, as one of them put it, "a seemingly endless army of cheap, unorganized workers, brought efficiently to their doorsteps by the government."[31] Millions more came undocumented, outside the program.

In a sense, then, Bracero updated Coleman Blease's 1929 border law, further channeling Mexican migrants into two distinct streams. In one stream were those outside the Bracero Program; they remained criminalized, subject to imprisonment and prosecution. The border patrol built more detention centers along the border and set up dispersed forward operating bases, which were used to intercept migrants and process them quicker for deportation. The number of apprehensions skyrocketed, with annual deportations by 1952 pushing close to a million.[32] In the other stream, Bracero workers were legal, but largely unprotected by labor law. Most lived in squalid conditions, overworked and denied many of the rights of basic citizenship, not to mention the more forceful worker protections put into place by the New Deal. "We used to own our slaves," said one Florida sugar planter in an exposé into the mistreatment of farmworkers, including those in the Bracero Program; "now we just rent them."[33]

5.

Slaves were supposed to be something that the United States didn't have. The United States stood, in 1944, on the threshold of enormous power, about to win a war that many described as a fight on freedom's frontiers against the forces of a new kind of totalitarianism. It was "the world's greatest war against human slavery," FDR said in his 1944 State of the Union address. The New Deal might have moved away from its early radicalism and put into place policies on behalf of large-scale corporate interests. But it still advanced a broadly social-democratic conception of citizenship. The fight against fascism, many thought, had to be about more than restoring an ideal of freedom as freedom from restraint. "We have come to a clear realization of the fact that true individual freedom cannot exist without economic security and independence," Roosevelt said in his 1944 remarks. "Necessitous men are not free men," he said, repeating a favorite phrase.

Most every other country agreed. "A true social democracy" was what the world needed, said the German novelist Thomas Mann in April 1945 from his exile in California, a "balance between socialism and democracy."[34] GERMANY IS FINISHED, COMMUNISTS DISTRUSTED, MAJORITY WANTS SOCIALISM ran a *Boston Globe* headline seven months later—a "vast majority," according to the article's on-the-ground reporter.[35] The Old World lay wrecked, destroyed by both mobilized fascism and hands-off laissez-faire. From the ruins, "common people have taken over political power. They intend to use it to obtain economic and social power as well." British, French, and Scandinavian people had voted in social democracy, "Holland and Belgium will shortly," said the *Globe*, and "Italy will take it too." So would Spain, when Franco was gone. In December 1948, the United Nations adopted its Universal Declaration of Human Rights, shepherded into being by Eleanor Roosevelt, which synthesized political and social rights and called for an end to racial discrimination in all its forms. As to Latin America, every nation followed the Mexican example and ratified postwar constitutions that included social rights.[36]

The men who would lead the United States to new heights of political and economic power, whatever their personal opinions, understood the kind of promises offered by the Universal Declaration to be useful in countering the Soviet Union, providing an ideological alternative to communism. As such, in Japan, Douglas MacArthur, the supreme commander for the Allied Powers, "instructed" the Japanese

prime minister to encourage unionization, while the drafting committee introduced social rights into Japan's new constitution, including the
right to work, unionize, and bargain collectively ("twenty years ahead"
of any such protections in the United States, said one observer).[37] For
his part, Harry Truman's special envoy, John Foster Dulles, inserted
into Washington's multinational peace treaty with Japan a pledge that
signatories would "strive to realize the objectives of the universal declaration of human rights." Dulles also included in the treaty a commitment to respect the rights promised by the United Nations, regardless
of "race, sex, language, or religion."

At home in the United States, though, "human rights"—whether
understood as civil rights ending segregation or social rights further-
ing economic democracy—were meeting strong opposition. Roosevelt,
in his 1944 address, proposed the adoption of a second "Bill of
Rights"—an "economic declaration of rights" that included all the
rights Mexico had been guaranteeing its citizens since 1917: the right
to health care, education, a living wage, decent housing, and social security.[38] FDR was still more than a year from his death, but, recovering
from the flu, he was too ill to address Congress in person, instead reading a portion of the text over the radio. Film footage of the broadcast
shows the president looking cadaverous. He'd win a fourth term later
in 1944 but wouldn't live to complete a year of it. His proposal that
the nation adopt a bill of social rights was gone shortly after.

ELEVEN

A Golden Harvest

*"To reopen the West's economic frontier
at a new moral level."*

By the end of World War II, the word "frontier" had started to shake off whatever negative associations had been attached to it. The United States had emerged from the war with unprecedented economic power and a restored sense of confidence. And as it did, the word once again returned to mean a line, not to stop at but to cross over, a challenge and an opportunity.

In the coming decades, the idea of the frontier migrated into nearly every scholarly discipline, including economics, agricultural science, politics, sociology, and even psychology: "frontier" was used to identify the terrain on which a proper ego was formed, as well as the field on which an unrestrained id was let loose. As a metaphor, it was put to great effect in literature, movies, and political speech. Roosevelt himself, before his death, started to use it not just to indicate a past that no longer existed but a future that might be attained. "New frontiers of the mind are before us," he said shortly after his last election as president.[1] In 1941, a physicist described research that was allowing for an "intensive attack" on a "new frontier": the impending splitting of the nucleus of an atom. Four years later, in July 1945, a month before the United States dropped atomic bombs on Hiroshima and Nagasaki, one of the builders of those bombs gave a report to Harry Truman: *Science, the Endless Frontier* described research and development as a "largely unexplored hinterland for the pioneer."

As Frederick Jackson Turner wrote half a century earlier—referring to something different, to the way the frontier allowed individuals to avoid submitting to complexity—"society became atomic."[2]

1.

With the fight against fascism won, leaders of what would come to be known as the Cold War against communism found it easy to hitch the idea of the frontier to a new politics of expansion. America's frontier was now on the Elbe, the river separating western Europe from the east, wrote John Knox Jessup, an editor of *Life* magazine, in a long 1951 essay titled "Western Man and the American Idea." Jessup was a key advisor to Henry Luce, the influential publisher of *Time*, *Life*, and *Fortune* who, earlier, in 1941, had coined the phrase "American Century." Even as World War II still raged, Luce commissioned a series of reports describing what the postwar world might look like. Jessup's lengthy treatise was meant to sum up the overarching philosophy behind that project.

Jessup understood the frontier not as a defensive perimeter but a civilizational zone separating freedom from slavery—from Soviet slavery, a challenge that defined America's postwar mission. At some point during the world war, he said, the United States accepted "responsibility for the fate of its parents' lands, for the mother and father of its own past."[3] That obligation was "beyond question": on "America almost alone has fallen the awful responsibility of holding open the door of history against the forces of evil until freedom is born anew all over the world." Drawing heavily on Turner, Jessup said that America's long frontier experience produced a new kind of human, a "horizontal man" capable of spreading the "brotherly love" of a true internationalism. Where Europe's "vertical man" gets bogged down in elaborating doctrine and reciting creeds, in arguing existentialism in Parisian cafés, the American treks across the plains and climbs the mountains unburdened by abstractions. He doesn't "stop to make a summa." "American democracy," as Turner had earlier written, "was born of no theorist's dream."[4]

In fact, the United States' security frontier would soon entail much more than the Elbe. By the late 1950s, it ran, starting in the northern Pacific, from Alaska around Japan, southern Korea, and Taiwan, across Southeast Asia (Indonesia to be added later, after its 1964 CIA-supported coup), back under Australia, New Zealand, Latin America, southern Africa (with more countries from that continent to be included as decolonization from Europe proceeded), up to the Persian Gulf, especially Iran and Saudi Arabia, to Turkey and Pakistan, then across the Elbe to Scandinavia, and back around to Canada. It was a considerable radius, and costly to secure, as Washington had pledged to do under the terms of the various mutual defense treaties FDR and Truman had signed. But this was also largely the range open to U.S. capital, which for decades after World War II enjoyed a profitable return on investment.

One of Luce's postwar surveys, borrowing a phrase Jacksonians often used to convey the boundless potential of the American continent, called on Washington to "enlarge the practical area of human freedom." By this, the authors explicitly meant freedom to invest and extract. "The horizon of the individual enterpriser, who is still the true source of wealth," the survey continued, should "be vastly widened."[5] Earlier, FDR said the world was fighting Nazism to protect Four Freedoms: freedom from want, from fear, of speech, of worship. Now Luce's team suggested adding a fifth freedom: "individual enterprise." And as if to underscore the imagery of the world as the American West, the Truman administration put the Department of the Interior—that is, the agency that oversaw the Bureau of Indian Affairs and managed the extraction of resources on domestic public lands—in charge of assisting third world governments within the sphere of U.S. influence to mine minerals and pump oil for the world market.[6]

In the early 1950s, the country was governed by a majority coalition, comprised of both Democrats and Republicans, that largely accepted the domestic and foreign agenda of the New Deal order. This agenda could be summed up in these eight points:

1. A strong federal government that superintended an economy organized around large-scale industrial and agricultural production;

2. Public welfare, including the acceptance of social rights and social democracy in allied countries;

3. At home, a commitment to the (slow) dismantling of the institutional and legal mechanics of segregation;

4. Abroad, decolonization, an end to European imperialism;

5. Containment of the Soviet Union, including maintaining superiority in the nuclear arms race, and pacification of third world socialist and nationalist governments allied (or potentially allied) with it;

6. An expansive (and expensive) diplomacy carried out under the umbrella of regional and international treaties and organizations, including the United Nations and NATO;

7. The restoration of Europe and Japan to their prewar industrial strength;

8. The provision of financial, technical, and military assistance to other, poorer countries, with the goals of promoting economic development and ensuring political stability.

This new international order came to be known, among other names, as liberal multilateralism.[7]

2.

Men like Luce and Jessup saw no contradiction between what they called "complete free trade"—that is, the lowering of tariffs and removal of obstacles limiting U.S. investment in allied nations—and New Deal corporatism. A postwar world of plenty would come about under the

direction of a strong state working in close collaboration with a hand-
ful of powerful corporations, advancing an aggressive agenda of domestic
reform and an equally aggressive foreign policy. Their vision was of an
expanding foreign-service bureaucracy to widen the world frontier,
an expanding military bureaucracy to contain the Soviet Union, an
expanding civil rights bureaucracy to advance racial justice, and an
expanding regulatory bureaucracy to rationalize corporate activity.

At the same time, though, a number of libertarian writers, including Laura Ingalls Wilder's daughter, Rose Wilder Lane, began to use the
frontier metaphor themselves to launch their campaign against such "an
ever spreading governmental bureaucracy." It was the "frontiersmen"
who first "broke loose from the economic 'controls' that restricted their
energies," Lane wrote in her 1943 libertarian manifesto *The Discovery
of Freedom* (published a year before Friedrich von Hayek's *The Road
to Serfdom*). They provided an example of self-emancipation that could
serve as inspiration for moderns who hoped to escape the New Deal
state. "Social Security is National Socialism," Lane said.[8] Another
libertarian call to arms also published in 1943, Isabel Paterson's *The
God of the Machine*, probably didn't mean to imply that there was a
dependent relationship between racial terror and the fetish of a minimal government. Still, the book nicely captured the Jacksonian worldview: "In the opinion of the frontiersman, the only good Indian was a
dead Indian. But the frontiersmen had no excessive attachment to government either."

The principles of what came to be called libertarianism aren't new
and can indeed be traced back to the Jacksonian period, to Andrew
Jackson's definition of a federal government reduced to "primitive simplicity," or back further, to Madison's belief that "diversity" is the source
of virtue and wealth.[9] Modern libertarians updated these ideals. With
Truman integrating the military, and the Supreme Court ruling that
school segregation was not legal, some feared that the expansion of
federal authority seemed unstoppable. Libertarians, in response, sought
to use the penalizing power of the market to stem the tide. Again, the
idea of the frontier proved useful. The economist James M. Buchanan,
who started his career in the 1950s and whose theories concerning

individual choice would win him a Nobel Prize, appreciated the role
the frontier played in breaking up collective identities.[10] "Why was the
frontier important?" Buchanan asked in an essay titled "The Soul of
Classical Liberalism." His answer: it provided the "guarantee of an exit
option, the presence of which dramatically limits the potential for inter-
personal exploitation." If the market were allowed to function free of
government intervention, it would work "precisely the same way as
the frontier"—it would provide an "exit option" from coercive relationships and thus weaken the "nanny state." The frontier was the very
soul of freedom.

There also existed a hidebound minority, both in Congress and the
legal profession, suspicious of diplomatic internationalism and out-and-
out hostile to domestic reform, especially to the twin threat of racial
equality and social democracy. Some congressmen, led by Dixiecrat
southerners and individual-rights absolutists, had become vigilant in
their efforts to stop any legislation or foreign treaty that might pave
the way toward either desegregation or economic rights. This minority
was especially fearful that the Truman administration would use all the
new international agreements it was signing and multilateral alliances
it was joining to do an end run around Congress. Conservatives
feared that international treaties would justify federal intervention in
domestic social life, to further the cause of racial and economic democracy. They said that internationalism provided a warrant to "control
and regulate all education, including public and parochial schools,"
to intervene in "all matters affecting civil rights, marriage, divorce,"
as well as in the economy, regulating "labor and conditions of employment."[11]

When the United Nations voted in December 1948 in favor of
adopting its Universal Declaration of Human Rights—which pledged
member states to guarantee the political, social, and civil rights of
their citizens—conservatives began to mobilize. The declaration was a
"blueprint for socialism," said a representative of the American Bar
Association.[12] Here, in examining the postwar backlash against New
Deal internationalism, the opposition between race and class—that is,

the question of whether backlashers were motivated by racial hatred or by desire to defend the economic hierarchy—doesn't hold up. Those who feared internationalism as a stalking horse for greater equality made little distinction between the threat of desegregation and the threat of social rights.

The effort to revise the Constitution in a way that limited the president's ability to cite international law to achieve domestic reform came to be called the Bricker Amendment campaign, for its main sponsor, Ohio's senator John Bricker. The American Bar Association was a strong supporter of the amendment. Social rights, one of its representatives told Congress, would "destroy in many respects vital parts of our free enterprise system."[13] Other backers of the Bricker Amendment focused on racial equality. One of them fretted that "Truman's Civil Rights Commission," unable to push desegregation through Congress, would get it "done by treaty, that is, through the back door." Here were the earlier fears voiced of the Freedmen's Bureau—the idea that a supra-bureaucracy would force "negroes into social equality"—carried forward and expanded, transposed onto the institutions of liberal multilateralism.*

Conservatives were particularly hostile to institutions like the Department of State, even though they were run by staunch anti-communists such as John Foster Dulles. For instance, the Bricker Amendment coalition

---

*The supporters of the Bricker Amendment were especially concerned about a 1919 Supreme Court ruling that foreign treaties—in this case, an agreement between Canada and the United States to protect migratory birds—might indeed override states' rights and grant power to the federal government that wasn't explicitly stated in the Constitution. The claim that "states alone were the repositories of the power to regulate migratory birds," as some conservatively interpreted the Constitution, was ludicrous on its face, revealing the speciousness of much of the "states' rights" legal reasoning and opening the door to expansionary interpretation of federal power.

It's fitting, at least as vivid imagery, that migratory birds became a flashpoint between New Dealers trying to create new multilateral institutions and conservatives holding dear to the Jacksonian sanctity of state sovereignty. Similar to two elements essential to modern economics—migrants and capital—birds not only couldn't be contained by borders but were too economically important to be left to individual states to regulate. In the 1920s, both sides in the debate about whether to exempt Mexico from immigration quotas often referred to Mexican workers as "birds of passage." Opponents of quotas argued that migrant laborers, like birds, came and went without leaving a trace. Those who wanted to keep "poverty-stricken" migrants out said, "Keep your Mexicans and your birds of passage out of the country."

tried to derail Truman's final peace treaty with Japan, which granted considerable authority to the United States to continue to police the Pacific but also committed signatory nations to "strive to realize the objectives of the universal declaration of human rights." Since the Senate hadn't yet ratified that U.N. declaration (the United States only voted in favor of it in the United Nations), conservatives charged that the treaty with Japan was a "sneak attack" on the Constitution, as the *Chicago Tribune* put it, a "roundabout approach" to get the United States signed on to social rights, desegregation, and other anti-racist principles. "In other words," the *Tribune* continued, "once the U.N. 'rights' get a foot in the American door, the Constitution and Bill of Rights can be rewritten to suit the Truman politicians."[14]

Congressional conservatives lost this battle. The treaty with Japan was ratified, after which their movement to amend the Constitution failed. But, in a way, they fought the larger war to a draw. In the coming years, the United States would fitfully desegregate, with liberals often using the pressure of fighting a (mostly cold) war on the frontiers of freedom to push forward reform at home. But social rights were never legitimated.

3.

One event, concerning Puerto Rico, is especially illustrative of the failure of social democracy to gain a legal foothold in the United States, even in a roundabout, "back door" sort of way. Possession of Puerto Rico, of course, represented unfinished business from an earlier moment of expansion, when the United States waged war on Spain in 1898. By this point, in the 1950s, Puerto Ricans had been granted citizenship, but the status of the island itself was unclear. Some residents—including members of a militant nationalist movement—wanted independence, while others wanted some kind of ongoing relationship with the United States, either in the form of a quasi-autonomous commonwealth or admittance into the union as a state.

Wherever one might stand on that question—independence, commonwealth, or statehood—all, or at least a vast majority, wanted social democracy. In 1952, Puerto Rican voters overwhelmingly approved a new constitution that recognized "the right of every person to obtain work" and the right of "social protection in the event of unemployment, sickness, old age, or disability." But since Puerto Rico was a colony, or a protectorate, its constitution had to be approved by the United States Congress.

Upon seeing a draft of the charter, Republicans and southern Democrats—the same ones pushing the Bricker Amendment—balked. "This is as different from our Bill of Rights as day from night," said Indiana representative Charles Halleck, who feared that if such language was allowed in the constitution of a "protectorate," the United States itself could be bound by its promises. "This is evil and will ultimately render null and void other protections granted to individuals," said another House member; "if we approve this, it will be one of the greatest blows ever struck against the freedom of men. It means the citizens will be wards of the government." Congressional members, in hearings, interrogated the drafters of Puerto Rico's constitution, wanting to know if they believed that social rights—to health care, employment, education, food, clothing, and housing—imposed "any possible obligation upon the United States of America to provide any of these benefits?" The constitution's drafters, caught off guard by the vehemence with which their interrogators reacted to the idea of "social rights," hedged. They answered that the idea was to create a set of cultural expectations that no one in a free society should starve or go without work or die from lack of health care. But such "expectations" were the last thing these congressional representatives wanted to create. Nevada senator George Malone complained of "so-called rights" that "are not legal rights as we have in our Constitution but are social and economic aims that could be dangerous."[15]

Halleck, seeing the Puerto Rican charter as yet another "roundabout approach" to legitimate social democracy, managed to cobble together a congressional majority, including both conservatives and liberals, that approved Puerto Rico's new constitution while stripping out all references to social rights. Liberals who were willing to cite international law, and use international pressure, to fight desegregation at home were fine with joining with conservatives to avoid any statutory recognition of social rights.[16] In the coming years, it would be the G.I. Bill of Rights, not FDR's Second Bill of Rights, that would provide millions of members of "the Greatest Generation" with publicly subsidized education, housing, health care, and other benefits. They just wouldn't be called social rights. And they'd receive them in exchange for their service as veterans, not as a right of citizenship.

4.

There were others who supported the creation of a postwar world system through which the United States could continue to expand its range of action, but they didn't think it should be dressed up in a color-blind universalism. In fact, Clare Boothe Luce, Henry's wife, wrote a long letter to her husband early in the 1940s, laying forth her own, quite distinct vision of what the "American Century" should look like. She argued that Washington should work to establish an unabashedly racially divided global order, ensuring that Anglo-Saxons had control of the world's supply of oil, rubber, iron, tin, coal, cotton, minerals, sugar, and other resources. Luce, who later served as Eisenhower's ambassador to Brazil and Italy, explicitly linked her realism to the closing of the frontier: the whole globe was "divvied up," she wrote in 1942, rebuking what she described as her husband's Pollyannaish belief that all could share in the world's unlimited bounty in peaceful cooperation. The world had limits, she said, and they had been reached and laid claim to, "every last jot and tittle of it, every last acre, stream, and mountain," even the "Antarctic wastes." "America will survive as a nation," she said, only if it preserved its "racial and cultural homogeneity" by putting up "strict barriers against further immigrations of Brown, Black, and Yellow peoples." She also wanted to keep out the "scum and sweepings of South Europe, the Levantine East, and Asiatic Russia."[17] Anglo-Saxons, Luce said, needed to put into place a world order where they would continue to have access to cheap labor and cheap resources in the darker parts of the world.

"A white man's peace" couldn't be imposed on a world that was "only half white," said one of her husband's American Century articles; "the remnant cords of white imperialism" had to be cut and all people and nations considered equal.[18] Clare Boothe Luce disagreed. A "white man's peace" was the only kind of peace that could be enforced in a world "half white." Clare lost out to Henry's American Century, which was, at least in its justification, color-blind and universal, confident that the frontiers of possibility were still open. Others, though, shared her doubts. The diplomat George Kennan thought the postwar order should be founded on more explicit Anglo-Saxon lines, especially when it came to ensuring that the poorer precincts of the world remained open to U.S. derricks, bulldozers, excavators, and harvesters. "We have about 50 percent of the world's wealth but only 6.3 percent of its population," Kennan wrote in a 1948 policy memo, and "our real task in the coming period is to devise a pattern of relationships which will permit us to maintain this position of disparity without positive detriment to our national security. To do so, we will have to dispense with all sentimentality and day-dreaming."[19]

And even those committed to a universal multilateralism had worries. Postwar policy makers remained haunted by the Great Depression, by fears of returning scarcity. Henry Stimson, FDR's secretary of war, born in 1867 and having lived through many booms and busts, captured the widespread optimism of the year 1947 when he said that by promoting prosperity abroad, the United States would ensure prosperity at home. But Stimson also conveyed some apprehension that success might not come easily: "We must all of us avoid the pitfalls of laziness, fear, and irresponsibility." "We must," he said—that "must" hinting at underlying anxiety—reach "new levels of peacetime production."[20] "We cannot go through another ten years like the ten years at the end of the twenties," Dean Acheson, who would later help put into place Truman's foreign policy but was then FDR's assistant secretary of state, told a congressional committee on postwar planning in 1944. And there were few appealing options to preventing a return to the chaos other than opening "foreign markets." "You could probably fix it," Acheson said, "so that everything produced" within the United States "would be consumed" within the United States. But such a system would, he argued in a sharply drawn exposition of a founding premise of Americanism, require so much government intervention that it "would completely change our Constitution, our relations to property, human liberty, our very conceptions of law."[21] Others conveyed a disquiet in less precise terms. "We share the belief of the American people in the principle of Growth," wrote the authors of a report issued by the Materials Policy Commission, set up to ensure that the United States maintained access to global resources.[22] The commission, however, confessed it couldn't give "any absolute reason for this belief," only noting that "to our Western minds" growth "seems preferable to any opposite, which to us implies stagnation and decay."

What that opposite might look like was sketched out by Franz Alexander, a Budapest-born, Berlin-trained psychoanalyst. Alexander's 1942 book, *Our Age of Unreason*, previewed an increasingly popular brand of social science that criticized modern life for its excessive interiority, for producing unmoored personalities—individuals who, subsumed into mass consumer and entertainment culture, were "at home everywhere and nowhere," as David Riesman would soon write in *The Lonely Crowd*. Previously, some New Dealers thought the end of the frontier might create a healthier form of socialization. But Alexander, as the head of Chicago's Institute for Psychoanalysis, said that its closing produced a new kind of slavery. Where an earlier age of heroic capitalism gave rise to the individual at the center of the liberal ideal, Alexander saw around him nothing but decomposing psyches running in place with no purpose or goal, isolated and alone: "They would all like to stop," but were compelled by the "invisible whip wielded by an invisible slave driver" they carried in their own minds. "The economic field is near to its saturation point and will no longer provide sufficient outlet for creative ambition and so becomes the arena of destructive competition," Alexander wrote. He wondered: "Are there new frontiers—

open territories worthy of the individualistic and productive forces of a great nation?"

Nelson Rockefeller, who had served as Roosevelt's and Truman's top Latin American envoy, wanted to believe there were. "With the closing of our own frontiers," he told the House Foreign Affairs Committee in 1951, "there is hope that other frontiers still exist in the world."[23] There was "frustration," he said, among the young people he had spoken with, a fear that there was no way to fulfill traditional individual initiative:

> These young people are seeking new opportunity, the chance to move out, to go to other parts of the world. Our country was settled by people with that dynamic urge to find new opportunities, and they found them for many years in the country. Now the opportunity seems to be in other parts of the world. . . . The young people of this country naturally assume that we are an integral part of a world scene, and they want to be identified positively with that world scene. I think they want to feel that we are not just working for our own limited interests as a Nation, but that we are working for interests plus the interest of the people of the world as a whole. I think psychologically that is a very important factor. I feel the same myself.

Postwar internationalism—the opening of the global economy under U.S. leadership—could be a new frontier, Rockefeller told Congress, allowing the next generation an opportunity to be ambitious and to believe itself good, to see no daylight between the pursuit of self-interest and the pursuit of a better world.

Dissents, doubts, and frustrations aside, postwar technological advances, especially in agricultural production, were spectacular. Many old New Dealers didn't imagine the promise of "growth" to stand in opposition to their efforts to establish an ethic of social solidarity. FDR's vice president, Henry Wallace—who would later break with the Democratic Party over its postwar turn toward anti-communism and launch a third-party bid for the White House—had worked with Nelson Rockefeller in the early 1940s to set up a program of agricultural research in Mexico. That program dramatically improved corn and wheat yields in Mexico and then expanded into the broader Green Revolution to triple grain production in Asia.[24] Walt Whitman's long-ago prediction that the United States would "feed the world" had, it seemed, come true, with progress achieved not by waging class war on property relations but by innovation, technology, and trials and errors that increased production. "The task before us," the historian Arnold Toynbee said in 1964, "is to reopen the West's economic frontier at a new moral level," and to use the "technological precocity" of the United States to help the whole world reap a "golden harvest."[25]

Harry Truman often invoked the country's frontier history in his battle against McCarthyite reactionaries to argue that the United States could both spend lavishly on a Cold War armaments program *and* continue funding New Deal social programs.[26] This double challenge, of fighting oppression abroad and advancing progress at home, he said, was part of the frontier tradition. The country was up to the task, Truman said shortly after winning the 1948 presidential election, "because there are now, as there have always been, more Americans who look ahead toward the broad horizon than who look backward toward times and places left behind." The nation had crossed a new meridian, Truman said, where it learned from "experience that we cannot leave the forces of a huge and complicated economy to take care of themselves." As long as that lesson wasn't lost, it would be possible to create a postwar world of uninterrupted progress, with "a steady growth in the standards of living" and an "ever-expanding economy" freed from cyclical crises. Conservative critics who said otherwise were living in the past. Endless innovations and never-ending growth were opening up new roads and "today's frontiers call for the same pioneering vision, the same resourcefulness, the same courage that were displayed by the men and women who challenged our geographical frontiers a century ago."

To be sure, U.S.-led internationalism during its golden age was profoundly skewed. Henry Luce won the political—or public relations—argument. But Clare's "race realism," as some today would call her kind of geopolitical white supremacism, was closer in truth to how the world's resources were actually distributed. With "less than 5 percent of world population," the United States, according to one analysis, consumed "one-third of the world's paper, a quarter of the world's oil, 23 percent of the coal, 27 percent of the aluminum, and 19 percent of the copper."[27] Between 1900 and the end of the Cold War, resource consumption in the United States "increased by a factor of 17," vastly outpacing "that of people living in the developing world." It took an enormous amount of violence, including the staging of serial coups—in Southeast Asia, Africa, the Middle East, and Latin America—to maintain those numbers, and the pretense of calling this arrangement "universalism" or "multilateralism" could only be maintained so long as the promise of endless economic growth remained credible.

"Our watchword is not 'holding our own,'" Truman said. "Our watchwords are 'growth,' 'expansion,' 'progress.' . . . There are still frontier days."

At the end of World War II, an ascendant United States, its dust storms behind it, had a claim to being a different kind of world power. It seemed to many as if the nation had overcome its obsession with laissez-faire to embrace a modern conception of citizenship—not, surely, social rights or social democracy, but still something close to the reforming spirit of the New Deal. Abroad, postwar reconstruction proved it was willing to spill blood saving the economies of potential commercial rivals (Great Britain and France) and spend its treasure rebuilding those of enemies (Germany and Japan). The Marshall Plan extended billions of dollars to restore Europe's economy, serving as the calling card of a foreign policy that justified itself with a credible conflation of selfishness and selflessness. "Mankind," Truman said as he reached the end of his presidency, "for the first time in human history can wipe poverty and ignorance and human misery clean off the face of the earth."[28]

The Henry Luces and Harry Trumans won the postwar debate. The idea of the frontier was reborn and the United States would work to create an open world and to bring down barriers. Still, in 1945, at the end of the war, the first significant physical barrier went up along the Mexican border: "4,500 lineal feet of chain link fencing," ten feet high and "woven of No. 6 wire," near Calexico, California.[29] The fence's posts and wire mesh had been recycled from internment camps that had been used to hold Japanese Americans during World War II.

TWELVE

Some Demonic Suction Tube

"You couldn't use standard methods to date the doom."

Then came Vietnam, which supporters and critics described as yet another frontier war. John F. Kennedy repeatedly used the metaphor to describe a proactive, aggressive foreign policy, especially to promote counterinsurgency campaigns in the third world. The United States had to secure Vietnam, Kennedy said, since China loomed "so high beyond the frontiers." As the war steadily escalated, soldiers in the field dubbed their air and ground operations "Sam Houston," "Daniel Boone," and "Crazy Horse" and cut the ears off dead Vietnamese as trophies. "Like scalps, you know," said one, "like from Indians."[1] "It was," the historian Richard Drinnon noted, "as if Cowboys and Indians were the only game the American invaders knew."[2] "Come on, we'll take you out to play Cowboys and Indians," writes the journalist Michael Herr in his book of Vietnam reportage, *Dispatches*, describing how a captain invited him to accompany a patrol. Wondering when exactly the war had begun, Herr writes: "You couldn't use standard methods to date the doom; might as well say that Vietnam was where the Trail of Tears was headed all along, the turnaround point where it would touch and come back to form a containing perimeter."

1.

Years before the escalation of U.S. involvement in Vietnam, Martin Luther King, Jr., had already started to criticize the frontier ideal as reinforcing deep-seated pathologies, providing mythic justification for militarism, masculine violence, and economic inequality. The Civil Rights Movement was then on the cusp of its greatest legislative achievements. King, though, was identifying a problem that couldn't be remedied through law. The United States, he said, was trapped in its own myth: America is "a nation that worships the frontier tradition, and our heroes are those who champion justice through violent retaliation"; retribution was held up as the "highest measure of American manhood."[3]

King had begun to use the "frontier" metaphor in the early 1960s, in response to JFK's repeated invocation of the image.[4] By then he had already started to identify as a socialist. "Something is wrong with capitalism as it now stands in the United States," King warned. "Rugged individualism," he said, was a faulty foundation for national identity, since over the years it had distracted from the fact that government does in fact redistribute wealth—upward. "This country has socialism for the rich," King said, and "individualism for the poor"; what was dispensed lavishly as "subsidies" to one kind of people was begrudged to another as "welfare." And such individualism was volatile, easily triggered. It led to fantasies that life was an endless game of cowboys and Indians, to alienation, social isolation, and free-floating aggression. "There is," he said, "an individualism that destroys the individual."[5]

Developing a critique that focused on capitalism's psychic hold over people, King used the idea of the frontier to put forward a counter value structure, an alternative vision of American history and morality. African Americans, he said, confronted a reality "as harsh and demanding as that of the pioneer on the untamed frontier."[6] That harshness forged character and weeded out frivolity; it sharpened "knowledge and discipline . . . courage and self-sacrifice." James Meredith, who in 1962 became the first African American to register at the University of Mississippi, was an exemplar. Meredith faced jeering mobs with a "noble sense of purpose" and with "the agonizing loneliness that char-

acterizes the life of the pioneer."[7] For King, then, nonviolent resistance
was more than a tactic. The ability to fight on the "social frontier," to
forge a path through the "wilderness of segregation" without losing
oneself to justifiable anger, without giving in to rage, he said, contained
the embryo of an alternative society, a way to free the nation from its
past, to overcome its cultish adherence to frontier violence and create
a beloved, social community.[8]

King had already, in the early 1960s, questioned the logic of the
nuclear arms race, and his wife, Coretta Scott King, was close to the
peace movement (as a student at Antioch College, Coretta supported
Henry Wallace's 1948 third-party, anti–Cold War presidential bid).
King was allied with JFK and the Democratic Party and he continued
to hope—even as late as 1962, after Kennedy had sent hundreds of
Green Berets into Southeast Asia—that Washington could avoid a war.
The costs of war, he knew, would be high, especially for African Americans. "Negroes *need* an international détente," he said.[9] An aggressive
foreign policy would pull out society's worst sentiments, including racism, King feared, while drawing away funds from progressive social legislation. Wars, hot and cold, would strengthen the power of southern
segregationists in Congress, who knew they could threaten to withhold
military funding to veto civil rights laws.

In August 1964, after Kennedy's assassination and following the
Gulf of Tonkin incident—when Washington falsely accused North Vietnam of attacking a U.S. Navy ship—Congress gave Lyndon Baines
Johnson authority to escalate military operations in Vietnam. The next
year, even as civil rights leaders were announcing plans for a march
from Selma, Alabama, to Montgomery, Johnson was ordering the implementation of Rolling Thunder, the daily bombing of Southeast Asia.
On March 7, 1965, John Lewis and Hosea Williams led protesters out
of Selma onto the Edmund Pettus Bridge, where they were brutally
beaten by police under the command of Sheriff Jim Clark (sparking
national outrage that led to the signing of the 1965 Voting Rights Act).
The next day 3,500 Marines landed at Da Nang. In August, during the
Los Angeles Watts riots that left thirty-four people dead, King pressed
LBJ to halt the bombing of North Vietnam. By this point, King was

looking for ways to join the struggle to end racism with the fight for a
more economically just society. And he knew that Vietnam threatened
both.[10]

King, though, kept his criticism of foreign policy muted, constrained
by his alliance with the Democrats. When the Student Nonviolent Coordinating Committee in 1966 started criticizing the war in Vietnam, it
earned this rebuke from the *Atlanta Daily World*, an African American newspaper: "Negroes must continue to be loyal to America, particularly when they are on the threshold of receiving full equality before
the law."[11] By early 1967, though, horrified by images of Vietnamese
children brutalized by U.S. soldiers and weapons, by "torn flesh, splintered bones," by "tiny faces and bodies scorched and seared" with
napalm and white phosphorus, King could no longer keep quiet.[12]

2.

On April 4, 1967, Martin Luther King, Jr., gave his "Beyond Vietnam"
speech in Riverside Church in Manhattan, to an overflow crowd of
thousands.[13] It was time, he said, to "break the betrayal of my own
silences." King didn't just condemn the United States' war in Southeast
Asia. He condemned all of it: the country's long history of expansion,
its "giant triplets of racism, materialism, and militarism," and a political culture where "profit motives and property rights are considered
more important than people."

In a way, King's speech was an answer to John Quincy Adams's 1836
denunciation of his Jacksonian colleagues, a call and response across
history. Who would pay for America's frontier wars? Adams asked. The
poor, King said. Would war, asked Adams, provide the social glue to
bind together the "motley compound" that made up the U.S. population? Yes, said King, "in brutal solidarity," but only so long as the killing continued. "Is there not yet hatred enough?" Adams asked. "Have
you not Indians enough" to exterminate? The United States, King said,
was the world's "greatest purveyor of violence. . . . This business of

burning human beings with napalm" was a "symptom of a far deeper malady," a sickness at the heart of the republic.

And just as Adams watched the Jacksonians use perpetual war on the frontier to reverse his policy of (as he wrote in his diary) "progressive and unceasing internal improvement," King watched Vietnam derail the struggle for justice: "It seemed as if there was a real promise of hope for the poor, both black and white, through the poverty program. There were experiments, hopes, new beginnings. Then came the buildup in Vietnam." And he watched this program get "broken and eviscerated as if it were some idle political plaything of a society gone mad on war."

"We are left," he said elsewhere, "standing before the world glutted by our own barbarity."

King's dissent wasn't just a break with the Cold War liberal consensus, which conditioned support for civil rights at home on backing anticommunism abroad. Rather, his protest entailed the refutation of an older, more primal premise. The nation was founded on the idea that expansion was necessary to achieve and protect social progress. Over the centuries, that idea was realized, again and again, through war. Extending the vote to the white working class went in hand with Indian removal; the military defeat of the Confederacy by the Union Army didn't just end slavery, but marked the beginning of the final pacification of the West, with the conquered frontier continuing as an important basis of Caucasian democracy. Millions of acres were distributed to veterans. By the time African Americans started entering the armed forces in significant numbers, with the war of 1898, there was no more frontier land to hand out. But military service remained one of the country's most effective mechanisms of social mobility, for African Americans as well as for working-class people in general, with the G.I. Bill of Rights providing education, medical care, and homeownership to veterans.

King's dissent, therefore, signaled a schism in American politics worthy of his namesake. To "go beyond Vietnam" didn't just mean splitting from the New Deal coalition by demanding an exit from Southeast

Asia. It meant breaking with the devil's bargain that had tempted even Du Bois, the idea that social progress could be achieved in exchange for support for expansion and militarism abroad. For King well understood that while war made progress possible, it also threatened progress, activating the backlashers, revanchists, and racists who run through U.S. history. The War of 1898 opened the military to more African Americans, giving them a mechanism to claim a place in the nation. The same year also witnessed, in Wilmington, North Carolina, white soldiers returning home and slaughtering African Americans, driving them from public office. For all that war turns reform into a transactional arrangement (some suffragists, for instance, traded their support for Woodrow Wilson's war in exchange for his support for their right to vote), and for all that war worked as a safety valve (helping to vent extremism outward), it also created the aggressive, security- and order-obsessed political culture King criticized.[14]

King paid a price for his opposition. He was rebuked by allies both white (who represented the liberal consensus that support for war abroad would allow progress at home) and black (who bet their hopes on that consensus), including Jackie Robinson, Roy Wilkins, and even Bayard Rustin. Newspapers around the country were near unanimous in their censure. The *Washington Post* essentially gave King notice that his services would no longer be needed. "He has diminished his usefulness," its editors said, describing his remarks as "sheer inventions of unsupported fantasy." "Linking these hard, complex problems," the *Los Angeles Times* lectured, in a piece with the catechetical headline DR. KING'S ERROR, will "lead not to solutions but to a deeper confusion."*

King continued to criticize the war, describing Vietnam as "some demonic, destructive suction tube," drawing resources, commitment, and attention outward even as it worsened domestic polarization. Racists killing brown people abroad became more racist; opponents

---

* *Selma*, a recent popular film, took this point to heart: that it's best to keep war abroad and social justice struggles at home separate, lest matters be confused. The film provides an up-close reenactment of the negotiations between King and LBJ over voting rights, without once mentioning or even alluding to Vietnam or how the war "eviscerated" King's program.

of racism, reacting to the killing, became more militant. As urban riots continued through 1967, King repeatedly pointed out that money spent on war could have been used to alleviate poverty at home, that political energy that could have been put to building a more just nation was squandered in yet another "divine, messianic crusade." The most destructive passions, worsened by war, might be channeled outward by war, as black and white soldiers united in brutal solidarity to kill foreigners. But, King said, the United States was fast approaching a point in time when it would no longer be able to avoid a reckoning with itself and when it would no longer be able to deflect the most destructive elements of its race hatred outward. "Our nation," he said, "is trying to fight two wars at the same time, the war in Vietnam and the war on poverty, and is losing both."

"There is such a thing as being too late," he said in his Riverside Church speech, warning that the United States, even if it did try to reverse course, might not be able to steer away from its self-destruction. "Over the bleached bones and jumbled residues of numerous civilizations are written the pathetic words, 'Too late.'"

Others around this time began to make similar arguments, that war simultaneously deepened domestic racism while directing much of its viciousness outward. In the 1950s, the historian William Appleman Williams was criticized for what some said was an overly materialist interpretation of American foreign policy, which held that U.S. expansion was driven by a need to find new markets. Vietnam, though, turned him into something like a mad Freudian: "Americans," he wrote, "denied and sublimated their violence by projecting it upon those they defined as inferior."

3.

The Confederate battle flag and other symbols of white supremacy, including the Klan hood and the burning cross, were already displayed in Vietnam before King's dissent. On Christmas Day 1965, for example, a number of white soldiers paraded the flag in front of the audience at conservative comedian Bob Hope's USO show at Bien Hoa Air Base; officers posed beside the banner and snapped pictures.[15] After King's 1967 speech, displays of the flag became more prominent. "We are fighting and dying in a war that is not very popular in the first place," Lieutenant Eddie Kitchen, a thirty-three-year-old African American stationed in Vietnam, wrote his mother in Chicago in late February 1968, complaining of "people who are still fighting the Civil War."[16] Kitchen, who had been in the military since 1955, reported a rapid proliferation of Confederate flags, mounted on jeeps and flying over some bases. Two weeks later he was dead, officially listed as "killed in action." His mother believed that he had been murdered by white soldiers in retaliation for objecting to the flag.

Kitchen's was one of many such complaints. An African American newspaper, the *Chicago Defender*, reported that southern whites were "infecting" Vietnamese with their racism. "The Confederate flags seem more popular in Vietnam than the flags of several countries," the paper wrote, judging by the "display of flags for sale on a Saigon street corner." Black soldiers who pushed back against such Dixie-ism suffered retaliation from white officers. Some were thrown in the stockade.[17] When Private First Class Danny Frazier complained to his superiors of the "damn flag" flown by Alabama soldiers in his barracks, they demoted him and ordered him to do demeaning work.

Then, one year to the day of his "Beyond Vietnam" speech, King was assassinated in Memphis, Tennessee. As protests and riots spread in cities across the United States, white soldiers in Vietnam raised Confederate flags in celebration. Commanding officers let them fly for days. At Cam Ranh Bay Naval Base, a group donned white robes and held a Klan rally. At Da Nang and elsewhere, they burned crosses. The Department of Defense, following these and similar incidents, tried to ban the Confederate flag on its bases and its theaters of war. But Dixiecrat politicians, who controlled the votes President Lyndon Johnson needed to fund the war, objected. The Pentagon backpedaled and withdrew its ban.[18]

Battle flags flew and crosses burned, and America's war in Southeast Asia became a different kind of race war, not just against the Vietnamese but within the ranks. The kind of violence witnessed in Florida in 1898 repeated itself but on a larger scale. On one base, an African American soldier reportedly bombed an officers' club in retaliation for the soused renditions of Confederacy on display every night.

Southern working-class soldiers, white and black, served in U.S. wars in disproportionate numbers, so these escalating fights over symbols of southern racist identity effectively marked the end of the pact of 1898. That pact, which had brought about national reconciliation between North and South, rested on two elements. First, the War of 1898 and the serial wars that followed allowed southerners to reclaim admission into the nation without having to renounce their white supremacy. On the contrary, the symbol of that supremacy, the Confederate flag, was unfurled over the nation's proliferating battlefields. Many could even imagine that that flag didn't represent racial domination and slavery but rather honor and grit, a fighting spirit that was helping to carry democracy forward. Second, the War of 1898 was the beginning of the process by which African Americans could claim citizenship by being willing to fight for the nation, with the military coming to serve as the country's most effective venue of class and race mobility and distributor of social services, such as education and welfare. The pact didn't suppress or transcend racial conflict so much as deferred it from one war to the next. Defeat in Vietnam, though, marked the end of this deferral.

The domestic effects of the Vietnam War were worse than even King could have imagined, as racist opposition to the Civil Rights Movement fused with hostility toward the anti-war movement to nationalize the Confederate flag. The banner was increasingly seen not just at gatherings of the fringe KKK and the John Birch Society but at "patriotic" rallies in areas of the country outside the old South: in Detroit, Chicago, California, Pennsylvania, and Connecticut. On Flag Day, June 14, 1970, pro-war demonstrators marched up Pittsburgh's Liberty Avenue with a large Confederate flag, demanding that "Washington . . . get in there and win."[19]

The battle flag, for many, remained an emblem of racist reaction to federal efforts to advance equal rights and integration. Yet the banner's meaning seeped more broadly into American society. Race, militarism, and class conflict merged into a wider "culture war," leading some in the rising New Right to rally around the St. Andrew's Cross to avenge both the South and South Vietnam. The Confederate flag stopped flying as the pennant of reconciliation, the joining of the southern military tradition to northern establishment might to spread Americanism abroad. It now was the banner of those who felt that the establishment had sacrificed that tradition, "stabbed it in the back." The battle flag became the banner not of a specific Lost Cause but of all of white supremacy's lost causes.

The working-class Floridian lieutenant William Calley, for instance, the only soldier convicted for taking part in the March 1968 My Lai Massacre, became the representational bearer of this aggrieved standard. He was popular throughout the country, especially in the South; his supporters rallied under the Confederate flag and Richard Nixon embraced Calley in his reelection campaign. As a result, the massacre of over five hundred Vietnamese civilians was transformed from a war crime into a cultural wedge issue, used to nationalize southern grievance and weaponize the wartime coarsening of sentiment for electoral advantage.[20] "Most people," said Nixon of Calley's actions at My Lai, "don't give a shit whether he killed them or not." "The villagers got what they deserved," agreed Louisiana senator Allen Ellender.[21]

With loss in Vietnam, the racial and ideological conflicts long held in check by war began to worsen. A switch flipped on King's demonic suction tube: the wind now blew inward, fanning the flames of reaction. King had said that the war was a domestic issue. After he left the White House in 1969, LBJ agreed, saying that were the United States to lose and South Vietnam fall, "we can have a serious backlash here at home."[22]

As to the Confederate flag, it is still carried into battle, including into the Persian Gulf. But it now competes with so many other racist symbols that its meaning has dimmed. As all of the country's catastrophic military interventions start to meld into one another—Vietnam, Iraq, Afghanistan, Syria, Libya—it conveys little more than free-floating resentment, a resentment that authorizes a right to inflict pain.[23] According to one report at the infamous Bagram Theater Internment Facility in Afghanistan, a platoon implicated in the torture of detainees and known as the "Testosterone Gang"—they were "devout bodybuilders" and were considered the facility's cruelest interrogators—hung the battle flag in their tent.[24]

4.

The story of the breakdown of the long postwar consensus is well known: loss in Southeast Asia, a decade of race conflicts and urban riots, assassinations, Watergate, and rising energy prices. During the Cold War, the United States didn't "enlarge the area of freedom," even if that freedom was only defined as the ability of corporations to extract, invest, and extend their dominion. Through the two decades following World War II, Washington helped execute dozens of anti-communist coups around the world—from Iran in 1953 to Indonesia in 1964 to Chile in 1973—meant to open the third world to U.S. capital. The result was the opposite, sparking ever greater waves of economic protectionism—the Mexican Revolution writ large across the globe—that, through nationalization of industry and high tariffs, shut out U.S. investment.

"Today, the belief in American exceptionalism has vanished with the end of empire, the weakening of power, the loss of faith in the nation's future," wrote Daniel Bell in 1975.[25] Fifteen years earlier, Bell had published his influential *The End of Ideology*, which held that the United States had moved beyond ideology, that New Deal radicalism had given way after World War II to a faith in technocratic improvement. In liberal America, wisdom was institutionalized in democratic structures; it was policy, not social conflict, much less ideology, that guided gradual progress. Now, though, impressed by the madness with which liberal technocrats drove the country into a war that escaped the bounds of reason, Bell offered something of a revision. How was it, he wondered, that a nation that had long believed itself to be unburdened by the past kept reenacting the past, especially the trauma of "frontier violence"? Why was Cowboys and Indians still the only game the country knew how to play?

Bell tried to answer. There had been a weightlessness to American identity, he said, the idea that the nation had freed itself from the obligations of history, along with a sense of deathlessness. No obstacles, not even mortality, stood in the way of growth. Christian righteousness had sanctified the "American mission" outward and had given the country "a special American metaphysical destiny." But defeat in Southeast Asia had brought the United States down to earth. "There is no longer a Manifest Destiny or mission," Bell wrote. The war, the lies by which it was justified and waged, had proven that "we have not been immune to the corruption of power. We have not been the exception. . . . Our mortality now lies before us." The United States was "caught up in the ricorsi of history."

The myth of limitlessness had created a uniquely American dilemma. On the one hand, in all the ways discussed above, the ability to move out in the world did help stabilize society. Even the New Deal, which cited a closed frontier to argue that a strong, regulatory state was needed to manage a complex society, was dependent on the opening of foreign markets. Those markets helped consolidate a high-tech, capital-intensive corporate sector that supported a domestic reform agenda. On the other hand, a blind belief in limitlessness destabilized society, driving the United States out beyond the limit (Octavio Paz, in 1970, described the United States as a "giant which is walking faster and faster along a thinner and thinner line") until it hit the limit in Vietnam, a war that broadcast a deep distrust throughout society, worsened domestic racial and class conflicts, and led to a breakdown of governing legitimacy.[26]

The end of American exceptionalism might, Bell wrote, prompt a more honest reckoning of the problems the country faced, allowing for the creation a more self-consciously social state, a "greater range" of policy choices, including something approximating European social democracy. But Bell thought it more likely that the instability generated by the war would continue. All the "issue politics," or what now

are called cultural "wedge issues," brought to the fore by Vietnam—
race, war, crime, drugs, sex, the price of gas and heating oil—would
create an opening for "all-or-nothing demagoguery."

Richard Nixon, of course, was the kind of politician Bell had in
mind. Nixon's "southern strategy" famously played to racist resentment. But it turns out, he also had a stratagem farther south, a "border
strategy."[27] As the historian Patrick Timmons has written, Nixon,
running for president in 1968, promised to get tough on illegal drugs—
the "marijuana problem," as he put it—coming in from Mexico. And
then, shortly after winning the White House, Nixon did put into place
"Operation Intercept," a short-lived, military-style, theatrical crackdown on the border. That the operation was run by two right-wing
personalities, G. Gordon Liddy and Joe Arpaio, highlights the continu-
ities between Nixon and the kind of demagoguery Bell warned, pre-
sciently, would become a staple of U.S. politics. Liddy went on to run
Nixon's "Plumbers," as the burglars who broke into the Watergate
Hotel were called, precipitating Nixon's downfall. Arpaio, the racist
sheriff of Maricopa County in Arizona who gratuitously imposed
humiliating, brutal, and often deadly conditions on his overwhelmingly
Latino prisoners, would become an early supporter of Trump.

Bell thought that the nation would be increasingly subjected to the
kind of stunts Nixon played on the border. Conservative demagogues,
he wrote, would be best positioned to take advantage of wedge issues.
But, forced inward by the "end of empire," they wouldn't be able to
build on this advantage—that is, they wouldn't be able to use foreign
policy to achieve a "critical realignment," a new set of moral ideals of
how the country should be organized that would outlast their presi-
dencies. By leveraging polarization to win, conservatives would only
worsen polarization, thus creating something like a permanent state of
disequilibrium.

Bell was half right, and half wrong. He didn't see Ronald Reagan
coming.

THIRTEEN

More, More, More

"Nothing is impossible."

Has any politician ever offered a simpler, more commonsense description of American freedom, of the right to limitlessness, than Ronald Reagan? Here he is on a campaign stop in a steel town on the Ohio River in early 1980, five years after the fall of Saigon, with Iranians holding U.S. citizens hostage and Nicaraguan revolutionaries challenging U.S. influence in the Western Hemisphere, and just a few months after Jimmy Carter had urged citizens to save gas by giving up unnecessary vacations: "Not too many years ago, all an American—caught someplace out in the world in a revolution or in a war—had to do was pin a little American flag on his lapel and he could walk right through the war or the revolution and no one would lift a finger against him. Not a hair of his head would be harmed because the world respected the U.S. and knew we would go to the ends of the earth to protect a single citizen of our country."[1]

Reagan almost seems to be rewriting Henry David Thoreau's 1851 essay "Walking," about the joys of aimless rambling through nature in "absolute Freedom," as a Cold War parable. The United States had escalated the war in Vietnam and helped radicalize (through economic policies that provoked unrest and security policies that repressed reformers) both Nicaraguan and Iranian societies. And yet the moral of Reagan's story is that the United States should not be held accountable, or bound in any way, by the chaos it creates beyond its border, while at the same time claiming the right to threaten more chaos. Reagan's rover, with his little flag lapel pin, strolls calmly through the gunfire.

1.

Ronald Reagan ran against Jimmy Carter's executive order to turn thermostats down in government buildings as if it were the British Royal Proclamation banning white settlement west of the Alleghenies. Carter wants us to be "miserable," Reagan told a crowd of steelworkers in Coraopolis, in Allegheny County, Pennsylvania, early in his campaign. Nearly immediately upon assuming the presidency in 1981, Reagan canceled Carter's thermostat order—an "excessive regulatory burden," Reagan said—and took Carter's solar panels off the roof of the White House. "More, more, more" was how the head of Reagan's energy transition team, a Houston oil-and-gas man, described what was coming.[2]

The country's previous political coalition, the New Deal, came onto the national stage talking about limits, with Franklin Roosevelt using the image of a closed frontier to put forward a new political common sense. Four decades later, that coalition exited the stage again talking about limits. "We believed that our nation's resources were limitless," Carter said in his famous 1979 Camp David "malaise" speech. In a way, Carter wasn't saying anything that Weyl, Chase, Tugwell, Perkins, Wallace, and even Franklin Roosevelt himself hadn't said years earlier. We used to think that there were no limits, which created a certain kind of psychological disposition ("a mistaken idea of freedom, the right to grasp for ourselves some advantage over others," as Carter put it); now that we had hit limits, we needed to adjust and develop a new conception of freedom based on a recognition of social dependency. The New Dealers could trace a clear line of cause (the closing of the frontier) to effect (the many ills of the Great Depression) to action: government intervention, in all its many forms. And if one intervention didn't work, try something else.

Carter, in contrast, was more hemmed in, his options narrowed by the fallout from defeat in Vietnam and skyrocketing energy costs. His Camp David speech reflected a widespread sense that the world had reached the "end of plenty," that capitalism had—either because of population growth or overconsumption of nonrenewable resources—hit the "limits of growth."[3] But Carter's remarks were a jumble. He had a hard time distinguishing the causes of the nation's problems from their effects: the oil crisis; inflation; Vietnam; Watergate; "special interests"; the assassinations of MLK, JFK, and RFK; "paralysis and stagnation and drift"; and a culture of "indulgence and consumption." And Carter couldn't deflect outward. Defeat in Southeast Asia, revolutions in Nicaragua and Iran, and rising economic nationalism had closed off much of the third world—the area of the world that had been within Washington's Cold War security perimeter during its height—to U.S. action, including investment.[4]

Still, even with its muddled analysis, the speech's frankness went over well with many, contrary to how it is remembered. Carter's poll numbers rose.[5] But he was unable to follow up with a clear policy philosophy, to explain how acknowledging limits was the first necessary step in building a better society, as Roosevelt did decades earlier. That gave Reagan his opening. As a Republican pollster put it, the speech set up "the counterpoint": more, more, more.[6]

2.

On any given day, Reagan could be as ugly as Nixon was before him, using racial resentment and the backlash caused by defeat in Vietnam for electoral advantage. Reagan kicked off his 1980 general election campaign at the Neshoba County Fair in rural Mississippi, near where three civil rights workers had been murdered sixteen years earlier, and announced his support for "states' rights," a not-so-subtle signal of sympathy for southern efforts to maintain some form of de facto racial segregation. "I believe in states' rights," he said, including restoring schools to local control. Complaining about the welfare system's "vast bureaucracy," Reagan sounded like Andrew Johnson complaining about the Freedmen's Bureau.[7] "It's time we told the rest of the world we don't care whether they like us or not," he said elsewhere on the trail, "we want to be respected." He ran on those "issue politics," the ones Daniel Bell said lent themselves to right-wing populism, against abortion, gun control, welfare, regulations, and environmental restrictions on oil drilling, promising to be tough on crime and to stem the disintegration of the family. "The family unit is deteriorating, eroding," he said. Reagan filled "the void," the *Los Angeles Times* wrote in early 1980, left by the departure of Alabama's racist George Wallace "from the national political scene." Meaning: Reagan appealed to white supremacy.[8]

In this sense, Reagan's New Right revolution fulfilled Bell's prediction that demagogues would be able to take advantage of the breakdown of the New Deal order. But Bell was wrong to think that a critical realignment wasn't possible, that the divisive and racially coded nature of "issue politics," of the kind that propelled Reagan to power, allowed only the politics of negativity and grievance mobilization. It's true that the New Right was fundamentally negative in nature, organized around rejectionism: of federal control of public lands, of regulations, of taxes, of union power, of government action to achieve racial, gender, and sexual equality, of gun control, of the idea of limits imposed by environmental concerns, of third world nationalism, of sex education in school. But the promise of limitlessness—of more, more, more—transformed that negativity into positive imagery, into an ideological realignment that reclaimed weightlessness, limitlessness, and deathlessness as American virtues. Reagan advanced a forward-looking Americanism that was, as he once put it, neither left nor right but rather up—"up to the maximum of individual freedom."

A restored ideal of freedom as freedom from restraint was both an effective demagogic tactic—which Reagan used, for example, when he promised his Mississippi audience freedom from federal oversight—*and* a moral appeal to a greater good, a way to conjure an inclusive, boundless Americanism, organized around an inexhaustible horizon, or frontier. "There are no limits to growth," Reagan said. "Nothing is impossible."

Throughout his eight years in office, Reagan frequently invoked the imagery of pioneers "pulling us into the future," pushing us "toward the far frontier," to transcend inconsistencies in his political coalition and to imagine the nation united in an exceptional history.[9] His policies could be quite savage in "freedom frontier" countries like Nicaragua, El Salvador, and Angola. But to the home crowd he played the sunny sheriff. And he did so with a twinkle of Brechtian irony, admitting that "life wasn't that simple" on the range, that there was a difference between "myth" and "reality." "The frontier," as one writer noted much earlier, had "become conscious of itself."[10] But it didn't matter. As Reagan, quoting the liberal historian Henry Steele Commager, put it: "Americans believed about the West not so much what was true but what they thought ought to be true."[11]

3.

In the years after Reagan's first election, the New Right spearheaded a remarkable restoration of markets and moralism, a post-Vietnam re-sanctification of the mission that many thought permanently de-sanctified. It was in the realm of foreign policy and diplomacy where much of the New Right's efforts at re-legitimation took place, where action could be taken to reestablish authority in the world and ideas could be rehearsed to justify that action. Conservative intellectuals brought early into the administration worked to correct the idea, which took hold after Vietnam, that U.S. power was immoral. Such an idea was confirmed by multiple sources: massacres in My Lai and Kent State, among others; the illegal war on Cambodia; investigations into covert operations around the world, into coups in Iran, Guatemala, and Chile;

the murder of Congolese leader Patrice Lumumba; and domestic surveillance and psych-ops programs used against U.S. citizens, including Martin Luther King.

Skepticism and cynicism spread, creating something more threatening than organized opposition: a culture of deep distrust, alternating between anger and jaundiced apathy and primed to believe the worst of the United States, either related to things Washington actually did—secretly bomb Cambodia for years, work to overthrow democratically elected leaders throughout Latin America and elsewhere—or was thought to have done, expressed in the proliferation of conspiracy theories to explain politics.

And so the country might need "a military response to the Soviets," as William Clark, Reagan's deputy secretary of state, wrote in 1981, in an influential policy memo that circulated through the administration. But it also needed "an ideological response." "Our struggle is for political liberty," Clark said.[12] A policy that emphasized "human rights," of the kind that Carter had begun to promote during his presidency, might, he thought, help with this ideological project. But some revision was needed. In the immediate postwar years, conservatives successfully prevented social rights from being legitimated within the United States (and from coming in in a "roundabout" way through the back door of colonialism, via Puerto Rico). But in most of the rest of the world, "human rights" *meant* social rights. New Right intellectuals therefore pushed for a redefinition, hoping to return to a purer "American" understanding, pared down to align with "individual rights." Richard Allen, Reagan's national security advisor, agreed, saying that "the notion of economic and social rights is a dilution and distortion of the original meaning of human rights."[13] "Life, liberty, property," Allen said, listing the things that should properly be considered human rights.

Ultimately, however, Clark thought the phrase "human rights" was unsalvageable. He recommended that the State Department "move away" from its use altogether and instead substitute "individual rights," "political rights," and "civil liberties." What Clark and others wanted was Andrew Jackson's understanding of "human rights": in the middle of Indian removal, Jackson had championed a minimalist definition of government power ("scarcely to be felt") in the service of a maximal defense of individual rights, which would entail the right to the property taken from the Indians after their removal. Like "freedom," the idea of "individual rights" could be deployed both as universal appeal—on behalf of people trampled down by tyranny*—and as racist dog whistle. It is impossible to extricate "individual rights"—to possess and to bear arms, and to call on the power of the state to protect those rights—from the bloody history that gave rise to those rights, from the entitlements settlers and slavers won from people of color as they moved across the land. "Individual rights," as Trent Lott acknowledged in 1984, "are things that Jefferson Davis and his people believed in."[14]

This reassertion of the ideal of individual rights corresponded to a broader ideological campaign run by corporations, conservative foundations, and libertarian donors. The story is well known: diverse intellectuals and activists, among them the economist Friedrich von Hayek and the novelist-philosopher Ayn Rand, established footholds in educational and cultural institutions, in universities and publishing houses, and cultivated generations of followers to carry their anti-statist revolution forward, to fight collectivism in all its forms.[15] When their moment came—when the crisis hit in the 1970s—they were ready, helping to push forth deregulation, privatization, and tax cuts. This revolution is often described as the triumph of the "Austrian" school, in that many of its most prominent economists, such as Hayek and Ludwig von Mises, hailed from Vienna. But the founders of the modern libertarian movements—including those mentioned earlier, Rose Wilder Lane, Isabel Paterson, and James Buchanan—understood their mission to apply "the idea of the frontier" to public policy.[16] The

---

* Clark, a libertarian rancher, pushed Reagan to take a more ideologically aggressive stance against the Soviet Union. "I prefer to speak of personal or individual rights," Clark said in 1981, in a meeting called to discuss how to use the language of rights to criticize revolutionary Iran while avoiding affirming the principle of social rights. Some at the meeting expressed concern that too great a stress on "individuality" limited the ability of the administration to advocate on behalf of ethnic "groups," such as "Jews in the Soviet Union" and "Armenians in Turkey." A Reagan official, though, said that "the important thing is to be out there pushing for individual rights. It is an effective way to fight communism. Emphasis on the individual is the best way to be forceful."

libertarian revolution proved to be enormously successful (counting among its achievements legal rulings granting the right of free speech to corporations), transforming the fields of economics, law, education, labor relations, and philosophy.

Increasingly politicized elites began to invest vast sums in any intellectual, lawyer, economist, or philosopher willing to tell them they were the new pioneers, that the individual was the sole source of virtue, the only creator of value, that the world was divided between makers and takers, that market solutions were the only effective solutions, and that new economic frontiers were always open to conquest. Decades earlier, similar "masters of industry," Frederick Jackson Turner pointed out, had proclaimed themselves pioneers and appropriated the symbols of the West to seize "new avenues of action and of power" and "to extend the scope of their dominion." And here they were again, CEOs singing, "Don't fence me in." *

Unfencing CEOs, though, was hardly the kind of "ideological response" that could justify Reagan's dramatic increase in military spending and support for third world anti-communist insurgencies. Coming up with a vision of the commonweal wasn't easy when so much of the New Right was bent on destroying the very idea of the commonweal. The richer were getting richer, the poor were becoming poorer, even as New Right policy intellectuals chipped away at welfare, attacked public education, and weakened unions. It's in this context, of a restored imperial presidency trying to reestablish U.S. power on a moral foun-

---

* The Koch brothers, for instance, began their involvement in national politics in 1980, as David Koch ran for vice president on the Libertarian Party ticket, pushing for an even more extreme deregulatory agenda than Reagan did and rallying his supporters around the so-called Sagebrush Rebellion. Sagebrush emerged in opposition to "end-of-plenty" legislation passed by Congress in the 1970s to better manage western public land, including the Endangered Species Act. Financed by big ranchers, land developers, miners, lumber companies, and independent oil mavericks, Sagebrush was a largely contrived movement to weaken environmental regulations and federal control, with "rebels" fashioning themselves as cowboy-hat-wearing frontier Jacksonians, waging war on federal despots. Reagan, too, supported Sagebrush, and in office he increased the amount of public land open to gas and oil drilling. Over the years, the Kochs have continued to finance so-called wise use campaigns, funding politicians and organizations aimed at privatizing federal land or transferring it to state authority (as well as reducing the size of protected natural reserves and federal land monuments, as the Trump administration has done with Bears Ears in Utah).

dation and of a committed cadre of conservative activists who would have been happy to strike the word "social" from the dictionary, that Reagan threw his support behind immigration reform.

4.

"You don't build a nine-foot fence along the border between two friendly nations," Reagan said on a campaign swing through Texas in September 1980. Taking a swipe at the Carter administration's plans to build a fence along heavily trafficked stretches of the border, he was making a play for Texas's Latino vote, which had gone eighty-seven percent for Carter four years earlier. "You document the undocumented workers and let them come in here with a visa," Reagan said, and let them stay "for whatever length of time they want to stay."[17]

Policy changes in the 1960s had by this point heated up the immigration debate. In 1963, Washington ended the Bracero Program, which for two decades had allowed millions of low-skilled Mexican workers to earn seasonal wages on U.S. farms.[18] In 1965, Congress passed the Immigration and Nationality Act. Mostly a liberalizing reform, the act is denounced today by nativists for repealing the explicitly racist quota system put into place in 1924. But the new law did also impose, for the first time, a limit on how many migrants could enter from Mexico. Then, in 1968, Congress set up a separate magistrate court system to try migrants for unlawful entry, allowing for a significant expansion in the number of people prosecuted, detained, and deported. Combined, these policy revisions further criminalized Mexican migration. The "legal" migrant stream slowed to a trickle.[19] The "illegal" one poured forth, as demand for Mexican labor increased.[20] According to the historian Ana Raquel Minian, the number of Mexicans arrested in the United States for entering unlawfully jumped from fifty-five thousand in 1965 to one and a half million in 1986.[21]

In one sense, the border was almost wide open during these years, with workers massing in the hundreds just south of San Diego as they waited for nightfall to come across. Leonard Chapman, head of the

Immigration and Naturalization Service between 1972 and 1977, warned of a "vast army" of migrants leading a "silent invasion." But he also believed immigration laws to be "absolutely unenforceable." "A police state is not the answer," Chapman, a retired four-star general, said. "No one wants to see our country hemmed in by a Berlin Wall. And we can't have a huge army of immigration officers stopping people on the streets to check for citizenship."[22] At the same time, though, crossing became ever more dangerous, as migration from Mexico became associated with organized crime, human trafficking, drugs, and gun running. Thieves stalked poor migrants in the canyons south of San Diego. In 1978, the city's police set up a decoy unit, with officers dressing like migrants to catch perpetrators. But they had to disband the unit because the decoy police were too often being shot at by other police and by border patrol agents.

During these years, the nature of migrant work changed. In addition to finding jobs in fields, factories, and restaurants, more laborers gathered on city street corners hoping to be hired for the occasional household job, for landscaping or one-off repairs, and more middle-class families hired undocumented women as live-in servants, often in peonage-like conditions. Throughout the borderlands, labor relations became more intimate, in the way that chattel slavery was intimate: some women found themselves trapped, sexually and emotionally abused.[23] Increasing militancy among farmworkers and Chicano-rights activists—high school students in El Paso, for instance, fighting for the right to speak Spanish—was met by white supremacist backlash.[24]

Conflict was especially acute in California, where Reagan served as governor from 1967 to 1975. As San Diego's sprawl began to push against agricultural fields, racist attacks on migrants increased. Vigilantes drove around the back roads of the greater San Diego area, shooting at Mexicans from the flatbeds of their pickups; dozens of bodies were found in shallow graves.[25] Anti-migrant violence was fueled by angry veterans returning from Vietnam, who carried out what they called "beaner raids" to break up migrant camps. Snipers took aim at Mexicans coming over the border.[26] Led by a twenty-seven-year-old David Duke, the KKK set up a "border watch" in 1977 at California's

San Ysidro point of entry, finding much support among border patrol agents.[27] Other KKK groups set up similar patrols in south Texas, placing leaflets with a printed skull and crossbones on the doorsteps of Latino residents, warning "aliens" and the federal government to fear the Klan.[28] Around this time, agents reported finding pitfall traps, modeled on the punji traps Vietnamese would set for U.S. soldiers, in the swampy Tijuana estuary, an area of the border vigilantes began calling "Little 'Nam."

The United States had just lost a war in Vietnam largely because it proved impossible to control a border dividing north and south. In fact, Secretary of Defense Robert McNamara, desperate to keep the North Vietnamese from infiltrating South Vietnam, had spent over five hundred million dollars on two hundred thousand spools of barbed wire and five million fence posts, intending to build a "barrier"—which came to be called the "McNamara Line"—running from the South China Sea to Laos.[29] That line failed. The first bulldozed six-mile strip quickly became overgrown with jungle, while the barrier's wooden watch towers were, the *New York Times* reported, "promptly burned down."[30]

Reagan, as president, had to strike a delicate balance. He had, after all, won the White House in no small part because of the Vietnam backlash. But now conservative activists were starting to demand that a similar barrier be put into place at home.[31] They called for a wall, or even a "moat," to be built along the border. Others started rehearsing complaints that have become mainstays of the immigration debate. They wanted the Constitution amended to disallow the children of migrants born in the United States to claim citizenship, and for the military to police the border "in full war gear."[32] Groups such as the Federation for American Immigration Reform, founded in the late 1970s, and Californians for Population Stabilization opposed any legislation providing "amnesty"—that is, a pathway to citizenship for those undocumented migrants already in the country—and demanded that the U.S. Census Bureau not count undocumented residents.

At the same time, though, Republican strategists started saying in 1983 that the party had to take a more forceful stand on the side of inclusion. "The Hispanic vote is not only essential to President Reagan's reelection chances in 1984, if he should run, but is also vital to the future of the party itself," they said.[33]

Reagan split the difference. To keep the exclusionists happy, his administration launched Operation Jobs, which sent federal agents into the workplace to capture and deport undocumented workers. Those captured complained of the brutality of the raids: "The agents detained us and piled us into camps in heaps," Everardo Leyva reported to a Mexican paper. "Then they gave us what was almost garbage to eat and there was nothing else to do but return home."[34] Reagan also placed hard-liners in key positions. Harold Ezell, for instance, organized "Americans for Border Patrol," which demanded tougher action against migrants, while he served as the western regional commissioner of the Immigration and Naturalization Service.[35] Ezell—who before his INS appointment was an executive with Der Wienerschnitzel, a fast-food chain—once had the border patrol line up three thousand undocumented workers alongside Interstate 5 in northern San Diego County as a warning to other migrants. "They should be afraid of us," he said. "The ones who are here illegally aren't supposed to love us."[36] In 1984, the border patrol saw the "single largest increase in personnel in the agency's 60-year history," with hundreds of new agents hired. On the roads and highways of the Southwest, it set up twenty-four-hour checkpoints.

Reagan might have dismissed Carter's plan for a fence, but his administration started pushing the idea that the border could be "sealed," and that the deployment of "high tech" equipment—infrared scopes, spotter planes, night goggles—might provide effective control. "New stuff," said a border patrol official, though some of the ground sensors set out were leftover matériel from Vietnam.[37] Reagan himself took a more pessimistic position in his reelection campaign than he did in 1980. "Our borders are out of control," he said in a debate.[38] A Reagan-appointed federal prosecutor even started an investigation into supposed voter fraud, asking California county officials to report the names of all voters who requested a bilingual ballot, an early shot in what by now has become a sustained campaign against the right of people of color to vote.[39]

With his eye on the longer game, however, Reagan hedged against the nativists then filling Republican ranks. Even as his administration was carrying out workplace raids that critics were comparing to Operation Wetback in the 1950s, he bet the party's fortunes on courting the Latino vote. "Hispanics are Republicans," Reagan once said, on the idea that they were inherently conservative, "they just don't know it."[40] Risking his own backlash, Reagan committed to immigration reform, including some kind of amnesty program for the country's undocumented residents.

But what to do with the growing numbers of radicalized veterans filling the ranks of white supremacist organizations, with the "watchers" and the vigilantes who prowled the border?

5.

Ronald Reagan's revival of the Cold War—especially his support for covert actions and anti-communist insurgencies in Nicaragua and Afghanistan—provided a solution. Those wars kept busy the contentious theocon, neocon, and paleocon factions of the New Right, which otherwise might have focused their fire on Reagan's many domestic compromises with the Democratic establishment, including on immigration. The White House empowered an interagency group of men, headed by Oliver North, to run foreign policy as if it were a revival of Buffalo Bill's Wild West Show. They called themselves the "cowboys." Iran-Contra, as the various scandals involving the cowboys became known, was as much a romance as a crime, a bid—and a successful one for a time—to reopen the frontier through counterinsurgency in Central America and elsewhere and to deflect extremists his campaign mobilized outward. There's no clearer example of this than the story of Thomas Posey and his organization, the Civilian Matériel Assistance, or CMA, a paramilitary group.

Posey was an archetypical backlasher, exactly the kind of revanchist LBJ warned about. Already steeped in right-wing Bircher and Klan politics, Posey was radicalized even further by Vietnam and adrift in the post-Vietnam drawdown. "Peacetime is miserable, sitting on my butt," he said.[41] Reagan's call to roll back communism in the third world gave Posey a chance to put himself back into action. Operating out of Flint City, he set out gallon pickle jars in local general stores and gun shops, asking for donations "to stop the communists in their tracks and send them back to Russia." Posey was part of a loosely organized network of Vietnam veterans and National Guardsmen, many of them also KKK'ers and Birchers, or *Soldier of Fortune* mercenaries tied into one or another of the covert ops the White House kept simmering in Africa or Asia. The main objective of this network was to try to find ways to bypass the congressional prohibition against sending military aid to the Nicaraguan Contras, the anti-communist insurgency trying to destabilize the Sandinista government. The prohibition was part of a broader post-Vietnam retrenchment, an effort to limit the White House's ability to wage unaccountable wars.

Posey's next step was to join with other Ku Kluxers and Vietnam vets to found the CMA, which over the next few years developed close ties with both Central American militaries and their CIA handlers. The CMA raised money to fund Reagan's Central American campaign and ran weapons and other supplies to the Contras in Honduras and to right-wing death squads in El Salvador. Members of the organization also trained and fought with the Contras in Nicaragua and helped them set up a second front in Costa Rica. By 1985, the CMA, which coordinated its work with Oliver North's cowboys, claimed thousands of members, the majority of them Vietnam veterans. The group had offices throughout the South, in Georgia, Louisiana, Alabama, Tennessee, Florida, and Mississippi, growing quickly through the region's many military and National Guard bases and VFW meeting halls.[42]

The CMA, though, wasn't just focused on Central America. By this point in the mid-1980s, hundreds of thousands of Central Americans were fleeing Reagan's wars in Nicaragua, Guatemala, and El Salvador and traveling to the United States every year, further inflaming the kind of anti-communist white supremacy that animated groups like the CMA. Ku Kluxers, Birchers, and Nazis didn't see much difference between communists over there, in Central America, and migrants entering here without papers. So at the same time that the CMA was shipping instructors and matériel to El Salvador and Honduras, it also began organizing vigilantes in Arizona to patrol the border (and to harass "sanctuary" activists, part of a network of church groups helping refugees fleeing Reagan's Central American wars).[43] This border activism came to national attention just as Congress was taking up Reagan's immigration reform. On the Fourth of July, 1986, about twenty CMA "border angels" dressed in camouflage fatigues and armed with AK-47s, under the command of J. R. Hagan (a Vietnam vet described as a "repo man and paramilitary buff" who boasted about how many Vietnamese he had killed), captured sixteen migrants crossing over the border just east of Nogales and held them at gunpoint before eventually handing them over to the border patrol.[44] The national press, including the *New York Times*, picked up the story, generating widespread condemnation of the vigilantes.

Posey, most likely coordinating his response with his contacts in the Reagan administration, moved to shut down the CMA's border operations. From the Alabama headquarters of the CMA, he repudiated the operation, dismantled the "border angels," and expelled Hagan, who would be charged by federal prosecutors with illegal-weapons possession. At the same time, however, the CMA increased its activities in Central America, its members keeping busy by bouncing around the region's anti-communist capitals, Tegucigalpa, Guatemala City, and San Salvador. The same month Hagan's border patrol caused a national outrage, the CMA sent a detachment of about a hundred Vietnam veterans to Honduras to train the Contras.[45]

Let's recap and describe the dependent relationship between foreign war and domestic radicalization in as schematic a fashion as possible: Loss in Vietnam radicalized a generation of veterans, pushing many into the ranks of white-supremacist groups. Ronald Reagan, as the standard bearer of an ascendant New Right, effectively tapped into this radicalization, which helped lift him to victory in his 1980 presidential campaign. Once he was in office, Reagan's re-escalation of the Cold War allowed him to contain the radicalization, preventing it from spilling over (too much) into domestic politics. Anti-communist campaigns in

Central America—a region Reagan called "our southern frontier"—
were especially helpful in focusing militancy outward.[46] But Reagan's
Central American wars (which comprised support for the Contras in
Nicaragua and death squads in El Salvador, Guatemala, and Honduras) generated millions of refugees, many, perhaps most, of whom fled
to the United States. As they came over the border, they inflamed the
same constituencies that Reagan had mobilized to wage the wars that
had turned them into refugees in the first place. For its part, the White
House continued to deflect, venting revanchism outward (back toward
Central America and other places in the third world, including Afghanistan). It was, to say the least, a highly volatile game Reagan and his
"cowboys" were playing, one that could only continue as long as the
frontier remained open.

In any case, the backlash was routed into foreign policy, at least for
now. And the White House was able to move ahead with the Immigration Reform and Control Act. That act beefed up enforcement, including a requirement that employers confirm the citizenship status of their
employees, which was applauded by conservative organizations such
as the Federation for American Immigration Reform. But it also created
a one-time-only five-year path to citizenship for many undocumented
residents, which included paying fees, taking a medical exam, learning
English, passing a civics test, registering for military selective service,
and demonstrating no felony and no more than two misdemeanor convictions.

Many migrant-rights advocates understood that the act's retroac-
tive, once-only amnesty was dangerously flawed.[47] The bill set a precedent by conditioning reform on the impossible-to-fulfill promise that
the border could be sealed through an expansion of police power. Still,
enough Republicans and Democrats came together over the objection
of an increasingly vocal nativist caucus to pass the legislation, which
Reagan signed into law on November 6, 1986.* As a result, an estimated 2.7 million undocumented residents became citizens.[48]

---

* That same day, the Iran-Contra story broke in a Lebanese newspaper, generating a scandal that nearly brought down Reagan's presidency. "No comment," Reagan said at the
signing in response to a reporter's request to confirm the story.

The United States was still "a beacon," as Reagan said in his farewell address, "a magnet for all who must have freedom, for all the pilgrims from all the lost places who are hurtling through the darkness, toward home."[49]

The Berlin Wall fell in 1989 and the Soviet Union collapsed in 1991, leaving the United States the world's lone superpower. It was a long time coming. "America has a hemisphere to itself," Thomas Jefferson wrote in 1813. "Half the globe," he said. Secretary of State Dean Acheson, at the dawn of the Cold War, pondered how to "create half a world, a free half." George H. W. Bush, Reagan's successor, got the whole thing. And having the whole thing meant there was no longer any divide, not even a moving, fleeting, zigzagging one, between inside and out. "When I talk with foreign leaders about new markets for American products, is it foreign policy or domestic?"[50] Both, Bush answered his own question. The frontier was now everywhere, but borders, in terms of limits, were nowhere. "We saw the frontier beyond the stars, the frontier within ourselves," Bush said in June 1989. "In the frontiers ahead, there are no boundaries."[51]

Six months later, in December 1989—a month after the collapse of the Berlin Wall— Bush invaded Panama to overthrow Manuel Noriega, a former ally turned enemy. Eight months after that, he sent hundreds of thousands of troops into the Persian Gulf to begin the liberation of Kuwait, a war that he defined as a self-help intervention. "You know," he told returning soldiers in March 1991, "you all not only helped liberate Kuwait, you helped this country liberate itself from old ghosts and doubts." "No one in the whole world doubts us anymore," he said. "What you did, you helped us revive the America of our old hopes and dreams." War, Bush said, was more than "just foreign policy." Driving Iraq out of Kuwait "reignited Americans' faith in themselves."[52]

It seemed, then, that the lingering effects of the dismal 1970s were over, that the New Right project of re-sanctifying the mission was successful, and that the "Reagan Revolution," having once again pointed the demonic suction tube outward, had achieved a critical realignment.

"Freedom," by the early 1990s, had become the keyword of a new moral order. In retrospect, the realignment was fragile. Reagan, for instance, got his immigration reform, but it wound up rebounding against the Republican Party, which couldn't convince a majority of Latino voters that its program of deindustrialization, social services cuts, and promotion of right-wing cultural issues had much relevance to their lives. Most continued to vote Democratic. In fact, perhaps as a result of Reagan's "amnesty," the Republicans even started to lose Reagan Country. George H. W. Bush in 1988 was the last Republican presidential candidate to carry California.

The Republican Party found itself in a bind. Continuing to lose California would be bad. Losing Texas and Florida, states with demographics similar to California, would be catastrophic. Some Republicans still believed they could win Latinos over on issues such as abortion and opposition to gay rights. Others, though, began to push draconian anti-Latino policies, including, in 1994, California's Proposition 187, which denied social services to undocumented residents. The proposition passed and did gather the energies of the state's anti-migrant forces around the governorship of Pete Wilson. But it too eventually backfired. Wilson was unable to turn nativism into a national movement, and California subsequently became one of the most Democratic states in the country. Republicans, meanwhile, continued their schism, rent between a leadership that imagined the party's future depending on winning over at least a portion of the Latino vote and a rank and file committed to making the United States as hostile a place as possible for migrants. As party activists began to put into place race-targeted voter-suppression initiatives and "show me your papers" laws in states like Arizona, they specifically pointed to Reagan's "amnesty" as a mistake not to be repeated.[53]

Reaganism, as an ideological realignment, hit its stride promising to overcome limits. But it would eventually hit its own limit in the cultural politics of immigration. Before that would happen, though, Reagan's successors would carry forth the promise: more, more, more.

FOURTEEN

The New Preëmptor

"Divided in grabbing . . . united in holding."

For most of the twentieth century, the United States' border with Mexico had served as the shadow side of the nation's frontier universalism, a two-thousand-mile-long margin to which racist extremism was relegated. "The world has been frontier for them from the first," Woodrow Wilson wrote in 1895 of a restless nation that looked out at the world and saw nothing but free range. But increasingly, in the last decades of the twentieth century, it was the border, not the frontier, that captured the national mood and concentrated its imagination. More Mexicans came in, without even the minimal protections afforded by the Bracero Program. Hundreds of thousands of Central Americans fleeing Reagan's wars were joining them. For the first time since the Mexican Revolution, politicians and pundits, mostly on the right, were singling out the border as a national security concern. Reagan restored the idea of the frontier. But he also warned of communists looking to "move chaos and anarchy toward the American border." In the early 1990s, immigration wasn't yet a completely partisan issue. Rank-and-file Democratic Party organizations, such as the American Federation of Labor and the United Farm Workers, worried that undocumented workers depressed wages.[1] "We advocate a firm, hard sealing of the border," the Democratic Party chair of the House Select Committee on Population, New York's James Scheuer, had recently said.[2] But a toxic sort of nativism was fast concentrating in the Republican Party.

And more industry was going out, setting up assembly plants in Mexico. This move over the border, part of what commentators were just beginning to call economic globalization, was actually held up by many as a way to escape the border. A "revolution without borders," was how George H. W. Bush described his goal of establishing a hemisphere-wide free-trade zone, "from the Arctic Circle to the Strait of Magellan," a shared, open community of "liberty, peace, and prosperity."[3] In particular, commentators argued that the North American Free Trade Agreement—a flashpoint in today's politics—would bring the xenophobes and extremists to heel. "This new global economy is our new frontier," Bill Clinton said, making the case that liberalized trade with Mexico would bring about civic renewal. "Our national destiny depends upon our continuing to reach out" to the world.[4] NAFTA, said one of his cabinet members, was "the moral equivalent of the frontier in the nineteenth century."[5]

NAFTA, though, didn't help the country rise above the border but rather hardened the border, transforming the line—and all the hatreds and obsessions that go with it—into a permanent fixture in domestic politics and a perennial source of nationalist grievance.

1.

In 1992, Clinton won the presidential election with 43 percent of the popular vote and held the fraying country together by applying Madison's theory with what at the time seemed like confidence: extend the sphere and you will have peace and prosperity. Clinton was Reagan's greatest achievement. He carried forward the Republican agenda by combining a postindustrial fatalism—regulation wasn't possible, austerity was unavoidable, budgets had to be balanced, crime was a condition of culture, not economic policy—with a folksy postmodern optimism, offering sunny bromides touting the "politics of inclusion" that endless growth would make possible. Refusing to rein in out-of-control derivatives, Clinton made sure Wall Street's Wild West remained unfenced. Clinton also served as a good steward of George H. W. Bush's legacy, keeping the defense budget high and continuing Bush's expansive use of the armed forces, including in Bosnia, Sudan, Afghanistan, and Kosovo. And Clinton increased the United States' military presence in the Persian Gulf, regularly launching air strikes into Iraq. By 2000, his administration was spending more than a billion dollars a year to bomb Iraq, on an average of three times a week.[6]

NAFTA, though, represents the clearest and most consequential through line linking the three presidents. Proposed by Reagan in 1980, negotiated by Bush after the fall of the Berlin Wall, North American free trade began to be pushed through Congress by Clinton just months after his inauguration. It should have been a moment of national self-assuredness. The United States had emerged victorious in the Cold War, the Soviet Union not just defeated but gone, off the map. Having waged successful wars in Panama and the Persian Gulf, the United States faced no challenger, not political, economic, or, most important, ideological. And yet a whiff of insecurity hung over the debate leading to the passing of the treaty. Bill Clinton was a minority president, having won when a third candidate, Ross Perot, split the vote running against free trade. Meanwhile, Mexico's president at the time, Carlos Salinas, had stolen his election outright, from none other than Lázaro Cárdenas's son, Cuauhtémoc Cárdenas, who had campaigned against economic liberalization and sought to return the country to his father's radicalism.[7] Pushing for NAFTA, then, became a way for both Clinton and Salinas to offset their political weaknesses with the support of large financial corporations. Salinas practically turned Goldman Sachs into a branch of the Mexican government, letting the financial firm's advisors prep the nation's economy to facilitate the passage of NAFTA.

For his part, Clinton saw the campaign to pass NAFTA as a chance to establish dominance over the Democratic Party base, throwing him-

self into the fight with an "all-consuming" passion. Clinton, wrote
Thomas Friedman about the president's commitment to NAFTA, always
seemed at his "most clearly defined when doing combat with traditional Democrats." It wasn't just the AFL-CIO and environmentalists
who opposed the deal; the Congressional Black Caucus did as well.
Clinton countered by touting free trade as a chance at cultural renewal,
part of, as one of his advisors said, "a subliminal debate going on in
the American psyche" over opportunity, mobility, and responsibility.
In particular, he linked NAFTA to an issue he would return to again
and again as president: race.

The early 1990s, especially in the wake of the Los Angeles riots,
were a fraught moment for race relations. Crime was up, as were
inner-city shootings, and twelve years of Republican rule had greatly
weakened proactive federal policies put into place in the 1960s and
1970s to tackle racism and poverty. So-called New Democrats like
Bill Clinton were increasingly invoking culture to explain social problems, focusing especially on the "pathologies" of young African American
men, their broken families, gun violence, poverty, and unemployment.
Just a few days before the congressional vote on NAFTA, for instance,
Clinton traveled to Memphis, Tennessee, and gave a now-infamous
speech in the same church where Martin Luther King presented his
last sermon. Clinton didn't just mimic King's cadences but spoke in
his voice, scolding the audience on the need to take personal responsibly for crime, guns, and their children. "I did not fight for the right of
black people to murder other black people with reckless abandonment,"
Clinton imagined King as saying. Elsewhere on that trip, Clinton
pitched NAFTA more directly. Economic expansion, not targeted federal intervention to destroy the structural foundation of racism, would
provide the wealth needed to bind communities and families together
and end "ghetto pathology."[8]

Remarks such as those Clinton offered in Memphis weren't meant
to win over black leaders to NAFTA. A week later, most members of
the Congressional Black Caucus voted against the deal. But by making
globalization part of the cultural critique of black men, Clinton was
giving Republicans and conservative Democrats another reason to vote

for the treaty. The official line was that global growth would help the country overcome poverty and racism. The unofficial line, though, the "subliminal" message, was clear: global competition would discipline the black underclass and help the Democratic Party break its dependence on groups like the Congressional Black Caucus. And if Clinton could beat the base on NAFTA, then he could beat it down the line on the other items on his agenda, including his dismantling of welfare (established in 1935 by FDR), strengthening of police power, and expansion of the prison system.[9]

Unions and civil rights leaders, along with environmental organizations and Ralph Nader–type public-interest groups, opposed NAFTA for progressive reasons: fear that the treaty would lead to a loss of jobs, put downward pressure on wages, and allow industries to skirt anti-pollution and other government rules. But the nation's pro-treaty political class, both Democrats and Republicans, liberals and conservatives, were happy to let nativists such as Patrick Buchanan and the occasionally unhinged Perot be the public faces of the opposition to free trade.

Buchanan had just come off his unexpectedly strong 1992 primary challenge to George H. W. Bush for the Republican nomination, where he called for a wall, or a ditch—a "Buchanan Trench," as he put it—to be built along the U.S.–Mexico border and for the Constitution to be amended so that the children of migrants born in the country couldn't claim citizenship. Buchanan took glee in making explicit the racism that Reagan mostly kept implicit, hitting all the resentments Reagan stirred up, including toward welfare recipients, third world socialists, gay-rights advocates, and environmentalists. He advocated policies that would stem "national suicide" or "race suicide" and defend the country's Judeo-Christian heritage. Buchanan lost his "America First" bid. But he did get the Republican Party to include in its platform, for the first time, a promise to build a "structure" along the border.

NAFTA, then, was sold as a way to beat back the darkness. Extend the sphere through free trade and you'll not only dilute the power of extremists—in this case Perot and Buchanan—you'll also give meaning to the republic. The nation's "moral character" was at stake, wrote the *New Republic*.[10] Earlier in the century, that magazine was the headquarters of intellectuals, like Weyl, who had socialized Turner's thesis and said that expansion wasn't the solution to every problem, that it was time to focus on problems at home and not deflect them forever outward on the frontier. In the early 1990s, its editors had gone full Turnerian. Buchanan and Perot, they said, represented "the cause of evil," in that they stood in the way of expansion. NAFTA, now that the Cold War was over, would allow the United States to continue to square the circle, to go on combining realism and idealism and defining its ambitions as virtues: "With each passing decade, the line between domestic and foreign policy becomes more blurry." The trade treaty represented an "internationalism" that combined "moral vision" and "national self-interest."

NAFTA liberalized trading and investment terms with both Canada and Mexico, but it was on Mexico that most of the debate fell, with free-trade campaigners such as Henry Kissinger selling the treaty as an actual extension of the Cold War, a way to finish up that war's unfinished business.

Mexico was not just any random third world country. As the birthplace of the twentieth century's first great social revolt against U.S. capital, it was where it all started, that arc of revolutionary nationalism leading to the global acceptance of social rights and protective economic policies that by the 1970s had shut out United States investment. Reagan's hard line in the third world had begun to reverse the tide. NAFTA was a chance to roll it completely back. Free trade would allow the United States to once again, as it did after the Civil War, "revolutionize" Mexico—and then revolutionize the rest of the Americas. "Mexico has been in the vanguard of the revolution sweeping the Western Hemisphere," Kissinger wrote of Salinas's economic reforms, "against statist left-wing attitudes."[11]

"Just a first step," Clinton said of the treaty.[12]

2.

The backstory to NAFTA starts three decades earlier, in 1965, the year Mexico City and Washington revised their nations' tariff schedules. Henceforth, Mexican assembly plants located on the border were allowed duty-free import of raw material and partially assembled components from the United States so long as the finished product was exported back to the United States; the United States, in turn, would assess tariffs not on the total value of imported items but only on the value of the part of the items that was added abroad.[13] These revisions, quietly done, began the disaggregation of the production process, turning the Mexican side of the borderlands into a belt of export assembly plants. Under the new terms, cloth cut in New York could be sewn into garments in Mexico, with the final product imported back into the United States, and companies would only have to pay tariffs on the value of the work done in Mexico.[14] Mexican workers received considerably lower wages than did their U.S. counterparts, so the money corporations saved by transferring production would be substantial.

Companies did the numbers and made the move. Seventy-four factories in 1968 grew to 147 in 1969 and then 454 in 1975. They included manufacturing plants of advanced-tech companies, such as Fairchild Camera and Instrument and Raytheon. At first these plants were hard to find, located in "unmarked sheds at the ends of dirt roads," as firms didn't want to attract attention as "runaways."[15] But as foreign investment in Mexico increased, there was no hiding. Soon, plants as imposing as penitentiaries were being built. By the end of the Cold War, there were 1,925 of them, holding half a million workers who sewed clothing, assembled electronics, and made cars, with $1 buying labor in Mexico that would cost $8.29 in the United States.[16] NAFTA was still years away, but the border was already transformed into a ribbon of industry, with thousands of squat, cavernous cinder-block buildings ringed with barbed wire and watchtowers, the majority clustered around the cities of Tijuana, Ciudad Juárez, Mexicali, Nuevo Laredo,

Reynosa, and Nogales.[17] Today, there are well over three thousand such plants, where workers make everything from T-shirts to TVs, pharmaceuticals to SUVs.

Mexican officials in 1965 didn't imagine border industrialization as a turn away from the legacy of the Mexican Revolution. Assembly plants certainly weren't sold as a break with the revolution's hallmark agrarian reform, which had distributed not just land but subsidies to peasant communities, while protecting them with tariffs against cheap corn and other food imported from the United States.[18] Rather, policy makers were mostly worried about the effect that the end of the Bracero Program, along with the U.S. imposition of immigration caps or quotas, would have on domestic employment. Suddenly, what Mexicans understood to be their own *válvula de seguridad*—the "safety valve" offered by migration north—had shut. So Mexico City proposed loosening investment and tariff rules in order to encourage the establishment of assembly plants on the border, which, by creating jobs, might offset the loss of north-of-the border employment. Assembly plants would also, many policy makers argued, diffuse productive technology and know-how throughout the economy, sparking a more robust industrialization and, by increasing exports, lower the country's persistent trade deficit.[19]

Neither did Lyndon Johnson, when he agreed in 1965 to revise the U.S. tariff code, imagine that he was undermining the economic order created by the New Deal. The New Deal state had long worked to keep wages low for certain key industries, and that's how Johnson's White House sold the tariff revisions.[20] "Where we used to bring low-pay Mexican labor to our country," said James Givens, a labor activist based in El Paso, "we now take the work to them."[21]

But 1965 was also the year that Johnson escalated the Vietnam War. B-52s would soon drop more bombs on North Vietnam, Laos, and Cambodia than were dropped in all of World War II. Those bombs, as King said they would, exploded at home, triggering a chain reaction that transformed the North American continent.

3.

The cost of the bombs the United States dropped in Southeast Asia, along with the troops it deployed and the price of other matériel, put sustained pressure on the U.S. dollar, leading to an extended economic crisis marked by inflation and low growth. The U.S. Federal Reserve responded, in 1979, by dramatically raising interest rates. What became known as the Volcker Shock, named after the Fed chair, Paul Volcker, eventually broke inflation but also broke much of everything else. In the United States, tight-money policy led to an overvalued dollar, which hit the Northeast and the Midwest industrial region hard, raising the price of exports and making the cost of the credit needed to modernize too expensive. Companies took advantage of the downturn to shutter their factories and begin capital's great migration south, either to the right-to-work and low-tax Southwest or over the border to Mexico. Between 1981 and 1984, the United States lost about two million union-wage industrial jobs. Reagan practically paid for the moving trucks, keeping interest rates high for as long as he could and offering other incentives to shift the economy from old-line manufacturing—including steel and car manufacturing—to high-tech weapons, finance, and services.[22]

The same high interest rates that led to the closing of factories also overwhelmed small farmers. Expensive money both increased the value of their existing debt and made new loans, essential to planting future crops, too pricey. Within a decade, the United States would lose upward of a million family farms. The result of what came to be known as the "farm crisis" was, as the journalist Joel Dyer documented in his book *Harvest of Rage*, "massive poverty and despair," increases in suicide, illness, crime, and political extremism.[23] Even before the full effects of the crisis hit, the federal government had largely abandoned its support of small farmers, shifting its priorities to encourage large-scale agro-industry to expand and then expand again. "Get big or get out," bankers and land university agronomists told farmers.[24] Where New Deal programs balanced the coexistence of family and corporate farms, now government policy showered its favors on big industrially efficient operations. "Farms became larger," writes agricultural economist John Ikerd, "and owned by fewer operators."[25] A number of policies—including federally subsidized crop insurance, loans, tax breaks, government-funded research, and credit advanced to countries to buy U.S. crops—all encouraged bigness, standardization, and industry consolidation. As farms merged, large swaths of the Great Plains were emptied of people: miles upon miles of huge, mechanized farms were punctuated by deserted small towns filled with boarded-up shops.[26] Today in western Kansas, for example, thirty-nine rural counties are home to less than ten people per square mile.

The same high interest rates that began the deindustrialization of the United States and devastated its small farmers were also used to pry open the Mexican economy. Similar to those of U.S. farmers, Mexico's loans were denominated in U.S. dollars. As the value of the dollar increased, thanks to the interest-rate shock, so too did Mexico's debt. The country came close to defaulting, until the International Monetary Fund stepped in. In exchange for new loans to cover its debt and prop up its currency, the government agreed to privatize state-owned companies, cut spending, remove controls on foreign investment, weaken labor law protections, and wind down the land reform. This deal, more than anything else, effectively began to end the nationalist model put in place by the Mexican Revolution and put the country on the road to NAFTA.

4.

The United States was already a decade into its farm crisis and deindustrialization when NAFTA was signed in 1993, so the effect of the treaty was felt as a continuation of changes under way. In Mexico, NAFTA was a blow. Up until the eve of the agreement going into effect, on January 1, 1994, Mexico City had continued to provide significant subsidies and tariff protections to small farmers. NAFTA swept this support away, not all at once but in significant batches, until soon the country's peasants faced U.S. behemoths like Cargill and Archer Daniels Midland unprotected, alone as if before the gods.

Earlier, in the 1960s, Mexican officials might not have imagined border industrialization as an assault on the country's peasantry. By the 1990s, though, a new class of Mexican technocrats looked out at the country's nearly thirty thousand collective farms, or *ejidos*, many of them run by indigenous communities, and saw nothing but relics, a people wallowing in the muck of the past and holding the country back. NAFTA was a chance to sweep it all away, after which Mexico could join the ranks of modern nations. "We're not France," Mexico's former foreign minister once said. "We can't afford to underwrite backward peasants just because they seem charming." As part of the prep leading up to the agreement's ratification, the Salinas government had amended Mexico's constitution, deactivating its most radical provisions.[27] The agrarian reform was declared over. Henceforth, no more property would be seized and redistributed to peasants. *Ejidos* would be allowed to sell or rent their holdings to private capital or to distribute their common land as private property to its members. These changes, justified in the name of turning peasants into small-property owners or moving them fully into wage labor, served as eviction notices: get out.* If peasant land was fertile, it would be combined by agricultural capitalists into large farms, to produce non-grain crops like strawberries and avocados for the U.S. market.[28] If it was hardscrabble, if it took a lot of work to coax out a corn harvest, the land would be abandoned. It was easier just to buy the cheap imported U.S. corn now sold in Mexican Walmarts.

In contrast, the United States, under the terms of NAFTA, got to keep its agricultural subsidies. For example, the 2014 U.S. Farm Bill allocated $959,000,000,000—nearly a trillion dollars—in spending over the course of nine years, with a significant share of subsidies going to a handful of Texas farmers (Nueces County alone, which sits close to the Mexican border, took in nearly twenty-one million dollars

---

*The NAFTA amendment of Mexico's constitution could be compared to the United States' 1887 Dawes Act, which privatized communal Native American land holdings: "In less than fifty years, some 150 million acres, or three quarters of the 1887 Indian land base, and generally the most productive, was lost," as smallholders sold or otherwise were forced to transfer their titles.

in 2016).[29] Mexican elites, for their part, were happy for the chance to bargain away their peasantry in order to attract capital, technology, and industrial jobs, eliminating nearly all subsidies and tariffs and opening up the country's market to U.S. agriculture.

Government officials promised that displaced campesinos would find jobs in the fast-expanding assembly sector in the border. That's not what happened. The border assembly sector eventually came to employ about a million Mexicans, but 4.7 million farming families had lost their land within a few years of NAFTA going into effect. Small corn, dairy, and pig farmers were wiped out by mechanized U.S. agro-industry.[30] Soon, a couple of hundred thousand Iowa farmers were growing twice as much corn as about three million Mexican peasants and selling it for half the price.[31]

Cheap corn, though, did not make food in Mexico more affordable. Once local peasant production was destroyed, the shelf price of imported food could rise as the world market saw fit. Mexico once had a vibrant dairy sector. But shortly after NAFTA went into effect, it became the number one importer of powdered milk. As tariff-free soda and junk food flooded Mexico, malnutrition and obesity increased in tandem (recently, Mexico was ranked as having the second-highest obesity rate in the world).[32] At the same time, an ever-greater percentage of Mexican corn, along with sugar and African palm, was being directed to produce biofuels (the demand for which was kept artificially high by yet more Washington subsidies), which took land out of use that might have produced local food.

Unable to compete, a majority of the NAFTA refugees either moved to Mexico City, where they tried to eke out a living in the informal economy, drifted into the drug trade, or migrated north, hoping to find work in the United States. Between 1994 and 2000, the yearly number of Mexicans traveling to the United States increased by 79 percent.

Over the years, these Mexican migrants have been joined by more and more Central Americans. Having barely survived Reagan's escalation of the Cold War in the 1980s, countries in Central America were pushed by Washington in the 1990s to open up their economies to mining, large-scale biofuel production, and transnational agricultural

corporations. Today, hunger stalks the land. More than half of Guatemalan children endure chronic malnutrition, a "free-trade" generation
raised with severe cognitive and physical difficulties. The World Food
Programme consistently ranks Guatemala as one of the most malnour-
ished countries in the world.[33]

5.

NAFTA freed investment and commodities, allowing them to cross the
borders at will. But the treaty didn't grant the same liberty to workers.
The text of the agreement didn't even include a guest-worker program.
In fact, increased worker mobility would have negated the whole point
of NAFTA, as Mexico would lose its main attraction for investors: surplus cheap labor. Rapid militarization of the border, which took place
exactly at the moment NAFTA went into effect, functioned as the system's own perverse anti-safety valve, limiting the range of movement
allowed to Mexican workers and ensuring that Mexico's comparative
advantage for the U.S. economy—low wages—remained intact.

The Clinton administration knew that NAFTA would lead to a spike
in undocumented migration, and planned accordingly.[34] It significantly
increased the budget and staff of the border patrol, supplying it with
ever more technologically advanced equipment: infrared night scopes,
thermal-imaging devices, motion detectors, in-ground sensors, and soft-
ware that allowed biometric scanning of all apprehended migrants.[35]
Stadium lights went up, shining into Tijuana. A substantial length of
what the administration didn't want to admit was a wall was built. "We
call it a fence," said a government official. "'Wall' has kind of a negative connotation." One stretch, running fifteen miles east from the
Pacific, was made up of old Vietnam-era steel helicopter landing pads
standing on end, the edges of which were so sharp that migrants trying
to climb over often severed their fingers.[36]

Especially consequential was a string of "operations"—with names
including Blockade, Gatekeeper, Hold-The-Line, and Rio Grande—that
militarized what had been relatively safe crossing routes in cities like

El Paso, San Diego, and Laredo.[37] Migrants were now forced over more treacherous ground to get into the United States, across either the creosote flatlands of south Texas or the gulches and plateaus of the Arizona desert. Trips that used to take days now took weeks, on arid sands and under a scorching sun. Clinton's INS Commissioner, Doris Meissner, said that "geography" was an "ally"—meaning that desert torments would work as deterrents.[38] No one knows how many people have died trying to get into the United States since NAFTA went into effect. Most die of dehydration, hyperthermia, or hypothermia. Others drown in the Rio Grande. Since about 1998, the border patrol has reported nearly seven thousand deaths, with groups like the Tucson-based Coalición de Derechos Humanos estimating that the remains of at least six thousand people have been recovered. These numbers certainly are just a fraction of the actual toll.[39] As one migrant-rights worker said of the difficulty of trying to come up with an accurate tally, "The desert is a big place."

People's desperation was bigger. They kept coming, though now a higher percentage stayed. The difficulty of the journey ended the long-standing practice of seasonal migration. Once here, workers stayed here. The number of permanent undocumented residents doubled and doubled again, passing ten million by the time Clinton left office.

Clinton did more than harden the border. He, along with a Republican Party courting nativists, hardened public opinion against migrants. In the congressional midterm elections that followed the NAFTA vote, many Democrats who had voted yes were voted out, paving the way for Newt Gingrich's ascension to Speaker of the House. The Republican majority largely supported NAFTA but began to politicize the issue of undocumented migrants, focusing on their refusal to assimilate and Latino crime. Republicans discussed ways that they might take away citizenship from "anchor babies," pass English-only laws, pull undocumented children from public schools, and deny access to public hospitals. Clinton, for his part, used this extremism to sound moderate and push his own hard line. "All Americans," he said in his 1995 State of the Union speech, should be "rightly disturbed by the large numbers of illegal aliens entering our country."

Promising "to speed the deportation of illegal aliens who are arrested for crimes," Clinton signed a number of extremely punitive crime, terrorism, and immigration bills into law, which created the deportation regime that exists today.[40] These laws closed down various routes for migrants to obtain legal status, eliminated judicial review, and required detention without bail. Essentially, the whole immigration bureaucracy— its agents, courts, and detention centers—was now geared toward expediting deportations, the numbers of which shot up tremendously. Migrants, including those with legal residency, could now be deported for any infraction, including misdemeanors, even if the transgression was committed decades earlier or the matter had already been settled in court. The White House saw this anti-migrant campaign as building on Clinton's various crime bills, which had cut into the Republican advantage on "law and order" issues. His advisor Rahm Emanuel urged him to target migrants in the "workplace," to set a goal of making certain industries "free of illegal immigrants" and achieving "record deportations of criminal aliens."[41] Even the legislation Clinton signed ending welfare targeted undocumented migrants, banning them from receiving many social services and prohibiting local jurisdictions from offering "sanctuary" to undocumented residents. "Before 1996, internal enforcement activities had not played a very significant role in immigration enforcement; afterward these activities rose to levels not seen since the deportation campaigns of the Great Depression," write the sociologists Douglas Massey and Karen Pren.[42]

By the time Clinton left the White House, corporations had their new frontier. Thanks to treaties like NAFTA, they were as free as they ever were. Mexican wages, though, were not much higher than they were in 1970, when the Federal Reserve Bank of Dallas estimated that the daily average wage for an unskilled Mexican worker was $2.84 a day.[43] Today, nearly a half century later, in an assembly plant run by Lexmark—a Chinese-owned, U.S.-based electronics corporation— employees, mostly women, work nine and a half hours a day for about six dollars. "It's not possible to live on these wages. It's not human," said a Lexmark worker, Susan Prieto Terrazas. "They are creating generations of slaves."[44] Wage depression in Mexico, in turn, puts downward pressure on pay in the U.S., which has been flat or declining for decades. "Since the late 1970s, wages for the bottom 70 percent of earners have been essentially stagnant," writes the economist Lawrence Mishell, "and between 2009 and 2013, real wages fell for the entire bottom 90 percent of the wage distribution."

Meanwhile, the border patrol had tripled its size to become the nation's second-largest law-enforcement agency, behind only the FBI.

Progressive critics, writing earlier in the twentieth century, would have recognized NAFTA as an extension of the Gilded Era confiscation of land and resources—yet another "great barbecue," divvying out the best portions of the continent's bounty to the rich. It is a reconstituted "preëmptor," as Walter Weyl in 1912 described elites who use the law to override local control. Corporations particularly like NAFTA-style treaties because they contain provisions that allow them to sue a country if it passes environmental and public health regulations that might impinge on "expected future profit." When Mexico City refused to issue a construction permit to a California-based toxic-landfill management firm, heeding community opposition and attempting instead to convert land that the company owned into an ecological reserve, the company sued and won a multimillion-dollar settlement.[45] By 2015, billions of dollars had been paid out to foreign investors under such suits, with claims of billions more pending.[46]

"Divided in grabbing," as Weyl wrote over a century earlier, corporations were still "united in holding."

The grabbing and holding has happened on both sides of the border, in different but interconnected ways. There's a shared hollowing out. A vacant western Kansas, sending 99 percent of its corn to Mexico, has its counterpart in rural Oaxaca and Puebla, or in highland Guatemala, which used to grow ample corn to feed its people but now largely doesn't. Villages in these regions are emptying too. The remaining residents of Oaxaca's Santa Ana Zegache are mostly women and older folk, as all the working-age men have gone north for jobs.[47]

There's no social "pathology" in the United States, to use Clinton's

term—drugs, crime, guns, depression, suicide, malnutrition, obesity—
that is not mirrored by similar problems in Mexico and Central America, problems that were either caused or worsened by Washington's
policies. Mara Salvatrucha, or MS-13, the "Central American" gang
that inflames U.S. nativists, was founded in the United States, in Los
Angeles prisons in the 1980s, by refugees fleeing Reagan's wars.* Likewise, the drug cartels that have overrun Mexico aren't just fueled by
U.S. demand for the product.[48] They are also a result of Washington's
multibillion-dollar militarized interdiction policy in Colombia, which
had the effect of spreading drug violence that had been contained to
the Andes north through Central America and Mexico.

Washington's policy south of its border with Mexico previewed the
later debacle it created in the broader Middle East, a region that also
has produced waves of refugees, inflaming regional politics. In North
America, U.S. economic policy has provoked one of the greatest migra-
tions in history, equal to that of the nineteenth-century march west
across the Alleghenies. But instead of having the force of natural law
at their backs and the welcoming sun of manifest destiny on their
brows, today's American migrants—a "sheer mass of humanity," as a
border patrol agent described NAFTA's first wave of refugees—are moving into a country that increasingly defines itself by what it hates.[49]

---

* Where Cuban and Nicaraguan migrants were considered "political refugees"—in flight
from leftist governments and thus given good treatment—Salvadorans and Guatemalans
were dealt with roughly. Many wound up in the penitentiary system. Treated as criminals,
they became criminals, organized by gangs, including what became known as MS-13, and
they continued that membership after being deported back to their home countries. (One
of the reasons Nicaragua doesn't suffer greatly from such gangs is that its refugees
weren't shuffled into the prison system and then deported home.)

FIFTEEN

Crossing the Blood Meridian

*"The struggle turns inward . . .
wars are followed by witch-hunts."*

1.

The border before NAFTA was no idyll. For more than a century, it gave liberty to nativist fantasy, letting vigilantes of one sort or another run wild. In 1990, members of a California group calling itself the Alliance for Border Control pointed their cars south, as many as five hundred at a time, and "lit up the border," collectively shining their headlights into Mexico. That same year, a group of San Diego high school students fashioned themselves into a neo-Nazi paramilitary group they called Metal Militia and began to stage "war games" on the border, hunting down and robbing migrants. The spree was notable in that it was covered by a new broadcasting network, Fox, on a show called *The Reporters*.[1]

Racism and nativism had not yet become Fox's bread and butter. The host of *The Reporters*, former *Newsday* investigative journalist Bob Drury, went for sensationalism—the episode was titled "Human Prey"—while depicting migrants sympathetically. Drury interviewed one vigilante who estimated that there were about ten militant groups in the San Diego County area who would "hunt, track, and stalk" migrants for sport. The film crew accompanied one such group as they captured a family, which included a baby and an elderly, terrified grand-mother. Drury linked the upsurge in border extremism to the earlier drawdown in Vietnam: many of the vigilantes were veterans. Others were young, sometimes teenagers who modeled their tactics, including the setting of booby traps, on Vietnam war movies. The most disturb-ing portions of Drury's report were his interviews with vigilantes. Dis-guised so as not to be recognized, they expressed unalloyed hate. "Grab a kid," one said, discussing his favored method of terrorizing migrants, and "nobody is going to do anything."

In the two years prior to the broadcast, a hundred migrants had been murdered in San Diego County. Hilario Castañeda, who was twenty-two, and Matilde Macedo, nineteen, were walking along a county back road when the teenage Kenneth Kovzelove, dressed in black, popped up from the bed of a passing pickup. "Die, die, die," Kovzelove yelled, firing his semiautomatic rifle and killing Castañeda and Macedo. Both victims were legal residents, farmworkers with visas. "So you guys were out specifically looking for Mexicans to kill?" Kovzelove was asked in interrogation. "Yes, sir," he replied.[2] Kovzelove was convicted of his murders, but most went unsolved. A third of the migrants killed were never even identified.

The border patrol, for its part, continued being what it had been since its founding: a frontline instrument of white supremacist power. Patrollers regularly engaged in beatings, murder, torture, and rape, including the rape of girls as young as twelve. Some patrollers ran their own in-house "outlaw" vigilante groups.[3] Others had ties with groups like the Klan.[4] Patrol agents also used the children of migrants, either as bait or as a pressure tactic to force confessions. When coming upon a family, border patrollers usually tried to apprehend the youngest in the group first, before the others dispersed, with the idea that the rest of the party would give themselves up so as not to be separated. "It may sound cruel," one patroller told a journalist, but it often worked.[5]

Separating migrant families was not official government policy in those decades. But border patrol agents left to their own devices regu-larly took children from parents, threatening that they would be sepa-rated "forever" unless one of them confessed that they had entered the country illegally. Mothers especially, an agent said, "would always break."⁶ Once a confession was extracted, children might be placed in foster care or left to languish in federal jails. Others were released into Mexico, alone, far from their homes—forced to survive, according to public defenders, by "garbage-can scrounging, living on rooftops and whatever."⁷ Ten-year-old Sylvia Alvarado, separated from her grandmother as they crossed into Texas, was kept in a small cinderblock cell for more than three months. In California, thirteen-year-old Julia Pérez, threatened with being arrested and denied food, broke down and told her interrogator that she was Mexican, even though she was a U.S. citizen. The border patrol released Pérez into Mexico with no money or way to contact her U.S. family.⁸

An investigation conducted by John Crewdson of the *New York Times* revealed that abuses weren't one-offs but part of a pattern, encouraged and committed by officers up the chain of command.⁹ The violence was both gratuitous and systemic, including "stress" techniques later associated with the war in Iraq. Migrants were stripped naked and placed for extended periods in extremely cold rooms. Others, being sent back to Mexico, were handcuffed to cars and made to run alongside to the border. Patrollers pushed "illegals off cliffs"—done, a patrol agent told a journalist, "so it would look like an accident."¹⁰

Officers in the patrol's parent agency, the Immigration and Naturalization Service, traded young Mexican women they caught at the border to the Los Angeles Rams in exchange for season tickets, and supplied Mexican prostitutes to U.S. congressmen and judges, paying for them out of funds the service used to compensate informants. Agents also worked closely with Texas agriculturalists, delivering workers to their ranches (including to one owned by Lyndon Baines Johnson when he was in the White House), then raiding the ranches just before payday and deporting the workers. "The ranchers got their crops harvested for free, the INS men got fishing and hunting privileges on the ranches, and the Mexicans got nothing," Crewdson wrote.

Agents reminded captives that they were subject to their will: "In this place you have no rights."¹¹ The border patrol institutionalized impunity, operating with little oversight. The remoteness of much of

the border region and the harshness of its terrain, the work that strad-
dled the line between foreign and domestic power, and the fact that
many of the patrollers were themselves veterans of foreign wars (or
hailed from regions with fraught racial relations, including the borderlands themselves) all contributed to a "fortress mentality," as one officer put it.[12] Patrollers easily imagined their isolated substations to be
frontier forts in hostile territory, holding off barbarians.[13] They wielded
awesome power over desperate people with little effective recourse.
Most captured migrants, beaten or threatened with a beating, signed
"voluntary departure agreements" and were "quickly repatriated."[14]
Between 1982 and 1990, Mexico City sent at least twenty-four protests to the U.S. State Department on behalf of Mexicans injured or
murdered by border patrol agents.[15]

Just as soldiers use racial epithets for the people they are fighting
overseas, border patrollers had a word for their adversaries: "tonks."
Pressed by lawyers in an abuse case to say what the word meant, patroller
after patroller claimed they didn't know. Finally, one witness admitted
that *tonk* is "the sound a flashlight makes when you hit someone over
the head."[16]

In neighborhoods filled with undocumented residents, the patrol
operated with the latitude of an occupying army. "Mind your own fucking business, lady, and go back into your house," one patroller ordered
a resident in Stockton, California, who came out on her balcony to see
him "kicking a Mexican male who was handcuffed and lying face-
down on the ground."[17] Agent power was limited by no constitutional
clause. There was no place patrollers couldn't search, no property
belonging to migrants they couldn't seize.[18] And there was hardly any-
body they couldn't kill, provided it was a poor Mexican. Between 1985
and 1990, federal agents shot forty migrants around San Diego alone,
killing twenty-two of them. On April 18, 1986, for instance, patroller
Edward Cole was beating fourteen-year-old Eduardo Carrillo Estrada
on the U.S. side of the border's chain-link fence when he stopped and
shot Eduardo's younger brother, Humberto, in the back. Humberto was
standing on the other side of the fence, on Mexican soil. A court ruled
that Cole, who had previous incidents of shooting through the fence at

Mexicans, had reason to fear for his life from Humberto and used justifiable force.[19]

It wasn't just the federal border patrol that engaged in such sadism, but local law enforcement as well. In 1980, a Texas lawyer affiliated with the United Farm Workers obtained videos of seventy-two interrogations of migrants that took place over the course of the previous seven years, recorded by the police department in McAllen, Texas. The images were disturbing: police took turns beating one handcuffed Mexican man, bashing his head on the concrete floor, punching, kicking, and cursing as he pleaded for mercy.[20] The tapes were made for enjoyment: as the officers gathered "night after night," they drank beer and watched "playbacks" of their interrogation sessions. It was, said one of the men involved, a bonding ritual used to initiate new recruits.[21]

Such was the border in the 1980s and 1990s, a zone of lawless violence and impunity over a century in the making. For the most part, though, the borderlands, with all their seething racism and militarized and paramilitarized cruelty, remained apart, a world away from the American heartland. News from the border, no matter how bloody, stayed beyond the nation's consciousness as Ronald Reagan once again launched the United States beyond the frontier and Bill Clinton made his pitch that no line separated U.S. interests from the world's interests.

2.

But the violence began to break through around 2000. Increasingly, reports of the vigilantism that had long existed but had long been ignored started drawing national attention.

Witnesses began to report seeing men wearing camouflage and driving civilian vehicles, shooting and killing migrants.[22] The body of one unidentified male was found with rope burns around his neck, as if lynched. Posses were capturing Mexicans and marching them by the score in coffles to be turned over to the border patrol. U.S. RANCHERS TAKE UP ARMS, ran a headline in the *Christian Science Monitor*.[23]

Soon, anonymous flyers were being distributed among campgrounds in the Southwest, inviting outsiders to bring their RVs, guns, and halogen spotlights to have some "fun in the sun" by joining a "Neighborhood Ranch Watch." By early 2001, the border started to attract even more white supremacists, Nazis, nativists, and members of the militia groups that had, after the first Gulf War, spread throughout the Midwest and West.

Then, suddenly, 9/11 interrupted this gathering of the tribes. The nation mobilized for war, first in Afghanistan and then Iraq. As it did, vigilantism declined. The attacks on the Pentagon and the World Trade Center were galvanizing, giving the country a renewed sense of purpose after what many had identified as a decade of post–Cold War self-indulgence. Earlier, many liberals and conservatives had pitched NAFTA as providing this purpose, as a continuation of the country's frontier universalism, a way to resist the temptations of isolation. But once the agreement was signed into law, a kind of deflation set in. There had been other treaties to support, including the one creating the World Trade Organization. But free trade, or at least its implementation, is ultimately small-bore, utilitarian stuff. The terms of economic agreements—establishing the minutiae of duty schedules, for example, or defining the distinction between cellulosic and starch ethanol—aren't matters that give meaning to national life. And a decade of free trade had neither created an international community of prosperous, peaceful nations nor overcome domestic political divisions. After the contested 2000 presidential election, the country was more polarized than ever.

And so, in the months after the terrorist attacks, the same political class that said that passing NAFTA was the moral equivalent of the frontier now said the same thing about invading Afghanistan and Iraq. The "Global War on Terror," as the United States' post-9/11 campaign came to be called, offered a chance for the nation to turn away from the border and look out at the world anew. The mission was re-sanctified. "We will extend the frontiers of freedom," George W. Bush pledged in the summer of 2004.

By that point, the extent of the catastrophe was coming into view.

Had the occupations of Afghanistan and Iraq not gone so wrong, perhaps Bush might have been able to contain the growing racism within his party's rank and file by channeling it into his Middle East crusade, the way Ronald Reagan broke up the most militant nativist vigilantes in the 1980s by focusing their attention on Central America. For over a century, from Andrew Jackson forward, the country's political leaders enjoyed the benefit of being able to throw its restless and angry citizens—of the kind who had begun mustering on the border in the year before 9/11—outward, into campaigns against Mexicans, Native Americans, Filipinos, and Nicaraguans, among other enemies.

But the occupations did go wrong. Bush and his neoconservative advisors had launched what has now become the most costly war in the nation's history, on the heels of pushing through one of the largest tax cuts in the nation's history. They were following the precedent set by Reagan, who in the 1980s had slashed taxes even as he increased the military budget until deficits went sky-high.[24] Yet news coming in from Baghdad, Fallujah, Basra, Anbar Province, Bagram, and elsewhere began to suggest that Bush had created an epic disaster. Politicians and policy intellectuals began to debate what was and wasn't torture and to insist that whatever "enhanced interrogation" was, the U.S. had a right to do it. Photographs from Abu Ghraib prison showing U.S. personnel cheerfully taunting and torturing Iraqis circulated widely, followed by reports of other forms of cruelty inflicted on prisoners by U.S. troops. Many people were coming to realize that the war was not just illegal in conception but deceptive in its justification, immoral in execution, and corrupt in its administration.

Every president from Reagan onward had raised the ethical stakes, insisting that what they called "internationalism"—be it murderous wars in impoverished third world countries or corporate trade treaties—was a moral necessity. But the disillusionment generated by Bush's war on terrorism, the velocity with which events revealed the whole operation to be a sham, was extraordinary. As was the dissonance. The war, especially the war to bring democracy to Iraq, was said to mark a new era of national purpose. And yet a coordinated campaign of deceit, carried out with the complicity of reporters working for the country's most respected news sources, had to be waged to ensure public support. The toppling of Saddam Hussein was to be a "cakewalk," and U.S. soldiers, said Vice President Dick Cheney, would "be greeted as liberators." But Cheney still insisted he needed to put into place a global network of secret torture sites in order to win the fight against terror. As thousands died and billions went missing, the vanities behind not just the war but the entire post–Cold War expansionist project—of more, more, more—came to a definitive end.

With the frontier closed, some turned back to the border. Sporadic violence—for instance, in Yuma County in 2004 a white supremacist killed a migrant while "hunting down Mexicans"—gave way to organized paramilitary extremism.[25] War revanchism usually takes place after wars end—the KKK after World War I, for example, or the radicalization of white supremacism after Vietnam. Now, though, it took shape as the war was still going on. And border paramilitarism began to pull in not only soldiers who had returned from this war but veterans of older conflicts, whose fears about the influx of migrants concerned not just the current war but all wars.

Vietnam vet Jim Gilchrist, for example, recalls the moment when, around the time the Abu Ghraib scandal broke, he had the idea to create a volunteer organization to secure the border. "Things came out that were in my head swimming around for years," Gilchrist said. "It was a culmination of fears building up." He asked, "What did all these people die for in World War II, Korea, and Vietnam?" It wasn't for open borders, to let in so many migrants that the United States would "turn into a country of mayhem."[26] Shortly after this realization, in early 2005, Gilchrist helped found the Minuteman Project, which began patrolling the desert looking for undocumented migrants. The project grew rapidly over the next three years, even as it splintered into different groups, among them the American Border Patrol, Mountain Minutemen, and the California Minutemen.

"Hunting down Mexicans" is old sport in the United States, going back at least to the years after the signing of the Guadalupe Hidalgo Treaty, when Mexican officials used that exact expression in their complaint to Washington about "committees of armed men" robbing and killing Mexicans in Texas.[27] Now the hunt was nationalized. Minuteman franchises started to harass day laborers gathered on city street corners far from the border, in places like Long Island's East End.[28] One mid-western detachment targeted Latinos in city parks. "The border is no longer in the desert," the founder of Kansas City's "Heart of America" Minuteman Civil Defense Corps chapter said. "It is all over America." By the end of 2006, according to one count, one hundred forty Minuteman branches had been established in thirty-four states.[29] At its height, the Minuteman Project alone claimed twelve thousand members, many of them veterans, retired border patrol agents, and other law-enforcement officers. It was also around this time, as Afghanistan and Iraq worsened, that Maricopa County's Sheriff Joe Arpaio shifted his focus away from a general law-and-order hard line to specifically target Mexican American communities and migrant workers. Throughout the country, violence directed at Latinos shot up.[30]

3.

As Bush lost control of his occupations, he lost control of his party. Having gotten their tax cuts and their wars, Republicans were struggling with the fallout from both. Many at the time thought that modern conservatism was on the wane, done in by its own ideological excess, a contradictory commitment to a militarized national security state and libertarian economics, to its fetish of individual freedom and its stoking of the culture war, including racial grievances. Bush won reelection in 2004. But the lesson many party leaders took from the victory—as they looked at the changing demographics of states like Arizona, Texas, and Florida—was once again that Republicans, to stay viable on a national level, would have to win over Latino voters. To that end, the White House hoped to replicate Reagan's immigration gambit. It put forth legislation that would further militarize the border but also allow, for those undocumented residents who qualified, a one-time path to citizenship.

The proposed reform electrified vigilantes, who mobilized to oppose

the legislation. This, in turn, revived the flagging conservative movement. A blast of nativist fanaticism helped to stay an unraveling
caused by the movement's already existing fanaticism, providing
new coherence, vitality, and a way forward that didn't include citizenship for millions of undocumented residents. "The struggle turns
inward," as the historian Richard Slotkin wrote, imagining a moment
when the United States would no longer possess the ability of regen-
erating itself through frontier violence; "Wars are followed by witch-
hunts."[31]

Vigilantes formed the core of a larger anti-migrant coalition, which
included growing numbers of allies in state legislatures and the U.S.
Congress: Alabama senator Jeff Sessions, relatives of victims of crimes
committed by undocumented migrants, families of soldiers killed in
action, returning veterans, and members of law enforcement, including border patrol agents.[32] Leaders of the Minuteman Project appeared
regularly on Fox News and talk radio to demand that Bush, instead of
pushing "amnesty," deploy the National Guard to the border and build
a wall along its entire length.

Bush tried to placate this rank-and-file rebellion by yet further
hardening the border. The 2006 Secure Fence Act appropriated billions of dollars to pay for drones, a "virtual wall," aerostat blimps,
radar, helicopters, watchtowers, surveillance balloons, razor ribbon,
landfill to block canyons, border berms, adjustable barriers to compensate for shifting dunes, and a lab (located at Texas A&M and run
in partnership with Boeing) to test fence prototypes. The number of
border agents doubled, and the length of border fencing quadrupled.
Operation Streamline detained, prosecuted, and tried migrants en
masse and then expedited their deportation (mostly using the immigration reform law Clinton signed in 1996). Agents from Immigration and Customs Enforcement (or ICE, as the post-9/11 reorganized
border patrol was called) seized children off school buses and
tracked undocumented residents deep in liberal states, including in the
Hamptons, New York, and in New Bedford, Massachusetts. All told,
throughout his eight years in office, Bush deported two million people.

To no avail. In 2007, the party's nativist wing killed his immigration bill.

"A police state is not the answer," General Leonard Chapman, the head of Nixon's and Ford's INS, had warned three decades earlier, of what it would mean for policy makers to continue to chase the illusion that the border could be completely sealed. John Crewdson, the *New York Times* journalist who reported on much of the border abuse described at the beginning of this chapter, also asked: "Who wants an American KGB?"[33] If despotism ever came to the United States, Chapman and Crewdson were saying in their own ways, it wouldn't be due to the usual explanations offered by the left and the right, in reaction to either a threatening workers' movement or the expansion of the nanny state. It would be the result of the country's exceptional border, of its impossible-to-satisfy desire to secure that border—a border that was policed not because of national security concerns but because "it is the demarcation between such desperate poverty and such massive wealth."[34]

In the years since, Chapman's and Crewdson's warnings have proved prophetic. "We have no intention of breaking up families of those who are already here," said Chapman in 1976.[35] But as immigration policy hardened over the decades, the breaking up of families and the targeting of children has occurred with increasing frequency. And still it wasn't enough for the border brutalists.

In the last months of the Bush presidency, with the grassroots rage that had assembled on the border spreading through the nation, and the country bogged down in Afghanistan and Iraq, the housing and credit markets began to collapse. Banks failed. Mortgage foreclosures and evictions spiked. Inequality and personal debt deepened as social services stretched thin. And still, no matter how many patrollers the government put at the border, no matter how many deportations Bush carried out, Mexicans and Central Americans kept arriving. As the historian Gordon Wood said of the Jacksonian period, everything seemed to be coming apart, unraveling. The main difference, though, was that the Jacksonians looked beyond the settlement line and saw nothing but possibility; the promise of free land, and all that went with it, allowed the nation to stitch itself back up. Now the United States looked out and saw nothing but peril.

And then the country elected a black man to the presidency.

4.

Barack Obama faced antagonism that, over the course of his eight years in office, seemed possessed by the ghosts of the Confederacy, along with those of the Mexican–American War, the Texas Secession, all the way back to the Paxton Boys. A number of historians have noted that the same people who hated Obama loved Andrew Jackson, described by more than one scholar as the first "Tea Party President."[36] That makes sense, for the intensity of the emotions stems from the same source: the frontier. Both presidents came up on the outer edge of the wave, the hither side of the nation's outermost jurisdiction: Jackson in the Cumberland Gap and western lands; Obama in Hawaii and Indonesia (a nation securely in the United States' sphere of Cold War influence). The difference, though, is that Jackson, as a cultural symbol, represented the settlers who drove the frontier forward, who won a larger liberty by dispossessing and enslaving people of color, a liberty that was then defined in opposition to the people they dispossessed and enslaved. Obama, the country's first African American president, invoked their victims, and so his opponents seized on the idea that he was an alien, raised, if not born, beyond the boundary.

Obama's election "packed an emotional wallop," as the historian Daniel Rodgers put it. But his administration produced "only a policy whimper," seeking to address the multiple calamities inherited from his predecessor not with radical solutions but on familiar terms. Major legislative initiatives—those that became law, like the Affordable Care Act and financial regulation, and those that didn't, such as a carbon cap-and-trade plan—were well within the bounds of what many Republicans not too long in the past would have found acceptable.[37] The Republican Party could have acceded to implementing in full the agenda

Obama laid out in any one of his eight State of the Union addresses, and yet little would have improved the precarious condition of the many millions who lived in poverty. Most striking was the Obama administration's refusal to think beyond 1990s-style free trade. Former NAFTA boosters, including the economist Paul Krugman, had turned skeptical, starting to notice the country's long-term wage stagnation. The "spoils of globalization," the New York Times admitted, have "gone disproportionally to the wealthy."[38] And yet Obama pushed through trade agreements with Panama, Colombia, and South Korea.[39] He kept reaching for a center that no longer existed, that he seemed to think he could reconstitute by the power of his rhetoric and the infiniteness of his patience.

In the meantime, the nativist right continued to coalesce. Under Bush, the diverse border vigilante groups expanded nationally and helped set federal policy. Under Obama, they merged with other right-wing organizations into what became known as the Tea Party.[40] Cross-fertilization occurred at every level, as anti-migrant Republicans rebranded themselves libertarians and anti-Latino organizations mobilized around fiscal "responsibility." Border Minutemen joined the Bundy family militia (which engaged in two armed standoffs on public land with federal authorities), while militia members did border reconnaissance with the Minutemen. In places like Cochise County, Arizona, long a preserve of right-wing rancher vigilantism, the Minutemen and the Tea Party merged.[41] "Build a wall and start shooting," said one featured speaker at a 2010 Phoenix rally. "Line 'em up. I'll torture them myself," he said. Cruelty, by this point, was a way of establishing symbolic dominance over foreigners. But it was also a badge of contempt for the political establishment and all its leaders and institutions.

The wars went on, and the military, with its outsized budget, still served as the country's most effective instrument of social mobility and provider of health care and education. But whereas Bush had framed militarism as an ideological struggle, Obama presented it as a matter of utility and competence.[42] As he did so, the country lost its ability to channel extremism outward, and the kind of chaos the United States had released in the Persian Gulf was increasingly mirrored at home, in an escalating spiral of jihadist massacres, mass school shootings, and white-supremacist and masculinist rampages.[43]

5.

By 2010, the United States had lost something more than the ability to vent extremism. For over a century, foreign relations had served as the arena where normative ideas about how to best organize society got worked out, where national leaders could harmonize potential conflicting interests between, say, the individual and society, or virtue and ambition. They could point outward and say that there, beyond the frontier, we'd rise above our differences.[44] When Bill Clinton started campaigning for NAFTA, the world, with the Soviet Union gone, was wide open, which made his insistence that free trade would lead to civic renewal sound credible and the claim that the treaty was the "moral equivalent of the frontier in the nineteenth century" hard to argue with.

Obama was fenced in. The collapse of America's moral and military authority, along with the bankruptcy of the free-trade growth model, meant that there was no aspect of foreign policy that he could use to articulate a larger vision of the common good, no realm of international relations that might help him overcome the polarization tearing the nation apart: not war, not humanitarian intervention, not trade, and certainly not the Trans-Pacific Partnership, a mega–trade deal described by one critic as "NAFTA on steroids."[45] Obama began pushing the TPP just as the campaign for his successor was getting under way, confirming for critics on the left and the right that the center had little to offer except more of the same.

With the country unable to imagine a future moving outward, fights over the people trying to move inward grew even more intense. Here too Obama tried to meet his opponents halfway. He signed an executive order, the Deferred Action for Childhood Arrivals (DACA), which provided protection to some undocumented residents who had entered the country as minors. But he also increased the funding and staff of the nation's various border, customs, and immigration agencies. The White

House was making the same bet Bush did, caught in the same "enforcement first" trap laid out decades ago, which insisted that the border had to be "sealed"—an impossible proposition—before reform could be passed. Obama hoped that stepping up border security would open a space for compromise. But the situation got away from him. A "surge" of Central American children—tens of thousands every year between 2009 and 2014—began arriving at the border, mostly from El Salvador, Honduras, and Guatemala.[46] Already hit hard by Reagan's Central American wars, these countries were battered anew by Washington-backed trade, anti-drug, and security policies. One reason the children came alone was because border militarization had closed relatively safe crossing routes, making it too perilous for families to travel together as a group.

In response, the White House diverted more resources to try to secure the border and stepped up deportations.[47] By 2016, the United States was spending more on border and immigration enforcement than on all other federal law-enforcement agencies combined. Still, as it did under Bush, immigration reform failed.

As the power of ICE and the border patrol grew, its impunity continued unabated. Since 2003, patrollers have killed at least ninety-seven people, including six children. Few agents were prosecuted.[48] According to a report by the ACLU, young girls have been physically abused and threatened with rape, while unaccompanied children apprehended by the border patrol experienced "physical and psychological abuse, unsanitary and inhumane living conditions, isolation from family members, extended period of detention, and denial of access to legal medical service."[49] The same kind of stress tortures that John Crewdson documented over thirty years earlier, including migrants being placed for extended periods of time in extremely cold rooms, continued to be used.[50] One seven-year-old Salvadoran girl who was trying to reunite with her parents in Long Island was captured in Texas in 2014 after a ten-day trek. She was kept in an "ice box" for fifteen days. "It was cold, very cold," she testified. "The lights were on all the time, and the floor was hard. I couldn't sleep. . . . I was hungry all the time."[51]

It's difficult to process this litany of abuse. The horrors blend into one another, as if the closing of the frontier has brought about a collapse of a sense of time. The violence that had been associated with moving outward in the world, which gave the illusion of leaving problems behind, now just accumulates. "We slash their bottles and drain their water into the dry earth," writes a border patroller, describing what he and his coworkers did when they came upon a stash of supplies tucked away by hiding migrants. "We dump their backpacks and pile their food and clothes to be crushed and pissed on and stepped over, strewn across the desert and set ablaze."[52]

Meanwhile, as Obama reached the end of his second term, right-wing grievances continued to spin in a circle, from migrants to health care, from taxes, war, and guns to Confederate flags, ISIS, Mexican cartels, and environmental regulations, from sharia law, energy policy, and gender pronouns to Central American gangs and Black Lives Matter. And finally back to migrants, to DACA recipients and Central American children. The backlashes to decades of disastrous policies piled up, one after the other, until the backlash to the backlashes came.

The nativism that rallied at the border under George Bush, and that for eight years was expressed in an almost psychotropic hatred of Barack Obama, crystallized into what some have described as "race realism": a rejection of the legitimating premises of the liberal multilateral order—especially the idea that all could sit at the table and enjoy the world's abundance, that the global economy should be organized around lines as open as possible, and that diversity rather than, say, Anglo-Saxonism, could serve as the foundation of political communities.* The frontier was closed, as Clare Boothe Luce wrote half a century earlier, resources were finite, and political systems should be based on an acceptance of those facts.

Such a worldview is often expressed as instinct rather than a worked-

---

* According to the *Washington Post* (March 20, 2018), in focus groups conducted by the social media data-harvesting firm Cambridge Analytica prior to the 2014 midterm elections, themes related to "race realism," including a proposal to build a "wall to block the entry of illegal immigrants," tested well among alienated "white Americans with a conservative bent."

out philosophy and has taken many forms in the United States, including a reflexive sympathy for law-enforcement agencies and racial resentment. But over the last few decades, the border has provided increasing coherence to the sentiment. In July 2014, for instance, residents of Murrieta, California, just north of San Diego, took to the streets for days, waving U.S. and Gadsden flags and hurling racist slurs, trying to stop buses carrying Central American children to a nearby federal facility. "We can't take care of others if we can't take care of our own," one protester said, offering a concise précis of what would soon be called Trumpism. The buses were turned back—the children shunted into some other federal detention center—and two years later, Murrieta residents, by a large margin, voted for Donald Trump.

America's exceptionalism was born on a frontier thought to be endless. Now the only thing endless is history's endless return, as veterans travel to the borderlands to rehearse how lost wars could have been won. Jim Gilchrist, one of the founders of the Minuteman Project, came home from the war in 1968. "There's not been one day" since, he says, that he hasn't "thought about Vietnam."[53] "We go out in two-man teams and we hit them like we did forty years ago in Vietnam," said another vigilante.[54] Other veterans patrolling the border fought in Iraq, in either the first or second Gulf War, or in Afghanistan—or in any of the other seventy-four countries where the United States has been conducting military operations since 2015.

Frederick Turner thought the ninety-ninth meridian, the place where the prairie meets the desiccated plains, as good a place as any to symbolically mark the frontier. Beyond this line, tenacious, inventive men started to figure out ways to irrigate dry land and began to think of history as progress, as moving forward toward an ever more bountiful future. It was here where the United States became liberal and internationalist, where it learned how to "feed the world."[55] The novelist Cormac McCarthy called this line the "blood meridian" and thought it signaled a different kind of boundary, across which the conceit of progress gave way to an infernal timelessness, to a land "filled with violent children orphaned by war," where soldiers and settlers got caught in a dervish swirl, moving in circles going nowhere. That place used to be out there, beyond the frontier. But the United States crossed the line so many times that it erased the line.

Now the blood meridian is everywhere, nowhere more so than the border itself, a place where all of history's wars become one war. Vigilantes often describe themselves as the rear guard of the Mexican–American War of 1846–48, standing against an enemy they believe is intent on retaking land they lost at the end of that conflict.[56] "Mexican migrants are attempting a reconquest," said one of the Minuteman founders, not by force but through migration.[57] It's a resonant word, "reconquest," or *reconquista*, and often invoked by vigilantes. The Spanish originally used the term to refer to their crusade, starting in 722 and ending in 1492 (a long war if ever there was one), to retake the Iberian Peninsula from Arab and Berber Muslims. Today, the border Minutemen imagine the descendants of those Muslims coming north. They say they often spot "Middle Eastern guys with beards" and find Arabic-English dictionaries in the sand.[58] "This is our Gaza," one Minuteman told a researcher.[59]

In the last years of the Obama presidency, as fallout from Iraq worsened and Central American children arrived, vigilantism surged anew in a more aggressive form. Its ranks were filled with younger, angrier men than its earlier version, outfitted with military hardware and desert camouflage, intent on stopping "fucking beaners," obsessed equally with ISIS, Central American gangs, Mexican cartels, and Black Lives Matter.[60] Most have done multiple stints in Afghanistan and Iraq. "For me, it is therapeutic to come down here and join my fellow veterans," said one veteran, who after four tours in Iraq was left with brain injury and stress disorder.

The desert calms his nightmares. Guarding the border, he told a journalist, helps make "new memories."[61]

EPILOGUE

The Significance of the Wall
in American History

The point isn't to actually build "the wall" but to constantly announce the building of the wall. "We started building our wall. I'm so proud of it. We started," Donald Trump tweeted. "What a thing of beauty." No wall—at least nothing beyond the miles of fortification that have been steadily increasing since the presidency of Harry Truman—is being built. Eight "prototypes" for Trump's wall do rise high out of the desert, just east of San Diego, at the Otay Mesa section of the border. Supposedly, one will be selected as a design for the wall, and Trump has said he'll pick the winner himself. But the Department of Homeland Security recently announced that none of the Otay Mesa models will be the basis of whatever gets built. Rather, it seems, these mock-ups, which cost a half-million dollars each, are meant to inspire future mock-ups: "The eight different prototypes are each anticipated to inform future border wall design standards in some capacity."[1] Still, they serve as a useful backdrop to nativist politicians, when they want to attack Congress for not building the wall or to demonize migrants by highlighting some crime they are accused of committing. "Yemenis, Iraqis, Pakistanis, Chinese, name your former Soviet satellite states, they all come in through Mexico," said San Diego's Republican House member Duncan Hunter, speaking at an anti-immigrant rally in front of the structures. And the monoliths do suggest permanence, a sense that, whatever Trumpism's political future, there they'll be.

In any case, the idea of a border wall might have missed its moment, considering that what is now called "the border" is just about everywhere, much like "the frontier" used to be. Immigration and defense officials are quick to say that the United States' true border is found not in Arizona and Texas but at Mexico's southern boundary with Guatemala.[2] There, Mexican agents, subsidized by Washington, police the first line of a multitiered border against Central American migrants heading north. In fact, all of South America is our "third border," according to one defense analyst, and so, says the Pentagon, is the Caribbean.

Likewise, the immigration posts that have proliferated at airports around the world are also now considered part of the U.S. border, as are all the random inspections that take place on Amtrak and Greyhound lines and airports within the country. Federal agents have "extraconstitutional powers" in what are called "border zones," defined as one hundred miles in from international boundaries, which covers as many as two hundred million citizens—about 65 percent of the country's population, and about 75 percent of its Latino residents.[3]

All of Michigan is a "border zone," as are Hawaii and Florida. "It really is kind of a Constitution-free zone," as one policy analyst put it. Border patrollers can seize vehicles anywhere in these zones, conduct inspections, and demand to see papers.[4] An ACLU spokesperson calls the checkpoints that are installed deep in the country, miles away from the actual international border, "borders themselves," meaning that they are intentionally set up to separate families and communities. In 2008, an internet project partly funded by the state of Texas started letting anyone, anywhere, be a border patroller, putting online a live feed from over two hundred border cameras. Hundreds of thousands of people logged on, not just to report suspicious activity but to create a social media community of virtual vigilantes.[5] "Where, exactly, are the boundaries of the American 'homeland'?" asks an analyst at the

American Enterprise Institute. "All over America," says the founder of the Kansas City border watch.

Wherever they are found, the borderlands, long the pride of place in frontier mythology, are no longer special. Every country has borders and boundaries, and now many of them have walls.[6] They have gone up everywhere since the one in Berlin came down: protecting the rich in Rio, containing Palestinians in the West Bank, separating India from Bangladesh, Greece from Turkey, and Belfast's Catholics from Protestants. Just as the harsh frontier environment of the flat Texas plains spurred new technological advances—the invention of the Walker Colt revolver helped settlers "fight Comanches and Mexicans without dismounting" from their horses, as the historian Walter Prescott Webb noted—the thriving global "border wall" industry has sparked high-tech security innovations. The state of Arizona, which in 2010 passed SB 1070, the strictest anti-immigration law in the country, has turned itself into a bazaar for "security wall" merchandise, hosting international expos staffed by a new kind of border Babbitts: engineers whose research is subsidized by public money, salesmen who pitch their products to besieged states, and the techies who back them up. "In that vast, brightly lit cathedral of science fiction in Phoenix, it isn't the guns, drones, robots, or fixed surveillance towers and militarized mannequins that startle me most," wrote the journalist Todd Miller after attending a convention filled with such gadgets.[7] Rather, it was "the staggering energy and enthusiasm, so thick in the convention's air" that impressed Miller. He left the convention center realizing he had just witnessed "a burgeoning new multibillion-dollar industry that has every intention of making not just the border but this entire world of ours its own."

The "great world frontier" is how historians and economists, not too long ago, described the spread of U.S.-style democratic development. Today we have walls the world over.

For over a century, the frontier served as a powerful symbol of American universalism. It not only conveyed the idea that the country was moving forward but promised that the brutality involved in moving forward

would be transformed into something noble. Frontier expansion
would break every paradox, reconcile every contradiction between, say,
ideals and interests, virtue and ambition. Extend the sphere, and you
will ensure peace, protect individual freedom, and dilute factionalism;
you will create a curious, buoyant, resourceful people in thrall to no
received doctrine, transcend regionalism, spread prosperity, and move
beyond racism. As horizons broaden, so will our love for the world's
people. As boundaries widen, so will our tolerance, the realization that
humanity is our country. There was no problem caused by expansion
that couldn't be solved by more expansion. War-bred trauma could be
rolled over into the next war; poverty would be alleviated by more
growth.

But today the frontier is closed, the safety valve shut. Whatever
metaphor one wants to use, the country has lived past the end of its
myth. Where the frontier symbolized perennial rebirth, a culture in
springtime, those eight prototypes in Otay Mesa loom like tombstones.
After centuries of fleeing forward across the blood meridian, all the
things that expansion was supposed to preserve have been destroyed,
and all the things it was meant to destroy have been preserved. Instead
of peace, there's endless war. Instead of a critical, resilient, and progressive citizenry, a conspiratorial nihilism, rejecting reason and dreading
change, has taken hold. Factionalism congealed and won a national
election.

A few do still have access to something that looks like a frontier, as
the kind of treaties and agreements represented by NAFTA has given
corporations their own endless horizon. Recently, the World Bank took
stock of the extreme concentration of global wealth, the emergence of
new technologies that reduce the need for human labor, and the ability
of investment to move across borders at will, and gave this advice to
the world's poorer nations: you need to keep employers happy by doing
away with "burdensome" rules. Countries with "high minimum wages,
undue restrictions on hiring and firing, strict contract forms, all make
workers more expensive vis-à-vis technology" and make businesses less
likely to invest.[8] The democratic utility of the frontier—whereby an
open range provided unprecedented numbers of common people unpre-

cedented freedom, helping them resist being subordinated to "system and control"—has been completely inverted. Now corporations have Turner's "gate of escape" written into international law, which they can use to trim the regulatory ambitions of national governments.

The fantasies of the super-rich, no less than their capital, have free range. They imagine themselves sea-steaders, setting out to create floating villages beyond government control, or they fund life-extension research hoping to escape death or to upload their consciousness into the cloud. Mars, says one, will very soon be humanity's "new frontier." A hedge-fund billionaire backer of Trump who believes "human beings have no inherent value other than how much money they make" and that people on public assistance have "negative value," a man so antisocial he doesn't look people in the eye and whistles when others try to talk with him, gets to play volunteer sheriff in an old New Mexico mining town and is thereby allowed to carry a gun in all fifty states.[9] Never before has a ruling class been as free—so completely emancipated from the people it rules—as ours.

For most everyone else, the area of freedom has contracted. A whole generation—those born in the 1980s—may never recover from the Great Recession that followed the 2007–08 crash.[10] Since that crash, unemployment has declined and the stock market has boomed but poverty has become entrenched. According to a recent report by the United Way, nearly fifty-one million U.S. households don't make enough "to survive in the modern economy," their monthly budgets unable to cover basic needs such as housing, food, and health care. Ranked against other high-income countries, the United States has the lowest life expectancy and the highest infant mortality. Ronald Reagan said nothing is impossible. For many, less and less is possible, including a decent education and a dignified retirement, or any retirement.[11]

Most every other industrial nation in the world has pursued "free trade" policies similar to those enacted by the United States since its farm crisis, some combination of outsourcing, privatization, and financial liberalization. But no other wealthy nation has experienced the kind of alienation, inequality, public health crises, and violence that have become routine in the United States.[12] That's because, as part of the post-Vietnam restoration, the United States didn't just restructure but also launched an assault on the social institutions—especially public services and unions—that might have moderated the effects of the restructuring. "You're the troops," Reagan told the New Right's frontline activists working to unwind as much of the New Deal as possible. "You're out there on the frontier of freedom."

In addition to the upheavals caused by the wars in Iraq and the financial crash, there is a realization that the world is fragile and that we are trapped in an economic system that is well past sustainable or justifiable. As vast stretches of the West burn, as millions of trees die from global warming–induced blight, as Houston and Puerto Rico flood, the oceans acidify, and bats, frogs, and flying insects disappear in uncountable numbers, any sentence from Cormac McCarthy's *The Road* could be plucked and used as a newspaper headline. A VAST LANDSCAPE CHARRED, AND A SKY FULL OF SOOT ran the title of a *New York Times* report on California's wildfires.

The wars might be endless, but the mission, in any of its forms, is no longer sanctified.

It's tempting to think that Trump's border wall represents a more accurate assessment of how the world works, especially when compared to the myth of the frontier. The *frontier* was, ultimately, a mirage, an ideological relic of a now-exhausted universalism that promised, either naïvely or dishonestly, that a limitless world meant that nations didn't have to be organized around lines of domination. All could benefit; all could rise and share in the earth's riches. The wall, in contrast, is a monument to disenchantment, to a kind of brutal geopolitical realism: racism was never transcended; there's not enough to go around; the global economy will have winners and losers; not all can sit at the table; and government policies should be organized around accepting these truths.

Accepting that there are, in fact, limits to growth—that the old model of politics, based on the idea that social conflicts could be solved by a constant flight forward, is no longer viable—could lead to a variety of political responses. In the United States, the New Deal built a new, humane ethic of social citizenship by recognizing that the frontier had closed. That vision, though to a degree eclipsed by the New Right, still accounts for much of what remains decent in the country.

But in a nation like the United States, founded on a mythical belief in a kind of species immunity—less an American exceptionalism than exemptionism, an insistence that the nation was exempt from nature, society, history, even death—the realization that it can't go on forever is bound to be traumatic. This ideal of freedom as infinity was only made possible through the domination of African Americans, Mexican Americans, Mexicans, and Native Americans, as slave and cheap labor transformed stolen land into capital, cutting the tethers and launching the U.S. economy into the stratosphere. And now, as we fall back to a wasted earth, the very existence of people of color functions as an unwanted memento mori, a reminder of limits, evidence that history imposes burdens and life contracts social obligations.

And so the wall offers its own illusions, a mystification that simultaneously recognizes and refuses limits. On the one hand, Trumpism fuels resentment that the United States has been too generous, that in a world of scarcity "we can't take care of others if we can't take care of our own," as that Murrieta resident protesting the arrival of Central American children put it. On the other hand, Trumpism encourages a petulant hedonism that forbids nothing and restrains nothing—the right to own guns, of course, but also to "roll coal," for example, as the rejiggering of truck engines to burn extraordinary amounts of diesel is called. The plume of black smoke emitted by these trucks is, according to such hobbyists, a "brazen show of American freedom"— and, since 2016, a show of support for Donald Trump.[13] Pulling out of the Paris Climate Accord will do little to boost corporate profits, as many have pointed out, but it has everything to do with signaling that the United States will not submit to limits. In a world as fragile as ours, such displays of freedom become increasingly cruel, until cruelty itself becomes a "brazen show of American freedom"—lifting restrictions on killing hibernating bears, say, or pardoning Joe Arpaio, or extolling torture.

Trump's cruelty takes many such forms, but it is most consistent in its targeting of Mexicans and Central American migrants.[14] We can think of his wall as refashioning the country into a besieged medieval fortress, complete with its own revered martyrs' cult. As a candidate, Trump campaigned with the victims (or families of victims) of crimes committed by undocumented residents, using their grief to stoke aggrievement. As president, one of his first acts was to establish a government office charged with providing support services to "victims of crimes committed by removable aliens."

There's no visa program aimed to help suffering people so measly that it can't be canceled by Trump with great fanfare. A program helping a few thousand Nicaraguans was eliminated, as were similar programs for Hondurans. The director of Trump's Citizenship and Immigration Services announced that his office was going to "start denaturalizing people"—that is, seeking out mistakes in the application process that let an immigrant become a citizen, then using them to take away citizenship—even though he admits that such errors are extremely rare. Along the border, more people than ever are being denied passports, on the suspicion that their birth documents are forged and that they were actually born in Mexico. According to the *Washington Post*, under Trump, "passport applicants with official U.S. birth certificates are being jailed in immigration detention centers and entered into deportation proceedings."[15] Trump wants to go even further: he's promised to sign an executive order ending birthright citizenship, which would entail a radical narrowing of the Fourteenth Amendment to the Constitution.

And then, in the summer of 2018, with midterm elections approaching, Trump calculated that he could turn the abuse of migrant children into a winning political issue. His attorney general, Jeff Sessions, announced that families arriving at the border would be split up, with the children taken away and the parents placed in jail and prosecuted as child-smugglers. Suddenly, it was as if all the many decades of long-ignored border brutalism came bursting forth, in a unbearable torrent of stories, photographs, videos, and audio clips: caged babies wailing for their parents, children injected with drugs to force them to sleep, abandoned Walmarts converted into detention centers. Outrage forced Trump to back down from the worst of his family separation policy. But he still used the public attention to insist on "zero tolerance" and used the protests against his policies to cultivate a sense of grievance among ICE and border patrol agents. It's a "good issue," he said, citing a nonexistent poll of public support for his policies.[16] As of mid-2018, the United States was holding almost 13,000 migrant children, mostly from Mexico and Central America, in borderland detention centers, a nearly tenfold increase from the previous year.[17]

Trump won by running against the entire legacy of the postwar order, including those policies that have generated, in the countries south of the border as well as in the Middle East, untold numbers of refugees (and, as might be expected, criminals): endless war, austerity, "free trade," unfettered corporate power, and extreme inequality.[18] Two years into his tenure, the war has expanded, the bombing has escalated, and the Pentagon's budget has increased. Taxes have been cut, deregulation accelerated, and the executive branch is staffed by ideologues who want to deregulate even more.

Public lands and resources are being privatized, tax cuts are continuing the class war against the poor, and judicial and executive agency appointments will increase monopoly rule. Unable to offer an alternative other than driving the existing agenda forward at breakneck speed, Trumpism cultivates an enraged refusal of limits—his appeal, to many, is his impunity, as Trump himself often points out—even as his pledge to build a border wall is founded on the idea that the world does have limits.

Whether that wall gets built or not, it is America's new symbol. It stands for a nation that still thinks "freedom" means freedom from restraint, but no longer pretends, in a world of limits, that everyone can be free—and enforces that reality through cruelty, domination, and racism.

Maybe after Trump is gone, what is understood as the political "center" can be reestablished. But it seems doubtful. Politics appears to be moving in two opposite directions. One way, nativism beckons; Donald Trump, for now, is its standard-bearer. The other way, socialism calls to younger voters who, burdened by debt and confronting a bleak labor market, are embracing social rights in numbers never before seen. Coming generations will face a stark choice—a choice long deferred by the emotive power of frontier universalism but set forth in vivid relief by recent events: the choice between barbarism and socialism, or at least social democracy.

A NOTE ON SOURCES AND OTHER MATTERS

RACE REALISM AND THE WALL

In a short story published in 1950, "The Wall and the Books," Jorge Luis Borges tells of Emperor Shih Huang Ti, who ordered China's Great Wall built and all the books in his kingdom burned. It's Borges, so every reason he gives for these two seemingly contradictory desires—to create and to destroy—is followed by another explanation that cancels out the first. Borges finally settles on the idea that both the building and the burning were driven by the emperor's desire to "halt death." Shih Huang Ti, at least according to Borges, lived in terror of mortality, prohibiting the word "death" from being uttered in his presence and searching desperately for an elixir of youth. Maybe, Borges guessed, Shih Huang Ti ordered the wall built to preserve his realm for eternity and the books burned to suppress the idea that nothing lasts for eternity. For if the history contained in books teaches anything, it is that our time on earth is fleeting. The emperor apparently sentenced anyone who tried to save a book to a lifetime of forced labor on his wall. "Perhaps the wall was a metaphor," Borges writes, since its construction "condemned those who adored the past to a task as vast, as stupid, and as useless as the past itself."

As to the United States, the biologist Garrett Hardin, a tenured professor at the University of California, Santa Barbara, was among the first to call for a wall to be built on the border with Mexico. "We might build a wall, literally," Hardin wrote in a 1977 essay titled "Population and Immigration: Compassion or Responsibility?" published in *The Ecologist*. Hardin was an early exponent of what today is called "race realism," the idea that a world of limited resources and declining white birth rates calls for hardened borders. Hardin's 1971 editorial in *Science*, titled "The Survival of Nations and Civilizations," makes the case:

> Can a government of men persuade women that it is their patriotic duty to emulate the rabbits? Or force them? If we renounce conquest and overbreeding, our survival in a competitive world depends on what kind of world it is: One World, or a world of national territories. If the world is one great commons, in which all food is shared equally, then we are lost. Those who breed faster will replace the rest. . . . In a less than perfect world, the allocation of rights based on territory must be defended if a ruinous breeding race is to be avoided. It is unlikely that civilization and dignity can survive everywhere; but better in a few places than in none.

Two centuries earlier, Benjamin Franklin and Thomas Jefferson were rhapsodic when they contemplated New World bountifulness: the idea that growth, including rapid population growth, would soon double "the numbers of mankind, and of course the quantum of existence and happiness." Self-styled "realists" such as Hardin made explicit what in Jefferson and Franklin was implicit: such joy was reserved exclusively for Anglo growth. Hardin would go on to describe his position as "lifeboat ethics," the idea that oars should be used not just as paddles but weapons, to swat away others trying to climb up on the boat. He would later advocate the "race science" of *The Bell Curve*.

Over the last few decades, as anti-migrant nativism has revitalized the conservative movement, the right has built a library of follow-up manifestos. Some of the early publications emerged out of the post-Vietnam "end of plenty" literature, and reveal overlap between the concerns of environmentalists, population controllers, English-language defenders, and anti-immigrant nativists. Hardin is an example of this overlap, as is John Tanton, who in the 1970s wrote an essay arguing for eugenics and helped found the nativist Federation for American Immigration Reform. Elena R. Gutiérrez, *Fertile Matters: The Politics of Mexican-Origin Women's Reproduction* (2009), discusses the increasing obsession of immigration restrictionists like Tanton with Mexican fertility rates. See also Laura Briggs, *How All Politics Became Reproductive Politics* (2017).

The novelist and environmentalist Edward Abbey, author of *The Monkey Wrench Gang*, had already expressed concerns about population growth, the rising birth rates of people of color, and the "Latinization" of the U.S. when in 1981 he called for the creation of a "physical barrier" and an expansion of the border patrol to include up to twenty thousand agents (a number that was considered a radical proposal at the time but today is only about half of the agents working for the border patrol and ICE combined). "These are harsh, even cruel propositions," said Abbey. But echoing Hardin, he wrote in a letter to the *New York Review of Books* (December 17, 1981) that the "American boat is full, if not already overloaded; we cannot afford further mass immigration. The American public is aware of this truth even if our 'leaders' prefer to attempt to ignore it. We know what they will not acknowledge." As xenophobia became a more central element of the conservative right, environmentalists, both mainstream and radical, moved away from linking their social critique to immigration concerns. Murray Bookchin, in 1988, called Abbey racist. See also Luis Alberto Urrea's criticism, "Down the Highway with Edward Abbey," in *Nobody's Son: Notes from an American Life* (1998).

Patrick Buchanan did the most to popularize the idea of a barrier on the southern border in his 1992 nomination challenge to George H. W. Bush. Today, most conservative personalities, such as Ann Coulter and the like, publish at least one anti-migrant call to arms. Earlier contributions to the genre include Palmer Stacy and Wayne Lutton, *The Immigration Time Bomb* (1985); Wayne Lutton, *The Myth of Open Borders* (1988); Lawrence Auster, *The Path to National Suicide* (1990); Roy Howard Beck, *The Case Against Immigration* (1996);

Peter Brimelow, *Alien Nation* (1996); John Tanton and Joseph Smith, *Immigration and the Social Contract* (1996); Samuel Francis, *America Extinguished* (2001); Buchanan, *The Death of the West* (2002); and Victor Davis Hanson, *Mexifornia* (2003). Also worth mentioning is Harvard political scientist Samuel Huntington's respectfully received *Who Are We? The Challenges to America's National Identity* (2004). Daniel Denvir's forthcoming *All-American Nativism* is an important overview of the rise of anti-migrant extremism.

The decision of the Republican Party to focus on suppressing the vote of Latinos and other people of color was based on mundane calculations: that if voter registration, turnout, and preference trends continued as they had been, then the Republican Party was in danger of losing Texas, Arizona, and Florida, along with its status as a national-level political organization. For voter suppression, as well as its targeting of Latinos, see Gregory Downs, "Today's Voter Suppression Tactics Have a 150 Year History," *Talking Points Memo* (July 26, 2018), and Ari Berman, "The Man Behind Trump's Voter-Fraud Obsession," *New York Times* (June 13, 2017). Rick Perlstein and Livia Gershon document Republican Party efforts at voter suppression of minority votes going back to 1961, including in Arizona's now infamous Maricopa County, where the future chief justice of the Supreme Court William Rehnquist ran Operation Eagle Eye, which forced "every black or Mexican voter" to take a literacy test and read a passage from the Constitution—an initiative that was expanded statewide, with the help of nearly all of the state's sheriffs, during Barry Goldwater's 1966 presidential run. Perlstein and Gershon, "Stolen Elections, Voting Dogs and Other Fantastic Fables from the GOP Voter Fraud Mythology," *Talking Points Memo* (August 16, 2018).

But there's an excess to the hatred, directed as it is at people who largely represent the ideals that nativists claim they value. Throughout the United States, Latinos have been re-energizing neighborhoods and populating downtowns, opening stores and pumping money into established small businesses. Strip-mall America would be even more barren if it weren't for Mexicans and Central Americans who have turned empty stores into *taquerías*, *carnicerías*, *pupuserías*, and other enterprises. It's

almost as if, by forcing Latinos into the shadows, the right wants to finish the hollowing-out started years ago with the ascendance of corporate
globalization. The hatred is also rooted, I think, in the kind of terror of
mortality that Borges attributed to Shih Huang Ti. Put simply, the United
States' dependence on the labor of people of color confirms the social
basis of existence, and thus the legitimacy of social rights. In a political
culture that considers individual rights sacrosanct, social rights are something viler than heresy. They imply limits, and limits violate the uniquely
American premise that it is all going to go on forever.

The fact alone that many Latin American Walmarts are unionized
should put an end to one of Ronald Reagan's favorite clichés: that Latinos were Republicans who didn't yet know it. After Barack Obama's
2012 re-election, many conservatives came to realize that neither appeals
to cultural wedge issues nor promises of immigration reform would
necessarily help the Republican Party when it came to Latino voters.
Latino voters are not loyal to Democrats because of the promise of
immigration reform, the *National Review*'s Heather MacDonald wrote,
but because they value "a more generous safety net, strong government
intervention in the economy, and progressive taxation." Over at the
American Enterprise Institute, Charles Murray agreed that Latinos were
not inherently conservative. They aren't more religious than other
groups, Murray pointed out, nor are they more homophobic, and they
are only marginally more opposed to abortion than the population at
large (though Murray did say that the Latino laborers who tend to his
house seem to be "hard-working and competent," which he took to be
synonymous with conservative).

Such realizations helped tip the balance of power within the Republican Party to the forces of what is now called Trumpism. In the wake
of George W. Bush's disastrous presidency, movement conservatives,
hamstrung by their own ideological excess and sensing they were losing a broader culture war, seized on the demonization of migrants (and
of naturalized Mexican and Central American citizens) as a way to
account for setbacks without having to resort to moderation. Right-
wing activists, thinkers, and politicians held Reagan's 1986 immigration reform, which provided a path to citizenship for about three million

undocumented residents, responsible not just for the Democratic takeover of California but for Barack Obama's election and reelection to the presidency. According to this line of thinking, Reagan's amnesty added (as a result of naturalized citizens being able to sponsor other family members for citizenship) fifteen million new citizens to the voting rolls. Republican representative Steve King, a leading nativist ideologue in the House, said that this supposed increase "brought about Barack Obama's election." Prior to the 2016 election, a majority of Republicans believed that millions of "illegal immigrants" had voted in 2008 and 2012 and were planning to do so again in 2016. There is no evidence to support any of these claims, yet such arguments justify ongoing efforts to suppress the vote of people of color. Recently, Fox's Tucker Carlson used such an argument to downplay Russian interference in U.S. domestic politics, accusing Mexico of "routinely interfering in our elections by packing our electorate."

THE FRONTIER

The literature on the U.S. frontier, along with scholarship on the Frontier Thesis, is vast. In addition to studies cited throughout, these books have been, in different ways, especially helpful: Patricia Limerick, *The Legacy of Conquest* (1987), and *The Frontier in American Culture* (1994), edited by James Grossman, with essays by Richard White and Patricia Limerick. Richard Slotkin's multivolume studies on the role of frontier violence in making and remaking American culture, starting with *Regeneration Through Violence* (1973), was indispensable. For the evolution of the idea: John Juricek, "American Usage of the Word 'Frontier' from Colonial Times to Frederick Jackson Turner," *Proceedings of the American Philosophical Society* (1966). Also: Warren Susman, *Culture as History* (1984); Sarah Deutsch, *No Separate Refuge: Culture, Class, and Gender on the Anglo-Hispanic Frontier in the American Southwest, 1880–1940* (1987); Richard White, *It's Your Misfortune and None of My Own: A New History of the American West* (1991); George Rogers Taylor, ed., *The Turner Thesis: Concerning the*

Role of the Frontier in American History (1972); Amy Greenberg, *Manifest Manhood and the Antebellum American Empire* (2005); Kerwin Lee Klein, *Frontiers of Historical Imagination* (1997); Adam Rothman, *Slave Country: American Expansion and the Origins of the Deep South* (2007); Walter Johnson, *River of Dark Dreams: Slavery and Empire in the Cotton Kingdom* (2013); Walter Prescott Webb, *The Great Frontier* (1952); and Henry Nash Smith, *Virgin Land* (1950). Patricia Limerick ("Turnerians All: The Dream of a Helpful History in an Intelligible World," *American Historical Review* [June 1995], vol. 100, no. 3, pp. 697–716) points out that Turner's thesis contains within itself what she calls the "Frontier Antithesis" and that every effort to move beyond Turner stumbles over the fact that such an effort is already in Turner.

THE BORDER

Equally vast is the scholarship, more important than ever, on the U.S.-Mexican border, the wider borderlands, NAFTA, and the militarization of immigration policy. Here, rather than name specific books or articles that are cited in the text, I want to acknowledge scholars who have been especially influential to this work: Liz Oglesby, Mae Ngai, Dara Lind, Kelly Lytle Hernández, John Crewdson, Ana Raquel Minan, Anabel Hernández, Douglas Massey, Karl Jacoby, Robin Reineke, Rachel St. John, Oscar Martínez, Adam Goodman, Natalia Molina, Samuel Truett, Elliot Young, David Bacon, Paul Kershaw, Todd Miller, Rebecca Schreiber, Paul Ortiz, Alicia Schmidt Camacho, Joseph Nevins, Patrick Timmons, Timothy Dunn, and the scholars of the *Refusing to Forget* memory project: Ben Johnson, Trinidad Gonzales, Monica Muñoz Martinez, Sonia Hernández, and John Morán González. Published after this book was finished, Monica Muñoz Martinez's *The Injustice Never Leaves You: Anti-Mexican Violence in Texas* provides a formidable challenge to the hagiography of the Texas Rangers, which, as the author shows, operated for much of its history like what, in other countries, would be called a death squad.

THE SAFETY VALVE

Starting in the early 1800s, there have been many versions of the argument that liberal capitalist democracy *requires* expansion to survive. In the early nineteenth century, British conservatives said that the reason why the United States was able to extend the vote to white workers was that it had the "safety-valve" of the wide-open West, which would weaken the threat that they would use the vote to vote in socialism. Over the centuries, other writers have stressed different kinds of expansion (landed, economic, ideological, political, and martial) along with the different social ills that expansion would solve (the overproduction and/or underconsumption of manufactured goods, population pressure, class conflict, property-rights-threatening radicalism, capitalist alienation, modernist ennui, and civic decay, among other maladies).

Frederick Jackson Turner was influenced, as a number of historians have shown, by Georg Wilhelm Friedrich Hegel. Born in Stuttgart six years before the signing of the Declaration of Independence, Hegel was both a philosopher of *dependency* (of individuals moving to a higher level of consciousness as they come to recognize their dependence on the people around them) and of *escape*. There was no internal solution, Hegel said, to the problem of "excessive wealth" and "excessive rabble." And so the philosopher who once posited master and slave locked in a psychic conflict as the parable of what the path to true freedom might look like now urged modern economic man to give in to his "inner dialectic" and flee forward to evade the conflict. Turner might also have drawn his civil society/state division from Hegel, who identified the United States as the only republic in the world that had expansion built into its foundational premise. With "no neighboring State," Hegel wrote in the early 1820s, the United States "has the outlet of colonization constantly and widely open, and multitudes are continually streaming into the plains of the Mississippi," ensuring the sources of discord are dispersed. Hegel, foreshadowing Turner, describes the Mississippi River valley as an ideal of civil society, as a vast integrated network of trade and trust where virtue existed *prior* to the arrival of the state.

Where Hegel offered a parable of master and slave, Marx theorized capitalism as a history of social alienation, of individuals and families losing control over their means of subsistence and becoming dependent on wages and obligated to pay rent. Marx, who once considered immigrating to pre–Civil War Texas, was, like Hegel and Turner, aware of the importance of the United States in the history of capitalism. "With the accumulation of rents in Ireland," he wrote in *Capital*, published in 1867, "the accumulation of the Irish in America keeps pace." And they can't all stay in Boston. Marx briefly entertained the idea that the frontier might help the masses forestall proletarianization, citing a French writer who said that in California workers can resist being attached, like a crustacean, to any one thing: "As mining did not turn out remunerative enough, I left it for the town, where in succession I became typographer, slater, plumber, &c. In consequence of thus finding out that I am fit for any sort of work, I feel less of a mollusk and more of a man."

After Hegel and Marx, came others who stressed the "inner dialectic" of expansion, including Rosa Luxemburg, Lenin, and Hannah Arendt. Also see Paul Baran, *The Political Economy of Growth* (1957); Baran and Paul Sweezy, *Monopoly Capital* (1966); Gabriel Kolko, *The Roots of American Foreign Policy* (1969); and Harry Magdoff, *The Age of Imperialism* (1969). No other single scholar contributed more to elaborating, in the years before and after Vietnam, the argument that liberal capitalism was driven to expand by its own internal contradictions than William Appleman Williams. Williams is often remembered as a diplomatic historian, yet he is better thought of as a critic of ideology and a theorist of liberalism; his most important contribution—what makes his work so enduringly generative but at the same time often misunderstood—was to identify the arena of foreign relations as where normative ideas concerning how best to organize society got worked out. Williams argued that over the long course of U.S. history, liberalism's prime contradictions—the tensions between community and private property, individualism and society, virtue and self-interest—were harmonized through constant expansion, first territorially then economically. Empire, he wrote in 1976, "was the only way to honor avarice and morality. The only way to be good *and* wealthy."

Likewise, Michael Paul Rogin's *Fathers and Children: Andrew Jack-*

son and the Subjugation of the American Indian (1976) is a remarkable synthesis of psychoanalysis and social history (of, in a way, Freud and Turner), which argues for the centrality of western expansion and indigenous dispossession in both capital accumulation and ego formation, and how both depended on constant expansion. Rogin coined the phrase "the American 1848," used to contrast the Jacksonian consensus, forged in frontier expansion and racist war, from Europe's increasingly socialized political culture, which emerged in the wake of the revolutions of 1848. Since the 1970s, social historians have found alternatives to the consensus (beyond the particular rivalries of individual "Jacksonians," such as Jackson and William Henry Harrison, for example, or politicians who identified as Whigs but shared the white nationalist, expansionist, and militarist Jacksonian ethos) in the oppositional cultures and organizations of skilled and unskilled urban laborers, in the radicalism of labor republicans and the militancy of abolitionists. But Rogin advises against "confusing" these counter-cultures "with elaborated political opposition." There might have been oppositional identities, based on class position, urban life, or place of origin. Perpetual war on the frontier might not have been the primary way urban workers identified with the nation. But, Rogin points out, "neither did a widely supported, lasting political alternative emerge from the conditions of the ante-bellum working class." The Jacksonian consensus wasn't watertight, but it did hold. Until it didn't. But see Daniel Walker Howe for an alternative opinion: "American imperialism did not represent an American consensus; it provoked bitter dissent within the national polity," in *What Hath God Wrought: The Transformation of America, 1815–1848* (2007), p. 705. See also Frederick Merk's *Manifest Destiny and Mission in American History: A Reinterpretation* (1995), p. 216, for how expansion, despite a lack of consensus, nonetheless unified nationalism. Among contemporary writers, Susan Faludi, in books such as *Stiffed* (1999) and *The Terror Dream* (2007), carries on the critical spirit of the New Left, linking the transformation of masculinity to broader historical shifts, including changes in the political economy of capitalism and the rise of endless militarism.

"HELLO, CAL," "HELLO, AL": WHY THERE IS
NO SOCIALISM IN AMERICA

Why has the United States proven so resistant to social rights, much less socialism? Over the years, many have answered: "the frontier," arguing that either the landed or ideological frontier worked to deflect or co-opt class conflict and create a steadfast commitment to individualized notions of freedom. But Leon Samson, writing in 1933, offered a wonderfully perverse reading of the frontier thesis to answer the question. First off, Samson said, the premise of such a question is wrong. Americans didn't have an aversion to socialism. They are socialists. The kind of Americanism produced on the frontier, Samson said, delivered substantively on all of socialism's promises: where the socialist harkens to a future of unalienated labor, a time when individuals can be fully human, the American "insists he is already 'human,' a full-blown free and final individual." Where the socialist says that the state, under equitable economic relations, will "wither away," the American performs this withering every day "all by himself," in frontier-produced rituals of informality: "'Hello, Cal'—'Hello, Al.' The American abolishes the state by shaking hands with the statesmen." There's not one concept within socialism—the need to overcome the dead hand of the past; the idea that labor is the source of value; a suspicion of bourgeois morality; and even class conflict and consciousness—that doesn't find a "substantive counter-concept" in frontier-forged Americanism.

An anti-war activist and intellectual who was chased out of Columbia University in 1917 by a patriotic mob for opposing the United States' entrance into World War I, Samson has also been chased out of memory. There is very little information about his life after publishing *Towards a United Front* in 1933. Not even Paul Buhle knows! In any case, Samson's larger point in trying to explain why the U.S. working class seems immune to the allure of socialism is that the frontier negates ideology, and then turns that negation into an ideology. As a result of the frontier, the United States was constantly moving toward and away from capitalism, simultaneously escaping and being overcome by "capitalist forces and forms." "This double movement," he wrote, "was the mainspring of American history," producing a psychic dissonance that Samson called "social neuroticism." Michael Denning discusses Samson's arguments in *The Cultural Front* (1998), p. 431.

OUR FRONTIER THEORIST PRESIDENTS

Theodore Roosevelt, Woodrow Wilson, and Ronald Reagan's contributions to frontier theory are well known. Less commented on are these presidents:

LBJ: After 1969, retired from a tortured presidency that had promised to expand the New Deal but wound up letting loose the forces that would break it, Lyndon Johnson often escaped to Las Pampas, an enormous ranch in the Mexican state of Chihuahua, 75 miles long and 45 miles wide and filled with Texan cattle. Intensive cycles of capital accumulation and imperial war often bring equally intensive bouts of nostalgia, and Johnson in Mexico, free from the burdens of Vietnam, could fantasize about rededicating himself to social reform. He enjoyed "the total isolation and rugged beauty of the place. He was moved by the poverty of some of the ranch hands, who almost invariably had large families." Through an interpreter, Johnson lectured the families on birth control. "If I became dictator of the world," he said, "I'd give all the poor on earth a cottage, and birth control pills—and I'd make damn sure they didn't get one if they didn't take the other." Those workers, however, had different ideas. They claimed that Johnson was in illegal possession of Las Pampas, which remained titled to Johnson's friend, former Mexican president Miguel Alemán. Pre-NAFTA Mexican law prohibited foreigners from owning such large ranches, and so the peasants demanded that it be confiscated, under the terms of the land reform, and turned into an *ejido* (for Las Pampas, see Leo Janos, "Last Days of the President: LBJ in Retirement," *The Atlantic* [July 1973]; Richard Severo, "Mexican Farmers Say Johnson Holds a Ranch There Illegally," *New York Times* [December 31, 1972]). A

Texan, and friends with a number of Mexican presidents, Johnson had long experienced the borderlands as an integrated economic zone. John Crewdson, in *The Tarnished Door* (1983), p. 154, reports that even after the Bracero Program had ended, LBJ had "arranged for the regular delivery of illegal Mexican farmworkers to the LBJ Ranch while its owner was living in the White House."

George H. W. Bush: Having helped broker the end of the Soviet Union, invaded Panama, driven Iraq out of Kuwait, and started advocating a free trade treaty that would cover all of the Americas, Bush thought that the era he presided over "just begs for a catchy name." "Here's one," he said, admitting that he "stole" the phrase from Nicaragua's Sandinistas: "*La revolución sin fronteras,* the revolution without frontiers." Earlier, Ronald Reagan had cited that phrase (more properly translated as "revolution without borders") as proof that the Sandinistas were inherently expansionist, to justify continued U.S. funding of the Contras. There's nothing unusual in a triumphant hegemon borrowing the language, ideas, and style of a recently defeated adversary. But there's a shabbiness about Bush's borrowing, especially considering Nicaragua's relative size and power to the United States, not to mention the ongoing miserable poverty of those Central American countries that supported Reagan's anti-communist crusade.

Bill Clinton: Clinton seized on the campaign for NAFTA as part of a drive for civic renewal, with free trade serving as the "moral equivalent of the frontier." A wide-open world became, as discussed in the book, a way for Clinton to trade in race baiting and to also rise above race baiting. Clinton, as many observers have noted, developed a signature populist style that often mimicked African American cadences to challenge New Deal constituencies, especially unions and civil rights leaders, to push through economic liberalization, end welfare, and pass punitive law-and-order legislation.

There's an origin story to the style: Twelve years after Reagan traveled into deep Mississippi and spoke up for "states' rights," Clinton, on the eve of Georgia's 1992 Democratic primary, made a pilgrimage to that state's Stone Mountain correctional facility, in the shadow of a bigger-than-Mount-Rushmore monument to the Confederacy, not far from the birthplace of the modern KKK. This blatant appeal to white supremacy is fairly well known. There, flanked by white neo-confederate politicians and standing in front of a well-ordered phalanx of about forty mostly African-American prisoners, Clinton delivered a "tough-on-crime" speech. Jerry Brown, also running for president, said Clinton's message was clear: "We got 'em under control, don't worry." Less well known is what happened just after. As Dee Dee Myers, a Clinton campaign advisor, tells it: upon leaving the prison, Clinton stopped to speak with an elderly African American woman. At this point in the campaign, Myers writes, Clinton had lost his stride and was having trouble finding his political voice. Apparently, though, the black vernacular in which this "fabulous little old lady" (as Myers describes her) spoke was clarifying: "I don't care what they say about you. I'm lookin' at you, and I know you're for me," she apparently told the candidate, who realized that he could win on populism, running against the party's educated "elites." "After that," Myers writes, Clinton "was like a jet-fighter pilot. . . . He was locked in on his target." So it was at Stone Mountain, with the chiseled likeness of Robert E. Lee looking down at him, where Clinton figured out how to synthesize white racism and African American populism, which he would then use to push through treaties like NAFTA, end welfare, and expand the prison system. For Myers's story, see "Clinton the Survivor," *Newsweek* (July 19, 1992); for Clinton at Stone Mountain, see Nathan Robinson, "Bill Clinton's Stone Mountain Moment," *Jacobin* (September 16, 2016); for the Jerry Brown quote, see Kofi Bueno Hadjor, *Another America* (1995).

Already in 1992, Stone Mountain was a battleground in the culture wars. As *Time* magazine ("Nixing Dixie," August 2, 1993) wrote just a few months after Clinton's visit, reporting on the backlash to removing Confederate symbols from public spaces: "Some whites fear that soon all Confederate monuments, cemeteries and even Georgia's Stone Mountain, with its huge granite memorials to Confederate heroes, will vanish." "Our culture is being eradicated," said Charles Lunsford, then spokesman for the Sons of Confederate Veterans.

Donald Trump: Donald Trump's German grandfather, Frederick, lived the frontier theory. He escaped an unhealthy Palatinate youth for New York in 1885 and followed the mining boom west to Seattle, then north to Alaska, before returning east to buy property on Jamaica Avenue, in Woodhaven, Queens, which became the foundation of the family's fortune. During the campaign, Trump broke Republican orthodoxy by declaring that he didn't "like" the term *American exceptionalism*, an opinion that was part of his supposed "realism," a rejection of multilateral globalists who were said to be selling out U.S. interests. Donald Trump, who was born in Queens, plumped in Brooklyn, and preened in Manhattan, is perhaps the least likely bearer of the frontier tradition (despite Frederick's legacy). But as president, he's updated the frontier theory to affirm not internationalism but resentment-driven domination. In a 2018 commencement speech at the Naval Academy, he said: "Our ancestors trounced an empire, tamed a continent, and triumphed over the worst evils in history. In every generation, there have been cynics and critics that try to tear down America. But in recent years, the problem grew worse. A growing number used their platforms to denigrate America's incredible heritage, challenge America's sovereignty. . . . We have been taken advantage of by the world. That is not going to be happening anymore." Where past presidents supported space programs by invoking the wide-open frontier (Reagan: astronauts were "pulling us into the future," pushing us "toward the far frontier"; George H. W. Bush: "We saw the frontier beyond the stars, the frontier within ourselves"), Trump, in calling for the creation of a Space Force as its own branch of the nation's armed forces, presents the universe as something like the last, final border: "Our destiny beyond the Earth is not only a matter of national identity, but a matter of national security. . . . When it comes to defending America, it is not enough to merely have an American presence in space. We must have American dominance in space."

Where other frontier-theorist presidents waxed lyrical about big skies and open ranges, Trump sings of a different symbol of the American West. Starting in the 1870s, a new invention began to spread over the prairie and plains, allowing ranchers to employ fewer and fewer hands even as they gained the ability to contain more and more livestock: barbed wire. "Barbed wire," Trump said, referring to one of the ways the active-duty soldiers he deployed to the border might keep out Central American asylum seekers, "can be a beautiful sight."

NOTES

INTRODUCTION

1. Turner's essay, "The Significance of the Frontier in American History," which is easily found on the internet, has been reproduced widely, including in a volume edited by John Mack Faragher, *Rereading Frederick Jackson Turner* (1994). All subsequent uncited Turner quotations are from this volume.
2. Frank Norris, "The Frontier Gone at Last," *The Responsibilities of the Novelist: And Other Essays* (1903), p. 83.
3. Woodrow Wilson, *The Course of American History* (1895), pp. 11, 15.
4. Over the years, the Turner thesis and other conceptualizations of the "frontier" have been applied to many countries that incorporated frontier experience into their national mythologies. The United States, however, is distinct both in its long history of expansion and in taking its frontier myth as an exemplary metaphor of capitalism. For applying Turner-like arguments to Russia: Mark Bassin, "Turner, Solov'ev, and the 'Frontier Hypothesis': The Nationalist Signification of Open Spaces," *Journal of Modern History* 65.3 (1993), pp. 473–511. For comparative settler societies: Lynette Russell, ed., *Colonial Frontiers: Indigenous–European Encounters in Settler Societies* (2001); Paul Maylam, in *South Africa's Racial Past* (2017), p. 52, points out that attempts to apply Turner's Frontier Thesis to South Africa render its racism explicit. For Brazil: Mary Lombardi, "The Frontier in Brazilian History," *Pacific Historical Review* (November 1975), vol. 44, no. 4, pp. 437–57; For comparative South America: Gilbert J. Butland, "Frontiers of Settlement

in South America," *Revista Geográfica* (December 1966), vol. 66, pp. 93–108; and David Weber and Jane Rausch, eds., *Where Cultures Meet; Frontiers in Latin American History* (1994).

5. For Hobbes's connection to the Virginia Company: Patricia Springborg, "Hobbes, Donne and the Virginia Company: Terra Nullius and 'the Bulimia of Dominium,'" *History of Political Thought* (2015), vol. 36, no. 1, pp. 113–64; and Andrew Fitzmaurice, "The Civic Solution to the Crisis of English Colonization, 1609–1625," *Historical Journal* (1999), vol. 42, pp. 25–51, as well as Fitzmaurice, *Sovereignty, Property and Empire, 1500–2000* (2014), p. 104.

6. "A Summary View of the Rights of British America," 1774, available at: http://press-pubs.uchicago.edu/founders/print_documents/v1ch14s10.html.

7. Loren Baritz, "The Idea of the West," *American Historical Review* (April 1961), vol. 66, no. 3, pp. 618–40.

8. Paul Horgan, *Great River* (1954), vol. 2, p. 638.

9. Walter Prescott Webb, *The Great Frontier* (1951), p. 126.

10. "General Jackson's Letter," dated February 12, 1843, and published in *Niles' National Register* (March 30, 1844), p. 70.

11. Flame throwers: Rick Perlstein, *Nixonland* (2010), p. 243; Bombs: "The Casualties of the War in Vietnam" (February 25, 1967), http://www.aavw .org/special_features/speeches_speech_king02.html.

12. Eliot Janeway, *The Economics of Crisis: War, Politics, and the Dollar* (1968), p. 114; Walter LaFeber, *The New Empire* (1961).

13. Frances FitzGerald, *Fire in the Lake* (1972), p. 371. Richard Slotkin's trilogy on the myth of the frontier in America is the fullest elaboration of such arguments.

14. William Appleman Williams, *The Great Evasion* (1966), p. 13.

15. Rukmini Callimachi, Helene Cooper, Eric Schmitt, Alan Blinder, and Thomas Gibbons-Neff, "'An Endless War': Why 4 U.S. Soldiers Died in a Remote African Desert," *New York Times* (February 20, 2018).

16. Wesley Morgan and Bryan Bender, "America's Shadow War in Africa," *Politico* (October 12, 2017), https://www.politico.com/story/2017/10/12/niger -shadow-war-africa-243695.

17. According to one report, spending on operations in Iraq and Afghanistan alone—not including the costs of wars in Pakistan, Yemen, Syria, Libya, and sub-Saharan Africa—will top six trillion dollars. "The largest portion of that bill is yet to be paid," the authors of the report write, referring to interest on deficit spending to finance the operations, as well as the long-term medical care and disability compensation for veterans and their families. Linda Bilmes, "The Financial Legacy of Iraq and Afghanistan: How Wartime Spending Decisions Will Constrain Future National Security Budgets," HKS Faculty Research Working Paper Series RWP13-006 (March 2013). Neta

Crawford's "U.S. Budgetary Costs of Wars Through 2016," Watson Institute, Brown University (September 2016), does include spending in Syria, Pakistan, and on Homeland Security: http://watson.brown.edu/costsofwar/files /cow/imce/papers/2016/Costs%20of%20War%20through%202016%20 FINAL%20final%20v2.pdf.

18. J. W. Mason, "What Recovery?" Roosevelt Institute (July 25, 2017), http:// rooseveltinstitute.org/wp-content/uploads/2017/07/Monetary-Policy-Report -070617-2.pdf; Larry Summers, "The Age of Secular Stagnation," *Foreign Affairs* (March–April 2017); Nelson Schwartz, "The Recovery Threw the Middle-Class Dream Under a Benz," *New York Times* (September 12, 2018), https://www.nytimes.com/2018/09/12/business/middle-class-financial-crisis .html; David Lazarus, "The Economy May Be Booming, but Nearly Half of Americans Can't Make Ends Meet, *Los Angeles Times* (August 31, 2018), http://www.latimes.com/business/lazarus/la-fi-lazarus-economy-stagnant -wages-20180831-story.html.

19. "Remarks Announcing Candidacy for the Republican Presidential Nomination" (November 13, 1979), http://www.presidency.ucsb.edu/ws/?pid=76116; "Second Inaugural Address" (January 21, 1985), http://avalon.law.yale.edu /20th_century/reagan2.asp.

20. Rudiger Dornbusch, *Keys to Prosperity* (2002), p. 66.

21. Though in real life they did: Mark Lause, *The Great Cowboy Strike: Bullets, Ballots, and Class Conflicts in the American West* (2018).

22. Sam Tanenhaus, *The Death of Conservatism* (2010), p. 99.

23. Andy Kroll, "How Trump Learned to Love the Koch Brothers," *Mother Jones* (December 1, 2017), describes the degree to which Trump, despite running against the Kochs, has fulfilled their deregulation agenda. As of this writing, though, Trump's proposal to impose tariffs on imports has strained his relationship with free-trade Republicans.

1. ALL THAT SPACE

1. Jonathan Hart, *Representing the New World* (2001), p. 149.

2. Alexander Young, *Chronicles of the Pilgrim Fathers* (2005), p. 36; Thaddeus Piotrowski, *The Indian Heritage of New Hampshire and Northern New England* (2008), p. 14.

3. Bernard Bailyn, *The Barbarous Years* (2012), p. 438.

4. James Kirby Martin, *Interpreting Colonial America* (1978), p. 29.

5. Frederick Jackson Turner often cited this document, though the English translation he used was slightly off, using "Indian tribes" for "*naciones indias*" and "region" for "*el vasto continente.*" An original Spanish version of the letter from Baron de Carondelet, dated December 1, 1794, is found in the

Wisconsin Historical Society, Draper Collection, mss 39 J 16–69. Thanks to Lee Grady, an archivist at the society, for making it available.

6. Octavio Paz, *El Arco y la Lira* (1956), p. 279.

7. David Weber, *The Mexican Frontier* (1982), p. 175.

8. John Fanning Watson, *Historic Tales of Olden Time* (1833), p. 229.

9. Watson, *Historic Tales of Olden Time*, p. 229.

10. Available at: https://founders.archives.gov/documents/Franklin/01-04-02 -0080.

11. Fred Anderson, *The War That Made America: A Short History of the French and Indian War* (2006), and Colin Calloway, *The Scratch of a Pen: 1763 and the Transformation of North America* (2007).

12. Robert Kirkwood, *Through So Many Dangers: The Memoirs and Adventures of Robert Kirk, Late of the Royal Highland Regiment* (2004), p. 66.

13. Norman O. Brown, *Love's Body* (1968), p. 30.

14. Jared Sparks, *The Works of Benjamin Franklin* (1840), vol. 7, p. 355.

15. Most historians date the Ohio Company to 1749, though the University of Pittsburgh's archives and special collections indicate its papers were drawn up a year earlier.

16. "Royal Proclamation Day" is marked in Canada both by the government and by native peoples, who use it as a basis to make claims on the state. Recently, Idle No More, a Canadian indigenous-rights grassroots organization that fights against the extension of fracking and mining, called for an international day of action to mark the proclamation's 250th anniversary. In the United States, a country that came into existence as the negation of the proclamation, no such influence or memorialization exists.

17. Kevin Kenny's *Peaceable Kingdom Lost: The Paxton Boys and the Destruction of William Penn's Holy Experiment* identifies the Paxton terror spree as the beginning of the end of Quaker authority in Philadelphia. For the prominence of "Ulster-Scots" in U.S. settler colonialism: Roxanne Dunbar-Ortiz, *An Indigenous Peoples' History of the United States* (2015), p. 51.

18. That Hans Nicholas Eisenhauer is the great-great-great-grandfather of Dwight D. Eisenhower is confirmed by ancestry records: Hans, with his first wife, had a son, Peter Eisenhauer. With Anna Dissinger, Peter had a son named Frederick Eisenhower (it is with him that the spelling of the name changes). Frederick, with Barbara Miller, had a son named Jacob F. Eisenhower, who was Dwight Eisenhower's grandfather. Thanks to Brendan Jordan for pinning this down.

19. Ezra Grumbine, "Frederick Stump: The Founder of Fredericksburg, Pa.," *Lebanon County Historical Society* (June 26, 1914), chapters 1–9.

20. Samuel Williams, "Tennessee's First Military Expedition (1803)," *Tennessee Historical Magazine* (1924), vol. 8, no. 3, pp. 171–90. For the Stump family

in Tennessee and Stump's alignment with the up-and-coming Jacksonians: Harriette Simpson Arnow, *Flowering of the Cumberland* (2013).

21. Washington lobbied London on behalf of veterans of the Seven Years' War, who were promised, but didn't receive, "bounty land" west of the Alleghenies in Ohio as compensation for their military service. In exchange for his advocacy on behalf of "his old soldiers," Washington received a percentage of their land. Washington himself was granted 20,000 Ohio acres for his wartime service against the French. Thomas Perkins Abernethy, *Western Lands and the American Revolution* (1937), and "Washington as Land Speculator," George Washington Papers, Library of Congress, https://www.loc.gov/collec tions/george-washington-papers/articles-and-essays/george-washington -survey-and-mapmaker/washington-as-land-speculator/. Also, see Archibald Henderson, *The Star of Empire: Phases of the Westward Movement in the Old Southwest* (1919), p. 47: "George Washington, acquiring vast tracts of western land by secret purchase, indirectly stimulated the powerful army that was carrying the broad-axe westward."

22. Caroline Winterer, *American Enlightenments: Pursuing Happiness in the Age of Reason* (2016), for New World bountifulness as a counter to Malthusian pessimism. Also: Antonello Gerbi, *The Dispute of the New World: The History of a Polemic, 1750–1900* (1973); and Lee Alan Dugatkin, *Mr. Jefferson and the Giant Moose: Natural History in Early America* (2009).

23. For the Jefferson quotations: *Memoirs* (1929), vol. 1, p. 437.

24. *The Writings of James Madison* (1807), vol. 7, p. 16.

25. See Carondelet's original Spanish version of the letter, found in the Wisconsin Historical Society.

26. For complaints by Spanish colonial officials in the Mississippi River valley that Anglos were impossible to "contain": Sylvia L. Hilton, "Movilidad y expansión en la construcción política de los Estados Unidos: 'Estos errantes colonos' en las fronteras españolas del Misisipí (1776–1803)," *Revista Complutense de Historia de América* (2002), vol. 28, pp. 63–96.

27. http://reevesmaps.com/maps/map380.jpg.

28. Jennifer Nedelsky, *Private Property and the Limits of Constitutionalism* (1994), p. 80.

29. Montesquieu, *Political Writings* (1990), p. 106. Noah Webster thought that the problem might be solved by editing the "great Montesquieu." Webster suggested inserting the word "property" wherever the French republican had used the word "virtue." By "property," Webster didn't mean the abstract right to possess. He meant actual land. "A general and tolerably equal distribution of landed property is the whole basis of national freedom," Webster wrote, in *An Examination into the Leading Principles of the Federal Constitution* (1787), p. 47.

30. Many scholars have emphasized the importance of Madison's Federalist No. 10 in revising republican thought to accommodate and justify expansion, including Charles Beard, *An Economic Interpretation of the Constitution of the United States* (1913). William Appleman Williams's "A Note on Charles Austin Beard's Search for a General Theory of Causation," *American Historical Review* (October 1956), vol. 62, no. 1, pp. 55–80, reviews Beard's interpretation of Madison. The quotes by Madison and Montesquieu used here draw from these works. Also see Andrew Hacker, *The Study of Politics* (1963), p. 81.

2. THE ALPHA AND THE OMEGA

1. Arístides Silva Otero, *La diplomacia hispanoamericanista de la Gran Colombia* (1967), p. 15. Also: Germán A. de la Reza, "The Formative Platform of the Congress of Panama (1810–1826): The Pan-American Conjecture Revisited," *Revista brasileira de política internacional* (2013), vol. 56, n. 1, pp. 5–21, http://www.scielo.br/scielo.php?script=sci_arttext&pid=S0034-73292013 000100001&lng=en&nrm=iso.

2. For more on *uti possidetis* and how it relates to modern ideals of sovereignty and the repudiation of the doctrine of discovery, including the sources of many the quotations here: Greg Grandin, "The Liberal Traditions in the Americas: Rights, Sovereignty, and the Origins of Liberal Multilateralism," *American Historical Review* (2012), vol. 117, pp. 68–91; also Alejandro Alvarez, *The Monroe Doctrine* (1924); Alejandro Alvarez, "The Monroe Doctrine from the Latin-American Point of View," *St. Louis Law Review* (1917), vol. 2 no. 3; and Juan Pablo Scarfi, *The Hidden History of International Law in the Americas* (2017). For more on Colombian republicanism, see Lina del Castillo, *Crafting a Republic for the World* (2018).

3. Leslie Rout, *Politics of the Chaco Peace Conference, 1935–1939* (1970).

4. Marcus Kornprobst, "The Management of Border Disputes in African Regional Subsystems," *Journal of Modern African Studies* (2002), vol. 40, no. 3, p. 375; Boutros Boutros-Ghali, *Les conflits de frontières en Afrique* (1972).

5. Graham H. Stuart, "Simón Bolívar's Project for a League of Nations," *Southwestern Political and Social Science Quarterly* (1926), vol. 7, no. 3, pp. 238–52.

6. Haitians, having led the first overthrow of New World slavery, felt depths of loneliness U.S. republicans couldn't come close to imagining. They were under constant economic siege by France, surrounded for decades by the Spanish empire, and unrecognized by Haiti's "sister republic," the United States. "We have dared to be free," the 1804 Haitian Declaration of Independence announced. "Let us be thus by ourselves and for ourselves." Wil-

liam Appleman Williams identifies an existential "isolation in time" as an element of the exceptionalism felt by U.S. republicans, a "deep sense of aloneness—of isolation." This was driven by a desire to distance themselves from other property-destroying revolutions—especially ones led by former slaves—but also by a sense that their efforts to achieve self-government in an ever-extending sphere were precedent-setting, that they were "challenging the wisdom of the gods" (*America Confronts a Revolutionary World* [1976], pp. 38–39). Caitlin Fitz, in *Our Sister Republics* (2016), points out that the sense of existential exceptionalism on the part of U.S. republicans, of the kind expressed by Jefferson in 1808, fully took shape a bit later, after Spanish-American independence movements got under way, when it became clear that the United States would be sharing the New World with other, perhaps many, republics.

7. The Federalist Papers can be accessed at the Yale School of Law Avalon Project. For this quote in Hamilton, No. 7: http://avalon.law.yale.edu/18th_century/fed07.asp.

8. George Bancroft, *History of the Formation of the Constitution of the United States* (1882), p. 503.

9. Peter Onuf, *Jefferson's Empire* (2000), p. 181.

10. The landed frontier was still open, but Monroe here already made the jump to thinking about limitlessness in terms of global trade: "Our experience," Monroe said, "ought to satisfy us that our progress under the most correct and provident policy will not be exempt from danger. Our institutions form an important epoch in the history of the civilized world. On their preservation and in their utmost purity everything will depend. Extending as our interests do to every part of the inhabited globe and to every sea to which our citizens are carried by their industry and enterprise, to which they are invited by the wants of others, and have a right to go, we must either protect them in the enjoyment of their rights or abandon them in certain events to waste and desolation." *Addresses and Messages of the Presidents* (1849), vol. 1, p. 478. For the quotation in the text, see *The Writings of James Monroe* (1903), vol. 7, p. 48.

11. As did James Madison, Wilson identified economic "interests" as being as much subjective as objective. "An apparent interest," he said, "produces the same attachment as a real one and is often pursued with no less perseverance and vigor." The United States comprised, Wilson wrote, a plurality of individual interests that "added together, will form precisely the aggregate interest of the whole." If the greater good can be no greater than the precise sum of individual interests, and if individual interests are forever mutable, how to form a stable government able to protect such subjective interests that wasn't tyrannical? If no such transcendent virtue could be established, higher than

the aggregate of individual interests, then what, asked the revolutionary Wilson, positing *the* revolutionary question, "is to be done?" Ratify the Constitution, he answered, and use largeness to protect liberty. James Wilson and Bird Wilson, eds., *The Works of the Honourable James Wilson* (1804), pp. 274–77. For the revolutionary alliance between "gentlemen" and "backcountry settlers" in Pennsylvania mentioned in this chapter's footnote: David Freeman Hawke, *In the Midst of a Revolution* (1961). Theodore Roosevelt also makes this argument in his chapter "In the Current of the Revolution: The Southern Backwoodsmen Overwhelm the Cherokees, 1776," of *The Winning of the West* (1889), vol. 1: "Each section had its own work to do; the East won independence while the West began to conquer the continent."

12. José Gaos, ed., *El pensamiento hispanoamericano* (1993), vol. 5, p. 168. For Bolívar's imagining of Panama as the center of a universal republic: Alvarez, *The Monroe Doctrine*, cited above. See also Jay Sexton, *The Monroe Doctrine* (2011), p. 80, on how the Jacksonians used Bolívar's invitation to the Panama Conference to solidify a racial nationalism.

13. Joseph Byrne Lockey, *Pan-Americanism: Its Beginnings* (1920), p. 388.

14. *The Writings of Thomas Jefferson* (1859), vol. 4, p. 419.

15. Onuf, *Jefferson's Empire,* p. 1.

16. Everett Somerville Brown, ed., *The Constitutional History of the Louisiana Purchase* (2000), p. 63.

17. Arthur Stanley Link, ed., *The Papers of Woodrow Wilson* (1970), vol. 8, p. 354.

18. Peter Onuf, *The Mind of Thomas Jefferson* (2007), p. 106.

19. David Ramsay, *An Oration on the Cession of Louisiana, to the United States* (1804), p. 21.

20. James McClellan, *Reflections on the Cession of Louisiana to the United States* (1803), p. 14.

21. As a political theorist, James Madison identified war as the most "dreaded" enemy of "public liberty" because it spread the "germ of every other" enemy: high taxes, debt, standing armies, "inequality of fortunes" through profiteering and fraud, and the corruption of manners and morals. As president (1809–17), faced with a choice between either a self-containing peace or a war to extend the sphere, Madison chose war. According to the historian Garry Wills, Madison "welcomed" the War of 1812 against the British: "He schemed to bring it on." The ultimate objective was to obtain Canada, and in that sense the war "seemed to gain nothing," according to Wills, *James Madison* (2015). But in a way it began everything, habituating northern manufacturers to the stimulus derived from militarism and launching Andrew Jackson, the avenger of the frontier and destroyer of the Creeks, into national politics.

22. Susan Dunn, *Jefferson's Second Revolution* (2004), p. 241.
23. Onuf, *The Mind of Thomas Jefferson*, p. 107.
24. Edward Everett, *Orations and Speeches* (1836), vol. 1, p. 197.
25. The quotations are from a letter Jefferson wrote to Indiana territorial governor William Henry Harrison, on February 27, 1803: *The Writings of Thomas Jefferson* (1859), pp. 472–73. The letter is available here: http://www.digitalhistory.uh.edu/active_learning/explorations/indian_removal/jefferson_to_harrison.cfm. Note that some transcriptions have "trading uses," not "trading houses." Harrison would become a national hero for defeating the Shawnee, who opposed U.S. expansion, at the 1811 Battle of Tippecanoe, an event that would precipitate the War of 1812 against the British. Based on his Indian-killing reputation, Harrison would be elected president in 1840, dying shortly after taking office.
26. Jefferson to Alexander von Humboldt, December 6, 1813, https://founders.archives.gov/documents/Jefferson/03-07-02-0011.
27. Jefferson to Alexander von Humboldt, December 6, 1813 (link above). Jefferson here was specifically referring to British support for Tecumseh's Rebellion, which was the definitive war for control of the Great Lakes region. The rebellion was ultimately put down by William Henry Harrison, the territorial governor of Indiana, to whom Jefferson issued his predatory-debt instructions. David Curtis Skaggs and Larry L. Nelson, eds., *The Sixty Years' War for the Great Lakes, 1754–1814* (2001); Kerry Trask, *Black Hawk: The Battle for the Heart of America* (2006); Richard White, *The Middle Ground: Indians, Empires, and Republics in the Great Lakes Region, 1650–1815* (1991).
28. Lewis Cass, "Removal of the Indians," *North American Review* (1830), p. 107.
29. Onuf, *The Mind of Thomas Jefferson*, p. 107.
30. Louis Hartz, *The Liberal Tradition in America* (1955), p. 7.
31. Loren Baritz, *City on a Hill* (1964), p. 99.
32. *The Writings of James Monroe* (1903), vol. 6, p. 274.
33. Ralph Louis Ketcham, *James Madison: A Biography* (1990), p. 145.

3. A CAUCASIAN DEMOCRACY

1. Indispensable: John Juricek, "American Usage of the Word 'Frontier' from Colonial Times to Frederick Jackson Turner," *Proceedings of the American Philosophical Society* (1966), vol. 110, no. 1, pp. 10–34.
2. *The Royal Standard English Dictionary* (1788).
3. J. M. Opal, *Avenging the People: Andrew Jackson, the Rule of Law, and the American Nation* (2017), p. 70.

4. Knox, according to Leonard Sadosky, *Revolutionary Negotiations: Indians, Empires, and Diplomats in the Founding of America* (2010), p. 158, was trying to define indigenous–federal relations by the "Westphalian states system"— that is, by recognizing indigenous sovereignty as a way of ending border, or boundary, conflicts. Others, such as Jefferson, thought that international law "must be adapted to the circumstance of our unsettled country," by which he meant the fact that as U.S. "sovereignty" increased, indigenous sovereignty would naturally decrease: "As fast as we extended our rights by purchase from them, so fast we extended the limits of our society, & as soon as a new portion became encircled within our line, it became a fixt limit of our society."

5. Lawrence Kinnaird, *Spain in the Mississippi Valley, 1765–1794* (1945).

6. R. Douglas Hurt, *The Indian Frontier, 1763–1846* (2002), p. 101, for North Carolina's 1783 "land grab" law, mentioned in the footnote.

7. Allan Kulikoff, *The Agrarian Origins of American Capitalism* (1992), p. 75.

8. William Reynolds, Jr., *The Cherokee Struggle to Maintain Identity in the 17th and 18th Centuries* (2015), p. 271.

9. Frederick Stump to Andrew Jackson, March 3, 1807, Library of Congress, Andrew Jackson papers, 1775–1874, available at: https://www.loc.gov /resource/maj.01007_0300_0301/?sp=1&q=%22frederick+stump%22. Steve Inskeep, *Jacksonland* (2015), discusses how Jackson's policies of dispossession, both as a private citizen and public citizen, enriched him and his associates.

10. Ned Sublette and Constance Sublette, *American Slave Coast: A History of the Slave-Breeding Industry* (2016), p. 396, for Jackson and slave trading, as well as for the larger history of the post-1808 internal slave trade. Jackson's clash with Dinsmore along with the quotations cited here is recounted in nearly every Jackson biography. *Letter from the Secretary of War, Transmitting the Information, in Part, Required by a Resolution of the House of Representatives, of 21st Inst. in Relation to the Breaking an Individual, and Depriving Him of His Authority Among the Creeks* . . . (1828), pp. 10–19. For other quotations: "James A. McLaughlin Jan. 30, 1843. Genl. Jacksons trip to Natchez, 1811," available at https://www.loc.gov/resource/maj.06165_0138 _0141/?st=text.

11. Opal, *Avenging the People*, p. 138.

12. Sublette and Sublette, *American Slave Coast*, p. 396; Josh Foreman and Ryan Starrett, *Hidden History of Jackson* (2018), p. 28.

13. *Journal of the Senate at the Second Session of the Ninth General Assembly of the State of Tennessee* (1812), p. 72, https://hdl.handle.net/2027/uiug .30112108189405.

14. Opal, *Avenging the People*, p. 138.

15. Robert Breckinridge McAfee, *History of the Late War in the Western Country* (2009), p. 492. For Jackson's assault on the Creeks, and the quotations used here, see Sean Michael O'Brien, *In Bitterness and in Tears: Andrew Jackson's Destruction of the Creeks and Seminoles* (2003); and Alfred Cave, *Sharp Knife: Andrew Jackson and the American Indians* (2017), p. 45.
16. *Speeches of the Hon. Henry Clay* (1842), p. 90.
17. Cave, *Sharp Knife*, p. 45.
18. The quotation is Sadosky's, in *Revolutionary Negotiations*, p. 194. By 1802, Jefferson "had committed the federal government to, at some point in the future, extinguishing all the Indian title within the boundaries of the State of Georgia, in exchange for Georgia's cession of its claims to the land that would become the states of Alabama and Mississippi."
19. Sadosky, *Revolutionary Negotiations*, p. 193, on removal originating in policies promoted by Jackson's ally, Willie Blount, while he was governor of Tennessee: "Blount's imagining of the removal of eastern American Indian populations to the western side of the Mississippi was only a more extreme version of a policy of dispossession and land acquisition that had been underway for most of the Jefferson administration."
20. For how race-based marginalization and exploitation continued in Spanish America despite formal constitutional equality, see Marixa Lasso, "Race War and Nation in Caribbean Gran Colombia, Cartagena, 1810–1832," *American Historical Review* (April 1, 2006), vol. 111, issue 2, pp. 336–61.
21. Arthur Schlesinger, Jr., *The Age of Jackson* (1945); Sean Wilentz, *Andrew Jackson* (2005). See Michael Rogin, *Fathers and Children* (1991), pp. xvii–xviii, for how Jacksonian hagiography corresponds to the cycles of American politics.
22. Wilbur Larremore, "The Consent of the Governed," *American Law Review* (March–April 1906), p. 166; Charles Maurice Wiltse, *John C. Calhoun, Nationalist, 1782–1828* (1968), p. 11.
23. Larremore, "The Consent of the Governed," p. 166.
24. Andrew Jackson to Tilghman Ashurst Howard, August 20, 1833, https://www.loc.gov/resource/maj.01084_0354_0357/?st=text.
25. *The Addresses and Messages of the Presidents of the United States* (1839), p. 423.
26. For the ways in which the elaboration of an ideal of states' rights and minimal government was used in defense of slavery: Manisha Sinha, *The Counterrevolution of Slavery: Politics and Ideology in Antebellum South Carolina* (2000); David Waldstreicher, *Slavery's Constitution* (2009); and Richard Ellis, *The Union at Risk: Jacksonian Democracy, States' Rights and the Nullification Crisis* (1989).

27. Cherokees wouldn't be removed until May 1838, when General Winfield Scott (who later would command U.S. troops against Mexico) forced them. out of their traditional homeland in southern Appalachia and drove them—an estimated 15,000 to 16,000 people—west on their Trail of Tears. Upward of 4,000 died along the way from illness, hunger, and exposure.

28. Francis Newton Thorpe, ed., *The Statesmanship of Andrew Jackson* (1909), pp. 190–92.

29. Cited in *Army and Navy Chronicle* (February 1, 1838), p. 69.

30. Caleb Cushing, *An Oration, on the Material Growth and Progress of the United States* (1839), p. 29.

31. In *Army and Navy Chronicle* (January 25, 1838), p. 55.

32. In *A Diary in America: With Remarks on Its Institutions* (1839), part 2, vol. 3, p. 205. Significantly, the 51,000 or so indigenous people just west of the Mississippi listed in this tally as *inside* the frontier were, just a year earlier, according to the Senate's Indian Affairs committee, said to be "outside of us, and in a place which will ever remain on the outside." The forts listed in this 1837 report—running in a zigzag pattern from Fort Brady in the north, at the near tip of Lake Superior, to Fort Adams, below Natchez, at Baton Rouge—provide a rough approximation of where the U.S. Army imagined the frontier, or "exterior line of defense," to be that year. The back-and-forth line stretched well east of the United States' political boundary at the time (as well as east of what was generally considered "Indian Country," created by removal, in Oklahoma). Western Indians within "striking distance" of the frontier line, according to the list of nations in the report, sprawled all the way to the first range of the Rocky Mountains, which faced the Great Plains, and included groups such as the Apache, who lived in Texas (which had by now broken from Mexico but had not yet been annexed by the United States). Not included in this list of latent warriors were those tribes who lived in the Rockies proper, or west of them, including the Utes, Paiutes, Shoshone, and Salish.

33. Rogin, *Fathers and Children*, p. 4.

34. *Niles' Weekly Register*, April 2, 1831, p. 83.

35. Juricek, "American Usage."

36. Thomas Frazier, *The Underside of American History* (1982), p. 71.

37. Frederick Hoxie, ed., *The Oxford Handbook of American Indian History* (2016), p. 605.

38. Rogin, *Fathers and Children*, p. 117.

39. *Winston Leader* (August 24, 1880).

40. "The Indian Question," *North American Review* (April 1873), p. 336.

41. "Report of the Commissioner of Indian Affairs," Department of the Interior (October 30, 1876), http://public.csusm.edu/nadp/r876001.htm.

42. In *A Diary in America*, p. 217.

43. *Army and Navy Chronicle* (February 1, 1838), p. 65.

44. Larremore, "The Consent of the Governed," p. 165.

4. THE SAFETY VALVE

1. "Steamboat Disasters," *North American Review* (January 1840), p. 40.

2. Emerson Gould, *Fifty Years on the Mississippi* (1889), p. 168.

3. *Hazard's Register of Pennsylvania* (June 27, 1835), p. 416.

4. Gordon Wood, *Radicalism of the American Revolution* (1991), p. 307.

5. Ronald Reagan later quoted this line from Channing, praising Joe Coors and the Heritage Foundation for leading the "New Right Revolution"; he hailed Angolan mercenaries as "freedom fighters" and toasted the Contras and Khmer Rouge, along with conservative cadres in the United States, as pushing a "forward strategy for freedom." *Public Papers of the Presidents of the United States: Ronald Reagan* (1988), p. 499.

6. T. Romeyn Beck, "Statistical Notices of Some of the Lunatic Asylums in the United States," *Transactions of the Albany Institute* (1830), vol. 1.

7. *Views and Reviews in American Literature* (1845), p. 39.

8. Charles Perkins, *An Oration, Pronounced at the Request of the Citizens of Norwich, Conn.* (1822), p. 19.

9. *Hampshire Gazette* (November 9, 1831), p. 3.

10. *Portland Daily Advertiser* (November 28, 1835), p. 2.

11. *The Life and Times of Frederick Douglass* (1993), p. 129.

12. John Codman, *The Duty of American Christians to Send the Gospel to the Heathen* (1836), p. 16.

13. *Jamestown Journal*, New York (August 8, 1845).

14. "To the Citizens of Portland," *Portland Weekly Advertiser*, Maine (July 9, 1833).

15. Manisha Sinha, *The Slave's Cause: A History of Abolition* (2016).

16. "Mr. Torrey's Case," *Emancipator and Free American* (February 11, 1842); *North American and Daily Advertiser* (November 12, 1840); "What Have the Abolitionists Done?" *The Emancipator* (June 28, 1838).

17. Debates over slavery advanced comparative sociology, as its defenders and critics looked to Europe to imagine the institution's future. Here's an example arguing why western expansion was necessary in order to keep chattel slavery viable: "When slavery in this country, therefore, shall have attained to that degree of density which exists in the semi-barbarous regions of Russia, Turkey, and China, it will fall without a struggle," which is why the "safety valve" provided by expansion into the "SouthWestern States" is needed in order to avoid such an outcome; "Extension of Slave Territory," *National Era* (March 11, 1847).

18. *Western Monthly Review* (January 1839), p. 359.

19. *Niles' National Register* (July 6, 1844), p. 303.

20. As reported in the "Proceedings of the London Convention," *The Emancipator* (September 10, 1840).

21. For the Free Soil movement: Eric Foner, *Free Soil, Free Labor, Free Men: The Ideology of the Republican Party Before the Civil War* (1995).

22. Frederick Evans, *Autobiography of a Shaker* (1869), p. 37.

23. Leon Samson, "Substitutive Socialism," *Toward a United Front* (1933), p. 7; John Commons, "Labor Organization and Labor Politics, 1827–1837," *Quarterly Journal of Economics* (February 1907), vol. 21, no. 2, pp. 324–25; Anna Rochester, in *Rulers of America* (1936), thought the open West depressed labor organizing.

24. In the 1920s, the agricultural economist Benjamin Horace Hibbard wrote that it was impossible to say what effect "the possibility of leaving the city for the frontier" had on labor disputes or in impeding the establishment of a labor party. He offered this cautious summation: "Without doubt the public lands served as a political and economic balance wheel; but, just as a well-adjusted machine gives no outward evidence of needing a balance wheel, so the functioning of the public domain in this capacity was imperceptible. Discontented groups of people were continually moving to the West.... It is not to be inferred that these people would have, in all cases, made trouble had they remained in the older settled parts of the country. They would, however, most assuredly have made a different country." In Hibbard's *A History of Public Land Policies* (1924), pp. 556–57.

25. Cushing, *An Oration*.

26. Robert J. Walker, *Letter of Mr. Walker, of Mississippi, Relative to the Reannexation of Texas: in Reply to the Call of the People of Carroll County, Kentucky, to Communicate His Views on that Subject* (1844). Walker served as secretary of the treasury during the annexation of Texas and the Mexican–American War and as governor of "bleeding Kansas" in the run-up to the Civil War, where he supervised the drafting of the territory's pro-slavery constitution.

27. Walker here cited completely fabricated 1840 census figures, which tallied an extremely high proportion of mental illness within the African American population, especially in the north. For the 1840 census: Dea Boster, *African American Slavery and Disability* (2013), p. 23, and Lynn Gamwell and Nancy Tomes, *Madness in America* (1995), p. 103.

28. W. E. B. Du Bois, *Black Reconstruction* (1935), p. 9.

29. The essay "Slavery in the United States" first appeared in the *Alphadelphia Tocsin*, the journal of a Fourierist utopian commune in Michigan, and was then reprinted in Evans's *Young America* on June 7, 1845: "Here, then, is

NOTES TO PAGES 80-85

our objection against *immediate* emancipation. It would place the blacks in a tenfold worse situation. It would fill our jails, penitentiaries, and poorhouses, and inflict a dreadful curse upon the white laborers in the north by reducing their wages, also by increasing the competition for labor. But shall we therefore perpetuate slavery? No! It cannot continue always. The increase of slaves is proportionally much greater than that of the whites, and if they be not released voluntarily they will emancipate themselves in coming time with the sword." But given their own territory, freed slaves "will then have a home of their own free from sharpers and shavers, with the means of becoming happy and independent by their own industry. Their rapid increase would be checked, for they would then have to provide for their own offspring. This, in our estimation, is the only way in which the negro's rights can be restored and justice done them. They have been violently deprived of their native home, and the least we can, or ought to do for them, is to give them another where they can dwell in peace. It is an indisputable but melancholy fact, that every government that has ever existed has reduced its laborers, who had not home of their own, to a state of slavery and destitution, tenfold more aggravated and abject than negro slavery now is; and that this condition has been rapidly developing itself among our northern white laborers. . . . Shall we then increase this class of our population three million at one fell stroke? No, God forbid! It would be madness to do it. . . . Why should we heap upon him a dreadful curse under the disguise of blessing him forever with freedom?"

30. "Ought we not be satisfied with the Mississippi?" James Monroe once asked Thomas Jefferson, expressing a short-lived worry that rapid expansion might create unforeseen dangers to the union.

31. David Lowenthal, *George Perkins Marsh: Prophet of Conservation* (2003), p. 102.

5. ARE YOU READY FOR ALL THESE WARS?

1. Randolph Campbell, *An Empire for Slavery: The Peculiar Institution in Texas, 1821–1865* (1991), p. 10.

2. Sublette and Sublette, *American Slave Coast*, p. 29; Randolph Campbell, *The Laws of Slavery in Texas: Historical Documents and Essays* (2010). See Karl Jacoby, *The Strange Career of William Ellis* (2016), for Mexico as a refuge for enslaved Texans.

3. Josiah Quincy, *Memoir of the Life of John Quincy Adams* (1859), p. 242.

4. John Quincy Adams, *Speech . . . on the Joint Resolution for distributing rations to the distressed fugitives from Indian hostilities in the States of Alabama and Georgia* (1836), for this and subsequent quotations.

5. Joseph Wheelan, *Mr. Adams's Last Crusade* (2008), p. 240. Adams's diaries are available here: http://www.masshist.org/jqadiaries/php/.

6. Steven Hahn, *A Nation Without Borders: The United States and Its World in an Age of Civil Wars, 1830–1910* (2016), p. 132.

7. Hershel Parker, *Herman Melville* (2005), vol. 1, p. 421. See Michael Rogin, *Subversive Genealogy* (1983), for a discussion of Melville's critique.

8. Martin Dugard, *The Training Ground: Grant, Lee, Sherman, and Davis in the Mexican War, 1846–1848* (2008).

9. Gene Brack, *The Diplomacy of Racism: Manifest Destiny and Mexico, 1821–1848* (1974). For Mexican perspectives on the menace, see Gene Brack, *Mexico Views Manifest Destiny, 1821–1846* (1975).

10. Peter Guardino, *The Dead March: A History of the Mexican–American War* (2017), p. 107.

11. Paul Foos, *A Short, Offhand, Killing Affair: Soldiers and Social Conflict During the Mexican–American War* (2002), p. 120.

12. William Earl Weeks, *Building the Continental Empire: American Expansion from the Revolution to the Civil War* (1997), p. 115.

13. Thomas Hietala, *Manifest Design: Anxious Aggrandizement in Late Jacksonian America* (1985), p. 155.

14. Weeks, *Building the Continental Empire*, p. 127.

15. *Congressional Globe*, February 26, 1847, p. 516.

16. David Weber, *Myth and the History of the Hispanic Southwest* (1988), p. 154.

17. Hietala, *Manifest Design*, p. xi.

18. *Message from the President of the United States* (1847), p. 17.

19. See the entry for "Standing Bear v. Crook," in Spencer Tucker, James Arnold, and Roberta Wiener, eds., *The Encyclopedia of North American Indian Wars, 1607–1890* (2011), p. 759.

20. Michael Rogin, "Herman Melville: State, Civil Society, and the American 1848," *Yale Review* (1979), vol. 69, no. 1, p. 72, for "the American 1848."

21. William Estabrook Chancellor, *Our Presidents and Their Office* (1912), p. 61.

22. Matthew Karp, *This Vast Southern Empire: Slaveholders at the Helm of American Foreign Policy* (2016).

23. Daniel Scallet, "This Inglorious War: The Second Seminole War, the Ad Hoc Origins of American Imperialism, and the Silence of Slavery," PhD dissertation, Washington University (2011), https://openscholarship.wustl.edu/cgi/viewcontent.cgi?article=1637&context=etd.

24. Erik France, "The Regiment of Voltigeurs, U.S.A.: A Case Study of the Mexican-American War," in Harriett Denise Joseph, Anthony Knopp, and Douglas A. Murphy, eds., *Papers of the Second Palo Alto Conference* (1997), p. 76.

25. James Oberley, "Gray-Haired Lobbyists: War of 1812 Veterans and the Politics of Bounty Land Grants," *Journal of the Early Republic* (Spring 1985), vol. 5, no. 1 pp. 33–58.

26. "The President and the Army," *American Review* (September 1847), p. 22.

27. Foos, *A Short, Offhand, Killing Affair*, p. 57.

28. Foos, *A Short, Offhand, Killing Affair*, p. 175.

29. Alex Gourevitch, *From Slavery to the Cooperative Commonwealth: Labor and Republican Liberty in the Nineteenth Century* (2014).

30. For Oregon's exclusion laws: Kenneth Coleman, *Dangerous Subjects: James D. Saules and the Rise of Black Exclusion in Oregon* (2017). Despite these laws, and even after the United States imposed its conqueror's peace on Mexico, some still hoped that western movement would carry liberty forward, and that Oregon might serve to counterbalance Jacksonian Texas. Oregon, argued Vermont senator Samuel Phelps in 1848, would be a "safety valve" for the east's "pent up" population of African Americans, who "should be thrown off," but "thrown off upon the rest of the world as freemen . . . to aid in the extension of civilization over our immense territorial domain." "Extract from a Speech Delivered in the Senate of the United States, June 2, 1848, by Honorable Samuel Phelps," *Vermont Historical Gazetteer* (1867), p. 61.

6. THE TRUE RELIEF

1. Montesquieu, *The Spirit of the Laws* (1949), vol. 2, p. 25.

2. Adam Gaffney, *To Heal Humankind: The Right to Health in History* (2017).

3. Christopher Abel, *Health, Hygiene and Sanitation in Latin America, c. 1870 to c. 1950* (1996), pp. 7–8.

4. Karl Polanyi, *The Great Transformation* (2001), p. 267.

5. In David S. Reynolds, "Fine Specimens," *New York Review of Books*, March 22, 2018.

6. Drew Gilpin Faust, *This Republic of Suffering* (2008), p. xiv.

7. Theda Skocpol, *Protection Soldiers and Mothers: The Political Origins of Social Policy in the United States* (1992).

8. Du Bois, *Black Reconstruction*, p. 179.

9. W. E. B. Du Bois, *John Brown* (1909), p. 28.

10. Veto message (February 19, 1866), http://www.presidency.ucsb.edu/ws/?pid=71977.

11. Du Bois, in his history of Reconstruction, shows Johnson more sympathy than he merits, describing his "transubstantiation" from "a poor white," who fought against economic privilege, into a postbellum white supremacist: Johnson was the "tragedy of American prejudice made flesh; so that the man

born to narrow circumstances, a rebel against economic privilege, died with
the conventional ambition of a poor white to be the associate and benefac-
tor of monopolists, planters and slave drivers."

12. *Trial of Andrew Johnson* (1868), vol. 1, p. 342.
13. Jack Beatty, *Age of Betrayal* (2008), p. 131.
14. Blair was "willing to concede the black man every legal right" he possessed
but refused to "grant him dominion over my conscience, or my society."
15. *Congressional Globe*, March 16, 1872, p. 144.
16. James McPherson, *Abraham Lincoln and the Second American Revolution*
(1992).
17. John Cox and LaWanda Cox, "General O. O. Howard and the 'Misrepre-
sented Bureau,'" *Journal of Southern History* (November 1953), vol. 19, no. 4,
pp. 427–56; James Oakes, "A Failure of Vision: The Collapse of the Freedmen's Bureau Courts," *Civil War History* (March 1979), vol. 25, no. 1,
pp. 66–76.
18. Howard's dispatch west, along with the closing of the bureau, is a complicated story, told in Eric Foner, *Reconstruction* (1988), and Oakes, "A Failure of Vision."
19. Oliver Otis Howard, *Autobiography of Oliver Otis Howard, Major General*
(1908).
20. Daniel Sharfstein, *Thunder in the Mountain: Chief Joseph, Oliver Otis Howard and the Nez Perce War* (2017).
21. *The Papers of Ulysses S. Grant* (2005), p. 69.
22. Boyd Cothran and Ari Kelman, "How the Civil War Became the Indian
Wars," *New York Times* (May 25, 2015).
23. Noam Maggor, *Brahmin Capitalism: Frontiers of Wealth and Populism in
America's First Gilded Age* (2017).
24. Vernon Parrington, *Main Currents in American Thought* (1927), p. 24; Maggor, *Brahmin Capitalism.*
25. John E. Stealey, *The Rending of Virginia* (1902), p. 616. Also Steven Stoll,
Ramp Hollow: The Ordeal of Appalachia (2017).
26. *North American Review* (1881), p. 533.
27. Link, ed., *The Papers of Woodrow Wilson,* vol. 9, pp. 273–74.
28. Fulmer Mood and Frederick Jackson Turner, "Frederick Jackson Turner's
Address on Education in a United States without Free Lands," *Agricultural
History* (1949), vol. 23, no. 4, pp. 254–59.

7. THE OUTER EDGE

1. Ray Allen Billington, *The Genesis of the Frontier Thesis* (1971), p. 170.
2. Charles McLean Andrews, *The Old English Manor: A Study in English Economic History* (1892), p. 3.

3. W. H. Stowell and D. Wilson, *History of the Puritans in England and the Pilgrim Fathers* (1849), p. 2,341.

4. George Bancroft, *The History of the United States*, (1846), vol 1, p. 40.

5. Woodrow Wilson, *The State* (1898), p. 509.

6. Andrews, *The Old English Manor*, p. 4.

7. Frederick Jackson Turner, "The West and American Ideals," in John Mack Faragher, *Rereading Frederick Jackson Turner* (1999), p. 142.

8. Arthur M. Schlesinger, Sr., *New Viewpoints in American History* (1922), p. 70.

9. Frederick Jackson Turner, "Middle Western Pioneer Democracy," *The Frontier in American History* (1921), p. 343.

10. *The Works of Hubert Howe Bancroft* (1890), pp. 184–85, 650.

11. Daniel Schirmer, *The Philippines Reader* (1987), p. 26.

12. Theodore Roosevelt, *The Winning of the West*, vol. 1 (1889), p. 90.

13. Roosevelt, *The Winning of the West*, vol. 1, pp. 1, 30.

14. Roosevelt, *The Winning of the West*, vol. 2 (1889), p. 107.

15. Roosevelt, *The Winning of the West*, vol. 1, p. 133.

16. Richard Slotkin, *Gunfighter Nation* (1992), p. 55.

17. Ray Allen Billington, "Young Fred Turner," in Martin Ridge, ed., *Frederick Jackson Turner* (2016), p. 17.

18. Billington, *The Genesis of the Frontier Thesis*, p. 12.

19. The very first historical question Turner asked in print, in 1889, came at the beginning of a short book based on his Johns Hopkins dissertation that focused on the fur trade: "The exploitation of the Indian is generally dismissed with the convenient explanatory phrase, 'The onward march of civilization.' But how did it march?" Later, Turner's argument about the frontier would downplay the violence that would be part of any honest answer. Here, though, just sixteen years out from having lived through the final removal of Native Americans from Wisconsin, Turner admitted that colonial relations, from the French to the English, were founded on coercive dispossession. But, despite his own experience, he held up Wisconsin as a kind of exception to that history, whereby peaceful commerce, not conquest, was the primary mode of settler–indigenous relations. Turner's conclusion even posits a kind of Wisconsin exceptionalism, which allowed the territory to serve as a refuge for victims of wars elsewhere, resulting in an increase of the Native American population. More and more native groups, including the Mascoutin, Pottawattamie, Sauk, Winnebago, Fox, and Chippewa, moved to Wisconsin, attracted by the lure of peaceful trade and coexistence. "They caused," Turner wrote, a "re-adjustment in the Indian map of Wisconsin." The study ends in the early 1800s, before Turner's father's namesake took the presidency and before removal destroyed what Turner, bypassing his own firsthand memories of government-orchestrated dispossession, imagined to be Wisconsin's

multicultural commercial utopia. Turner, "The Character and Influence of the Indian Trade in Wisconsin: A Study of the Trading Post as an Institution," *Wisconsin Historical Society* (1889), p. 53.

20. This quotation is a composite of two Wilson citations. The first ("Steadily, almost calmly, they extended") comes from Wilson's "The Course of American History," a lecture given in 1895 and published in *Mere Literature, and Other Essays* (1896), p. 226. The second ("this great continent, then wild and silent") is from a review essay, "Mr. Goldwin Smith's 'Views' on Our Political History," published in *The Forum* (December 1893), p. 495.

21. "Born Modern: An Overview of the West," http://www.gilderlehrman.org /history-by-era/development-west/essays/born-modern-overview-west.

22. Quoted in Billington, *Frederick Jackson Turner* (1973), p. 123, and cited to Huntington Library, Manuscripts Division: HEH TU File Drawer E, Folder. Another influence on Turner was an 1865 essay by E. L. Godkin, *The Nation*'s founding editor, which described western settlement as producing a know-nothing smugness, an indifference to art and literature, a disrespect of learning and abstract thought, and a fetish for material success, such that the "prosperous management of a dry-goods store will be taken as strong indication of ability to fill the post of Secretary of the Treasury." Turner kept some of this criticism. But, just a few short sentences after noting the "anti-social" nature of frontier life and its "antipathy to control," Turner transmutes this antipathetic individualism into something like Hegel's Absolute Spirit: "From the conditions of frontier life came intellectual traits of profound importance. . . . The result is that to the frontier the American intellect owes its striking characteristics."

23. Turner fully elaborates his ideal of a pre-state civil society, based on a just-so balance of individualism and cooperation, in a 1918 lecture, "Middle Western Pioneer Democracy," cited above. As a crystallization of a number of premises that undergird Americanism, it is worth quoting at length: "From the first, it became evident that these [pioneers] had means of supplementing their individual activity by informal combinations. One of the things that impressed all early travelers in the United States was the capacity for extra-legal, voluntary association. . . . This power of the newly arrived pioneers to join together for a common end without the intervention of governmental institutions was one of their marked characteristics. The log rolling, the house-raising, the husking bee, the apple paring, and the squatters' associations whereby they protected themselves against the speculators in securing title to their clearings on the public domain, the camp meeting, the mining camp, the vigilantes, the cattle-raisers' associations, the 'gentlemen's agreements,' are a few of the indications of this attitude. . . . America does through informal association and understandings on the part of the people many of

the things which in the Old World are and can be done only by governmental intervention and compulsion. These associations were in America not due to immemorial custom of tribe or village community. They were extemporized by voluntary action. The actions of these associations had an authority akin to that of law. . . . If we add to these aspects of early backwoods democracy, its spiritual qualities, we shall more easily understand them. These men were emotional. As they wrested their clearing from the woods and from the savages who surrounded them, as they expanded that clearing and saw the beginnings of commonwealths, where only little communities had been, and as they saw these commonwealths touch hands with each other along the great course of the Mississippi River, they became enthusiastically optimistic and confident of the continued expansion of this democracy. They had faith in themselves and their destiny. And that optimistic faith was responsible both for their confidence in their own ability to rule and for the passion for expansion. They looked to the future. . . . Just because, perhaps, of the usual isolation of their lives, when they came together in associations whether of the camp meeting or of the political gathering, they felt the influence of a common emotion and enthusiasm. Whether Scotch-Irish Presbyterian, Baptist, or Methodist, these people saturated their religion and their politics with feeling. Both the stump and the pulpit were centers of energy, electric cells capable of starting widespreading fires. They *felt* both their religion and their democracy, and were ready to fight for it. This democracy was one that involved a real feeling of social comradeship among its widespread members."

24. John O'Sullivan, in his 1845 essay that coined the phrase "manifest destiny," said that how the United States came into the possession of the continent, including the taking of much of Mexico, happened "without agency of our government . . . in the natural flow of events, the spontaneous working of principles, and the adaptation of the tendencies and wants of the human race to the elemental circumstances in the midst of which they find themselves placed." John O'Sullivan, "Annexation," *United States Magazine and Democratic Review*, (July–August 1845), vol. 17, no.1, pp. 5–10.

25. Turner, "Middle Western Pioneer Democracy," p. 303.

26. Turner, "The West and American Ideals," p. 298.

27. Frederick Jackson Turner, "Social Forces in American History" (1921), p. 319.

28. Turner, "The West and American Ideals," p. 300.

29. Turner, "Social Forces in American History," p. 318.

30. Turner, "The West and American Ideals," p. 305.

31. Turner, "The West and American Ideals," p. 299.

32. Quoted in Limerick, "Turnerians All: The Dream of a Helpful History in an Intelligible World," p. 706.

33. Turner, "Social Forces in American History," p. 318.
34. "Contributions of the West," in Faragher, *Rereading Frederick Jackson Turner*, p. 92.
35. "Contributions to American Democracy," in Turner, "Middle Western Pioneer Democracy," p. 261.
36. "The Ideals of America," *Atlantic Monthly*, vol. 90 (December 1902): 721–34.
37. "The Ideals of America," p. 726.
38. The seizure of the Philippines, Guam, and Puerto Rico undercut efforts, such as Turner's, to purge Anglo-Saxon supremacy from Americanism. The Supreme Court ruled in 1901 that the rights found in the Constitution didn't cover the new possessions, since they were based on "certain principles of natural justice inherent in Anglo-Saxon character." "Foreign in a domestic sense" was how the court defined Puerto Rico, echoing its earlier 1831 ruling that the Cherokees were "domestic dependent nations." At the same time, with millions of central and southern European workers arriving in the United States, immigration debates likewise identified Anglo-Saxons as possessing unique racial "mental and moral qualities," as Senator Henry Cabot Lodge, Sr., said in 1896, which allowed for self-government.
39. Turner, "Social Forces in American History," p. 315.
40. Christina Duffy Burnett and Burke Marshall, eds., *Foreign in a Domestic Sense: Puerto Rico, American Expansion, and the Constitution* (2001), especially Mark Weiner's essay, "Teutonic Constitutionalism," pp. 48–81, for the "constitutional questions" raised by conquest discussed in the footnote. For the phrase "foreign in a domestic sense," see *Supreme Court Reporter*, vol. 21, October 1900 Term (1901), p. 967.
41. After the war, in a long 1919 letter summing up his relationship to Woodrow Wilson, Turner says he was even more eager to enter the European conflict than Wilson was but deferred to the president until public opinion in the country could catch up. He even suggests that he wanted a more aggressive, interventionist policy toward Mexico than the one followed by Wilson, who dispatched troops twice into that country. "I hadn't his patience with Mexico, and believed that his course there encouraged German arrogance to us," Turner wrote. Wendell Stephenson, "The Influence of Woodrow Wilson on Frederick Jackson Turner," *Agricultural History* (October 1945), vol. 19, no. 4, pp. 249–53.
42. Turner, "Middle Western Pioneer Democracy," p. 357.
43. Ronald Fernandez, *The Disenchanted Island: Puerto Rico and the United States in the Twentieth Century* (1996), p. 56.
44. Link, ed., *The Papers of Woodrow Wilson*, vol. 32, p. 187.
45. United States, *Report of the Industrial Commission* (1901), p. 198.

46. Adam Hochschild, "When Dissent Became Treason," *New York Review of Books* (September 28, 2017).

47. Turner, "Middle Western Pioneer Democracy," p. 359.

48. The Equal Justice Initiative puts the number of lynchings since Reconstruction (after 1877) at over 4,400 (https://eji.org/national-lynching-memorial).

49. Turner had a great influence on socialists such as Scott Nearing. Nearing, also prosecuted for opposing Wilson's war, included a lengthy historical analysis of wealth concentration in the United States in his address to the jury. "Two generations ago," Nearing wrote, "the country's adjustment to life included a *safety valve* in the form of a frontier. The frontier meant cheap grazing land, free agricultural land, free timber and free minerals. Today each first-class piece of land in the United States has its price." *The Coal Question* (1918), p. 11. Also *The Trial of Scott Nearing* (1919), p. 188.

50. Edmund Morris, *The Rise of Theodore Roosevelt* (2010), p. 824.

51. Marcus Klein, *Easterns, Westerns, and Private Eyes: American Matters, 1870–1900* (1994), p. 110; Owen Wister, "The National Guard of Pennsylvania," *Harper's Weekly* (September 1, 1894), pp. 824–26.

52. Michael Duchemin, *New Deal Cowboy* (2016); Holly George-Warren, *Public Cowboy No. 1: The Life and Times of Gene Autry* (2007).

8. THE PACT OF 1898

1. Ron Andrew, *Long Gray Lines: The Southern Military School Tradition, 1839–1915* (2001), p. 2.

2. Cothran and Kelman, "How the Civil War Became the Indian Wars."

3. Cothran and Kelman, "How the Civil War Became the Indian Wars."

4. Richard White, *It's Your Misfortune and None of My Own: A New History of the American West* (2015), p. 100.

5. Matthew Westfall, *The Devil's Causeway: The True Story of America's First Prisoners of War in the Philippines* (2012), p. 138.

6. Quotation from Cleveland's first draft of his comments, cited in Walter LaFeber's doctoral dissertation, "The Latin American Policy of the Second Cleveland Administration," University of Wisconsin, Madison (1959), p. 224.

7. Richard Wood, "The South and Reunion, 1898," *The Historian* (May 1969), vol. 31, pp. 415–30.

8. Wood, "The South and Reunion, 1898," p. 421.

9. United Spanish War Veterans, *Proceedings of the Stated Convention of the . . . National Encampment* (1931), vol. 33, p. 73.

10. Kristin Hoganson, *Fighting for American Manhood: How Gender Politics Provoked the Spanish–American and Philippine–American Wars* (1998), p. 74.

11. United Spanish War Veterans, *Proceedings of the Stated Convention of the . . . National Encampment*, p. 69.

12. Quotations are in Hoganson, *Fighting for American Manhood*, p. 73. See also Joseph Fry, *The American South and the Vietnam War: Belligerence, Protest, and Agony in Dixie* (2015).

13. Robert Bonner, *Colors and Blood: Flag Passions of the Confederate South* (2004), p. 165. See particularly Bonner's chapter "Conquered Banners."

14. Gaines M. Forster, *Ghosts of the Confederacy: Defeat, the Lost Cause, and the Emergence of the New South* (1987); Ralph Lowell Eckert, *John Brown Gordon: Soldier, Southerner, American* (1993), p. 329; and *Minutes of the . . . Annual Meeting and Reunion of the United Confederate Veterans* (1899), p. 27.

15. Edward Ayers, *The Promise of the New South* (2007), p. 332.

16. Ayers, *The Promise of the New South*, p. 329.

17. *Minutes of the . . . Annual Meeting and Reunion of the United Confederate Veterans*, p. 27.

18. *Minutes of the . . . Annual Meeting and Reunion of the United Confederate Veterans*, p. 111.

19. United Spanish War Veterans, *Proceedings of the Stated Convention of the . . . National Encampment*, p. 73.

20. For the Philippines: Paul Kramer, *The Blood of Government: Race, Empire, the United States, and the Philippines* (2006), pp. 102–44; for Haiti: Mary Renda, *Taking Haiti: Military Occupation and the Culture of U.S. Imperialism, 1915–1940* (2004), pp. 155–56; for the Dominican Republic: Bruce Calder, "Some Aspects of the United States Occupation of the Dominican Republic, 1916–1924," PhD thesis, University of Texas, Austin (1974), pp. 153–55.

21. "Statement of Mr. William Joseph Simmons," *The Ku-Klux Klan: Hearings Before the Committee on Rules*, House of Representatives, Sixty-Seventh Congress, First Session (1921), pp. 66–73.

22. House of Representatives, *The Ku-Klux Klan: Hearings Before the Committee on Rules*, p. 68.

23. Jack Foner, *Blacks and the Military in American History: A New Perspective* (1974), p. 76.

24. Willard Gatewood, *Black Americans and the White Man's Burden, 1898–1903* (1975), p. 54.

25. Barbara Foley, *Spectres of 1919* (2003), p. 133.

26. David Blight, *Race and Reunion* (2009), p. 352.

27. "Our Patriotic Rebels," *Brooklyn Daily Eagle*, August 26, 1917.

28. Link, ed., *The Papers of Woodrow Wilson*, vol. 37, p. 128.

29. James Scott Brown, *President Wilson's Foreign Policy* (1918), p. 301.

30. Laurent Dubois, *Haiti: The Aftershocks of History* (2012), p. 226; Hans Schmidt, *Maverick Marine* (2014), p. 84.

31. Thomas's letters to his fiancée, Beatrice, are perhaps the largest intact collection of such documents, providing rare insight. The collection is available thanks to the work of the historian Michael Schroeder and can be found here: http://www.sandinorebellion.com/USMC-Docs/Images-ThomasLetters /EmilThomasCollectionTranscripts-REV.pdf. Also: Schroeder's "Bandits and Blanket Thieves, Communists and Terrorists: The Politics of Naming Sandinistas in Nicaragua, 1927–36 and 1979–90," *Third World Quarterly* (2008), vol. 26, no. 1.

32. For the information about Okinawa in the footnote, see William Griggs, *The World War II Black Regiment That Built the Alaska Military Highway* (2002), p. 9, and Irving Werstein, *Okinawa* (1968), p. 162.

33. *The Crisis*, April 1952, p. 242.

34. John Coski, *The Confederate Battle Flag* (2009), p. 112.

35. As editor of the NAACP's *The Crisis*, Du Bois supported Woodrow Wilson, first in 1912 for the presidency and then later as he went to war. Du Bois had no illusions about Wilson. But with lynchings on the rise in the early twentieth century and the Klan regrouping, he had modest hope that the educated president "will not advance the cause of an oligarchy in the South." Wilson, though, didn't just fail to suppress racists but activated them. Later, in 1920, Du Bois published an essay, "The Souls of White Folk," a withering condemnation of war. All those Anglo supremacists Du Bois had to endure, including Wilson and Theodore Roosevelt—these "super-men and world-mastering demi-gods"—had joined with Europe to bring about an unparalleled devastation. "From beating, slandering, and murdering us the white world turned temporarily aside to kill each other," Du Bois wrote, and "we of the Darker Peoples looked on in mild amaze." Brandeis historian Chad Williams is writing a book on an 800-page manuscript Du Bois, who died in 1963, left unpublished, titled "The Black Man and the Wounded World." Du Bois had worked on the study, based on extensive interviews with African American veterans, for decades.

9. A FORTRESS ON THE FRONTIER

1. Rachel St. John, *Line in the Sand: A History of the Western U.S.–Mexico Border* (2011), p. 3.

2. Michael Pearlman, *Warmaking and American Democracy* (1999), p. 101.

3. Karp, *This Vast Southern Empire*, p. 120.

4. St. John, in *Line in the Sand*, p. 41, writes: "Mimicking earlier arguments about U.S. manifest destiny . . . expansionists naturalized their calls for

annexation. They argued that Arizona and Sonora were part of a shared landscape that the border artificially divided."

5. Kris Fresonke, *West of Emerson: The Design of Manifest Destiny* (2003), p. 80.

6. "United States v. Erick Bollman and Samuel Swartwout," *Reports of Cases, Civil and Criminal in the United States Circuit Court of the District of Columbia* (1852), p. 385.

7. Joseph Rice, *The Hampton Roads Conference* (1903), pp. 10–11, 18–19, https://babel.hathitrust.org/cgi/pt?id=loc.ark:/13960/t3zs34s29;view=1up;seq=1. For the quotation in the footnote: Ted Worley, ed., "A Letter Written by General Thomas C. Hindman in Mexico," *Arkansas Historical Quarterly* (1956), vol. 15, no. 4, pp. 365–68, which provided details about the short-lived Confederate colony in Mexico. See also Andrew Rolle, *The Lost Cause: The Confederate Exodus to Mexico* (1965).

8. John Mason Hart, *Empire and Revolution: The Americans in Mexico Since the Civil War* (2006), especially chapter 1, "Arms and Capital," is invaluable in describing this history of claims and investment.

9. For Cushing's role on the Claims Commission, see Allison Powers, "Settlement Colonialism: Law, Arbitration, and Compensation in United States Expansion, 1868–1941," doctoral dissertation, Columbia University (2017). Cushing, one of the first theoreticians of social steam, put theory to practice, helping to execute his advocacy for expansion through policy and diplomacy. As President John Tyler's ambassador, he negotiated the United States' first treaty with China, opening that country's markets to U.S. exports. After his service in the Mexican War, he was appointed U.S. attorney general, where he used the office to push through the infamous Kansas-Nebraska Act, which escalated the fight between slavers and abolitionists. The act, which enraged abolitionists and worsened relations between free and slave states, was based on the Jacksonian doctrine of "popular sovereignty," which gave white settlers the right to decide for themselves if their territory was to be free or slave—in other words, explicitly defining freedom as the freedom of white men to decide if they were going to enslave black men, women, and children. As attorney general, in an effort to appease southern states, he made sure that for enslaved people there was no escape valve, vigorously enforcing fugitive slave laws that mandated that fleeing slaves be returned to their southern masters, even interpreting the law to hold that it extended over Indian territory. Later, after the Civil War, Cushing speculated in real estate in Baja California and helped U.S. claimants make financial demands on Mexico. In 1868, he traveled to Colombia on one of his last diplomatic initiatives, negotiating a "right-of-way" for a proposed canal through Panama (then still a province of the South American nation).

10. Hart, *Empire and Revolution,* p. 41.

11. *Monthly Bulletin of the International Bureau of the American Republics,* July–December 1899, p. 475.

12. *Monthly Bulletin of the International Bureau of the American Republics,* p. 473.

13. Richard Griswold del Castillo, *The Treaty of Guadalupe Hidalgo: A Legacy of Conflict* (1992), p. 83.

14. Stuart Banner, *How the Indians Lost Their Land: Law and Power on the Frontier* (2005), p. 185.

15. Philip Russell, *The History of Mexico* (2011), p. 277.

16. Yaqui removal had started as early as the 1860s, after the defeat of Napoleon III's occupation (the Yaqui had fought on the side of the French). But a 1903 report by the Mexican War Department urged an acceleration of the dispossession. The report laid out three options that the state could take to break Yaqui resistance: extermination, deportation, or colonialization of their homeland. The government effectively implemented all three recommendations. Francisco Troncoso, *Las guerras con las tribus yaqui y mayo* (1905). Also: Evelyn Hu-DeHart, "Peasant Rebellion in the Northwest: The Yaqui Indians of Sonora," *Riot, Rebellion, and Revolution,* Friedrich Katz, ed. (1988), pp. 168–69.

17. William Carrigan and Clive Webb, *Forgotten Dead: Mob Violence Against Mexicans in the United States* (2013).

18. Katherine Benton-Cohen, *Borderline Americans* (2009), pp. 83–84.

19. Benjamin Johnson, *Revolution in Texas: How a Forgotten Rebellion and Its Bloody Suppression Turned Mexicans into Americans* (2003), for the Plan de San Diego conspiracy and for how the Texas Rangers facilitated property dispossession.

20. The webpage for the memory project is found here: https://www.refusing toforget.org/the-history.

21. Shawn Lay, *War, Revolution, and the Ku Klux Klan* (1985), p. 35.

22. For the information in the footnote: David Dorado Romo, *Ringside Seat to a Revolution: An Underground Cultural History of El Paso and Juárez, 1893–1923* (2005), p. 223.

23. St. John, *Line in the Sand,* p. 183.

24. Linda Gordon, *The Second Coming of the KKK* (2017); Shawn Lay, "Revolution, War, and the Ku Klux Klan in El Paso," University of Texas, El Paso, PhD thesis (1984), p. 101.

25. See Nancy MacLean, *Behind the Mask of Chivalry: The Making of the Second Ku Klux Klan* (1994), for the comparison of the Klan with European fascism.

26. Hiram Wesley Evans, "The Klan's Fight for Americanism," *North American Review* (March–May 1926), pp. 33–63.

27. House of Representatives, *The Ku-Klux Klan: Hearings Before the Committee on Rules*, p. 6.

28. Shawn Lay, "Imperial Outpost on the Border: El Paso's Frontier Klan No. 100," in *Invisible Empire in the West* (2004): see also Lay's "War, Revolution, and the Ku Klux Klan in El Paso," from which much of the discussion here on El Paso draws.

29. Lay, "War, Revolution, and the Ku Klux Klan in El Paso," p. 69.

30. Mae Ngai, *Impossible Subjects: Illegal Aliens and the Making of Modern America* (2003), discusses the Klan in the early U.S. Border Patrol. See also Miguel Antonio Levario, *Militarizing the Border* (2012), p. 167; F. Arturo Rosales, *Chicano!* (1996), p. 26; David Bradley and Shelley Fisher Fishkin, *Encyclopaedia of Civil Rights in America* (1997), p. 125; and George Sánchez, *Becoming Mexican American: Ethnicity, Culture, and Identity in Chicano Los Angeles* (1993), p. 59.

31. "Protect Mexicans, Hughes Tells Neff," *New York Times* (November 17, 1922); Mark Reisler, "Passing Through Our Egypt: Mexican Labor in the United States, 1900–1940," PhD thesis, Cornell University (1973), p. 243; "Protecting Mexicans in the United States," *New York Times* (November 18, 1922); "Mexicans and Negroes Flee," *New York Times* (November 16, 1922); "Mexico Protests Texas Mob Threat," *New York Times* (November 16, 1922).

32. "Texans Will Fight Quota on Mexicans," *New York Times* (December 4, 1927).

33. Greg Bailey, "This Presidential Speech on Race Shocked the Nation," *History News Network* (October 26, 2016), https://historynewsnetwork.org/article/164410. For this period in general: Kelly Lytle Hernández, *City of Inmates* (2017); Hans Vought, *The Bully Pulpit and the Melting Pot* (2004); Natalia Molina, *Fit to Be Citizens? Public Health and Race in Los Angeles, 1879–1939* (2006); and S. Deborah Kang, *The INS on the Line: Making Immigration Law on the US-Mexico Border, 1917–1954* (2017).

34. Kelly Lytle Hernández, *Migra!* (2010), pp. 56–57, details the social status of the U.S. Border Patrol's first recruits and makes the argument of the border patrol institutionalizing racism. She also convincingly argues that the patrol allowed its agents to use "selective immigration enforcement" to establish some leverage with large ranchers. They might focus on liquor smuggling and other "morality" issues, while occasionally letting the landowners know that continued access to cheap labor depended on their goodwill. Also: Hernández's "Entangling Bodies and Borders: Racial Profiling and the United States Border Patrol, 1924–1955," PhD dissertation, UCLA (2002).

35. Lay, "War, Revolution, and the Ku Klux Klan in El Paso," p. 75.

36. Kelly Lytle Hernández, "How Crossing the U.S.-Mexico Border Became a

Crime," *The Conversation* (May 1, 2017), based on her *City of Inmates*, https://theconversation.com/how-crossing-the-us-mexico-border-became-a -crime-74604.

37. "The Perils of the Mexican Invasion," *North American Review* (May 1929).

38. Abraham Hoffman, *Unwanted Mexican Americans in the Great Depression: Repatriation Pressures, 1929–1939* (1974), p. 43; Robert McKay, "The Federal Deportation Campaign in Texas: Mexican Deportation from the Lower Rio Grande Valley During the Great Depression," *Borderlands Journal* (Fall 1981), vol. 5.

39. Sánchez, *Becoming Mexican American*, p. 211.

40. As the scholars David Bateman, Ira Katznelson, and John Lapinski point out, the first decades of the twentieth century witnessed the return to power of what they call the "Southern Nation," founded on an even sharper commitment to white identity. Bateman, Katznelson, and Lapinski, eds., *Southern Nation: Congress and White Supremacy After Reconstruction* (2018).

41. Quoted in Joseph Nevins, *Operation Gatekeeper and Beyond* (2010), p. 242. Roxanne Dunbar-Ortiz, *Loaded: A Disarming History of the Second Amendment* (2018), p. 125, recounts the story of Harlon Carter, as does Mark Ames, "From 'Operation Wetback' to Newtown" (December 17, 2012): https://www.nsfwcorp.com/dispatch/newtown/.

10. A PSYCHOLOGICAL TWIST

1. Walter Weyl, *The New Democracy* (1912), p. 35. Subsequent quotations from Weyl are drawn from this edition and can be found here: https://archive .org/stream/newdemocracy00weyl/newdemocracy00weyl_djvu.txt.

2. Lewis Mumford, *The Golden Day* (1926), passim. Another pre–Great Depression essay critical of the influence of the frontier on American life and intellectual thought is John Dewey's "The American Intellectual Frontier," *New Republic* (May 10, 1922); it's a good example of the modernist backlash against the Frontier Thesis but also of the degree to which that thesis set the range of debate. See also "Exit Frontier Morality," *New Republic* (January 2, 1924).

3. Stuart Chase, *A New Deal* (1932), full text available via Hathi Trust, at: https://hdl.handle.net/2027/mdp.39015063999323.

4. Rexford Tugwell, *The Democratic Roosevelt* (1957), p. 56.

5. Earlier in 1931, the governor of Wisconsin, Philip La Follette, began his first inaugural address also with a lengthy summary of the Frontier Thesis, using the Wisconsinite Turner to reclaim the legacy of the state's stalled progressive movement: "Today we cannot seek a new freedom and a new opportunity

in some new territory. We must find our freedom and make our opportunity through wise and courageous readjustments of the political and economic order to the changed needs and conditions of our times." Roosevelt's text is here: http://teachingamericanhistory.org/library/document/common wealth-club-address/.

6. David Siemers, *Presidents and Political Thought* (2010), p. 145.
7. *Public Papers of the Presidents of the United States: F. D. Roosevelt, 1936* (1938), vol. 5, p. 195.
8. Cass Sunstein, *The Second Bill of Rights* (2009), p. 18.
9. *Public Papers of the Presidents of the United States: F. D. Roosevelt, 1935* (1938), vol. 4, p. 47.
10. "No More Frontiers," *Today* (June 26, 1935).
11. Turner, "The West and American Ideals," p. 293.
12. Steven Kesselman, "The Frontier Thesis and the Great Depression," *Journal of the History of Ideas* (April–June 1968), vol. 29, no. 2, pp. 253–268.
13. Frances Perkins, *People at Work* (1934), pp. 11, 26–27.
14. Hansen, born and raised on the Dakota plains and often described as the "American Keynes," was one of FDR's most important advisors; he argued that extensive expansion based on settlement and colonialism continued outward on the "world frontier" even after the closing of the United States' western frontier. The exhaustion, though, of that global frontier led to an era of "secular stagnation." Hansen was making the case for guided capital expansion regulated by a progressive government: "We do not have a choice between 'plan and no plan,'" he wrote in 1941, "we have a choice only between democratic planning and totalitarian regimentation." As an advisor to FDR, he helped design Social Security and drafted the Employment Act of 1946, which was to be the "Full Employment Act" until Republicans and conservative Democrats trimmed its ambitions.
15. "NRA Held New Frontier," *Los Angeles Times* (November 11, 1933).
16. *The Social Frontier* was the title of a journal promoting progressive education that began publishing in the 1930s; the phrase was used to mean: "The age of individualism and laissez-faire in economy and government is closing and a new age of collectivism is emerging."
17. For the origins of the New Deal's cultural pluralism applied to New Mexico: Suzanne Forrest, *The Preservation of the Village: New Mexico's Hispanics and the New Deal* (1998), pp. 76, 222. Tugwell's commencement address, discussed in the footnote, is found in "Your Future and Your Nation," *New Mexico Quarterly* (1935), vol. 5, no. 3.
18. Mae Ngai, *Impossible Subjects: Illegal Aliens and the Making of Modern America* (2004), pp. 83–86. Also: Kang, *The INS on the Line*, p. 71. As discussed later in the chapter, agricultural workers were mostly left out of the

New Deal's protection of labor rights. But Perkins did what she could to support farm unions, including those organized by Mexican migrants. In 1936, when California growers accused striking Mexican migrants of being manipulated by Mexican diplomats, Perkins intervened on behalf of the workers.

19. Later, the New Deal's petro-corporatism in Saudi Arabia, which focused the interests of the major oil companies toward the Middle East, allowed FDR some leeway in recognizing the legitimacy of Mexico's nationalization program. For Saudi Arabia, see Robert Vitalis, *America's Kingdom: Mythmaking on the Saudi Oil Frontier* (2009).

20. Under Wilson, U.S. diplomats began to work actively on behalf of the U.S. petroleum industry, protesting what the industry called a radical extension of the doctrine of "eminent domain." The United States had long recognized a similar doctrine, applied over the years to confiscate land, often from indigenous peoples, to build projects considered vital to the national interest, especially railroads. But Mexico extended that doctrine to "subsurface" property (that is, oil and minerals) to allow the confiscation of private property, including that held by foreigners. Through the 1920s, Washington, in response, had turned Mexico into a pariah state. Christy Thornton's forthcoming *Revolution in Development: Mexico and the Governance of the Global Economy* will focus on these contested notions of property rights. Also: Grandin, "The Liberal Traditions in the Americas."

21. However, Gene Autry's 1939 movie *South of the Border* paints an unflattering vision of Cárdenas's Mexico, of nationalized oil derricks left idle and revolutionaries drunk on ideology, threatening the possibility of creating a Pan-American anti-Nazi alliance and leaving Mexicans with nothing but "misery and want."

22. For Mexico's influence on the New Deal, and for the information in this paragraph: Tore Olsson, *Agrarian Crossings: Reformers and the Remaking of the U.S. and Mexican Countryside* (2017). The discussion that follows draws mostly from this excellent work.

23. John Francis Bannon, *Bolton and the Spanish Borderlands* (1974), p. 328.

24. Olsson, *Agrarian Crossings*, pp. 77–78.

25. Joseph Harsch, "America's Foreign Policy Restated," *Christian Science Monitor* (January 18, 1939).

26. Thomas Ferguson and Joel Rogers, *Right Turn: The Decline of the Democrats and the Future of American Politics* (1986). See also Steve Fraser and Gary Gerstle, eds., *The Rise and Fall of the New Deal Order* (1989), especially the essay by Thomas Ferguson, "Industrial Conflict and the Coming of the New Deal: The Triumph of Multinational Liberalism in America."

27. The New Deal, the historian David Kennedy writes, could have better spent its resources on developing city-based capital-intensive industries. Instead,

the framework offered by the Frontier Thesis didn't just produce the kind of sharp analysis of someone like Tugwell but a sentimentalism that would be harnessed to corporatism. "Nostalgia," Kennedy writes, "intellectual inertia, and political pressure beckoned the New Dealers backward, to the cornfields and hay-meadows and pastoral idylls of national mythology—and into the welcoming arms of a lean and hungry agricultural lobby." David Kennedy, *Freedom from Fear: The American People in Depression and War, 1929–1945* (1990).

28. "FSA, Farmers' Union Attacked by Cotton Head," *Atlantic Constitution* (November 24, 1942).

29. Jack Temple Kirby, *Rural Worlds Lost* (1987), pp. 57–58. Donald Holley, *Uncle Sam's Farmers: The New Deal Communities in the Lower Mississippi Valley* (1975), p. 196.

30. Olsson, *Agrarian Crossings*, p. 56.

31. Jefferson Cowie, *Capital Moves: RCA's Seventy-Five-Year Quest for Cheap Labor* (2001) p. 106.

32. Shortly after Bracero went into effect, the Mexican government, fearing its own labor shortage, said it would pull out of the program if Washington didn't do more to stem the flow of undocumented workers, as historian Kelly Lytle Hernández documents. The Roosevelt administration complied. The federal government launched what the chief supervisor of the border patrol described as an "intensive drive on Mexican aliens." Agents were pulled off the Canadian border and amassed on the southern line. Washington dramatically increased the budget and staff of the border patrol and worked out protocols with the Mexican government to create a unified trans-border deportation system. "Special Mexican Deportation Parties"—rapid-response units—targeted, caught, and deported undocumented workers, Hernández writes, along the border but also as far north as Minnesota, Chicago, and North Dakota, handing them off to Mexican authorities who then "train-lifted" them into Mexico's interior to prevent them from slipping back into the United States. Kelly Lytle Hernández, "The Crimes and Consequences of Illegal Immigration: A Cross-Border Examination of Operation Wetback, 1943 to 1954," *Western Historical Quarterly* (2006), vol. 37, no. 4, pp. 421–44.

33. Truman Moore, *The Slaves We Rent* (1965); Dale Wright, *They Harvest Despair* (1965). The quotation comes from a 1960 CBS special report broadcast between Thanksgiving and Christmas, called *Harvest of Shame* and anchored by Edward R. Murrow, which also focused on farmworkers who were U.S. citizens.

34. "World Needs 'True Social Democracy,'" *Washington Post* (April 15, 1945).

35. William Shirer, *Boston Globe* (November 4, 1945).

36. Grandin, "The Liberal Traditions in the Americas: Rights, Sovereignty, and the Origins of Liberal Multilateralism."

37. "Women, Workers, Farmers" were doing well in Japan, *The Tennessean* reported on May Day 1951, which included the quoted comparison with the United States. For the drafting of the Japanese constitution, including its inclusion of social rights: John Dower, *Embracing Defeat: Japan in the Wake of World War II* (1999).

38. Henry Wallace, in his 1934 book *New Frontiers*, believed an interpretation of the Constitution as it was written could serve as a basis of social rights, recommending that the United States simply redefine the meaning of "property . . . in a way that will fairly meet the realities of today."

11. A GOLDEN HARVEST

1. "Roosevelt Urges Peace Science Plan," *New York Times* (November 21, 1944).

2. Frederick Jackson Turner, "The Problem of the West" (1921), p. 212.

3. John Knox Jessup, "Western Man and the American Idea," *Life* (November 5, 1951).

4. Turner, "The West and American Ideals," p. 293.

5. "Fortune Magazine Proposes Four-Point Post-War Program," *Bankers' Magazine* (May 1942); Raymond Leslie Buell, *The United States in a New World: A Series of Reports on Potential Courses for Democratic Action* (1942).

6. Megan Black, "Interior's Exterior: The State, Mining Companies, and Resource Ideologies in the Point Four Program," *Diplomatic History* (2016), vol. 40, no. 1.

7. Selecting Google Ngram (https://books.google.com/ngrams) for "liberal multilateralism," "liberal universalism," and "liberal internationalism" returns the comparative popularity over time of each descriptor.

8. Caroline Fraser, *Prairie Fires: The American Dreams of Laura Ingalls Wilder* (2018), p. 450. For the Paterson quote: *The God of the Machine* (1943), p. 65.

9. Milton Friedman strikes a Turnerian note when he celebrates frontier civil society mutualism, which kept the state at bay between 1800 and 1929, in *Free to Choose* (1981), p. 28.

10. "James M. Buchanan, Economic Scholar and Nobel Laureate, Dies at 93," *New York Times* (January 9, 2013); Nancy MacLean, *Democracy in Chains* (2017); James M. Buchanan, "The Soul of Classical Liberalism," *Independent Review* (2000), vol. 5, no. 1.

11. Frank Holman, *Story of the "Bricker" Amendment* (1954), p. 38.

12. Holman, *Story of the "Bricker" Amendment*, p. 151.

13. *Treaties and Executive Agreements: Hearings Before a Subcommittee of the Committee on the Judiciary, United States Senate, Eighty-Third Congress* (1953), p. 584. For the 1919 migratory birds case, see Edwin Borchard, "Treaties and Executive Agreements: A Reply," *Yale Law Journal* (1945), vol. 54, no. 3, pp. 616–64; for the quote in the footnote: House of Representatives, *Hearings Before the Committee on Immigration and Naturalization . . . Relating to the Temporary Admission of Illiterate Mexican Laborers* (1920), p. 174.

14. See "Sneak Attack on the Constitution," *Chicago Daily Tribune* (December 9, 1951). For how this mobilization, which apparently began with an idea put forth by the American Bar Association, was sparked by the signing of the U.N. Universal Declaration of Human Rights: "Curb on President's Treaty Role Voted, 8–4, by Senate Committee," *New York Times* (June 5, 1953); for the testimony of the ABA president: *Treaties and Executive Agreements: Hearings Before a Subcommittee of the Committee on the Judiciary, United States Senate, Eighty-Third Congress* (1953), p. 584.

15. "Vote on Constitution of Puerto Rico Bogs," *New York Times* (May 14, 1952); "Puerto Rican Code Approved by House," *New York Times* (May 29, 1952); "Hit Red Tinge in Puerto Rico Constitution," *Chicago Daily Tribune* (May 15, 1952). The politics surrounding Puerto Rico's 1952 constitution concerned not just "social rights" but fundamental issues related to questions of sovereignty, which played out in complicated ways within Puerto Rico. José Trías Monge, who was the chief justice of Puerto Rico's Supreme Court, describes some of the larger context here: *Historia constitucional de Puerto Rico,* vol. 4 (1983) and *Puerto Rico: The Trials of the Oldest Colony in the World* (1999).

16. Rick Halpern and Jonathan Morris, eds., *American Exceptionalism?* (1997), p. 92. The legal theorist Cass Sunstein points out that the time to have included social rights in the U.S. Constitution would have been either the 1930s or the 1960s, with Lyndon Baines Johnson's Great Society program. But in neither period did the country see any "serious debate about constitutional amendments. There was no significant discussion of adding social and economic rights to the American Constitution." After World War II, Washington did sign on to the U.N. Universal Declaration of Human Rights, which obligated states to guarantee both social and individual rights. Since then, the United States has retreated, refusing, for instance, to sign any treaty that might in any way promise health care. To do so, wrote the Heritage Foundation in 1993, would be "foolish" since "abundant health care, housing, and food are byproducts of wealth created by private individuals pursuing a profit," not products of a state intervening to redistribute private profit.

17. "A Luce Forecast for a Luce Century," in the Clare Boothe Luce Papers at

the Library of Congress (January 1, 1942). Thanks to Nikhil Singh for passing this on.

18. *Bankers' Magazine*, "Fortune Magazine Proposes Four-Point Post-War Program."

19. Department of State, "Report by the Policy Planning Staff" (February 24, 1948), https://history.state.gov/historicaldocuments/frus1948v01p2/d4.

20. Henry L. Stimson, *On Active Service in Peace and War* (1947), p. 654.

21. The quotation is found in the U.S. Congress's *Post-War Economic Policy and Planning* (1944), p. 1082, but it was first cited by William Appleman Williams, in his chapter "The Nightmare of Depression and the Vision of Omnipotence," in *The Tragedy of American Diplomacy* (1962), p. 236.

22. *Resources for Freedom: A Report to the President* (1952), p. 3.

23. *Preliminary Hearings Before the Committee on Foreign Affairs, House of Representatives* (1951), p. 376.

24. Leon Hesser, *The Man Who Fed the World* (2006), p. 66. Rockefeller's Mexico program was led by plant pathologist Norman Borlaug, who would later win the Nobel Prize and be associated with the anti-Malthusian idea that human innovation could always stay a step ahead of the environment's carrying capacity; Paul Sabin, *The Bet: Paul Ehrlich, Julian Simon, and Our Gamble over Earth's Future* (2013).

25. Preface to Webb, *The Great Frontier.*

26. Address in Cheyenne, Wyoming (May 9, 1950), http://www.presidency.ucsb.edu/ws/index.php?pid=13477; Truman, *The American Frontier: Address by Harry S. Truman, President of the United States, July 28, 1951* (1951).

27. Betsy Taylor and David Tilford, "Why Consumption Matters," in Juliet Schor and Douglas Holt, eds., *The Consumer Society Reader* (2000), p. 472.

28. Address Before the National Conference on International Economic and Social Development (April 8, 1952), http://www.presidency.ucsb.edu/ws/index.php?pid=14453.

29. Hernández, *Migra!*, p. 130. The point then, as it is now, was to force undocumented workers to take more deadly routes, as did five Mexicans who skirted this fence in 1952 and died of dehydration in California's Imperial Valley, near Superstition Mountain. Wayne Cornelius, "Death at the Border: Efficacy and Unintended Consequences of U.S. Immigration Control Policy," *Population and Development Review* 27 (December 2001), pp. 661–85.

12. SOME DEMONIC SUCTION TUBE

1. Quotations, including JFK's "high beyond," from Richard Drinnon, *Facing West: The Metaphysics of Indian-Hating and Empire-Building* (1980).

2. See also Milton Bates, *The Wars We Took to Vietnam* (1996).

3. Martin Luther King, Jr., *Why We Can't Wait* (2011), p. 34.

4. Martin Luther King, Jr., "The Church on the Frontier of Racial Tension" (April 19, 1961), digital.library.sbts.edu/bitstream/handle/10392/2751/King -ChurchOnFrontier.pdf; King, "Fumbling on the New Frontier," *The Nation* (March 3, 1962).

5. *The Papers of Martin Luther King, Jr.* (1992), vol. 6, p. 291.

6. *The Papers of Martin Luther King, Jr.*, vol. 7, p. 273.

7. In *The Radical Reader* (2003), edited by Timothy McCarthy and John Campbell McMillian, p. 376.

8. Tommie Shelby and Brandon Terry, *To Shape a New World: Essays on the Political Philosophy of Martin Luther King, Jr.* (2018).

9. *The Papers of Martin Luther King, Jr.*, vol. 7, p. 414.

10. David Garrow, *MLK: An American Legacy* (2016).

11. Daniel Lucks, *Selma to Saigon: The Civil Rights Movement and the Vietnam War* (2014), p. 4.

12. The quotations are from William Pepper's illustrated essay, "The Children of Vietnam," *Ramparts* (January 1967). Apparently the photographs and text in this essay moved King to speak out.

13. David Garrow, "When Martin Luther King Came Out Against Vietnam," *New York Times* (April 4, 2017).

14. An example of what by the early 2000s had become an entirely transactional relationship between war abroad and social services (through federal spending) at home: after 9/11, New York senator Hillary Clinton traded her vote in favor of George W. Bush's 2002 war authorization for domestic funding: "I'm sitting there in the Oval Office, and Bush says to me, 'What do you need?' And I said, 'I need twenty billion dollars to rebuild, you know, New York,' and he said, 'You got it.' And he was good to his word." And so was she, voting for Bush's war.

15. James E. Westheider, *Fighting on Two Fronts: African Americans and the Vietnam War* (1999).

16. Thomas Borstelmann, *The Cold War and the Color Line* (2001), p. 215; *Jet* (April 4, 1968), p. 9.

17. *Jet* (May 16, 1968).

18. For the Confederate flag in Vietnam after King's murder: James Westheider, *The Vietnam War* (2007), p. 182; Jason Sokol, *The Heavens Might Crack: The Death and Legacy of Martin Luther King Jr.* (2018); John Jordan, *Vietnam, PTSD, USMC, Black-Americans and Me* (2016), p. 26; Coski, *The Confederate Battle Flag.*

19. *Democrat and Chronicle* (June 14, 1970), p. 39.

20. The Floridian Calley was extremely popular in the South, as Joseph Fry points out in his recent book, *The American South and the Vietnam War:*

Belligerence, Protest, and Agony in Dixie (2015); Joan Hoff, *Nixon Reconsidered* (1995), p. 222.

21. The campaign to depict Calley as an honorable warrior scapegoated by elites could point to history for support. Calley did nothing worse than did the Texan Joseph Duncan, who, in March 1906 as head of the 6th U.S. Infantry, led the slaughter of between eight hundred and one thousand Filipinos, the majority of them women and children. Duncan received a personal telegram from President Roosevelt: "I congratulate you and the officers and men of your command upon the brilliant feat of arms wherein you and they so well upheld the honor of the American Flag." The Texan was eventually promoted to the rank of brigadier general, buried with honor at Arlington. Calley had the bad fortune of committing his atrocity just as the pact of 1898 was unraveling. "Roosevelt Congratulates Troops," *Mindanao Herald* (March 17, 1906), p. 1; "Medals for Valor," *Mindanao Herald* (June 2, 1906), p. 3; "Medal for Dajo Jero," *Mindanao Herald* (July 14, 1906), p. 2.

22. Leo Janos, "The Last Days of the President," *The Atlantic* (July 1973).

23. Greg Grandin, "Secrecy and Spectacle: Why Only Americans Are Worthy of Being Called 'Torturable,'" *The Nation* (December 17, 2014).

24. Tim Golden, "In U.S. Report, Brutal Details of 2 Afghan Inmates' Deaths," *New York Times* (May 20, 2005).

25. Daniel Bell, *The Public Interest* (Fall 1975).

26. Paz, *Claude Lévi-Strauss: An Introduction* (1970), p. 97.

27. Patrick Timmons, "Trump's Wall at Nixon's Border: How Richard Nixon's Operation Intercept Laid the Foundation for Decades of U.S.–Mexico Border Policy, Including Donald Trump's Wall," *NACLA Report on the Americas* (2017), vol. 49.

13. MORE, MORE, MORE

1. William Endicott, "Reagan Selling a Return to the 'Good Old Days,'" *Los Angeles Times* (May 6, 1980).

2. Ronnie Dugger, *On Reagan* (1983), p. 86.

3. Here's Secretary of State Henry Kissinger in 1974, a year after the end of the Vietnam War: "The U.S. economy will require large and increasing amounts of minerals from abroad, especially from less developed countries. That fact gives the U.S. enhanced interest in the political, economic, and social stability of the supplying countries. Wherever a lessening of population pressures through reduced birth rates can increase the prospects for such stability, population policy becomes relevant to resource supplies and to the economic interests of the United States."

4. See Paul Ehrlich, *The Population Bomb* (1968), for an example of an

argument that stressed the need to create a reformed, environmentally sustainable economic model. Many establishment economists reacted with incredulity to the kind of arguments put forth by the Club of Rome's 1972 *The Limits to Growth*, which held that capitalism was careening to catastrophe. "The very hint," as a recent survey put it, "of an overall global limitation as suggested in the report *The Limits to Growth* has generally been met with disbelief and rejection by businesses and economists" (Fereidoon P. Sioshansi, ed., *Energy, Sustainability and the Environment* [2011], p. 93). But high-level U.S. policy makers, such as Henry Kissinger, used the idea of impending scarcity and overpopulation to justify a hostile stance to developing nations, a stance that would culminate in Reagan's counterinsurgent drive into the third world. Electing Reagan, Kissinger said in his 1980 Republican National Convention speech, would "guarantee our access to vital minerals and raw materials at a fair price." Such neo-Malthusianism also was reflected in increased vigilantism on the U.S.-Mexico border.

5. Kevin Mattson, "A Politics of National Sacrifice," *American Prospect* (March 23, 2009).

6. David Nyhan, "The Can-Do President," *Boston Globe* (August 26, 1981).

7. Here's Reagan at the Neshoba County Fair: "They have created a vast bureaucracy, or a bureaucratic structure—bureaus and departments and agencies—to try and solve all the problems and eliminate all the things of human misery that they can. They have forgotten that when you create a government bureaucracy, no matter how well intentioned it is, almost instantly its top priority becomes preservation of the bureaucracy. . . . Bureaucracy has [welfare recipients] so economically trapped that there is no way they can get away. And they're trapped because that bureaucracy needs them as a clientele to preserve the jobs of the bureaucrats themselves." The transcript, and a recording of his remarks, are reproduced at the *Neshoba Democrat*, November 15, 2007, available here: http://neshobademocrat.com/Content /NEWS/News/Article/Transcript-of-Ronald-Reagan-s-1980-Neshoba -County-Fair-speech/2/297/15599. Reagan supporters strongly deny that these remarks—including his pledge to return schools to local control— were signaling white supremacy. But see Joseph Crespino, *In Search of Another Country: Mississippi and the Conservative Counterrevolution* (2007). According to Crespino, members of Reagan's campaign couldn't remember him using the phrase "states' rights" before Neshoba. During the campaign, Reagan even dared to float tentative criticism of the 1964 Civil Rights Act, saying that it "might be setting a precedent for infringing upon everybody's individual freedom." In "Reagan Goes After Carter, Woos Chicanos," *Boston Globe* (September 17, 1980.

8. Endicott, "Reagan Selling a Return to the 'Good Old Days.'"

9. From Reagan's remarks on the Challenger explosion; in *Public Papers of the Presidents of the United States: Ronald Reagan* (1990), p. 1199.

10. Norris, "The Frontier Gone at Last," p. 73.

11. *Public Papers*, vol. 1 (1984), p. 45.

12. William Clark is identified as the official author of this memo, though Aryeh Neier, *Taking Liberties* (2005), p. 185, tags Elliott Abrams, who also pushed human rights to be identified as individual rights, as its "actual author."

13. Jerry Wayne Sanders, *Empire at Bay: Containment Strategies and American Politics at the Crossroads* (1983), p. 22.

14. Euan Hague, Heidi Beirich, and Edward H. Sebesta, eds., *Neo-Confederacy: A Critical Introduction* (2008), p. 28.

15. Daniel Stedman Jones, *Masters of the Universe: Hayek, Friedman, and the Birth of Neoliberal Politics* (2012); Quinn Slobodian, *Globalists: The End of Empire and the Birth of Neoliberalism* (2018); Daniel Rodgers, *Age of Fracture* (2003); David Harvey, *A Brief History of Neoliberalism* (2005); Nancy MacLean, *Democracy in Chains* (2017); Wendy Brown, *Undoing the Demos* (2015); M. Olssen and M. A. Peters, "Neoliberalism, Higher Education and the Knowledge Economy: From the Free Market to Knowledge Capitalism," *Journal of Education Policy* (2005), vol. 20, no. 3, pp. 313–45; Keith Sturges, *Neoliberalizing Educational Reform* (2015); LaDawn Haglund, *Limiting Resources: Market-Led Reform and the Transformation of Public Goods* (2011); Philip Mirowski, *Never Let a Serious Crisis Go to Waste: How Neoliberalism Survived the Financial Meltdown* (2013); Jamie Peck, *Constructions of Neoliberal Reason* (2010).

16. "Idea of the frontier" is how Stuart Butler, a Heritage Foundation analyst who spearheaded much of Reagan's deregulatory agenda, described the libertarian agenda. In Jones, *Masters of the Universe*, p. 320. For the Koch brothers and Sagebrush: "Libertarian Candidate Backs Drive to Regain Land," *New York Times* (July 15, 1980); "Third Party Challengers," *Newsweek* (October 15, 1980). Such Koch-funded groups, including Americans for Prosperity Nevada, were allied with the Bundy family militia, which staged armed standoffs in Nevada and Oregon, including the forty-one-day siege at Oregon's Malheur National Wildlife Refuge. See Jack Healy and Kirk Johnson, "The Larger, but Quieter Than Bundy, Push to Take Over Federal Land," *New York Times* (January 10, 2016); William deBuys, "Who Egged On the Bundy Brothers?" *The Nation* (May 18, 2016). Charles Wilkinson, *Crossing the Next Meridian: Land, Water, and the Future of the American West*, published in 1992, describes the work of environmentalists who fought to take back the West from what he calls the "lords of yesterday." Many of these activists, including Wilkinson, had hoped Bill Clinton's 1992 election would

help create a "new American land ethic." Within a year, Wilkinson subsequently wrote, the Clinton administration gave up the fight. "The Lords of
Yesterday Are Back and They Want America's Public Land," ran a recent
headline in *Mountain Journal*.

17. "Reagan Breaks GOP Tradition, Woos Chicanos," *Chicago Tribune* (September 17, 1980).

18. The Kennedy administration had begun to wind down Bracero largely in
response to a series of damning exposés, including Edward Murrow's CBS
broadcast *Harvest of Shame* and Truman Moore's book *The Slaves We Rent*,
which revealed the dismal conditions under which farm laborers (denied
the protection offered by the New Deal's National Labor Relations Act)
worked. These reports focused on *both* Mexican migrants and U.S. citizens,
including many African Americans. "This scene is not taking place in the
Congo. It has nothing to do with Johannesburg or Cape Town. It is not
Nyasaland or Nigeria. This is Florida. These are citizens of the United
States, 1960," began *Harvest of Shame*. By shutting down Bracero—which
covered only Mexican migrants—the White House appeared to be doing
something to address the issue.

19. The 1965 Hart-Celler Act, which went into effect in 1968, imposed a total
quota of 120,000 on the entire "Western Hemisphere." That number was
further reduced in 1976. Ben Mathis-Lilley, "The Law That Villainized Mexican Immigrants," *Slate* (August 10, 2015), provides a good overview. http://
www.slate.com/articles/news_and_politics/politics/2015/08/mexican
_illegals_how_the_hart_celler_act_and_its_conservative_supporters.html. At
this point, before the post-Vietnam sort-out, nativists were found equally in
the Republican and Democratic parties.

20. A decade earlier, in 1952, in addition to affirming the racist quotas of the
1924 immigration law, the McCarran-Walker Act, passed by a Democratic
Congress over Truman's veto, made it easier to try migrants for unlawful entry
by removing their right to grand jury oversight and a jury trial.

21. Ana Raquel Minian, *Undocumented Lives: The Untold Story of Mexican
Migration* (2018). The numbers come from "Stanford Scholar Examines the
Spike in Unauthorized Mexican Migration in the 1970s," press release, Stanford University (May 14, 2018), https://news.stanford.edu/press-releases
/2018/05/14/analyzing-undocumented-mexican-migration-u-s-1970s/.

22. L. H. Whittemore, "Can We Stop the Invasion of Illegal Aliens?" *Boston
Globe* (February 29, 1976).

23. John Crewdson, "Abuse Is Frequent for Female Illegal Aliens," *New York
Times* (October 23, 1980).

24. Justin Akers Chacón and Mike Davis, *No One Is Illegal* (2006) provides an
excellent overview of the intersection of anti-immigration laws and white

vigilantism on the border. Also Crewdson's two reports: "Farmhands Seeking a Union Walk 400 Miles to See Texas Governor," *New York Times* (April 5, 1977), and "The New Migrant Militancy," *New York Times* (April 16, 1978).

25. Jonathan Freedman, "In an Area Growing Too Fast, Anger Is Taken Out on the Weak," *Los Angeles Times* (February 19, 1990).

26. California Legislature, "International Migration and Border Region Violence" (June 22, 1990), https://digitalcommons.law.ggu.edu/cgi/viewcontent.cgi?referer=https://www.google.com/&httpsredir=1&article=1086&context=caldocs_joint_committees.

27. Regarding the KKK's presence on the California border in the 1970s, Carter's INS director, Leonel Castillo, said that it was mostly a stunt, that the organization never had more than twelve people at the border at one time. But its members would hold a press conference, and protesters from the Chicano movement would show up and "completely outnumber them." And then newspapers would send reporters to cover the confrontation and they "outnumbered everybody" and the Klan got its profile raised. Castillo here is describing mass-media contretemps. Institutionally, though, the KKK had more than a few sympathizers within the border patrol, who welcomed the Klan's arrival on the border. One agent told a reporter that when the Klan showed up at the border with their "White Power" T-shirts, they were given the "red-carpet treatment" and encouraged to capture migrants. Three years later, one of the Klan border watch organizers, Tom Metzger, won the Democratic nomination for southern Los Angeles's House seat, to unsuccessfully challenge the Republican incumbent. John Crewdson, *The Tarnished Door: The New Immigrants and the Transformation of America* (1983), p. 196; Institute of Oral History, University of Texas at El Paso, interview #532, Leonel Castillo, https://digitalcommons.utep.edu/cgi/viewcontent.cgi?article=1565&context=interviews. See also Kathleen Belew, *Bring the War Home: The White Power Movement and Paramilitary America* (2018), p. 37.

28. "Klan There but Where?" *Austin American Statesman* (November 1, 1977).

29. Peter Brush, "The Story Behind the McNamara Line," *Vietnam* (February 1996), https://msuweb.montclair.edu/~furrg/pbmcnamara.html; Terry Lukanic, comp., *U.S. Navy Seabees-The Vietnam Years* (2017), p. 43.

30. "U.S. Will Construct Barrier Across DMZ," *New York Times* (September 7, 1967).

31. "The Illegales: Americans Talk of Fences," *Los Angeles Times* (October 9, 1977); "In Defense of an El Paso 'Wall,'" letter to the editor, *New York Times* (November 22, 1978).

32. "Wild Schemes for Slowing Illegal Aliens," *San Diego Tribune* (March 31, 1986).

33. Phil Gailey, "Courting Hispanic Voters Now a Reagan Priority," *New York Times* (May 19, 1983). According to Kathleen Belew, in *Bring the War Home*, it was around 1983 when white-supremacist groups underwent a transformation, largely driven by the fallout from Vietnam. In the past, organizations such as the Nazis and the KKK imagined themselves as pressure groups, working to keep the country as white as possible. Now, though, in the 1980s, they took a more oppositional, apocalyptical stance, their political analysis turning darkly, and baroquely, conspiratorial. Belew estimates that the extremist racist movement counted twenty-five thousand members and another six hundred thousand or so who either bought or read the movement's literature. The numbers are from an essay Belew wrote in the *New York Times* called "The History of White Power," (April 18, 2018).

34. Frederick Kiel, "Mexicans Outraged Over 'Operation Jobs,'" UPI (May 2, 1982).

35. "INS Official—Private War on Illegal Aliens," *Los Angeles Times* (April 28, 1986).

36. Reagan's straddle on the issue of immigration is symbolized by Ezell himself. After helping to sell Reagan's 1986 immigration "amnesty" to other hard-liners, Ezell used his INS office to intimidate undocumented residents from applying for the amnesty. He then went on to spearhead California's Proposition 187. Kate Callen, "Harold Ezell: INS Point Man for Amnesty Program," UPI (May 4, 1988).

37. "High-Tech War Against Aliens," *Newsday* (April 23, 1983).

38. "Transcript of the Debate," *Philadelphia Inquirer* (October 22, 1984).

39. Earl Shorris, "Raids, Racism, and the I.N.S.," *The Nation* (May 8, 1989).

40. Stacey L. Connaughton, *Inviting Latino Voters* (2005), p. 42.

41. I discuss Iran-Contra at length in *Empire's Workshop*. See also Belew, *Bring the War Home*, pp. 77–99, for a discussion of Posey and the CMA in detail, including its relationship to Reagan's 1983 invasion of Grenada, which, as Belew demonstrated, likewise focused the concentration of white-supremacist mercenaries.

42. The "Iran" part of Iran-Contra—which entailed members of the Reagan administration selling high-tech missiles to the Ayatollah's Iran and diverting the money to the Contras—wouldn't be revealed to the public until late 1986, when the story broke in the press. The CMA was part of the "Contra" part of Iran-Contra, which had been reported on since around 1984 and included the creation of a sprawling, grassroots fundraising network that brought together all the fringe elements of the right—radicalized vets, Klan members, *Soldier of Fortune* mercenary types, right-wing Christians, Latin American Nazis, southern conservative businessmen, like Texas oilman Ross Perot, and Middle East sheiks and sultans—to support the cause of anti-

communism in Central America. Eventually, Posey and other leaders of the CMA were charged with violating the United States' Neutrality Act, but the case was dismissed by a federal judge who said that they couldn't have violated the act, since that act only applied to countries with which the United States was at peace. "By no stretch of the imagination can the United States be said to have been 'at peace' with Nicaragua," Judge Norman Roettger ruled. "The facts show that, although Congress may have abstained from supporting the Contras . . . the executive branch did not abstain." Posey and his co-defendants were represented by Doug Jones, now Alabama's Democratic senator.

43. Kristina Karin Shull, "'Nobody Wants These People': Reagan's Immigration Crisis and America's First Private Prisons," PhD dissertation, University of California, Irvine (2014).

44. "Verdict in Sanctuary Trial," *Hartford Courant* (May 13, 1986); "Alien Arrests Uproar," *Los Angeles Times* (July 11, 1986); "Anti-Communism Called the Thread Binding Group That Captured Aliens," *New York Times* (July 11, 1986); "Private Wars," *Wall Street Journal* (June 14, 1985); "Plea on Firearms Charge," *New York Times* (July 29,1987).

45. For Posey and the CMA: S. Brian Willson, *Blood on the Tracks* (2011), pp. 188–89, 394; Peter Kornbluh, *Nicaragua: The Price of Intervention* (1987); Freddy Cuevas, "Contras Seek Training from Vietnam Vets," *Sunday Rutland Herald* and *Sunday Times Argus* (July 6, 1986); Ken Lawrence, "From Phoenix Associates to Civilian-Military Assistance," *Covert Action Quarterly* (Fall 1984), no. 22, pp. 18–19; *Who Are the Contras?* Washington, D.C.: U.S. Congress, Arms Control and Foreign Policy Caucus (1985); "6 Cleared of Illegal Aid to Contras," *Chicago Tribune* (July 14, 1989). See also Belew, *Bring the War Home*, pp. 77–99.

46. For "our own southern frontier:" *Public Papers of the Presidents of the United States: Ronald Reagan* (1988), p. 352.

47. The bipartisan Simpson-Mazzoli Act was largely based on the recommendations of the bipartisan Select Commission on Immigration and Refugee Policy, which was established by Congress in 1978 and issued its report in 1981. Carter, though, floated a similar reform: increasing the size of the border patrol; fining employees who hire undocumented workers; and a one-time limited amnesty that provided legal status but not citizenship to undocumented residents. "The Illegales: Americans Talk of Fences," *Los Angeles Times* (October 9, 1977).

48. "In total, over 3 million people applied for temporary residency, and nearly 2.7 million people received permanent residency in the United States as a result of IRCA. IRCA remains the largest immigrant legalization process conducted" in U.S. history; "Lessons from the Immigration Reform and Con-

trol Act of 1986," Migration Policy Institute (August 2005), http://www
.migrationpolicy.org/pubs/PolicyBrief_No3_Aug05.pdf.

49. "Reagan's Farewell Address" (January 12, 1989), https://www.nytimes.com
/1989/01/12/news/transcript-of-reagan-s-farewell-address-to-american
-people.html.

50. *Public Papers of the Presidents of the United States: George Bush, 1991*
(1992), p. 1378.

51. Bush made these remarks in a speech given in Wyoming, heavy with frontier
imagery straight from Turner. The topic of the speech was environmental-
ism, and Bush was trying to strike that middle ground, emphasizing limitlessness while still admitting that some government policy was needed to protect
nature. In light of current Koch-funded fossil-fuel absolutism, and considering that Bush did preside over successful policy responses to serious environmental problems, the speech seems well outdated: "But whether restoring a
forest or the air that flows above it, nature needs our help. . . . We've hardly
scratched the surface of what God put on earth and what God put in man."

52. *Public Papers of the Presidents of the United States: George Bush, 1991*
(1992), p. 280. For "revolution without frontiers," see "Remarks at the Beacon Council Annual Meeting" (September 30, 1991), http://www.presidency
.ucsb.edu/ws/?pid=20042.

53. For example, Edwin Feulner, the founder and former president of the Heritage Foundation, "Skip the Amnesty Sequel" (July 17, 2013), https://www
.heritage.org/immigration/commentary/skip-the-amnesty-sequel; "Steve King
Says Ronald Reagan's 1986 'Amnesty Act' Led to 15 Million Votes for Barack
Obama," *Politifact* (May 29, 2013), http://www.politifact.com/truth-o-meter
/statements/2013/may/29/steve-king/steve-king-says-ronald-reagans-1986
-amnesty-act-le/.

14. THE NEW PREËMPTOR

1. Walter Mears, "Immigration a Hot Political Potato," *Philadelphia Tribune*
(October 14, 1994).

2. "2 Dispute Chairman on 'Sealing' Border," *Washington Post* (December 22,
1978).

3. Bush actually borrowed, intentionally, a Sandinista slogan, *revolución sin
fronteras*, which he translated as "revolution without frontiers" but would
be better rendered as "revolution without borders." "Remarks at the Beacon
Council Annual Meeting," http://www.presidency.ucsb.edu/ws/?pid=20042.

4. "Remarks at the Dedication of the John F. Kennedy Presidential Library
Museum in Boston, Massachusetts" (October 29, 1993), http://www

.presidency.ucsb.edu/ws/index.php?pid=46039; Gwen Ifill, "Clinton Pushes Trade as New Frontier," *New York Times* (October 30, 1993).

5. Thomas Friedman, "Scholars' Advice and New Campaign Help the President Hit His Old Stride," *New York Times* (November 17, 1993).

6. Anthony Arnove, ed., *Iraq Under Siege: The Deadly Impact of Sanctions and War* (2002), p. 17; Chip Gibbons, "When Iraq Was Clinton's War," *Jacobin* (May 6, 2016). Earlier, in the 1980s, Clinton had been one of the few governors willing to send National Guard troops abroad; Arkansas guardsmen went to Grenada, as part of Reagan's invasion of that island, and Chile, where they trained with Augusto Pinochet's military.

7. Ginger Thompson, "Ex-President in Mexico Casts New Light on Rigged 1988 Election," *New York Times* (March 9, 2004); Paul Krugman, "The Uncomfortable Truth About NAFTA: It's Foreign Policy, Stupid," *Foreign Affairs* (November/December 1993).

8. In Memphis, Clinton used the phrase "public pathology" to refer to black-on-black crime. "Ghetto pathology" comes from Ta-Nehisi Coates, "The Black Family in the Age of Mass Incarceration," *The Atlantic* (October 2015), https://www.theatlantic.com/magazine/archive/2015/10/the-black-family-in-the-age-of-mass-incarceration/403246/.

9. Friedman, "Scholars' Advice and New Campaign Help the President Hit His Old Stride."

10. "For NAFTA," *New Republic* (October 11, 1993).

11. As national security advisor and secretary of state in the 1970s, Kissinger helped contain Latin America, supporting a series of right-wing coups and death-squad states across the continent that eliminated a generation of nationalists. Reagan, in the 1980s, built on Kissinger's work, going far in opening up Latin America. Now, in the 1990s, "free trade" offered a chance to consolidate "the revolution," as Kissinger said to Mexico's president Carlos Salinas. As an informal advisor to George H. W. Bush, Kissinger had been working to get Mexico on board with Bush's trade proposal, which was meant to be the first step in a hemisphere-wide free-trade zone (over a 1991 lunch, Kissinger urged Salinas to move fast on trade, since the Democratic Party, in reaction to the rise in poll numbers that victory over Saddam Hussein gave George Bush, would begin to push a protectionist line). After Bush lost reelection, Kissinger and his consultant firm, Kissinger Associates, began advising Clinton, urging him to put NAFTA ahead of health care on his first-year agenda. In his public lobbying for NAFTA, aside from arguments specific to Mexico, Kissinger pushed free trade with exactly the same arguments that he used earlier to push for the first Gulf War: both were needed to stay engaged with the world, to maintain a willingness to act by taking action.

For Kissinger and the first Gulf War: Grandin, *Kissinger's Shadow* (2015). For free trade: "With NAFTA, U.S. Finally Creates a New World Order," *Los Angeles Times* (July 18, 1993); Also: Carlos Salinas de Gortari, *México, un paso difícil a la modernidad* (2013). For Kissinger and Clinton: Jeff Faux, *The Global Class War* (2006).

12. Michael Wilson, "The North American Free Trade Agreement: Ronald Reagan's Vision Realized," Heritage Foundation (November 23, 1993), https:// www.heritage.org/trade/report/the-north-american-free-trade-agreement -ronald-reagans-vision-realized.

13. U.S. International Trade Commission, *Imports Under Items 806.30 and 807.00 of the Tariff Schedules of the United States* (1980), pp. 6–8; Kathryn Kopinak, "The Maquiladorization of the Mexican Economy," *The Political Economy of North American Free Trade*, Ricardo Grinspun and Maxwell A. Cameron, eds. (1993), pp. 141–61; "Mexico Starting Industrial Plan," *New York Times* (May 30, 1965).

14. Cowie, *Capital Moves*.

15. "Things Look Up for Mexico as U.S. Firms Cross the Border," *U.S. News & World Report* (July 1, 1968).

16. United States International Trade Commission, *Production Sharing: U.S. Imports Under Harmonized Tariff Schedule Provisions . . .* (1994), chapter 4, pp. 2–4.

17. U.S. Environmental Protection Agency and the Mexican Secretaría de Desarrollo Urbano y Ecología, *Integrated Environmental Plan for the Mexican–U.S. Border Area (First Stage, 1992–1994)* (1992), p. B-5 (appendix).

18. "Free Industrial Zone Booms on Mexican Border," *Los Angeles Times* (June 12, 1967); "Mexico Pushes Apparel in Border Cities," *Women's Wear Daily* (June 5, 1968); see also Michael Van Waas, "The Multinationals' Strategy for Labor: Foreign Assembly Plants in Mexico's Border Industrialization Program," PhD dissertation, Stanford University (1981). Mexico's Minister of Industry Octaviano Campos Salas said that he got the idea for a border "free trade" zone after a 1964 trip to Asia, where he realized that Mexico could be "an alternative to Hong Kong and Puerto Rico for free enterprise"; see his op-ed: *Wall Street Journal* (May 25, 1967). Also important to understanding the long historical context of NAFTA is Paul Kershaw's "Arrested Development: Postwar Growth Crisis and Neoliberalism in the US and Mexico, 1971–1978," PhD dissertation, New York University, department of history (2014).

19. Cowie, *Capital Moves*, pp. 100–27.

20. For Johnson and Mexico's border industrialization program: Michael Van Waas, "The Multinationals' Strategy for Labor," pp. 149–50.

21. Cowie, *Capital Moves*, p. 111.

22. Robert Reich, "Reagan's Hidden 'Industrial Policy,'" *New York Times* (August 4, 1985).

23. Joel Dyer, *Harvest of Rage* (1997); D. J. Mulloy, *American Extremism: History, Politics and the Militia Movement* (2004); Michael Kimmel and Abby L. Ferber, "'White Men Are This Nation': Right-Wing Militias and the Restoration of American Masculinity," *Rural Sociology* (2000), vol. 65, no. 4, pp. 588–92; Sean P. O'Brien and Donald P. Haider-Markel, "Fueling the Fire: Social and Political Correlates of Citizen Militia Activity," *Social Science Quarterly* (June 1998), vol. 79, no. 2, pp. 456–65.

24. Nick Reding, *Methland: The Death and Life of an American Small Town* (2009), p. 187.

25. "Twinkies, Carrots, and Farm Policy Reality," *Civil Eats* (December 19, 2017), https://civileats.com/2017/12/19/twinkies-carrots-and-farm-policy-reality/.

26. Corie Brown, "Rural Kansas Is Dying," *New Food Economy* (April 26, 2018).

27. "The Reform of Article 27 and Urbanisation of the Ejido in Mexico," *Bulletin of Latin American Research* (1994), vol. 13, no. 3, pp. 327–335. Also: Gavin O'Toole, "A Constitution Corrupted," *NACLA* (March 8, 2017).

28. For the footnote: David Case and David Voluck, *Alaska Natives and American Laws* (2012), p. 116.

29. Christopher Collins, "Top 1 Percent of Texas Commodity Farmers Get Quarter of $1.6 Billion in Subsidies," *Texas Observer* (November 15, 2017).

30. Center for Economic and Policy Research, "Did NAFTA Help Mexico? An Update After 23 Years" (March 2017), http://cepr.net/images/stories/reports/nafta-mexico-update-2017-03.pdf?v=2.

31. "Wave of Illegal Immigrants Gains Speed After NAFTA," *NPR Morning Edition* (December 26, 2013), https://www.npr.org/2013/12/26/257255787/wave-of-illegal-immigrants-gains-speed-after-nafta; Kristina Johnson and Samuel Fromartz, "NAFTA's 'Broken Promises': These Farmers Say They Got the Raw End of Trade Deal," *The Salt* (August 7, 2017), https://www.npr.org/sections/thesalt/2017/08/07/541671747/nafta-s-broken-promises-these-farmers-say-they-got-the-raw-end-of-trade-deal.

32. "The Trade Deal That Triggered a Health Crisis in Mexico," *The Guardian* (January 1, 2018).

33. "How Guatemala Finally 'Woke Up' to Its Malnutrition Crisis," *PBS NewsHour* (June 25, 2014); "The True Cost of a Plate of Food: $1 in New York, $320 in South Sudan," *The Guardian* (October 16, 2017).

34. See, in general, David Bacon, *The Right to Stay Home* (2014), and Bacon, "NAFTA, the Cross-Border Disaster," *American Prospect* (November 7, 2017).

35. The Clinton administration built miles of fortified fences but mistakenly ran one section into Mexican territory, prompting a call by the Mexican government to take it down. As the *Washington Post* reported: "James Johnson, whose onion farm is in the disputed area, said he thinks his forefathers may have started the confusion in the nineteenth century by placing a barbed-wire fence south of the border. No one discovered their error, and crews erecting the barrier may have used that fence as a guideline. 'It was a mistake made in the 1800s,' Johnson said. 'It is very difficult to make a straight line between two points in rugged and mountainous areas that are about two miles apart.'" Alicia Caldwell, "U.S. Border Fence Protrudes into Mexico," *Washington Post* (June 29, 2007).

36. Washington might be able to, as Benjamin Forgey wryly noted of the pads, "wall off the country" with its leftover war matériel. "The Great Walls of America," *Washington Post* (June 1, 1996).

37. On the night of September 18, 1993—still three months away from Clinton signing the agreement into law—hundreds of residents from Ciudad Juárez and El Paso filled El Paso's Civic Center to discuss opening up twenty-five miles of their border to trade and commerce. The next morning, though, they woke to find hundreds of green-and-white border patrol vehicles arrayed along the border, fifty yards to one-half mile apart, as helicopters buzzed overhead. Operation Blockade, as this display of men and equipment was called, was designed to shut down informal migration at the point of entrance, as opposed to apprehending migrants once they entered the country. It was executed on the orders of a local border patrol officer—a former Vietnam vet named Silvestre Reyes, who used the operation as a springboard to win, as a Democrat, El Paso's seat in the House of Representatives—but it quickly became national policy. Timothy J. Dunn, *Blockading the Border and Human Rights: The El Paso Operation That Remade Immigration Enforcement* (2009); Joseph Nevins, *Operation Gatekeeper: The Rise of the "Illegal Alien" and the Making of the U.S.–Mexico Boundary* (2002). Hernández, in "The Crimes and Consequences of Illegal Immigration," documents an earlier case where a local initiative taken by a border patrol agent became national policy, when patroller Albert Quillin of south Texas launched an operation that would serve as a model for Operation Wetback.

38. Dunn, *Blockading the Border*, p. 205.

39. Nigel Duara, "In Arizona, Border Patrol Doesn't Include Dozens of Deaths in Tally of Migrants Who Perish," *Los Angeles Times* (December 15, 2016); Todd Miller, "Over 7,000 Bodies Have Been Found at the U.S.-Mexican Border Since the '90s," *The Nation* (April 24, 2018).

40. Dara Lind, "The Disastrous, Forgotten 1996 Law," *Vox* (April 28, 2016).

41. In December 1996, Rahm Emanuel, a White House advisor, wrote a memo

urging Clinton to step up his anti-migrant rhetoric. Clinton's "law and order" policies had cut into the Republican advantage on the issue, but Emanuel wanted Clinton to go further to "claim and achieve record deportations of criminal aliens." Emanuel also recommended that Clinton target migrants in the "workplace." "Halfway through your term," Emanuel said, "you want to claim a number of industries free of illegal immigrants." Emanuel wrote his memo *after* Clinton won his 1996 reelection, so his recommendation was what he thought should be the long-term position of the Democratic Party. Clinton agreed. "This is great," he wrote on the memo's margin.

42. "Unintended Consequences of US Immigration Policy: Explaining the Post-1965 Surge from Latin America," *Population and Development Review* (2012), vol. 38, no. 1, pp. 1–29.

43. Robert Ford, "U.S.-Mexico Border Assembly Plant Number Growing," *Austin Statesman* (February 19, 1970).

44. Alana Semuels, "Upheaval in the Factories of Juarez," *The Atlantic* (January 21, 2016). Also: "Stingy by Any Measure," *The Economist* (August 16, 2014).

45. "Metalclad NAFTA Dispute Is Settled," *Los Angeles Times* (June 14, 2001). The Department of State threatened to punish El Salvador for setting up a seed-exchange program, which was meant to give local farmers a chance to not become dependent. See Edgardo Ayala, "Salvadoran Peasant Farmers Clash with U.S. over Seeds," *Inter Press Service* (July 5, 2014); Paul Krugman, "No Big Deal," *New York Times* (February 27, 2014).

46. Richard Roman and Edur Velasco Arregui, *Continental Crucible: Big Business, Workers and Unions in the Transformation of North America* (2015), p. 137.

47. Shasta Darlington and Patrick Gillespie, "Mexican Farmer's Daughter: NAFTA Destroyed Us," *CNN Money* (February 9, 2017).

48. In 2000, his last full year in the White House, Bill Clinton enacted Plan Colombia, a military-aid pipeline that channeled billions of dollars to one of the most repressive governments in the hemisphere. Washington had already been sending considerable money to security forces in Mexico, Central America, and Colombia, but Clinton's initiative was a considerable upgrade, meant to target Andean cocaine production. Plan Colombia did break up established Colombian transportation cartels, but it did nothing to stop the flow of drugs north. New start-up cartels and gangs in Central America and Mexico stepped into the vacuum, and drug violence that had largely, in the 1990s, been concentrated in Colombia telegraphed north and engulfed the region.

49. Bacon, *The Right to Stay Home*. For NAFTA's effects: Bacon, "NAFTA, the Cross-Border Disaster"; Katherine McIntire Peters, "Up Against the Wall,"

Government Executive (October 1, 1996), http://www.govexec.com /magazine/1996/10/up-against-the-wall/427/.

15. CROSSING THE BLOOD MERIDIAN

1. Gloria Romero and Antonio Rodríguez, "A Thousand Points of Xenophobia," *Los Angeles Times* (May 21, 1990); "Boy Won't Be Charged for Border Games," *Los Angeles Times*, (June 21, 1990); "TV Show on Border Brings Calls for Inquiry," *Los Angeles Times* (May 10, 1991); "Teen Sentenced to Six Years," *Los Angeles Times* (May 30, 1991), p. 29. *The Reporters'* segment is available on YouTube: https://www.youtube.com/watch?v=FM609 mv6BOw.

2. The interrogation quote is from *The Reporters*, but the case was widely covered in the print press: For example: "Youth Will Be Tried as Adult in 2 Slayings," *Los Angeles Times* (April 28, 1989).

3. John Crewdson, "Violence, Often Unchecked, Pervades U.S. Border Patrol," *New York Times* (January 14, 1980). Crewdson's reporting from the late 1970s through the early 1980s on the border for the *New York Times*, much of it reproduced in *The Tarnished Door: The New Immigrants and the Transformation of America* (1983), is harrowing.

4. Crewdson, *Tarnished Door*, p. 196.

5. John Crewdson, "A Night on Patrol," *New York Times* (April 22, 1977).

6. Crewdson, *Tarnished Door*, p. 170.

7. John Crewdson, "Border Sweeps of Illegal Aliens Leave Scores of Children in Jails," *New York Times* (August 3, 1980).

8. Crewdson, *Tarnished Door*, p. 170.

9. Crewdson, "Violence, Often Unchecked, Pervades U.S. Border Patrol."

10. Crewdson, *Tarnished Door*, p. 196.

11. Increasing numbers of undocumented laborers arrived to work the fields of a booming agricultural industry, even as the sprawl of San Diego overran those fields with ranch houses, swimming pools, and golf courses. As migrants pitched their makeshift tents (since few farms provided adequate worker housing) on the outskirts of new suburbs, in the creek beds of state and federal parks, they suffered increased racist violence. There were random slurs and jeers directed at groups of men shaping up for day jobs, but also increasing incidents of organized hatred; Crewdson, *Tarnished Door*, p. 196; Freedman, "In an Area Growing Too Fast, Anger Is Taken Out on the Weak"; Human Rights Watch, *Brutality Unchecked: Human Rights Abuses Along the U.S. Border with Mexico* (1992); for footnote, see Francisco Cantú, *A Line Becomes a River* (2018), p. 32.

12. Sebastian Rotella and Patrick McDonnell, "A Seemingly Futile Job Can Breed

Abuses by Agents," *Los Angeles Times* (April 23, 1993), http://articles.latimes.com/1993-04-23/news/mn-26329_1_level-border-patrol-agent.

13. Patrollers turned one such substation, in Harlingen, Texas, into a torture center. According to Human Rights Watch, between 1984 and 1992 "physical abuse" there was coupled "with due process abuses meant to terrorize victims of brutality." *Brutality Unchecked*, p. 30.

14. Operations of the Border Patrol: Hearing before the Subcommittee on International Law, Immigration, and Refugees of the Committee on the Judiciary, House of Representatives, One Hundred Second Congress, second session, August 5, 1992 (1992), p. 209. Also: American Friends Service Committee, *Sealing Our Borders: The Human Toll* (1992).

15. Operations of the Border Patrol, p. 208.

16. For "Tonk": Shorris, "Raids, Racism, and the I.N.S.," and John Carlos Frey, "Cruelty on the Border," *Salon* (July 20, 2012), https://www.salon.com/2012/07/20/cruelty_on_the_border/; Martin Hill, "Border Violence: Has the INS Crossed the Thin Line?" *San Diego Magazine* (June 1985).

17. Human Rights Watch, *Brutality Unchecked*.

18. Shorris, "Raids, Racism, and the I.N.S."

19. Judith Cummings, "Border Patrol Is Troubled by Attacks on Agents," *New York Times* (May 19, 1985); Patrick McDonnell, "A Year Later, Mexican Youth Still Haunted by Border Shooting," *Los Angeles Times* (April 21, 1986). Another example: In June 1992, in the middle of the day in a remote Arizona canyon, border patrol agent Michael Andrew Elmer shot Dario Miranda Valenzuela, who was unarmed, in the back, and left him to die. Elmer, who had earlier bragged about "shooting off the leg" of another migrant, was acquitted for the murder. He said he had mistaken Miranda's canteen for a gun. Miranda's family won a civil suit. Rhonda Bodfield, "Elmer Case Settled for $600,000," *Tucson Citizen* (June 5, 1995); Tessie Borden, "Border Agent Was Boastful," *Arizona Daily Star* (July 22, 1992).

20. William Scobie, "Video Films Trap Brutal Border Cops of Texas," *The Observer* (May 3, 1981).

21. James Harrington, "I'm Leaving the Texas Civil Rights Project, but Not the Fight," *Texas Observer* (January 6, 2016); Scobie, "Video Films Trap Brutal Border Cops of Texas."

22. "Mexico Asks UN for Help to Stop Ranch 'Posses' Hunting Migrants," *The Independent* (May 20, 2000); "UN Envoy Is Sent to Investigate Rio Grande Shootings by Posses of Vigilante Ranchers," *The Independent* (May 24, 2000); "Border Clash," *Time* (June 26, 2000). In early 2000, Sam Blackwood, a seventy-six-year-old south Texas rancher, shot and killed a migrant named Eusebio de Haro; de Haro, after spending two one-hundred-plus-degree days hiking into the United States, had approached the rancher on

his property and asked for water. Blackwood, who had chased de Haro down the road in his jeep and then shot him, was convicted of a Class A misdemeanor. John W. Gonzalez, "Rancher Convicted in Immigrant's Death," *Houston Chronicle* (August 25, 2001); Agustin Gurza, "America, Tear Down This Wall," *Los Angeles Times* (November 28, 2000). A spokesperson for the National Network for Immigrant and Refugee Rights blamed Clinton's militarization of the border for the rising vigilantism: "There's a climate of violence that's being created by the presence of armed agents, infrared sensors, helicopters with night-vision scopes and guns—a real sense from the U.S. government that there's actually a war being waged," leading people "to imagine immigrants as the enemy." See William Booth, "Emotions on the Edge," *Washington Post* (June 21, 2000), and Pauline Arrillaga, "'Climate of Violence' Leads to Death in Texas Desert," *Los Angeles Times* (August 20, 2000).

23. "Violence Up as Border Bristles with Guns," *Christian Science Monitor* (June 19, 2000).

24. By some estimates, Reagan's 1981 tax cut was the largest in U.S. history.

25. Evelyn Nieves, "Citizen Patrols as Feared as Smuggling Rings Along Border," *Milwaukee Journal Sentinel* (January 4, 2004); Government Accountability Office, "Countering Violent Extremism: Actions Needed to Define Strategy and Assess Progress of Federal Efforts" (April 2017), https://www.gao.gov/assets/690/683984.pdf.

26. Jennifer Delson, "One Man's Convictions Launched a Border Crusade," *Los Angeles Times* (April 11, 2005). Gilchrist founded the Minuteman Project with Chris Simcox, an Arizona anti-migrant activist currently serving a nineteen-year prison sentence for sexually assaulting three girls under the age of ten.

27. Carrigan and Webb, *Forgotten Dead*, p. 46.

28. Julia Mead, "Anti-Immigrant Group Active on East End," *New York Times* (April 23, 2006).

29. Miriam Jordan, "Anti-Immigration Activists Roil the Heartland," *Wall Street Journal* (July 16, 2007).

30. In Long Island, where teenagers burned a Mexican family out of their home and bodies of migrants began to turn up in the woods separating townships, stalking Latino migrants became a blood sport. A pack of teenagers out "hunting Mexicans" stabbed an Ecuadoran man to death. Southern Poverty Law Center, "Anti-Latino Hate Crimes Rise for Fourth Year in a Row" (October 29, 2008), https://www.splcenter.org/hatewatch/2008/10/29/anti-latino-hate-crimes-rise-fourth-year-row; Albor Ruiz, "Rising Hate Crime a National Shame," *New York Daily News* (November 3, 2008); Kirk Semple, "A Killing in a Town Where Latinos Sense Hate," *New York Times* (November 13, 2008). In 2009, Shawna Forde, leader of the Minutemen American Defense,

led two other militia members in a raid on the house of Raul Flores and his daughter Brisenia Flores, in Arivaca, Arizona, a town ten miles north of the border, killing both. Ford believed Flores was a cartel member.

31. Slotkin, *Regeneration Through Violence*, p. 564.
32. Barry Scott Zellen, *State of Recovery: The Quest to Secure American Security After 9/11* (2013).
33. Crewdson, *Tarnished Door*, p. 333.
34. John Crewdson, "Border Region Is Almost a Country Unto Itself, Neither Mexican Nor American," *New York Times* (February 14, 1979).
35. Chapman was a contradictory figure. He worked to make "illegal alien" a household phrase and brought a militarist's sensibility to border security, warning about high Mexican birth rates and "silent invasions." He ordered immigration agents to target workplaces, but also prohibited searching people at random. He seemed aware of what the implications of that militarism would be for the country's constitutional system. The episode "General Chapman's Last Stand" of Malcolm Gladwell's podcast, *Revisionist History* (http://revisionisthistory.com/episodes/25-general-chapman's-last-stand), focuses on Chapman, mostly to highlight the Mexican Migration Project—led by Douglas Massey, Jorge Durand, David Lindstrom, Silvia Giorguli Saucedo, Karin Pren, Alondra Ramírez López, and Verónica Lozano—which has shown how efforts to police the border to limit migration have had a contradictory effect. As discussed earlier, such policing efforts limit mobility and circulation, ending seasonal or one-off circular migration and increasing the population of permanent undocumented residents. For his quotations: Whittemore, "Can We Stop the Invasion of Illegal Aliens?"
36. Michael Barone, "In Terms of Geography, Obama Appeals to Academics and Clinton Appeals to Jacksonians," *U.S. News & World Report* (April 2, 2008); Jonathan Chait, "The Party of Andrew Jackson vs. the Party of Obama," *New York* (July 5, 2015); Robert Merry, "Andrew Jackson: Tea Party President," *American Spectator* (October 7, 2011).
37. Ezra Klein, "Obama Revealed: A Moderate Republican," *Washington Post* (April 25, 2011).
38. "Still Flying High," *New York Times* (December 25, 2006). For Krugman's second thoughts, see "Trouble with Trade," *New York Times* (December 27, 2007). Also: William Greider, "Paul Krugman Raises the White Flag on Trade," *The Nation* (March 14, 2016).
39. Lori Wallach, "NAFTA on Steroids," *The Nation* (June 27, 2012).
40. Gaiutra Bahadur, "Nativists Get a Tea-Party Makeover," *The Nation* (October 28, 2010).
41. "Tea Party Rolls into Arizona," *Human Events* (March 30, 2010), http://humanevents.com/2010/03/30/tea-party-rolls-into-arizona/.

42. But Obama still accepted the legitimating premises of the Global War on Terror, so much so that he refused efforts to hold any official in the Bush administration responsible for torture or extrajudicial assassinations. Indeed, Obama set his own dangerous precedent by claiming the authority to kill by drone. And he launched his own ruinous intervention in Libya. As with Iraq before it, the United States' military operation in Libya—as part of a NATO assault that led to the downfall of Muammar Gaddafi—had terrible consequences, spreading jihadism down into sub-Saharan Africa and, along with the civil war in Syria, sending millions of refugees into Europe, driving a right-wing reaction through the member states of the European Union. For Obama and extrajudicial assassination by drone: Mattathias Schwartz, "A Spymaster Steps Out of the Shadows," *New York Times* (June 27, 2018).

43. The United States, with its military spread out across the world and its round-the-clock, unaccountable bombing and extensive covert operations, has effectively abolished the idea of "peacetime." As a number of scholars have shown, endless war creates volatile forms of masculinity and free-floating hatreds. Many studies confirm the relationship between war and domestic radicalization, especially between the first Gulf War and the spread of militia and patriot groups. Examples: Jan Kramer, *Lone Patriot* (2007), p. 67; Steven Cermak, *Searching for a Demon* (2012); Abby Ferber, *Home-Grown Hate* (2004); Nadya Labi, "Rogue Element: How an Anti-Government Militia Grew on an U.S. Army Base," *New Yorker* (May 26, 2014). Also Belew, *Bringing the War Home*, and Mary Dudziak, *Wartime: An Idea, Its History, Its Consequences* (2012), p. 86, for how the first Gulf War served as a rupture in the national experience of past wars, which, from frontier wars to World War II, could be seamlessly integrated into a national narrative of progress. Also: Kenneth Stern, *A Force Upon the Plain: The American Militia Movement and the Politics of Hate* (1996); Jerry Lembke, *The Spitting Image: Myth, Memory, and the Legacy of Vietnam* (2000); Daniel Levitas, *The Terrorist Next Door: The Militia Movement and the Radical Right* (2002); Hugh Campbell, Michael Mayerfield Bell, and Margaret Finny, eds., *Country Boys: Masculinity and Rural Life* (2006); Michael Kimmel and Abby Ferber, "'White Men Are This Nation': Right-Wing Militias and the Restoration of Rural American Masculinity"; and Chip Berlet, "Mapping the Political Right: Gender and Race Oppression in Right-Wing Movements"; Evelyn Schlatter, *Aryan Cowboys: White Supremacists and the Search for a New Frontier, 1970–2000* (2009); Leonard Zeskind, *Blood and Politics: The History of the White Nationalist Movement* (2009); and Steven Cermak, *Searching for a Demon* (2012). Billions of dollars that are spent on war could fund social services, while municipalities try to cover their budgets by fining and ticketing their poorest residents, leading some neighborhoods to

feel like they are under occupation. As citizens marched to protest the increase in police killing of young, unarmed African American men, they were greeted by phalanxes of police officers armored with surplus gear from the country's wars. It was hard, many noted, to tell the police in Ferguson, Missouri, from the troops in Fallujah. For the political economy of municipal militarization: Walter Johnson, "The Economics of Ferguson," *The Atlantic* (April 26, 2015), https://www.theatlantic.com/politics/archive/2015/04/fergusons-fortune-500-company/390492/; Mark Thompson, "Why Ferguson Looks So Much Like Iraq," *Time* (August 14, 2014). A number of murders by right-wing racists during the Obama years are well known, including the June 2015 massacre of nine African Americans at Emanuel African Methodist Episcopal Church in Charleston, South Carolina. But quite a few slaughters, such as those in Oregon, Colorado, and Louisiana committed by survivalists, misogynists, racists, and white supremacists, were largely ignored. Government Accountability Office, "Countering Violent Extremism."

44. In the summer of 2017, Donald Trump, citing George H. W. Bush's 1990 invasion of Panama as a positive precedent, repeatedly pushed his national security staff to launch a military assault on crisis-plagued Venezuela. Trump was serious; he brought up the idea in meeting after meeting. Everyone he spoke with, though, including his military and civilian advisors and foreign leaders, forcefully dismissed the proposal. An invasion of Venezuela might be riskier than the one Bush used to good political effect in Panama, as a prelude to the first Gulf War. But rejection of the idea out of hand has, I think, less to do with objective tactical considerations and more with the fact that, because the U.S. is trapped in an endless war, it can't use one-off particular wars to reorder domestic and international politics, the way Panama did. In the past, the United States often returned to Latin America to regroup after periods of military overreach in the rest of the world. Reagan had his Grenada. Bush had Panama. Trump, for now, is denied his Venezuela.

45. Wallach, "NAFTA on Steroids." Ernesto Londoño and Nicholas Casey, "Trump Administration Discussed Coup Plans with Rebel Venezuelan Officers," *New York Times* (September 8, 2018), https://www.nytimes.com/2018/09/08/world/americas/donald-trump-venezuela-military-coup.html.

46. Dara Lind, in *Vox*, provides excellent coverage of border issues, including the militarization of immigration policy. See her overview "The 2014 Central American Migrant Crisis" (May 13, 2015), https://www.vox.com/cards/child-migrant-crisis-unaccompanied-alien-children-rio-grande-valley-obama-immigration/are-children-who-come-into-the-us-illegally-eligible-for-legal-status.

47. ABC News, "Obama Has Deported More People Than Any Other President" (August 29, 2016). Based on governmental data found here, https://www.dhs

.gov/immigration-statistics/yearbook, the author's insistence that "the Obama administration has deported more people than any other president's administration in history" seems overstated, especially since the mechanisms of deportation, especially during the Hoover, Roosevelt, Truman, and Eisenhower administrations, worked differently. But the point is taken.

48. Sarah Macaraeg, "Fatal Encounters; 97 Deaths Point to Pattern of Border Agent Violence Across America," *The Guardian* (May 2, 2018), https://www.theguardian.com/us-news/2018/may/02/fatal-encounters-97-deaths-point-to-pattern-of-border-agent-violence-across-america.

49. ACLU Border Litigation Project and the University of Chicago Law School, International Human Rights Clinic, "Neglect and Abuse of Unaccompanied Immigrant Children by U.S. Customs and Border Protection" (May 2018), https://www.dropbox.com/s/lplnnufjbwci0xn/CBP%20Report%20ACLU_IHRC%205.23%20FINAL.pdf?dl=0.

50. This ACLU page (https://www.aclusandiego.org/cbp-child-abuse-foia/) provides links to other recent reports conducted by a variety of organizations—including No More Deaths, the Women's Refugee Commission, and the National Immigrant Justice Center—on ongoing border patrol abuse and impunity.

51. Ed Pilkington, "'It Was Cold, Very Cold': Migrant Children Endure Border Patrol 'Ice Boxes,'" *The Guardian* (January 26, 2015), https://www.theguardian.com/us-news/2015/jan/26/migrant-children-border-patrol-ice-boxes.

52. Cantú, *A Line Becomes a River*, p. 32.

53. Jim Gilchrist and Jerome Corsi, *Minutemen* (2006), p. 13; see also Derek Lundy, *Borderlands* (2010), p. 187.

54. David Neiwert, *And Hell Followed with Her: Crossing the Dark Side of the American Border* (2013), p. 126; Lundy, *Borderlands*, p. 187.

55. David Nye, *America as Second Creation: Technology and Narratives of New Beginnings* (2004), p. 210. Also: Wallace Stegner, *Beyond the Hundredth Meridian: John Wesley Powell and the Second Opening of the West* (1954).

56. J. R. Hagan, who set up the border watch under the auspices of what turned out to be Iran-Contra, said that he had "mowed people down" in Vietnam and that he'd "do it again" to fight communism. "Verdict in Sanctuary Trial Fails to Deter Supporters of Movement," *Hartford Courant* (May 13, 1986).

57. "*Minuteman Alista Voluntarios,*" *La Opinión* (May 27, 2005). Another example: "People across that border are probably still sitting around campfires talking about how they lost the war to us," another militia member reported, acknowledging that whites "took this land by conquest"; Harel Shapira, *Waiting for José: The Minutemen's Pursuit of America* (2013), p. 3. Gilchrist and Corsi, *Minutemen*, pp. 146–52, for how border militia imagine the reconquest taking place.

58. Peter Holley, "These Armed Civilians Are Patrolling the Border to Keep ISIS Out of America," *Washington Post* (November 25, 2015).
59. Shapira, *Waiting for José*, p. 12.
60. Shane Bauer, "Undercover with a Border Militia," *Mother Jones* (November/ December 2016). Right-wing internet sites constantly report on the Urdu-English or Arabic-English dictionaries being found on the border.
61. Tim Gaynor, "Desert Hawks," Al-Jazeera America (October 26, 2014), http:// projects.aljazeera.com/2014/arizona-border-militia/.

EPILOGUE

1. Daniel Van Schooten, "Bad Actors Among Border Wall Contractors," *Project on Government Oversight* (April 17, 2018), http://www.pogo.org/blog /2018/04/bad-actors-among-border-wall-contractors.html.
2. Todd Miller, *Border Patrol Nation: Dispatches from the Front Lines of Homeland Security* (2014), draws attention to this new way of thinking about the border.
3. "The Constitution in the 100-Mile Border Zone," ACLU fact sheet, https:// www.aclu.org/other/constitution-100-mile-border-zone.
4. Tanvi Misra, "Inside the Massive U.S. 'Border Zone,'" *City Lab* (May 14, 2018), https://www.citylab.com/equity/2018/05/who-lives-in-border-patrols -100-mile-zone-probably-you-mapped/558275/.
5. The project, funded by the state of Texas, has since ended. See Joana Moll and Cédric Parizot, "The Virtual Watchers," *Exposing the Invisible*, https:// exposingtheinvisible.org/resources/the-virtual-watchers.
6. "Our Walled World," *The Guardian* (November 19, 2013). Michael Flynn, "Where's the U.S. Border?" unpublished paper, cited in Todd Miller's "Wait— What Are U.S. Border Patrol Agents Doing in the Dominican Republic?" *The Nation* (November 19, 2013); Miller, *Border Patrol Nation*; "All of Michigan Is an ICE 'Border Zone,'" *Metro Times* (February 2, 2018), https:// www.metrotimes.com/news-hits/archives/2018/02/02/all-of-michigan-is-an -ice-border-zone-here-are-the-rights-all-immigrants-should-know.
7. Miller, *Border Patrol Nation*, p. 43.
8. Ivana Kottasová, "The 1% Grabbed 82% of All Wealth Created in 2017," *CNN Money* (January 22, 2018), http://money.cnn.com/2018/01/21/news /economy/davos-oxfam-inequality-wealth/index.html. The report was produced by OXFAM "using data from Credit Suisse's Global Wealth Databook."
9. Jane Mayer, "The Reclusive Hedge-Fund Tycoon Behind the Trump Presidency: How Robert Mercer Exploited America's Populist Insurgency," *New Yorker* (March 27, 2017), https://www.newyorker.com/magazine/2017/03/27 /the-reclusive-hedge-fund-tycoon-behind-the-trump-presidency. The program

that allowed Mercer to play sheriff has reportedly been terminated. Isobel Thompson, "Bob Mercer, Glorified Mall Cop, Has a Badge—and Lots of Guns," *Vanity Fair* (March 28, 2018), https://www.vanityfair.com/news/2018 /03/robert-mercer-volunteer-policeman-gun-control; Sean Illing, "Cambridge Analytica, the Shady Data Firm That Might Be a Key Trump-Russia Link, Explained," *Vox* (April 4, 2018), https://www.vox.com/policy-and-politics /2017/10/16/15657512/cambridge-analytica-facebook-alexander-nix -christopher-wylie; Vicky Ward, "The Blow-It-All-Up Billionaires," *Huffington Post* (March 17, 2017), https://highline.huffingtonpost.com/articles/en /mercers; Michael Wolff, *Fire and Fury* (2018).

10. Tami Luhby, "Millennials Born in 1980s May Never Recover from the Great Recession," *CNN Money* (May 23, 2018), http://money.cnn.com/2018/05/22 /news/economy/1980s-millennials-great-recession-study/index.html.

11. Peter Whoriskey, "'I Hope I Can Quit Working in a Few Years': A Preview of the U.S. Without Pensions," *Washington Post* (December 23, 2017).

12. For a convincing argument concerning the structural transformation of the political economy, one that goes beyond questions of poverty and inequality and highlights the limitations of how progressives think about reform: James Livingston, *No More Work: Why Full Employment Is a Bad Idea* (2016). Livingston (influenced by, among others, the New Dealer Stuart Chase, especially his 1934 book, *The Economy of Abundance*) argues that labor has become disassociated from capitalist profit: "Since the 1920s, socially necessary labor—what it takes to reproduce the material rudiments of civilization as we know it—describes a smaller and smaller proportion of everyday transactions. Every year, we produce more output without any increase of inputs (whether of capital or labor), and this holds true globally, not just within the United States." The quotation is from "Why Work?" *The Baffler* (June 2017), https://thebaffler.com/salvos/why-work-livingston. For Livingston's take on how this shift fuels social violence: "Guns and the Pain Economy," *Jacobin* (December 18, 2012), https://www.jacobinmag .com/2012/12/guns-and-the-pain-economy. See also Victor Tan Chen, "All Hollowed Out: The Lonely Poverty of America's White Working Class," *The Atlantic* (January 16, 2016); Peter Temin, *The Vanishing Middle Class: Prejudice and Power in a Dual Economy* (2017); Thomas Ferguson, Paul Jorgensen, and Jie Chen, "Industrial Structure and Party Competition in an Age of Hunger Games: Donald Trump and the 2016 Presidential Elections," working paper #66, Institute for New Economic Thinking (January 2018), https://www.ineteconomics.org/uploads/papers/Ferg-Jorg-Chen -INET-Working-Paper-Industrial-Structure-and-Party-Competition-in-an -Age-of-Hunger-Games-8-Jan-2018.pdf; "Statement on Visit to the USA by Professor Philip Alston, United Nations Special Rapporteur on Extreme

Poverty and Human Rights" (December 15, 2017), https://www.ohchr.org
/EN/NewsEvents/Pages/DisplayNews.aspx?NewsID=22533; Samuel Steb-
bins, "Despite Overall Sustained GDP Growth in U.S., Some Cities Still Hit
Hard by Extreme Poverty," *USA Today* (April 23, 2018), https://www
.usatoday.com/story/money/economy/2018/04/23/cities-hit-hardest
-extreme-poverty/528514002/; I. Papanicolas, L. R. Woskie, and A. K. Jha,
"Health Care Spending in the United States and Other High-Income Countries," *Journal of the American Medical Association* (March 13, 2018), vol.
319, no. 10, pp. 1024–1039. See also Adam Tooze, *Crashed: How a Decade
of Financial Crises Changed the World* (2018).

13. Hiroko Tabuchi, "'Rolling Coal' in Diesel Trucks, to Rebel and Provoke,"
New York Times (September 4, 2016); Brian Beutler, "Republicans Are the
'Rolling Coal' Party," *New Republic* (June 5, 2017), https://newrepublic.com
/article/143083/republicans-rolling-coal-party.

14. Dara Lind, "Trump on Deported Immigrants: 'They're Not People. They're
Animals,'" *Vox* (May 17, 2018), https://www.vox.com/2018/5/16/17362870
/trump-immigrants-animals-ms-13-context-why.

15. The passport denials started under George W. Bush, continued through the
Obama administration, and increased dramatically under Trump. Kevin
Sieff, "U.S. Is Denying Passports to Americans Along the Border, Throwing
Their Citizenship into Question," *Washington Post* (September 13, 2018),
https://www.washingtonpost.com/world/the_americas/us-is-denying
-passports-to-americans-along-the-border-throwing-their-citizenship-into
-question/2018/08/29/1d630e84-a0da-11e8-a3dd-2a1991f075d5_story
.html.

16. See the transcript of Trump's call with a person he thought was a U.S. senator, published in *Business Insider* (June 30, 2016), https://www.businessinsider
.de/trump-prank-phone-call-transcript-john-melendez-bob-menendez-air
-force-one-2018-6?r=US&IR=T. See also John D. Feeley and James D. Nealon,
"The Trump Administration Shoves Honduran Immigrants Back into Danger," *Washington Post* (May 9, 2018); Masha Gessen, "Taking Children
from Their Parents Is a Form of State Terror," *New Yorker* (May 9, 2018). But
to underscore how Trump merely turns structural cruelty into spectacular
cruelty, Barack Obama's ambassador to El Salvador had announced a similar policy. Greg Grandin, "Here's Why the U.S. Is Stepping Up the Deportation of Central Americans," *The Nation* (January 21, 2016).

17. Caitlin Dickerson, "Detention of Migrant Children Has Skyrocketed to
Highest Levels Ever," *New York Times* (September 12, 2018), https://www
.nytimes.com/2018/09/12/us/migrant-children-detention.html.

18. Jonathan Chait, "Trump Has Now Broken Every One of His Economic Populist Promises," *New York* (May 11, 2018). As of this writing, the White

House is selling its renegotiation with Mexico and Canada of NAFTA, or what it is now calling the United States–Mexico–Canada Agreement, as a break with the terms of Clinton-era economic globalization. Yet the proposed new treaty—still to be ratified by the three countries—will enshrine into international trade law provisions that had originally been found in the rejected Trans-Pacific Partnership, including measures that "strengthen and lengthen patent and copyright monopolies." Trump, of course, campaigned against the TPP. See Dean Baker, "Trump's Reality-TV Trade Deal," *The Nation* (October 3, 2018), https://www.thenation.com/article/trumps-reality-tv-trade-deal/.

ACKNOWLEDGMENTS

Thomas Jefferson believed his ancestors "possessed a right, which nature has given to all men, of departing from the country in which chance, not choice has placed them, of going in quest of new habitations, and of there establishing new societies, under such laws and regulations as to them shall seem most likely to promote public happiness." First acknowledgment goes to the millions who are forced to try to claim this fundamental right, and to the frontline advocates in organizations such as No More Deaths/No Más Muertes, the Colibri Center for Human Rights, the South Texas Human Rights Center, the Undocumented Migration Project, *Las Patronas*, and the Desert Angels, among many others, who are trying to help them do so. I'm also grateful to the many friends and colleagues who over the years discussed different versions of the arguments presented here, including those who answered specific questions or read parts of the work, including Ned Sublette, Constance Sublette, Ben Johnson, Liz Oglesby, Paul Kershaw, Mae Ngai, Sinclair Thomson, Christy Thornton, Ernesto Semán, Corey Robin, Barbara Weinstein, Ada Ferrer, Walt LaFeber, Lloyd Gardner, Dan Denvir, Doug Henwood, Patrick Timmons, Nikhil Singh, Alejandro

Velasco, and Marilyn Young, whom I miss very much. Brendan Jordan's help was essential, researching out-of-the-blue questions and fact-checking the manuscript (but all errors mine . . .). Paul Kershaw answered key questions about NAFTA and Mae Ngai about immigration policy. Roxanne Dunbar-Ortiz graciously helped identify useful maps. Liz Oglesby read parts of the manuscript, sharing her unparalleled knowledge about both Clinton-era "punishment as deterrence" policies and Central America's political economy. And Robin Reineke took time out from her important work with the Colibri Center to answer questions. Thank you to all. Gratitude also to *The Nation*, where some of the arguments laid out in this book first appeared, and its editors Katrina vanden Heuvel, Roane Carey, Richard Kim, Sarah Leonard, and Lizzy Ratner. Appreciation also to Tom Engelhardt, who published an early version of chapter 8 at his indispensable tomdispatch.com. And thanks to Miguel Tinker-Salas and Ray Craib, who invited me to present early versions of some of the arguments offered here, at, respectively, Pomona's Ena H. Thompson Lectures and Cornell's Carl Becker Lecture Series.

Five times now I've worked with Sara Bershtel, and each time I'm amazed anew. She has the formidable ability, and a considerable amount of patience, to transform a muddled idea into a muddled manuscript, and then into a less muddled book. Sometimes I think I don't want to write an email without first running it by her. This time around, Grigory Tovbis invaluably helped sharpen the editing and argument. Thanks also to friends and family, especially Tannia Goswami and Toshi Goswami. And, above all, to Manu and Eleanor, who make every day a joy. May Eleanor and her generation live in a better world.

INDEX

Page numbers in *italics* refer to maps.

NAFTA and, 233–46
wall and, 8, 148–49, 224–25,
  267–69, 272–73, 275
Mexican migrants, 159–66, 177, 182,
  191n, 222–24, 232, 236, 238–39,
  243–66, 274–76
Mexicans, 1, 8, 83, 91–92, 94–95, 99,
  150, 155–67, 242–43
Mexico, 17, 26, 31, 33, 40, 55–56, 60,
  63, 75, 80–81, 84–87, 115, 127,
  151–58, 163, 178, 198, 213, 233,
  237–48, 268
  Constitution of 1917, 178–79, 184,
    242
  French occupation of, 152–54
  independence from Spain, 84
  Indian removal and, 84–87
  Revolution, 101, 156–57, 178–79,
    181, 211, 232, 237, 239, 241
  slavery abolished in, 84, 156
  Spanish rule of, 26, 152
  Texas secession from, 40, 85–87,
    152
  U.S. annexation of territory of, 31,
    55, 63, 75, 80, 91–92, 93, 97, 128,
    151–52
Mexico City, 92, 153n, 154–55, 243,
  247
Michigan, 63–64, 87, 95, 268
Middle East, 199, 248, 255, 275
migratory birds treaty, 191n
militarism, 66, 96–99, 189, 202, 204,
  206, 210, 261
military spending, 8, 88–89, 97, 143,
  203, 221, 234, 255, 261, 275
militias, 254, 261
Miller, Todd, 269
Millerism, 71
Mind of the South, The (Cash), 139
Minian, Ana Raquel, 222
Minneapolis Journal, 135
Minnesota, 63
Minuteman Project, 256–58, 261,
  265–66
Mises, Ludwig von, 220
Mishell, Lawrence, 247
Mississippi, 87, 136, 163, 216–18, 227
Mississippi River, 13, 17, 19, 24–26,
  35–36, 38–39, 43, 49, 51, 58–62
  59, 66–70, 85, 115, 119

Mississippi valley, 17, 21, 43, 49,
  54–55, 75, 95, 173
Missouri, 87, 103, 106
Missouri River, 26, 119
Moby-Dick (Melville), 89
Modoc, 133
Mohegan Nation, 55
Money, Hernando De Soto, 136
Monmouth, Battle of, 89
Monroe, James, 35–36, 38, 46, 48,
  54–55, 87n
Montana, 63, 134
Montesquieu, 27–29, 100
Morán González, John, 157
Morgan, J.P., 154
Mormons, 71
Morrill Land-Grant Acts (1862),
  110
Morris, Gouverneur, 28–29
Mountain Minutemen, 256
Mounted Rifles, 157
MS-13. *See* Mara Salvatrucha
Mumford, Lewis, 170
Muñoz Martinez, Monica, 157
Murrieta protests of 2014, 265, 273
Muslims, 266
My Confession (Chamberlain), 90n
My Lai Massacre, 210, 218

Naco, Arizona, 149
Nader, Ralph, 236
Napoleon, 38
Napoleon III, 152
Napolitano, Janet, 149
Natchez, 7, 22, 62
Natchez Trace, 51–53, 58, 96, 107
National Association for the
  Advancement of Colored People
  (NAACP), 146
National Cotton Council, 181
National Gazette, 73
National Guard, 143, 162, 227
National Health Service (UK), 102
National Labor Relations Act (1935),
  181
national parks, 174
National Recovery Administration, 175,
  179
National Rifle Association, 166–67
National Woman's Party, 130

ABOUT THE AUTHOR

GREG GRANDIN is the author of *The Empire of Necessity*, which won both the Bancroft and Beveridge Prizes in American history; *Fordlandia*, which was a finalist for the Pulitzer Prize, the National Book Award, and the National Book Critics Circle Award; and a number of other widely acclaimed books, including *Kissinger's Shadow*, *Empire's Workshop*, *The Last Colonial Massacre*, and *The Blood of Guatemala*. After teaching at New York University, he joined the Department of History at Yale University in 2019. A recipient of fellowships from the Guggenheim Foundation and the New York Public Library, Grandin has served on the United Nations Truth Commission investigating the Guatemalan civil war and has written for *The Nation*, the *London Review of Books*, and *The New York Times*.